Language Planning and Policy in Native America

BILINGUAL EDUCATION & BILINGUALISM
Series Editors: Nancy H. Hornberger (*University of Pennsylvania, USA*) and Colin Baker (*Bangor University, Wales, UK*)

Bilingual Education and Bilingualism is an international, multidisciplinary series publishing research on the philosophy, politics, policy, provision and practice of language planning, global English, indigenous and minority language education, multilingualism, multiculturalism, biliteracy, bilingualism and bilingual education. The series aims to mirror current debates and discussions.

Full details of all the books in this series and of all our other publications can be found on http://www.multilingual-matters.com, or by writing to Multilingual Matters, St Nicholas House, 31-34 High Street, Bristol BS1 2AW, UK.

Language Planning and Policy in Native America

History, Theory, Praxis

Teresa L. McCarty

Foreword by
Richard E. Littlebear

MULTILINGUAL MATTERS
Bristol • Buffalo • Toronto

Library of Congress Cataloging in Publication Data
McCarty, T.L.
Language Planning and Policy in Native America: History, Theory, Praxis/
Teresa L. McCarty.
Bilingual Education & Bilingualism: 90
Includes bibliographical references and index.
1. Indians of North America—Languages—Social aspects. 2. Indians of North America—Education. 3. Indians of North America—Education—Planning. 4. Education, Bilingual—United States. 5. Language planning—United States. 6. Language policy—United States. 7. Intercultural communication. I. Title.
PM108.8.M33 2012
306.44'97308997-dc23 2012036458

British Library Cataloguing in Publication Data
A catalogue entry for this book is available from the British Library.

ISBN-13: 978-1-84769-863-6 (hbk)
ISBN-13: 978-1-84769-862-9 (pbk)

Multilingual Matters
UK: St Nicholas House, 31–34 High Street, Bristol BS1 2AW, UK.
USA: UTP, 2250 Military Road, Tonawanda, NY 14150, USA.
Canada: UTP, 5201 Dufferin Street, North York, Ontario M3H 5T8, Canada.

Copyright © 2013 Teresa L. McCarty.

All rights reserved. No part of this work may be reproduced in any form or by any means without permission in writing from the publisher.

Front cover: Winona Castillo, age 13, and Hubert McCord, age 84, of the Fort Mojave Tribe of Needles, California. Mr. McCord is the only male tribal member who is a fluent singer of Mojave bird songs, a core cultural expression. Through a community-driven language documentation project focused on the bird songs, he and other Elders are teaching the language to Mojave youth like Winona (see p. 181). Mr. McCord's gesture in the photograph signifies affection, pride, and a forward-looking optimism for the next generation. It also conveys this book's larger message that language revitalization is not about 'saving' languages in an abstract sense, but is about strengthening intergenerational relationships and building community. Special appreciation goes to Hubert McCord, Winona Castillo, Katherine Castillo, and Natalie Diaz of the Fort Mojave Tribe, and to photographer Jeston Morris.

The policy of Multilingual Matters/Channel View Publications is to use papers that are natural, renewable and recyclable products, made from wood grown in sustainable forests. In the manufacturing process of our books, and to further support our policy, preference is given to printers that have FSC and PEFC Chain of Custody certification. The FSC and/or PEFC logos will appear on those books where full certification has been granted to the printer concerned.

Typeset by Techset Composition Ltd., Salisbury, UK.

Dedication

*To the memory of my parents,
Virginia Heckert Doulin and James Lawrence McCarty*

*And to the memory of our forebears in the Irish diaspora,
who, out of love for their children,
left the Irish language behind.*

Le cion agus le mórmheas

As tribal leaders our responsibilities are numerous. However, the reclamation and restoration of our heritage language and culture has visibly strengthened our Nation immeasurably. I am convinced this work is the single most important effort we have initiated to ensure the perpetuation and long-term survival of our Tribal Nation.

Chief Thomas Gamble,
Miami Tribe of Oklahoma, October 2009

Contents

	Dedication	v
	Statement by Miami Tribe of Oklahoma Chief Thomas Gamble	vi
	Acknowledgements	ix
	Foreword by Richard E. Littlebear	xiii
	Preface	xvii
1	Contextualizing Native American LPP: Legal–Political, Demographic and Sociolinguistic Foundations	1
	First Peoples, First Principles: Tribal Sovereignty	2
	Peoples, Populations and Lands	4
	Native American Languages	8
	Assessing Language Vitality and Endangerment	17
	Contemporary Native American Language Use in Public and Communal Spaces	21
2	Conceptualizing Native American LPP: Critical Sociocultural Foundations	32
	LPP Goals and Approaches	32
	A Critical Sociocultural Perspective on Language Planning and Policy	39
	Safety Zone Theory	42
3	Native American Languages In and Out of the Safety Zone, 1492–2012	46
	Print Literacy as a Colonizing Tool	48
	Colonial Schooling: The 'Slow Match' of Forced Cultural Transformation	50
	Subverting the Safety Zone	56
	Policy Turnabout: 'To Preserve, Protect, and Promote Native American Languages'	60
	Repatriating the Spoken Word	62

4 Indigenous Literacies, Bilingual Education and Community
       Empowerment: The Case of Navajo   65
   Situating Navajo LPP   66
   Indigenous Community-controlled Schooling: Possibilities
       and Constraints   84
   Navajo Language 'at a Crossroads'   87

5 Language Regenesis in Practice   91
   neetawaapantamaanki iilinwiaanki meehkamaanki niiyoonaani:
       Searching for Our Talk and Finding Ourselves
       Written with Daryl Baldwin, George M. Ironstrack and Julie Olds 92
   'Language Can Come Home Again': Wôpanâak
       Language Reclamation   106
   'We Wanted Language Learning to be Family Based': The
       California Master–Apprentice Language Learning Program   111
   'We Decided to Raise *Mohawk* Children': Kanienkeha Regenesis   119
   'The Hawaiian Language Shall Take Its Rightful Place among
       the Languages of the World': Hawaiian-medium Education   128
   'Harmonizing without Homogenizing': Navajo Immersion
       and Academic Success   139
   Reimagining Possibilities for Indigenous Mother Tongues   150

6 Language in the Lives of Indigenous Youth   156
   *Teresa L. McCarty with Mary Eunice Romero-Little, Larisa
       Warhol and Ofelia Zepeda*
   Research on Native American Youth Language Practices   157
   Youth Language Practices, Ideologies, and Desires   161
   Toward Linguistic and Cultural Continuance   178

7 Planning Language for the Seventh Generation   183
   From Ideologies of Contempt to Ideologies of Valor:
       The Victories of Native American LPP   184
   Standardization and Language Restrictionism   186
   Domesticating Dangerous Diversity   192
   Counter-Possibilities for Native Languages and Cultures in School 194
   Completing the Circle – Native American Linguistic
       and Educational Sovereignty   200

Appendix 1: Native American Languages Act of 1990/1992   203
Appendix 2: Esther Martinez Native American Languages
Preservation Act of 2006   211
Appendix 3: 2 December 2011 Executive Order on American
Indian/Alaska Native Education   214
References   221
Author Index   253
Subject Index   258

Acknowledgements

This book was germinated in the summer of 2000, when Lucille J. Watahomigie and I were co-teaching in the 22nd Annual American Indian Language Development Institute (AILDI). Lucille was then directing the acclaimed Hualapai Bilingual–Bicultural Education Program at Peach Springs, Arizona and, with Professor Ofelia Zepeda, I was codirecting AILDI. Lucille, Ofelia and I grew up together professionally in AILDI, and over the years we saw the concerns of Institute participants evolve from language maintenance to language recovery. It was in this context that Lucille and I proposed a book on Native American language education to Multilingual Matters. To get the book started, we conducted interviews with several esteemed Native American language educators; excerpts from some of those interviews are included in the chapters that follow. Time and events took both of us away from the book project and our co-authorship, but I am deeply grateful to Lucille for her early involvement in the project, and for her mentorship and friendship over the years. For participating in the initial interviews conducted with Lucille Watahomigie, I thank Stephen Greymorning, Darrell Kipp, Dorothy Lazore, Soloman Ratt, Christine Sims, and Roseanna Thompson.

As this authorial history suggests, I am also deeply indebted to Multilingual Matters for staying with the project all these years. I especially thank Managing Director Tommi Grover for his unflagging encouragement and support, and Series Editors Nancy Hornberger and Colin Baker for their wonderful feedback and faith in this work over more than 12 years. I also thank the anonymous reviewers commissioned by Nancy and Colin, who provided extremely helpful recommendations on an earlier version of the book. To Acquisitions Editor Laura Longworth, Production Manager Sarah Williams, and Marketing Manager Elinor Robertson, many thanks for your graciousness and expertise in getting the book under production and for seeing it through to the end. I also thank editorial managers Hannah Turner, Nick Barber, and their fine (and very patient) editorial team at Techset.

As the book's cover image suggests, this is a *peopled* account of language planning and policy, and I owe a huge debt of gratitude to those who shared inspirational stories of language reclamation and detailed feedback on earlier versions of the book manuscript. I want to especially thank long-time Navajo-language educator, mentor and friend Wayne Holm, for providing 30+ pages of detailed feedback, particularly on Chapter 4, and for leading me back to *the* Navajo language resource, 'YounganMorgan'; 'Aha Pūnana Leo cofounder and Indigenous-language policy advocate William H. (Pila) Wilson, for equally substantive and valuable feedback on the book as a whole and Hawaiian-medium education in particular; Leanne Hinton, co-founder of the California Master–Apprentice Language Learning Program and a model of engaged scholarship, for bringing me up to date on Native California language recovery; Louellyn White, Assistant Professor of First Peoples Studies at Concordia University, for perceptive cultural and ethnographic insights on the Akwesasne Freedom School and a much-needed update on Mohawk language revitalization; MIT Linguistics Professor Norvin Richards, for reading and responding to the section of Chapter 5 on Wôpanâak language reclamation and offering very helpful feedback on the Wôpanâak program's genesis and implementation; and Myaamia Project Director Daryl Baldwin and Education Coordinator George Ironstrack, who hosted me at Miami University, for extensive verbal and written feedback that led me to rethink (and ultimately rewrite) the entire book. I also thank Miami University Coordinator of Miami Tribe Relations Bobbe Burke for meeting with me to discuss the unique tribe–university relationship undergirding the Myaamia Project, and Daryl Baldwin, George Ironstrack and Miami Tribe of Oklahoma Cultural Resources Officer Julie Olds for co-authoring the section of Chapter 5 on Miami language regenesis.

I extend humble thanks and deep respect to Miami Tribe of Oklahoma Chief (*akima*) Thomas Gamble, who provided the powerful statement that begins the book on p. vi.

I am extremely grateful to Richard E. (Dick) Littlebear, president of Chief Dull Knife College and an icon in the field of American Indian education, who took a phone call from me one summer day in 2009, and kindly agreed to write such an eloquent Foreword for the book. Dr Littlebear has long been known for his clear-eyed yet optimistic view of the power of Native families and communities to 'take back' Native American education, including the language socialization of Native children. It is an incredible honor to have Dr Littlebear's words introduce readers to the book.

For the precious photo image on the book's cover, I thank Mr Hubert McCord, Winona Castillo and her mother Katherine Castillo, and Natalie Diaz of the Fort Mojave Tribe of Needles, California; and photographer Jeston Morris of Arizona State University. *Miiwanych 'ahotk.*

To my long-term co-researchers and friends, Mary Eunice Romero-Little and Ofelia Zepeda, I extend my deep appreciation for our work together, and for your co-authorship of Chapter 6. To Bryan McKinley Jones Brayboy, my Arizona State University (ASU) Center for Indian Education academic partner and friend, I am ever grateful for our many fruitful collaborations, some of which are represented in the pages of this book. To dear friends and colleagues Perry Gilmore and K. Tsianina Lomawaima, thank you for engaging my work over many years and for sharing insights from your ground-breaking scholarship.

I am sincerely appreciative to colleagues at Puente de Hózhǫ́ Trilingual Magnet School, whose language revitalization efforts are discussed in Chapter 5: Bilingual/ESL Director Michael Fillerup, Principal Dawn Trubakoff and Diné teachers Amy Begay, Josie Begay James, Ilene Ryan, Irene Tsosie and Pamela White-Hanson.

Although they cannot be named, I am enormously grateful to the youth whose 'lives with Indigenous languages' are explored in Chapter 6. The sometimes trenchant yet ever-hopeful and informative testimony shared by these young people should dispel misguided notions of youth as disinterested in their heritage languages or as intentionally orienting away from their cultural communities. Youth clearly care about the future of their languages and their tribal nations. They deserve all the recognition and support we adults can muster.

The story of language revitalization told here has been greatly aided by visual media. For assistance with photographs and maps I thank Daryl Baldwin, Karen Baldwin, Kristina Fox, George Ironstrack, Bradford Kasberg, Aaron Lane and Andrew J. Strack of the Myaamia Project and the Myaamia Heritage Museum and Archive; Scott Braley for the photograph of 2012 Breath of Life workshop participants in California; Kauanoe Kamanā and William Wilson of 'Aha Pūnana Leo for photographs of Nāwahī Laboratory School in Hilo, Hawai'i; Louellyn White for photographs of the Mohawk Akwesasne Freedom School; Leroy Morgan and Monty Roessel for photographs of Rough Rock Community School that appear in Chapter 4; the Library of Congress for historic images used in Chapter 1; and David McKnight, Nancy Shawcross and Elton-John Torres of the University of Pennsylvania Rare Book and Manuscript Library for the image of the Eliot Bible in Chapter 5. To Shearon Vaughn of Chart Room Graphics goes a huge and heartfelt 'thank you' for the many attractive maps and graphics created specifically for this book.

Special appreciation is due to the language revitalization exemplars who shared generously of their wisdom throughout the writing of the book: Joshua and Gella Fishman, Dónall Ó Riagáin, Tove Skutnabb-Kangas and Bernard Spolsky. To Dónall, many thanks (*agus mórchion*) for helping me express the book's dedication in my heritage language.

There are others whose scholarship has guided the writing of this book, several of whom also commented on earlier drafts and sections of the book: David Beaulieu, Steve Bialostok, Tamara Borgoiakova, Mary Carol Combs, Serafin Coronel-Molina, Kathryn A. Davis, Donna Deyhle, Ofelia García, Mary Hermes, Kendall King, Tiffany Lee, Wesley Leonard, Allan Luke, Stephen May, Lois Meyer, Sharon Nelson-Barber, Sheilah Nicholas, Sonja Novak-Lukanovič, Simon Ortiz, Django Paris, Susan Penfield, Lizette Peter, Vaidehi Ramanathan, Jon Reyhner, Monty Roessel, Irene Silentman, Elizabeth Sumida Huaman, Beth Blue Swadener, John Walsh, Sam No'eau Warner, Terrence Wiley, Harry Wolcott, K. Laiana Wong, Lily Wong Fillmore, Leisy Wyman and Akira Y. Yamamoto. To the students in my ASU graduate seminars who piloted earlier versions of the book (some of whom are now professors), thank you and best wishes on your scholarly journeys: Jeffrey Banner, Haiying Dong, Daisy Fredericks, Ayfer Gokalp, Brenda Herrera, Mary Hubbell-Ansera, Rochelle Jones, Rosalva Lagunas, Karen Lilly, Man-chiu Lin, Gabriel Martinez, Chelsea Mead, John Ng'asike, Jeston Morris, Erin Nolan, Lusia Nurani, Kristin Silver, Mi-jung Song, Susanna Steeg, Hanqiong Xu and Eman Yarrow.

To my ASU graduate research assistants, Ran Chen, Jeston Morris, Erin Nolan, and Kristin Silver, special thanks for your assistance with references, transcriptions, photographs and with other research and editorial support.

This work was completed while I was a faculty member at ASU, and was greatly aided by a generous endowment from Alice Wiley Snell and Richard Snell of Phoenix, Arizona. It has been an honor to steward language education policy scholarship in your name. A grant from the US Department of Education Institute for Education Sciences supported the collection and analysis of youth data examined in Chapter 6. A sabbatical release from ASU and a National Endowment for the Humanities Residential Fellowship through the School for Advanced Research (SAR) in Santa Fe, New Mexico enabled me to re-analyze the youth data reported in Chapter 6 and to complete the book revisions during the 2011–2012 academic year. For supporting my sabbatical, special thanks go to ASU School of Social Transformation Director Mary Margaret Fonow and former Social Science Dean Linda Lederman. For incalculable intellectual and moral support on the youth language work that was the focus of my SAR fellowship, I thank SAR President James Brooks, Vice President John Kantner, Director of Scholar Programs Nicole Taylor, and fellow SAR scholars Rebecca Allahyari, Margaret Bruchac, Kitty Corbett, Linda Cordell, Dean Falk, Linda Garro, Aimee Garza, Janice Gould, Craig Janes, Nancy Owen Lewis, Jennifer McCarty, Nancy Mithlo, Malena Mörling, Kelsey Potdevin, Douglas Schwartz, Woosen Argaw Tegegn and Julie Weise. To SAR staff who encouraged and offered assistance with the research undergirding this book – Flannery Davis, Laura Holt, Jason Ordaz, Lisa Pacheco, and Jean Schaumberg – I extend my sincere appreciation. A special note of gratitude goes to SAR Board of Management Director Steven J. Bolin and Vice Chair Glen W. Davidson.

Finally, I would venture to say that no project of this scope gets completed without a great deal of family support. To my stepdaughter and stepson Jennifer and Stuart Martin; sisters Julie McCarty and Valerie Mussi; nieces Casma Mussi, Kate Pitchford and Amity Roebke; cousin Jill Bace; aunt Jo Ann Brinnon; brotherly in-laws Ed Bace, George Mussi, and Greg Roebke; and my Phoenix family – Caren Creutzberger, Karyn Gitlis, Jan Kegelman, Diana Pardue and Diane Zipley – thank you for your ever-constant love and encouragement. To my husband, John Martin: words of gratitude sometimes fail when there is so much for which to be grateful. Thank you for listening, for sharing your own brilliant scholarship, and for standing by me – and the work – all these years.

Any failures in the book are, of course, entirely my own.

Ahéhee'.

Foreword

Richard E. Littlebear

Teresa McCarty's *Language Planning and Policy in Native America* is a book that I have always wanted to read and learn from. However, it did not exist. Finally, after three decades of my involvement in Native American language issues, the book I always wanted to refer to has finally been written. Let me share some of my journey as it relates to languages and also tell why I am glad this book has been written.

Prior to 1980, I was against the teaching of Native American languages. All my associations, experience and learning up to that point indicated that, in order to make a living in the United States, one had to learn the English language and *only* the English language. Then I became a bilingual education director at a BIA (Bureau of Indian Affairs) contract school. Because I was bilingual in the Cheyenne language and college educated, it was a job I was qualified for, it seemed. So, even though I was philosophically opposed to the teaching of our Cheyenne language, I took the job. It was the beginning of a slow-motion epiphany that eventually resulted in my becoming an ardent advocate of speaking, teaching and learning our Cheyenne language. This eventually led me to become an advocate for all of our Native American languages and Indigenous languages worldwide. But, there were some glitches in this epiphany, which is the reason it occurred in slow motion.

Nevertheless, I got more and more interested in bilingual education and bilingualism as they pertained to education and cognition. I started reading about languages. Most of the research I read then dealt with studies on behalf of languages other than Native American ones. The information available about our languages was mainly linguistics-oriented. The linguistic terminology was usually arcane and way above my vocabulary level. Encountering this situation contributed to the pauses in the epiphany.

Even though I was a novice, I intuitively sensed that the research and the linguistic information were not quite appropriate for the needs of the Native American classroom situations I was then working with. These needs were lesson plans, curriculum development, classroom materials, stories and professional development related to teaching our own languages. This research, which only marginally touched on Native American languages, usually treated our languages as anachronisms. Linguistics, as near as I could tell, dealt with our languages like laboratory specimens, ready for dissecting, categorizing, sorting and classifying. I think that the discipline of linguistics has changed to become more conscious of the need to maintain our languages.

However, as is usually the case with Native Americans, the languages of the first people here in this hemisphere were being dealt with peripherally and last. In fact, as I recall, even the Bilingual Education Act of 1968 had to be later modified to include Native American languages. This modification is a fortuitous afterthought because it brought to the forefront the dire predicaments of our languages.

I continued reading about language issues even though many of the books and articles did not specifically relate to my own Cheyenne language or to other Native American languages. For instance, much classroom-oriented research had been done for the Spanish language and other minority languages. I figured that, since this research was about language issues, then some of the issues might be relevant to our own Native American languages.

As I read, I would always be thinking, 'How does this topic relate to my Cheyenne language?' Thinking this way allowed me to make the connection between this research on other languages and my language. In the meantime, I gained a lot of knowledge about first and second language acquisition and the academic, economic, political and social issues that surrounded it.

Later, I got to thinking, 'There is something missing', and as I became more sophisticated in language issues, I came to the conclusion that that the missing piece was a comprehensive, research-based scrutiny of our own Native American languages. With McCarty's book, I did not have to be thinking, 'How does this relate to my Cheyenne language?' The information is all relevant because, to paraphrase McCarty's words, throughout the book there is the interplay of language practices at the micro level of everyday social interaction with larger macro forces that shape and are shaped by these practices. This book satisfies the need to approach our languages as more than just instruments of communication; we must view them equally as repositories of our psyches and the carriers of our ethos.

Finally, we have *Language Planning and Policy in Native America*, a book that is up to date and intensively, even excruciatingly, researched about our own languages. The whole book contains remarkable information. I would re-read portions of it and think, 'I knew this but I was not able to articulate it in either of my languages'.

For instance, I was wondering why languages end up in one of the categories discussed in Chapter 1. Then I recalled an incident from my own life. I had been away from speaking my language for about 12 months when I returned to the Cheyenne-speaking community where I was born and raised. Even though my brain was able to function in Cheyenne, there was a slight disconnect with the mechanism that produced Cheyenne language sounds. I would unintentionally mispronounce Cheyenne words and, for those errors, was ridiculed by my peers and by some of the people who were older than me.

I almost stopped speaking Cheyenne because of this ridicule and belittlement. Being called a *ve'ho'keso* (little White boy) by other Cheyenne people was the ultimate insult at that time. However, as I reflected on this situation, I made the conscious decision at the age of 15 that I was not going to be deprived of speaking my own language, even though I had become highly proficient in speaking a foreign language, English.

So I endured the ridicule and am thankful that I did because, in less than a week, I was back to speaking the Cheyenne language as if I had never left it for almost a year. I am glad I made the decision to continue speaking the Cheyenne language way back then because personally, spiritually, economically, socially, academically and intellectually, both of my languages, Cheyenne and English, have immeasurably enriched my life.

Recalling this incident in my life made me realize the myriad factors that can lead to language shift and language death. I had almost caused them within my own life.

I also found Chapter 6 most interesting because it addresses a segment of Native American society that hardly ever gets mentioned in relation to language issues: our youth. The youth in this chapter spoke about the additive and positive nature of being bilingual. I share their viewpoint. To paraphrase a statement from one of the youth in Chapter 6, 'For me, the Cheyenne language is important because it is my language and I should speak my language rather than other people's language ... When I speak the Cheyenne language, I think it makes me more Cheyenne and I can show to people that I am Cheyenne'. My identity as a Cheyenne is daily positively reinforced because I speak Cheyenne. I want our youth to have the same experience.

Later in the book, McCarty writes, 'Although much has been written on language shift and reclamation, studies from the perspectives of speakers themselves are relatively rare, [and] even rarer are studies centered on youth'. We must pay attention to the research that McCarty and her colleagues have gathered as it pertains to our Native American youth because these researchers have enabled youth to voice their opinions in this book.

We pay a lot of well-deserved attention to our elders and that is good. However, if an elder cannot transmit his or her language to the youth, the death of language is imminent. Ultimately, we are going to have to depend on our youth to carry on our languages. The issues discussed in Chapter 6 are much needed because we need to strategize about getting our youth to value our languages, especially since they are shifting away from them. I value both of the languages that I speak for the following reasons.

I know that being proficient in writing the English language and being able to speak it fluently has enabled me to make a living in this society. Parallel to that, being proficient in the writing and reading of the Cheyenne language and being fluent in it have reinforced my belongingness to the

Cheyenne-speaking community and have made me a positively contributing member of my country and my tribe. To put it more succinctly: the English language is for physical maintenance; the Cheyenne language is for spiritual sustenance.

Had I had this book three decades ago, I would not have made so many missteps in language program planning. So I know this book is going help language teachers, aides, policy-makers and planners guide our youth back to our languages. If we cannot get our youth to help us save our languages then we may have to resort to a defensive stratagem used by the Cheyenne people.

In the days before 25 June 1876, Cheyenne warriors would initiate a defensive rear-guard action by attaching a length of leather strap to a wooden stake. They would pound this stake into the ground and tie the strap to themselves. Pounding the stake into the ground was their declaration that, for as far as the strap reached, they were going to defend that piece of ground to the death. They were going to do this so that their loved ones would escape and survive. Sometimes seeing the Cheyenne warriors stake themselves to the ground was enough to deter the enemy from attacking because they knew they were up against Cheyenne warriors determined to fight to the death.

I tell this story because it is time that we too symbolically stake ourselves to the ground and defend our Indigenous languages. We who speak them should value them enough to defend them to prevent language death. Let us emulate Cheyenne warriors and continue defending our languages. Let us inform all that, when we stake ourselves to the defense of our languages, we are not going to relent. This book offers us additional ammunition, so to speak, in the defense and regenesis of our languages.

Dr McCarty, you have done a great service to all the advocates of our Native American languages.

Lame Deer, Montana, August 2009

Preface

> *If we have our Native language, we are unique and it identifies us, and we are spiritually whole. We have the complete circle.*
> Roseanna Thompson, Education Director, Mississippi Band of Choctaw Indians, interview, 29 June 2000

When I began working in the field of American Indian education more than 30 years ago, the issues were different than they are today. Invited by the Diné (Navajo) school board at Rough Rock, Arizona to join a bilingual–bicultural curriculum development project there, I worked with Diné educators to create culturally and linguistically relevant teaching materials that would support children's first-language development in Navajo while they acquired English as a second language. The educational goal was to promote bilingualism, biliteracy and bi/multiculturalism. Later, while employed by the National Indian Bilingual Center and as a faculty member and codirector of the American Indian Language Development Institute, I had the opportunity to work with parents, educators and tribal leaders throughout the United States, Canada and Latin America on curriculum development projects with similar aims.

Education in 21st century Native America is still concerned with providing linguistically and culturally responsive curriculum and instruction, but increasingly the goal is teaching Indigenous languages as second languages. Rough Rock is a case in point. Whereas virtually all Rough Rock students came to school speaking Navajo as a first language in the 1980s, Rough Rock teachers today report that fewer than a third of their students enter school speaking Navajo – and the number grows smaller every year. As Bernard Spolsky observed more than a decade ago, although the reservation as a whole remains widely Navajo speaking, 'Navajo parents, especially younger Navajos living in more urbanized settings, now speak to their children in English' (Spolsky, 2002: 142).

The causes of community-wide shift from an Indigenous or minoritized language to the dominant or 'alpha' language are complex, and are examined in detail throughout this book. Here, I want to emphasize the consequences, for, unlike speakers of colonial languages, which have 'massive symbolic domination' (Kroskrity, 2011: 181), Indigenous communities have no external pool of speakers to turn to as a language acquisition resource. 'The loss of the indigenous language is terminal', Sam No'eau Warner warns (1999a: 72). Yet, as we will see, even languages whose last native speaker has passed away can be – and are being – recovered and revived. The challenges are daunting, but the determination, hopefulness and impact of these revitalization projects are inspiring to behold.

Even as more Native American children enter school speaking English as a primary or sole language, they often speak a variety influenced by the Native language and are subjected to school labeling practices that stigmatize them as 'limited English proficient' or 'language-delayed'. This subtractive view of children's cognitive and linguistic abilities has a long history in Indigenous education and is a prime cause of language loss and of education disparities. Native American students are more than twice as likely as their White counterparts to be placed in remedial education programs, often on the basis of language. On average, American Indian and Alaska Native students are 117% more likely than their White peers to be pushed out or to leave school before completing a high school degree (National Caucus of Native American State Legislators, 2008). Data on Native Hawaiian education shows similarly drastic drops in literacy achievement following the banning of Hawaiian-medium schooling in the late 19th century (Wilson and Kamanā, 2006). Thus, the shift to English has *not* transformed long-standing educational disparities for Native American students or the structural inequalities those disparities reflect and reproduce.

How did the present sociolinguistic and educational situation come about? What does it entail for language planning and policy (LPP) at the local, tribal, state, national and international levels? How are dynamic situations of language shift and reclamation experienced by Native children and youth? What lessons do Native American experiences hold for larger issues of education reform, linguistic and cultural diversity, and Indigenous- and minority-language rights?

These are the questions that anchor this book. The geographic focus is the United States. However, recognizing the colonial origins of contemporary dominant-nation borders, much of the analysis can be and is extended outside the land claimed by the US, in particular Canadian Indigenous settings. Throughout the book, I explore the interplay of language practices at the micro level of everyday social interaction with larger meso and macro forces that shape and are shaped by those practices. Language planning and language policy – deliberate attempts to regulate and monitor the acquisition, status, use and development of language(s) – are implicated in all of these processes.

Perspective and Stance

I begin with four underlying assumptions. The first is that linguistic and cultural diversity is an inherently enabling condition for individuals, families, communities and society. To expand on Ruiz's (1988) notion of language as a resource, language is an irreplaceable intellectual, social, cultural and scientific resource to its speakers and to humankind. The great polyglot linguist Kenneth Hale described linguistic diversity as 'perhaps the most important enabling condition for minimally fettered creation of precious products of human intellectual labor' (Hale, 1995: 24). The loss of local languages, Hale contended, means the 'irretrievable loss of diverse and interesting intellectual wealth, the priceless products of human mental industry' (Hale, 1995: 24). As K. David Harrison writes in his study of what happens when languages die, the disappearance of a language 'is an erosion of ideas, of ways of knowing' (Harrison, 2007: 7). Even Hale's analysis does not go far enough, Harrison contends; we 'simply do not know what we stand to lose with the loss of a single language' (Harrison, 2007: 7). Language 'is the means of cultural memory', writes Kenyan literary scholar Ngũgĩ wa Thiong'o (2009: 40). And, in his path-breaking book, *Reversing Language Shift*, Joshua Fishman similarly describes languages and the cultural systems they represent as 'things of beauty ... encapsulations of human values [that] deserve to be fostered and assisted' (Fishman, 1991: 33).

For the people and communities who claim endangered languages, however, the issues go far deeper. References to a 'vanishing fund of human knowledge', linguistic anthropologist Paul Kroskrity points out, elide 'key connections to the larger role of threatened languages in the sociocultural lives of their speakers', including the fight for sovereignty and the places of origin and identifications associated with the language (Kroskrity, 2011: 180). Reflecting on his native Cheyenne, Richard Littlebear, whose words grace the Foreword to this book, notes that 'embedded in the language are the lessons that guide our daily lives. We cannot leave behind the essence of our being' (Littlebear, 2004: 20). The Native language is a 'gift', Hualapai educator Lucille Watahomigie writes; 'it must be cherished, nurtured, and treated with respect to honor the giver' (Watahomigie, 1998: 5). 'We believe that First Nations, Inuit and Métis languages are sacred and are gifts from the Creator', the Task Force on [Canadian] Aboriginal Languages and Cultures affirms (2005: 3). Similar metaphors can be found in Native American tribal language policies: 'The Yaqui language is a gift from Itom Achai, the Creator of our people', the Yaqui (Yoeme) tribal language policy begins, 'and, therefore, shall be treated with respect' (Zepeda, 1990: 250). These statements represent deeply held beliefs or ideologies about language that, as linguistic anthropologist Alexandra Jaffe notes in her study of Corsican language policy, are 'a real part of people's experiences of what it means to speak, or know, or own a language' (Jaffe, 2011: 221).

A second assumption I bring to this book is that language planning – in particular, efforts to revitalize endangered mother tongues – must be driven by Indigenous community members themselves. In the pages that follow, readers will find wide-ranging examples of Indigenous language revitalization. In bringing forth these varied accounts, my goal is to speak to issues of concern across a spectrum of language loss and revitalization experiences – from those of smaller, diasporized communities with few or even no native speakers, to those whose language is considered 'moribund' because speakers are beyond child-bearing age, to those in which there are still many child speakers, but fewer and fewer with each passing year. My hope is that, through these varied examples, the book will provide insights for LPP scholars as well as practitioners working under many types of sociocultural and sociolinguistic conditions.

A third assumption is that schools and educators have a strategic role to play in the promotion and revitalization of Indigenous mother tongues. It is widely agreed that schools alone cannot 'save' endangered languages (see, e.g. Hornberger, 2008), and indeed, as Jaffe (2011) notes, schools create new communities of practice very different from those in which Indigenous languages traditionally thrived. Schools 'cannot turn back the language loss that has been going on for hundreds of years', observes Littlebear (1990: para. 10), as school-based programs often lack the 'feedback loops' to speakers outside the classroom (Hill, 1993: 89). Nor is school-based revitalization viable, desired, or appropriate in all settings. Where it *is* a locally viable and desired option, schools and their personnel can work in alliance with families and communities to provide opportunities for Indigenous-language learning and use. Although they are 'extremely contentious spaces' (Rockwell & Gomes, 2009: 105), schools can be and have been appropriated as platforms for a multitude of language planning goals and activities – from orthographic standardization, to materials development, to teacher preparation, to the elevation of the status of Indigenous languages within the community and beyond.

A fourth assumption is that language issues are, at their heart, 'people' issues. Languages and their associated cultural systems are 'inextricably linked to the people from whom the language and culture evolved', Warner points out (1999a: 89). When we speak of language loss and revitalization, we should be ever mindful of the living, breathing children, families and communities those abstractions reference. Moreover, languages are not so much *re*placed as *dis*placed – 'crowded out by bigger languages' and their speakers (Harrison, 2007: 5). Language shift thus indexes multilayered power inequities. In this sense LPP is not merely or even primarily about language *per se* – that is, it is not about 'saving' an abstraction called language – but is rather about the self-determination of a people, social justice, and the restoration of personal and communal well-being.

Finally, let me say a few words about who I am to write this book. The repatriation and revitalization of an oppressed language is an avowedly anti-colonial project. This book and my work are unabashedly grounded in that stance. I come to this work as a non-Indigenous, native English-speaking educator and anthropologist, fully recognizing that the stakes for me are far different than they are for the Native people with whom I work. My purpose in writing is to bring together, in an accessible and useful way, knowledge from interdisciplinary research, LPP practice, and my own experience with diverse Indigenous communities. The book's anchoring questions derive from a growing body of scholarship in applied linguistics, Indigenous studies, and educational and linguistic anthropology, and from a growing Indigenous/minority language rights movement with which I have been closely aligned for many years. Throughout the book, I have sought to write as a listener, teller and 'allied other' (Kaomea, 2004; see also Brayboy & Deyhle, 2000). Through concrete examples I have also sought to show how Indigenous and non-Indigenous language planners can work (and are working) productively together on the decolonizing project of language reclamation. This is, as a consequence, a *peopled* examination, and in the pages that follow, readers are introduced to those who are on the frontlines of Native American LPP every day.

In his book, *Language Policy*, Spolsky proposes that 'students of language policy fall naturally into two main groups: the optimists who believe [language] management is possible and the pessimists who assume that language is out of control' (Spolsky, 2004: 223). 'The record seems to favor the pessimists', Spolsky admits (2004: 223). I nonetheless throw my lot in with the optimists. This is not to deny the gravity of language endangerment or the challenges it presents. Rather, it is to acknowledge the enormous efforts being made in the fight for Indigenous linguistic, cultural, and educational self-determination, and the promise those efforts hold for the continuance of individual cultural communities and the sustainability of human diversity worldwide.

A Few Key Usages and Terms

Naming

There are no neutral names, categories, labels or terms (Skutnabb-Kangas & McCarty, 2008: 3). Many terms used to reference Native peoples in the United States – American Indian, Alaska Native and Native Hawaiian – refer less to any subjective identifiers than to federal acknowledgement (or its lack) of the singular status of Native Americans as inherent sovereigns. Throughout the book, I use the terms Indigenous, Native, American Indian, First Nations and Native American to refer to those whose ancestry within the land area now claimed by the United States and Canada predates colonial invasions, and whose oral and written traditions place them as the first occupants of ancestral homelands. However, readers should recognize that Indigenous self-designations are the most precise identifiers; 'it is these names rather than any externally imposed labels that most accurately reference Indigenous identities' (McCarty & Zepeda, 2010: 324).

I also use a capital 'I' and 'N' when referring to Indigenous/Native peoples and their languages. I continue to be perplexed that this usage seems to require justification within some discourse communities. This usage signals the inherent sovereignty of Native Americans and distinguishes them as peoples, in the same way that initial capital letters are used with reference to Europeans and Anglo Americans. This usage is also consistent with conventions adopted by national and international organizations such as the Indigenous Language Institute in Santa Fe, New Mexico, the American Indian Language Development Institute at the University of Arizona and within the United Nations.

Literacy

The approach to literacy taken here is based on a notion of literacy as a social and cultural practice (Gee, 2012; Rockwell, 2005; Street, 2008), and a pedagogy of multiliteracies that recognizes 'the increasing multiplicity and integration of significant modes of meaning-making, where the textual is also related to the visual, the audio, the spatial, [and] the behavioral' (New London Group, 1996: 64). Literacy is never ideologically neutral but is embedded within sociocultural contexts and the discursive practices and power relations those contexts reflect and refract. This approach draws upon Brian Street's (2008: 4) 'alternative, ideological model of literacy [that] offers a more culturally sensitive view of literacy practices as they vary from one context to another', but extends that model in important ways.

Specifically, I argue that alphabetic or print literacy is only one facet of what 'counts' as literate practice. In Indigenous communities, literacy is more accurately construed as 'the ability to interpret the complex system of cultural symbols' – print and nonprint – that enable community members to participate actively and appropriately in communicative events (Benjamin *et al.*, 1996: 116). The Navajo Blessingway ceremony, for instance – a core cultural practice that epitomizes Diné values, ways of knowing and worldview – involves intricate, finely detailed literary performances by ritual specialists who spend years, even a lifetime, in apprenticeship to acquire this knowledge. Part of the ritual is the creation by the specialist of a sand painting – an elaborate visual representation made from multicolored sand. This visual text and the performative context in which it is created are essential parts of the patient's healing that invoke shared symbolic understandings of the relationship of humans to each other and to the spiritual and physical world. Reciprocally, those who are the beneficiaries of the specialist's services – the patients, their families and communities – spend lifetimes learning the nuanced meanings the ritual performances embody and enact.

This is what Ngũgĩ wa Thiong'o calls *orature*: 'a total aesthetic system, with performance and integration of art forms as two of its defining qualities' (wa Thiong'o, 2009: 44). Such oral performances, I argue, as well as more informal but culturally regulated storytellings, song texts, prayers and didactic teachings, constitute literacy 'practices' and 'events' (cf. Goodman & Wilde, 1992; Heath, 1982, 1983; Menezes de Souza, 2002; Street, 2001). Ofelia Zepeda describes the relationship between alphabetic or print literacies and orature as a continuum 'grounded in familial and community relationships' (Zepeda, 1995a: 5). This broader view of literacy, which includes non-graphocentric texts, carries with it expanded possibilities for community-based revitalization and empowerment. This theoretical and praxis-based approach to literacy is more fully developed in Chapters 1 and 4.

Linguistic enumeration, scaling, and staging

It is nearly impossible to find accounts of language revitalization and endangerment that do not invoke numbers: of languages, of speakers and of language-use contexts or domains. Indeed, it is these very characteristics – diminished numbers of language varieties, speakers and domains – that place languages on the endangered list to begin with (see, e.g. Moore, 1999: 65). As we will see in Chapter 1, linguistic enumeration is often associated with classificatory schemas, rankings and stages of language vitality and endangerment. While the numbers and rankings can be helpful, they can be problematic as well, engendering a false sense of languages as uniform, bounded or 'artefactualized objects' (Blommaert, 2008), obscuring the complexity of language practices in everyday life, and disguising the hybridity, heteroglossia and 'elasticity of speakerhood' (Moore *et al.*, 2010: 11). As linguistic anthropologist Robert Moore and his colleagues ask:

> Do we count people who speak the language *sometimes*, or only people who use it *all the time*? Do people who are *learning* the language at a later age, including adults, count? What do we do with people who grew up bilingually and can be said to belong to language group X *as well as* language group Y? (Moore *et al.*, 2010: 11)

The emphasis on enumeration and ranking may also 'inadvertently undermine the goals of advocacy', cautions linguistic anthropologist Jane Hill (2002: 120). Daryl Baldwin, director of the Myaamia Language Project discussed in Chapter 5, notes that counting and ranking can convey a 'doom and gloom message' that can paralyze language recovery efforts (see also Wesley Leonard's [2011] discussion of this for Miami). '[T]he way that you talk about [language loss and revitalization] has unintended consequences for tribes that are ... losing their speakers', Baldwin notes (personal communication, 19 August 2009).

These issues are discussed more fully in the chapters to come. For now, I want to cue readers to some of the problems surrounding enumeration, classification and 'staging', and urge caution in interpreting these representations of language vitality and shift.

What counts as a heritage language or mother tongue?

Native American LPP is a unique case that does not fit easily within conventional scholarly discourses about heritage languages and mother tongue schooling (see, e.g. McCarty, 2008a). Some scholars and activists object to the use of the term 'heritage' with regard to Native American languages, as it may be taken to mean a language 'spoken by an immigrant ancestor' or one that is no longer vital or relevant (William H. Wilson, personal communication, 27 July 2009). Some scholars also object to the use of 'mother tongue' when the language is acquired as a second language (i.e. through language revitalization efforts). My position is that, even though many Native American languages are no longer acquired by children as first languages, they are nonetheless languages of heritage, affinity and identity, and in this sense can and should be considered mother tongues (Skutnabb-Kangas & McCarty, 2008: 11). There are thousands of 'new' speakers who claim Indigenous languages in precisely this way (cf. O'Rourke & Walsh, 2012). Similarly, an Indigenous language can be conceived as a heritage or community language on the basis of personal and collective affiliation with it (McCarty, 2008a). Foregrounding their status as mother tongues also mutes potentially negative or backward-looking conceptions of Indigenous languages as things of the past with little utility in the present or future. In some places, then, I use 'heritage language' or 'heritage mother tongue' to reference Indigenous languages.

As succeeding chapters demonstrate, Native American languages are very much alive in the context of grass roots language planning and use. This is the notion of Indigenous heritage languages developed here – a view of Native languages and speech communities as dynamic, vital and emplaced – and, even under the weight of monumental pressure, refusing to be silenced.

About the Book

The book begins with an outline of the distinctive legal–political and demo-sociolinguistic context for Native American LPP. A defining feature of that context is tribal sovereignty, 'the powers of self-government, self-definition, self-determination, and self-education' (Wilkins & Lomawaima, 2001: 249), including the right to maintain and develop Indigenous mother tongues. Chapter 1 also provides an introduction to the diversity of Native American peoples, landscapes and language systems. A concluding section illustrates this diversity through examples of contemporary Indigenous-language use in public and communal spaces.

Drawing on concepts from the fields of anthropology, critical language studies and American Indian/Indigenous studies, in Chapter 2 I lay out a theory of LPP as a sociocultural process. Here, LPP is conceived not only as official acts and texts, but as the language-regulating social practices in which people engage, consciously and unconsciously, every day. This theoretical framework allows us to critically examine relationships among language, power and inequality, while also positioning LPP research and practice as a platform for advocacy, justice and social change. Building on a theoretical construct developed by K. Tsianina Lomawaima (2002, 2012) and elaborated in our work together on American Indian education policy and practice (Lomawaima & McCarty, 2002, 2006), I analyze Native American LPP as a contested field in which authorizing agents (in particular, the federal government) have systematically sought to distinguish and manage Indigenous cultural differences deemed 'safe' and thus tolerable, from those deemed so dangerously different as to threaten national interests. Lomawaima and I (2006) refer to this as *safety zone theory*. Medium-of-instruction policies, we argue, lie at the heart of education practices designed to ferret out 'safe' from 'dangerous' cultural difference (see also Lomawaima, 2012).

In Chapter 3, I trace the contours of the metaphorical safety zone from the first encounters between Native peoples and Europeans to the present day. From a policy of 'expedient tolerance' toward Native languages, to explicit policies intended to eradicate those languages, to the benign promotion of now-endangered Indigenous mother tongues, a critical-historical analysis of US language policy reveals the ways in which Native American languages have been positioned inside and outside a zone of perceived 'safe' cultural difference. However, Native people have not been passive recipients of federal policies; they have actively and creatively countered and reshaped metaphorical safety zone boundaries. These victories, and the on-the-ground work to recover and reclaim Indigenous mother tongues, are part of the story told in Chapter 3 as well.

Chapter 4 situates this historical and theoretical framework in a case study of Navajo, a language with almost as many speakers as all other Native American languages combined. As is true throughout much of Native North America, within the Navajo Nation the coterminous rise of bilingual–bicultural education and community-controlled schooling has been the centerpiece of a larger movement for Indigenous self-determination and linguistic rights. The Navajo case provides a multifaceted perspective on the ways in which grass roots Indigenous LPP challenges and subverts safety zone boundaries. Because Navajo has a relatively long history as a written language, this case provides the opportunity to consider the role of print literacies in these processes as well.

Chapter 5, in many ways, constitutes the heart of the book. The goal of this chapter is to put a human face on the project of language revitalization, presenting revitalizers 'as named individuals' (Kroskrity, 2011: 182), and examining the ways in which they construct language regenesis in social practice. The chapter explores a cross-section of family-, community-, school- and university-based approaches to this work; photographs and other visual representations are an important part of this examination. From formerly 'sleeping' languages such as Miami (an account co-authored with Miami language revitalizers Daryl Baldwin, George Ironstrack and Julie Olds), to California Native languages with a handful of elderly speakers but with many dedicated language apprentices, to the Mohawk freedom schools in present-day New York and southeastern Canada, to immersion schools in Hawai'i and in Navajo country, the chapter examines the initiatives by which revitalizers open new 'ideological and implementational spaces' (Hornberger, 2006a) for language reclamation, and with what effects.

Chapter 6, co-written with Mary Eunice Romero-Little, Ofelia Zepeda and Larisa Warhol – my co-investigators on a large-scale study of Native American language shift and retention – addresses the youngest stakeholders in this work: Native American youth. What do young people have to say about their heritage mother tongues? How do they construct language policy in everyday social practice? What can we learn from research with youth to inform broader LPP efforts? A close inspection of Indigenous youth language practices and environments reveals them to be much more complex than is often credited, raising thorny issues of fluency and 'dysfluency' (Meek, 2011), and simultaneously countering stereotypes of youth as disinterested in their heritage mother tongues. We relate these findings to Ortiz's (1992) notion of cultural continuance, which acknowledges the hybridity of contemporary youth language and cultural practices, enabling them to be re-envisioned as resources rather than liabilities for language regenesis.

Chapter 7 brings this examination of Native American LPP full circle. Drawing on Indigenous oral traditions that tell of the 'seventh generation' – alternately conceived as the present generation or as generations to come – I reflect on the victories of Indigenous self-determined LPP alongside the tests of those of those victories (both literal and figurative) within the present language policy environment. Focusing on school-based revitalization, the chapter considers the challenges emanating from twin movements for standardization and English-only. I offer a framework for the implementation of 'strong' Native language and culture programs, which, abundant research shows, are associated with high levels of language revitalization and academic success. The chapter closes with the possibilities for Indigenous linguistic and educational sovereignty these and other community-driven revitalization efforts represent.

A Special Note to You, the Reader

Writers can never fully anticipate who will read their words, and over more than a decade of this book's germination, I have imagined several audiences for it. For those of you who are new to the field, I have felt it important to lay out LPP foundations as I have come to understand them through my scholarship and work with Indigenous communities. For both new and established LPP scholars, I have sought to theorize and apply this knowledge to sociolinguistic contexts about which much has been written – Native North America – but not yet gathered under cover of a single volume.

However, this book is not intended solely for academics. I have also written this for educators, language planners, policy-makers, activists, scholar-practitioners, and tribal leaders – the large and varied group of individuals who undertake and influence language planning 'on the ground'. For you, I hope you will find here fresh insights and LPP strategies as well as confirmation of your own good ideas and practices. I expect you will find disconfirmation of some widely held stereotypes and public policy assumptions, and a few cautionary tales as well.

Some of you may represent what publishers call a 'general audience' – readers with an interest in Native American issues, the role of language in society, both, or more. I hope this book will answer some of your questions and perhaps even motivate you to lend your support to Indigenous community-driven LPP.

Finally, with every word, I have been acutely aware of the Indigenous youth, families and communities whose work and lives constitute the main storyline of the book. For you, I hope these pages resonate with your experiences and convey authenticity, solidarity and respect. Your work gives inspiration to others who are striving for linguistic and social justice – encouraging us all, in Ortiz's (1992) words, to 'fight back' and 'fight on'.

Phoenix, Arizona, July 2012

1 Contextualizing Native American LPP: Legal–Political, Demographic and Sociolinguistic Foundations

> *The very persistence of viable languages speaks immensely to the vitality of Native life in the United States.*
> Medicine, 2001: 52

I begin this chapter with this statement by Lakota anthropologist, educator and language activist Beatrice Medicine because she situates the dynamic cultural context for Native American language planning and policy so perceptively and well. Despite 'generations of pressure to change', Medicine argues, the 'nexus of sociolinguistic manifestations' within diverse Native communities persists – a sign, she adds, that Native cultures continue to thrive (Medicine, 2001: 51–52).

This chapter provides an overview of diverse Native American communities and the 'sociolinguistic nexus' at their heart. I begin with tribal sovereignty, a defining status of Native peoples that implicates critical questions of identity, authority and self-determination (Wilkins & Lomawaima, 2001: 4), including rights to language. This is followed by a demographic and sociolinguistic sketch of contemporary Native American communities and linguistic groups. Within this discussion, I introduce readers to the ways in which Native American languages have been described numerically, classified linguistically and 'staged' in terms of vitality and endangerment. I stress, however, that the numbers and classificatory schemas are, as multiple scholars have noted (including those who posit the numbers and classifications), imperfect representations of what constitutes 'speakerhood' that greatly simplify the complexity of language use and change 'on the ground'. That complexity is addressed in detail in subsequent chapters. Because enumeration and classification are common practices, both in the scholarly literature and in public discourse on language endangerment, it is important that we understand them and what they are attempting to do. The chapter concludes with illustrations of Native American language use in the public sphere, including education, arguably the most significant – if contested – domain for Native language use historically and today.

First Peoples, First Principles: Tribal Sovereignty

Understanding Native American language planning and policy (LPP) requires, first and foremost, understanding the unique legal and political status of Native peoples in the United States. As indicated in the Preface, the term Native American encompasses diverse American Indian, Alaska Native and Native Hawaiian peoples. Although each of these peoples has encountered the US sociopolitical system in different ways, all are descendants 'from the populations which inhabited the country ... at the time of ... colonization ... and ... irrespective of their legal status, retain some or all of their own social, economic, cultural, and political institutions' – the internationally recognized definition of Indigenous peoples (International Labour Organisation, 1989, Article 1.1.b).

From a legal–political perspective, at the core of this collective identity is the principle of tribal sovereignty: the 'right of a people to self-government, self-determination, and self-education', including the right to linguistic and cultural expression according to local languages and norms (Lomawaima & McCarty, 2006: 10). Like the sovereignty of US states and the federal government, tribal sovereignty is not absolute; the political realities of tribal–federal–state relations, 'competing jurisdictions, local histories, circumscribed land bases, and overlapping citizenships', all constrain, but do not negate, the exercise of sovereignty (Wilkins & Lomawaima, 2001: 5).

Examples of tribes' sovereign powers include 'the right to determine their membership, administer justice through tribal courts, govern their citizens, and regulate the use of their land base' (Lomawaima & McCarty, 2006: 10). At the federal level, recognition of tribal sovereignty in the linguistic and educational realm includes the 1990/1992 Native American Languages Act and the 2006 Esther Martinez Native American Languages Preservation Act (both discussed in Chapter 3). At the state level, Indigenous linguistic and educational sovereignty is reflected in such policies as Hawai'i's constitutional recognition of Hawaiian as co-official with English (Wilson, 2013 [in press]); Montana's 1999/2005 Indian Education for All Act requiring public schools to implement programs that fulfill the state's constitutional commitment 'to the preservation of [American Indians'] cultural heritage' (Ngai & Koehn, 2010: 50–51); New Mexico's Indian Education Act, designed to increase the number of Native American teachers and school leaders and provide resources for Native language and culture instruction in the state's public schools (Jojola *et al.*, 2010); Arizona's 2012 partnership between tribal governments and the state department of education to enable tribal control of Native-language teacher certification; and Alaska's 2012 Senate Bill 130, which establishes an Alaska Native Language Preservation and Advisory Council to assess the status of Alaska Native languages and make recommendations to the governor and state legislature on new or reorganized language education programs. At the tribal level, educational and linguistic sovereignty is expressed in tribal language policies, education codes and legislation such as the 2005 Navajo Sovereignty in Education Act (discussed in Chapter 4).

Tribal sovereignty predates the US Constitution and is therefore inherent (Wilkins & Lomawaima, 2001: 5). Tribal sovereignty is also recognized in the U.S. Constitution, which grants Congress the power to regulate commerce with foreign nations and tribes, and authorizes the President to negotiate treaties with foreign nations and Indian nations. From the first encounters between Native peoples and Europeans, the two groups operated on a government-to-government basis, with the US government acting toward Native peoples 'much as it would with foreign nations, using a mixture of diplomacy, treaties, and warfare' (Snipp, 2002: 2). (A similar government-to-government relationship exists between First Nations, Inuit and Metís peoples and Canada's federal, provincial and territorial governments.)

Between 1779 and 1871, the US government signed more than 400 treaties with American Indian tribes, of which 120 had education-related stipulations. Through those treaties, Native peoples relinquished certain rights and possessions – most critically, land – in exchange for certain federal guarantees such as education and health and other social services. The tribal–federal relationship was subsequently formalized in federal legislation, judicial decisions and the various agencies charged with overseeing 'Indian affairs', including the Bureau of Indian Affairs (BIA) within the US Department of the Interior. This is the basis of the tribal–federal relationship; it is a legally and morally codified relationship of *trust responsibility* that is both voluntary and contractual, and entails the 'federal responsibility to protect or enhance tribal assets [including linguistic and cultural assets] through policy decisions and management actions' (Wilkins & Lomawaima, 2001: 65; emphasis in original). It is an obligation and a legal–political relationship unlike that of any other US ethnolinguistic group (Lomawaima, 2003).

Over the years, the federal government has repeatedly violated its trust responsibility, and tribal and federal powers have frequently been at odds. Further pitting the 'uneven ground' (Wilkins & Lomawaima, 2001) of tribal sovereignty is the fact that the sovereignty of some tribes is recognized by states but not by the federal government; some tribes (e.g. many in California) have been denied recognition as sovereigns by both states and the federal government and are thereby disenfranchised from trust-related government services. Native Hawaiians, whose internationally recognized sovereign kingdom was illegally overthrown by the US government in 1893 and who were not officially incorporated into the US political system until Hawaiian statehood in 1959, are still fighting for federal recognition of their sovereign status. Alaska Natives, who include American Indians and Aleut, Inupiat and Yup'ik peoples, also share a distinct experience vis-à-vis state and federal governments, and some ethnic groups indigenous to Alaska (e.g. Siberian Yup'ik and Aleut peoples) have members in present-day Russia.[1] Nevertheless, all Native Americans share a distinct status as Indigenous peoples and a singular relationship with the US government in which culture, language, politics and legal status are inextricably linked (Lomawaima & McCarty, 2006: 7). As we will see in the chapters that follow, the tribal–federal relationship has shaped and continues to shape the possibilities for Native American language education in profound and far-reaching ways.[2]

Peoples, Populations and Lands

No one can know for certain the numbers of Native peoples or language varieties present in the Western hemisphere when Christopher Columbus made landfall in the Bahamas on 12 October 1492. Population estimates for the part of the hemisphere that is now the coterminous United States and Canada range from a low of 900,000 proposed by the anthropologist Alfred Kroeber in 1939, to a high of 12.3 million proposed by the anthropologist Henry F. Dobyns in 1966 (Thornton, 1987: 26). In *American Indian Holocaust and Survival,* the anthropologist Russell Thornton places the pre-Columbian estimate in this geographic area conservatively at 7+ million (Thornton, 1987: 32).

Following the European invasion, European-introduced diseases and the seizure of Indigenous lands plunged Native populations – and languages – into drastic decline. In 2012, the US Census Bureau reported 5.2 million American Indian and Alaska Native people (1.7% of the total population), and 1.2 million people identified as Native Hawaiian and 'other Pacific Islanders' (0.4% of the total population; Hixson *et al.,* 2012; Norris *et al.,* 2012).[3] Native Americans reside in every US state and territory, representing 565 federally recognized tribes and 617 reservations and Alaska Native villages (see Figure 1.1). There are also numerous Hawaiian Homelands or Homesteads, 'similar to American Indian reservations, with a 50% Native Hawaiian blood quantum requirement for leases' (Wilson, 2013 [in press]).

As Table 1.1 shows, the most populous American Indian nation is Cherokee, with more than 800,000 individuals identifying as Cherokee 'alone or in some combination' with one or more other tribal/ethnic groups. Navajo, with a population of more than 330,000, has the largest land base, with a reservation the size of Ireland spread across three southwestern states (see Figure 1.1). Most Native nations are smaller geographically and in terms

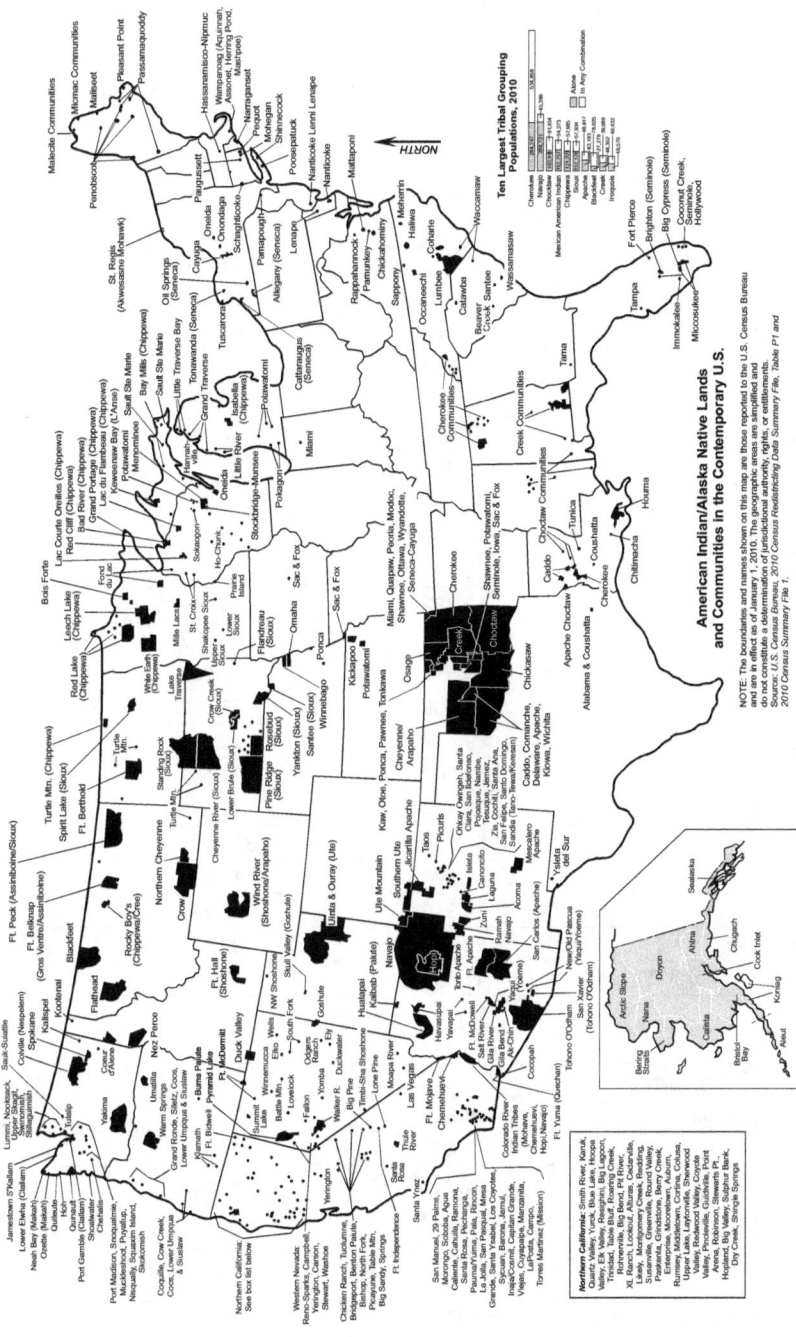

Figure 1.1 American Indian/Alaska Native lands and communities in the contemporary United States (graphics by Shearon Vaughn)

Table 1.1 'Selected tribal groupings' of the American Indian and Alaska Native population in the 2010 US Census (Norris et al., 2012: 17)

Tribal group	Number reporting 'American Indian and Alaska Native alone' (one tribal grouping)	Number reporting 'American Indian tribal grouping alone or in any combination with one or more other races'
Alaskan Athabaskan	15,623	22,484
Aleut	11,920	19,282
Apache	63,193	111,810
Arapaho	8,014	10,861
Blackfeet	27,279	105,304
Cherokee	284,247	819,105
Cheyenne	11,375	19,051
Chickasaw	27,973	52,278
Chippewa	112,757	170,742
Choctaw	103,910	195,764
Cree	2,211	7,983
Creek	48,352	88,332
Crow	10,332	15,203
Hopi	12,580	18,327
Iroquois	40,570	81,002
Inupiat	24,859	33,360
Kiowa	9,437	13,787
Lumbee	62,306	73,691
Menominee	8,374	11,133
Navajo	286,731	332,129
Osage	8,938	18,576
Paiute	9,340	13,767
Potawatami	20,412	33,771
Pueblo (non-Hopi Pueblos)	49,695	62,540
Seminole	14,080	31,971
Shoshone	7,852	13,002
Sioux (Lakota, Dakota)	112,176	170,110
Tohono O'odham	19,522	23,478
Ute	7,435	11,491
Yakima	8,786	11,527
Yaqui (Yoeme)	21,679	32,595
Yuman (multiple tribal groups)	7,727	10,089
Yup'ik	28,927	33,889
American Indian or Alaska Native tribes not specified	693,709	1,545,963

of their membership (see Table 1.1). As elsewhere in the Americas, economic disparities are profound, with more than a quarter of American Indian and Alaska Native people living below the federal poverty line, a figure double that of the US population as a whole (Ogunwole, 2006: 12). Importantly for considerations of language and education, the median age of the Native American population (31.9) is significantly younger than that of the non-Hispanic White population (40.1) (US Census Bureau, 2007: 7).

While many Native American people live in rural villages and on reservation lands, the majority of the American Indian/Alaska Native population (67% to 92%, depending on how one 'counts') lives outside of these areas, and only about 48,000 individuals reporting Native Hawaiian ancestry reside within Hawaiian Homelands (Hixson et al., 2012: 19; Norris et al., 2012: 13).[4] Moreover, there is often a great deal of transmigration of individuals and families back and forth between urban and rural/reservation areas. Tables 1.2 and 1.3 show the 2010 Census figures for the 12 US cities and counties, respectively, where the largest numbers of American Indian/Alaska Native and Native Hawaiian and Other Pacific Islanders reside. As these tables and Figure 1.1 illustrate, the largest *proportion* of the American Indian, Alaska Native and Native Hawaiian population resides in western states, although states with the largest *number* of American Indians and

Table 1.2 Twelve US cities reporting the largest American Indian and Alaska Native populations in the 2010 Census (Norris et al., 2012: 11)

Place	Total population	American Indian and Alaska Native population, alone or in combination with other tribes/'races'	
		Rank	Number
New York, NY	8,175,133	1	111,749
Los Angeles, CA	3,792,621	2	54,236
Phoenix, AZ	1,445,632	3	43,724
Oklahoma City, OK	579,999	4	36,572
Anchorage, AK	291,826	5	36,062
Tulsa, OK	391,906	6	35,990
Albuquerque, NM	545,852	7	32,571
Chicago, IL	2,695,598	8	26,933
Houston, TX	2,099,451	9	25,521
San Antonio, TX	1,327,407	10	20,137
Tucson, AZ	520,116	11	19,903
San Diego, CA	1,307,402	12	17,865
		Total:	**461,263**

Table 1.3 Twelve US counties reporting the largest Native Hawaiian and Other Pacific Islander population in the 2010 Census (Hixson et al., 2012: 9)

County	Total population	Native Hawaiian and Other Pacific Islander population, alone or in combination with other tribes/'races'	
		Rank	Number
Honolulu County, HI	953,207	1	233,637
Hawai'i County, HI	185,079	2	62,487
Los Angeles County, CA	9,818,605	3	54,169
Maui County, HI	154,834	4	42,364
San Diego County, CA	3,095,313	5	30,626
Clark County, NV	1,951,269	6	27,088
Sacramento County, CA	1,418,788	7	24,138
King County, WA	1,931,249	8	23,664
Alameda County, CA	1,510,271	9	22,322
Salt Lake County, UT	1,029,655	10	20,824
Orange County, CA	3,010,232	11	19,484
Kauai County, HI	67,091	12	17,374
		Total:	578,177

Alaska Natives include California, Oklahoma, Arizona, Texas, New York, New Mexico, Washington, North Carolina, Florida and Michigan. Hawai'i is home to the largest number of Native Hawaiians and 'Other Pacific Islander' peoples (Hixson *et al.*, 2012: 6; Norris *et al.*, 2012: 6–7).

Native American Languages

Spoken languages

Counting languages is problematic, not only because the sources are suspect (see Krauss [1998] on census counts in particular), but also because the project of enumeration is an ideological one. As Moore *et al.* (2010: 2) point out, the numbering of languages privileges a conception of languages 'as neatly-bounded, abstract, autonomous grammatical systems', diverting attention 'from the speech-community dynamics of language contact and change' and obscuring the complex dynamics of 'actual language-in-use'. Enumeration also confounds issues of dialect difference: '[W]hen are two varieties so different that they should be considered separate languages, and when should they be considered dialects of the same language?', asks

Grenoble (2011: 28; see also Bradley, 2011: 67). Yet the numbers are not entirely without worth; on a worldwide scale, they tell us 'that language endangerment is a major issue ..., and that it is not too late to do something about it' (Bradley, 2011: 68). Used carefully, then, the numbers provide one, admittedly incomplete, index of Native American linguistic endangerment and diversity.

Estimates of the number of languages indigenous to what is now the United States and Canada range from 300 to 600 (Krauss, 1998; McCarty & Watahomigie, 2004; Yamamoto, 2007). These figures reflect as many as 60 language families. Adding to this diversity are the pidgins and creoles that emerged prior to and following the European invasion, including trade languages such as Chinook Jargon in the Pacific Northwest, Hawaiian Creole English in Hawai'i, and Mobilian Jargon along the Gulf of Mexico. Throughout North America, long-standing Indigenous sign languages are also used, as are a multitude of Indigenous Englishes.

At the end of the 20th century, the linguist Michael Krauss (1998) estimated that 210 Native American languages were still being spoken in what is now the United States and Canada, including 175 in the United States alone (see also Goddard, 1996a, 1996b; Yamamoto, 2007; Zepeda & Hill, 1992). Recent estimates by the American Community Survey – a national demographic questionnaire associated with the US Census Bureau – report 169 Native American languages in the United States, excluding Hawaiian and languages spoken by peoples indigenous to Latin America and to American-affiliated Pacific Island territories (Siebens & Julian, 2011: 1). Table 1.4 provides an overview of major Native American language groups; Table 1.5 shows the recent census counts for 'most commonly spoken' Native American languages.

As Table 1.5 shows, the 2010 US Census Bureau reported approximately 372,000 to 397,000 speakers of Native American languages, almost half of whom were speakers of Navajo. The census also reported that only 5.4% of those living within American Indian/Alaska Native tribal areas spoke a tribal language, and of these, most were elderly (Siebens & Julian, 2011: 3). According to the Census Bureau, 'Over 1 in 5 ... people aged 65 and over spoke [a Native American] language, ... while about 1 in 10 people aged 5 to 17 did so' (Siebens & Julian, 2011: 3). (These statistics, of course, do not tell us 'how much' or 'how well' the languages are spoken.) Figure 1.2 shows the location of reported speakers of Native American languages in the 2010 census. Alaska, Hawai'i and the southwestern United States reported the majority of Native-language speakers, with nine counties within the states of Alaska, Arizona and New Mexico reporting half of all American Indian/Alaska Native-language speakers (Siebens & Julian, 2011: 5).

While helpful in providing a sense of the locations of Native American speech communities, as we will see in subsequent chapters, the US Census data greatly underestimate what Medicine called 'the persistence of viable

Table 1.4 Examples of the diversity of Native American languages (Goddard, 1996a; McCarty & Watahomigie, 2004; Mignon & Boxberger, 1997)

Language family grouping	Examples and locations of speakers*
Algonquian	Abenaki, Chippewa, Miami-Illinois, Ojibwe, Wôpanâak (*Great Lakes region, northeastern United States, Oklahoma*); Kickapoo, Omaha, Shawnee (*central states, and for Kickapoo, northern Mexico*); Arapaho, Blackfeet, Cheyenne, Cree (*northern Plains, including parts of southern Canada*)
Athabaskan	Athabaskan (*western Subarctic*); Carrier–Chilcotin (*northeast Plateau*); Hupa, Tlingit (*California, north Pacific Coast, Alaska*); Kiowa-Apache (*Plains*); Navajo, Western Apache (*Southwest*)
Caddoan	Arikara, Pawnee, Wichita (*eastern Plains*)
California Penutian	Maidu, Miwok, Patwin, Wintu (*northern California*)
Chinook–Tsimshian	Chinook (*northwest Pacific Coast/Washington and Oregon*)
Klamath–Sahaptin	Klamath, Modoc, Sahaptin, Warm Springs, Yakima (*northwest Plateau/Washington and California*)
	Tsimshian (*western Canada, Alaska*)
Chimakuan	Quileute (*northwest Pacific Coast*)
Salishan	Coeur d'Alene, Columbia, Flathead, Quinault, Shuswap (*northwest Plateau and Coast*)
Eskimoan	Yup'ik, Inuit–Inupiaq (*Alaska and the Circumpolar North, including Canada, Greenland and Eastern Russia*)
Aleut	Western and Eastern Aleut, Copper Island Aleut Creole (*Alaska*)
Hokan	Karuk, Washo (*northern California*)
Yuman	Cocopa, Havasupai, Hualapai, Ipai, Kumeyaay, Maricopa, Mohave, Quechan, Tipai, Yavapai (*Arizona, southern California, Baja California*)
Salinian–Seri–Shastan	Shasta (*northern California*)
Pomoan	Central, Eastern, Kashaya, Northern, Northeastern, Southern Pomo (*central and northern California*)
Iroquoian	Cherokee (*southeastern United States, Atlantic Coast, Oklahoma*); Mohawk, Onondaga, Oneida, Seneca (*eastern Great Lakes, northeastern United States, southeastern Canada*)
Muskogean	Choctaw, Chickasaw, Creek, Seminole (*southeastern United States, Oklahoma*)
Natchez	Natchez (*Gulf Coast*)

Table 1.4 (Continued)

Language family grouping	Examples and locations of speakers*
Polynesian	Hawaiian, Samoan, Tahitian, Tongan (*Hawaiian Islands, Samoa, American Samoa, Tahiti, Tonga*)
Micronesian	Chamorro, Chuukese, Kosrean, Marshallese, Palauan, Saipanese, Yapese (*Guam, Chuuk, Kosrae, Marshall Islands, Palau, Saipan, Yap*)
Uto-Aztecan	Comanche (*Plains*); Hopi, O'odham, Southern Paiute, Yaqui/Yoeme (*southwestern United States, northern Mexico*); Bannock, Chemehuevi, Paiute, Shoshone (*Great Basin area, Nevada, California*)
Tanoan	Tewa, Tiwa, Towa/Jemez (*Arizona, New Mexico*)
Kiowan	Kiowa (*Plains*)
Siouan	Hidatsa, Mandan, Osage, Ponca, Winnebago (*eastern Plains*); Assiniboine, Crow, Teton, Yankton (*western Plains, including Canada*); Dakota/Lakota (*central and northern Plains, including Canada*)
Yuchi (Euchee)	Euchee (*Gulf Coast, Oklahoma, South Carolina*)

* Location information includes Indigenous homelands and current locations resulting from forced relocation.

[Native American] languages' (2001: 52). The map in Figure 1.2, for example, does not reflect the presence of Native people in urban areas, where, as Tables 1.2 and 1.3 suggest, many speakers of Native American languages are likely to reside. Also excluded from these data are 'new speakers' – individuals who are learning and/or using their heritage language for a variety of everyday purposes, but who are not native speakers (O'Rourke & Walsh, 2012). Often these are members of small, diasporized Native nations that have been forcibly (and multiply) removed from traditional homelands. Grinwald and Bert (2011: 49–52) offer a list of the types of speakers who might be excluded from census data and other language surveys: 'rememberers', 'ghost speakers' who deny knowledge of a socially stigmatized heritage language but whose linguistic abilities might be reactivated under conducive circumstances, and 'neo-speakers' or new language learners. In Chapter 5, we will learn more of the perspectives and experiences of new speakers. Their presence throughout Native America, as well as that of speakers living outside of federally designated Native American lands, is denoted by the background shading of the map in Figure 1.2.

Finally, the census data completely invisibilize speakers of diverse Native American Englishes, creoles and pidgins. As anthropologist Anthony Webster points out with reference to his research on the uses of Englishes among Navajo poets, Native Americans can and do 'own' English (Webster, 2011: 61). Although a full discussion of these varieties is outside the scope of this

Table 1.5 Most commonly spoken Native American languages reported in the 2010 census (Siebens & Julian, 2011: 2)

Language	Number of speakers reported	Primary location of speakers in the United States
Navajo	169,471	Arizona, New Mexico, Utah
Hawaiian	27,160	Hawai'i
Yup'ik	18,950	Alaska
Dakota/Lakota	18,616	Minnesota, Montana, Nebraska, South Dakota, North Dakota
Apache	13,063	Arizona, New Mexico
Keres	12,945	New Mexico
Cherokee	11,610	Oklahoma, North Carolina
Choctaw	10,343	Mississippi, Oklahoma
Zuni	9,686	Arizona, New Mexico
Ojibwe	8,371	Michigan, Minnesota, Wisconsin
O'odham (Pima)	7,270	Arizona
Inupik	7,203	Alaska
Hopi	6,634	Arizona
Tewa	5,176	Arizona, New Mexico
Muskogee (Creek)	5,064	Southeastern United States, Oklahoma
Crow	3,705	Montana
Shoshone	2,211	Idaho, Wyoming, Utah
Cheyenne	2,156	Oklahoma, Montana, Wyoming
Tiwa	2,009	New Mexico, Texas
'Unspecified' American Indian language(s)	8,298	—
'Other' Native North American language(s)	47,238	—
Total	**397,179**	—

book, their presence adds to the complexity, heteroglossia and hybridity of the 'sociolinguistic nexus' within Indigenous communities. Native American Englishes are 'beautiful Englishes and intimate grammars', Webster maintains, 'and it is time to understand them as Native American languages' (Webster, 2011: 8; see also Leap, 1993; Wong, 1999a).

Indigenous multimodal literacies

Adding to the complexity and heterogeneity of Native American speech communities is the multimodal nature of literacies in use. Well before Europeans arrived, autochthonous non-graphocentric literacies flourished.

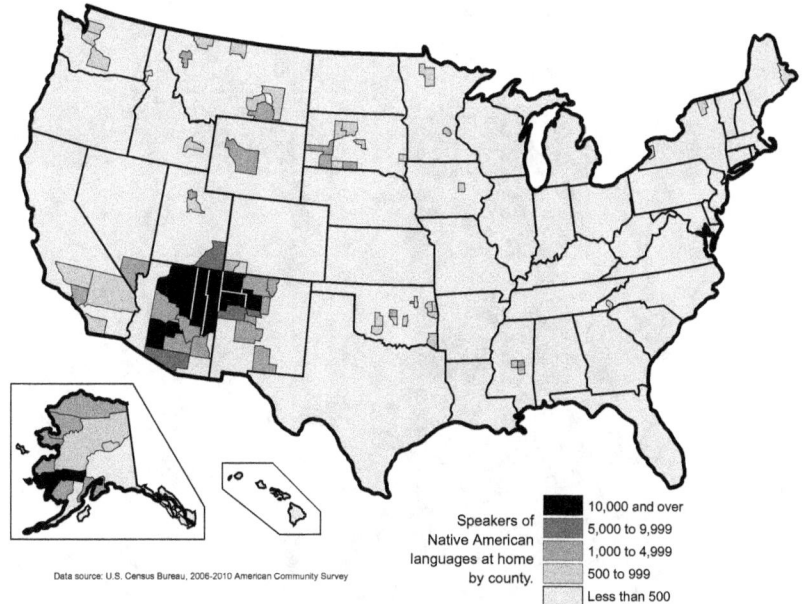

Figure 1.2 Native American language speakers, by US county, as reported in the 2010 US Census (Siebens & Julian, 2011: 4; graphics by Shearon Vaughn)

As Mi'kmaq scholar Marie Battiste relates, winter counts (pictographic calendars),[5] wampum and calendar sticks used 'ideographic symbolization of concepts and ideas ... to record and store valuable knowledge ... on available natural materials such as birch bark, rocks and shells' (Battiste, 1986: 25). All of this comprises Indigenous multimodal literacies that interact with and depend upon a collective oral tradition.

At the same time, print literacy has a long history in many Native American communities. Yup'ik, Navajo, Cherokee and many Algonquian languages have had alphabetic or syllabic writing systems for nearly two or more centuries. The Cherokee silversmith Sequoyah (whose Anglo name is believed to be George Guess or Gist) spent a decade creating his famous syllabary, which he completed in 1821 (Cherokee Nation Language Planning Committees, 2008: 4; see Figure 1.3). The syllabary has 85 characters, both invented and borrowed from the Roman and Greek alphabets, representing this Iroquoian language's sound system. Two years before Sequoyah completed his syllabary, a missionary-produced Cherokee spelling book using a version of the Roman alphabet was developed. In 1828, the Cherokee Nation, then headquartered in New Echota, Georgia, obtained a printing press and publication began of the first American Indian newspaper, the *Cherokee Phoenix* (see Figure 1.4).[6]

Figure 1.3 Sequoyah (George Guess or Gist), with a likeness of his 1821 Cherokee syllabary (Lithograph by Thomas L. McKenney and James Hall, ca 1836, Library of Congress Prints and Photographs Division, Washington DC, http://www.loc.gov/pictures/item93504544)

The extant historical record contains many examples of Indigenous print literacies in diaries, correspondence, land claims documents and biblical tracts – precious resources that, as Chapter 5 shows, have become invaluable documentation for contemporary language reclamation efforts. For other Native languages, practical writing systems have been developed in the past 30–40 years, often as an outgrowth of bilingual education programs or in tandem with language revitalization efforts (see Francis & Reyhner, 2002 for examples and a discussion). Orthographies for Indigenous languages vary widely, with some using adaptations of the Roman alphabet and others using their own symbols, including syllabaries.

It is nevertheless the case that the authority of Indigenous languages is widely recognized as residing in the spoken word (Dinwoodie, 1998: 193;

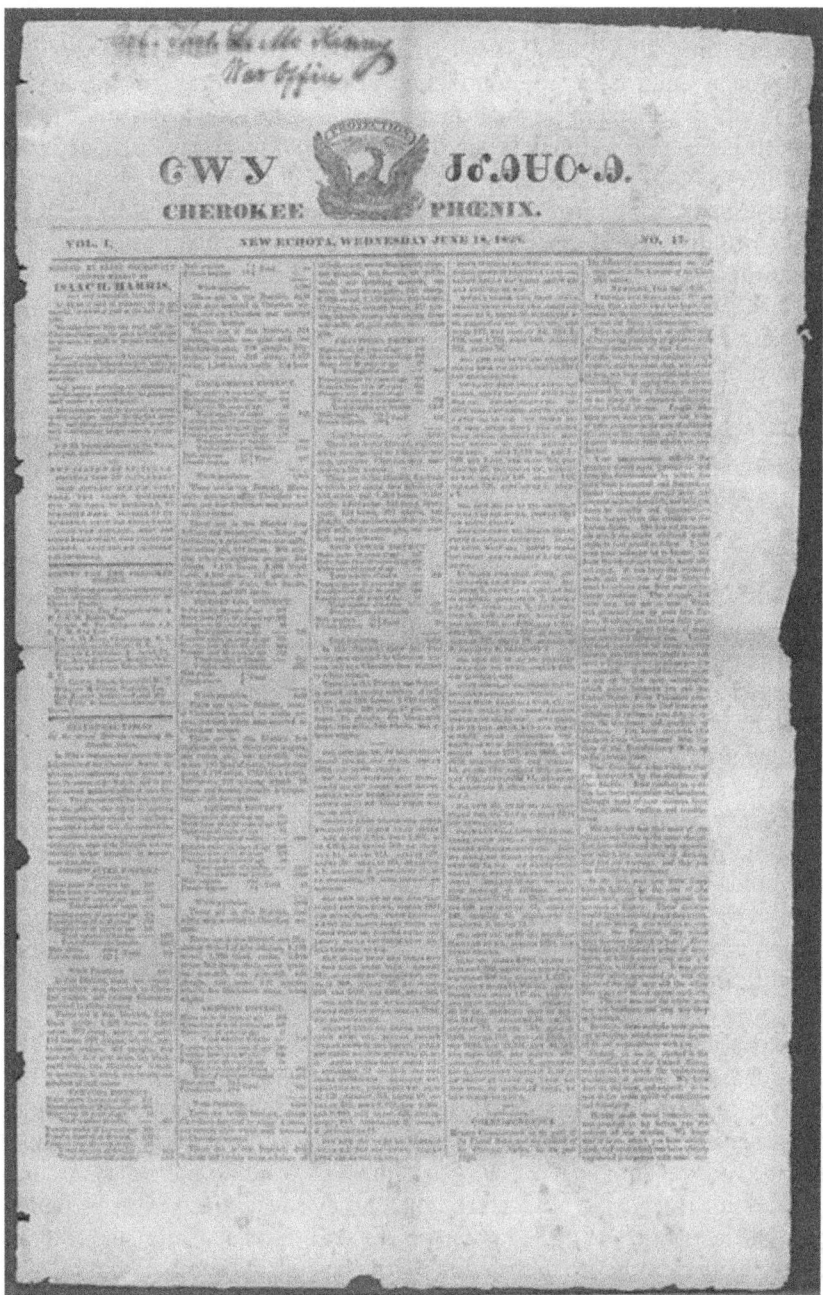

Figure 1.4 An early edition of the *Cherokee Phoenix* newspaper, which included the first census of the Cherokee Nation (American Treasures of the Library of Congress, Washington, DC, http://www.lc.gov/exhibits/treasures/trr125.html)

Zepeda, 1995a). 'It must not be forgotten', says Acoma scholar and activist Christine Sims, 'that the primary function of these tribal languages has always been their use as the foundation of essentially oral tribal societies. That is where the validation of these languages resides' (Sims, 2005: 105). Reflecting this, many Pueblo language programs have explicitly rejected print literacy as an educational and LPP goal out of concern for 're-strengthening the spoken language, first, as a language of communication in family and community contexts' (Sims, 2011: 158). Other tribal programs have found Indigenous-language literacy problematic because written texts '[violate] basic features associated with spoken [language] performance', and because of 'lingering uncertainties regarding the usefulness of a written Indian language or of knowing how to write it, concerns about the ways ... literacy will redistribute access to knowledge and affect seniority and status within the Tribe, and personal dissatisfaction with the representation of [the Indigenous-language] "text" when presented on the printed page' (Leap, 1993: 33).

In a telling account of the ways in which these issues may unfold, Sims (2008) describes the tensions and dilemmas that arose when New Mexico state authorities required standardized (written) assessments of Pueblo students' oral language proficiency. She writes: '[H]ere was a situation in which tribal language proficiency was being proposed as a standard process to be developed and used by all [Pueblo] language communities', with potentially damaging effects on students' language learning attitudes as well as the communal values informing the program (Sims, 2008: 336–37).

> Student participation in traditional ceremonies, helping elders and traditional religious leaders ... is an important aspect of language use that would be difficult to capture in a single test ... Again, the question has been raised about how this critical aspect of language use and its application in real-life circumstances can be determined by 'proficient' or 'nonproficient' labels. (Sims, 2008: 337)

In this case, the community response was to seek time and resources to construct 'a more appropriate process for reporting information about the progress of students' language learning' and to rededicate LPP efforts to strengthening young people's spoken language use in settings such as those described above (Sims, 2008: 339). Benjamin, Pecos and Romero discuss similar issues for the Pueblo of Cochiti, where, they say, literacy must be understood in the context of 'the oral nature of Cochiti society [and] the abilities needed by its members to understand particular cultural symbols and thereby participate in Cochiti intellectual tradition' (Benjamin *et al.*, 1996: 116; see also Pecos & Blum-Martinez, 2001).

Reflecting this broader view of literacy, Tohono O'odham linguist Ofelia Zepeda has proposed the metaphor of a literacy continuum. According to

Zepeda, the literacy continuum encompasses the 'traditional knowledge of storytelling, the rhythm of traditional narratives, the oral structures of those narratives and the importance of this type of literature' in Indigenous communities – knowledge that influences and interacts with the use of print literacies (Zepeda, 1995a: 15).[7] Later in the book we will explore examples of the literacy continuum in practice.

Assessing Language Vitality and Endangerment

We have seen in the foregoing discussion that the 'sociolinguistic nexus' in Native American communities encompasses a broad array of spoken language varieties linked to heterogeneous language ideologies and multimodal literacies. This section considers the classification schemas that have been developed to describe and evaluate the relative vitality of these sociolinguistic resources. Typically, the schemas use one or more factors indicative of trajectories of language shift: (1) the number and relative proportion of speakers in a population; (2) the nature and extent of intergenerational language transmission; (3) extant domains for using the heritage mother tongue; and (4) the potential for language regeneration (e.g. language documentation resources, official policies supporting or restricting language use, and the availability of teaching materials and heritage-language education programs). Of these factors, Grenoble argues that the characteristics of the pool of speakers are most important – not only numbers of speakers, but also their distribution intergenerationally and their proportions in the larger population (Grenoble, 2011: 38).

One of the most frequently cited classifications has been proposed by Krauss (1997, 1998), who places Native American languages within an A–E framework, as follows:

- *Class A*, languages still spoken by all generations and 'learned by practically all children';
- *Class A-*, languages learned by 'nearly all or most children';
- *Class B*, languages spoken by the parent generation and older, 'but learned by few or no children';
- *Class B-*, languages spoken by adults in their 30s 'but not by younger parents, and probably no children';
- *Class C*, languages spoken by 'middle-aged adults and older, forties and up';
- *Class C-*, languages spoken by adults in their 50s and older;
- *Class-D*, languages spoken by adults in their 60s and older;
- *Class D*, languages spoken by adults in their 70s and older;
- *Class D-*, languages spoken by adults in their 70s and older, 'fewer than 10'; and
- *Class E*, languages with no living speakers, described by Krauss as 'extinct' (Krauss, 1997: 25–26).

As discussed below, others describe 'class E' languages as 'sleeping' or 'dormant', a less terminal metaphor intended to differentiate languages without speakers but with the potential for future use based on linguistic documentation and the presence of a living heritage-language community (Leonard, 2007: 23; 2011).

Within Krauss's schema, scholars have placed the vast majority (80%) of Native American languages within classes B–D (see Figure 1.5). Based on this assessment, Krauss warns that, 'unless there is radical change and success at

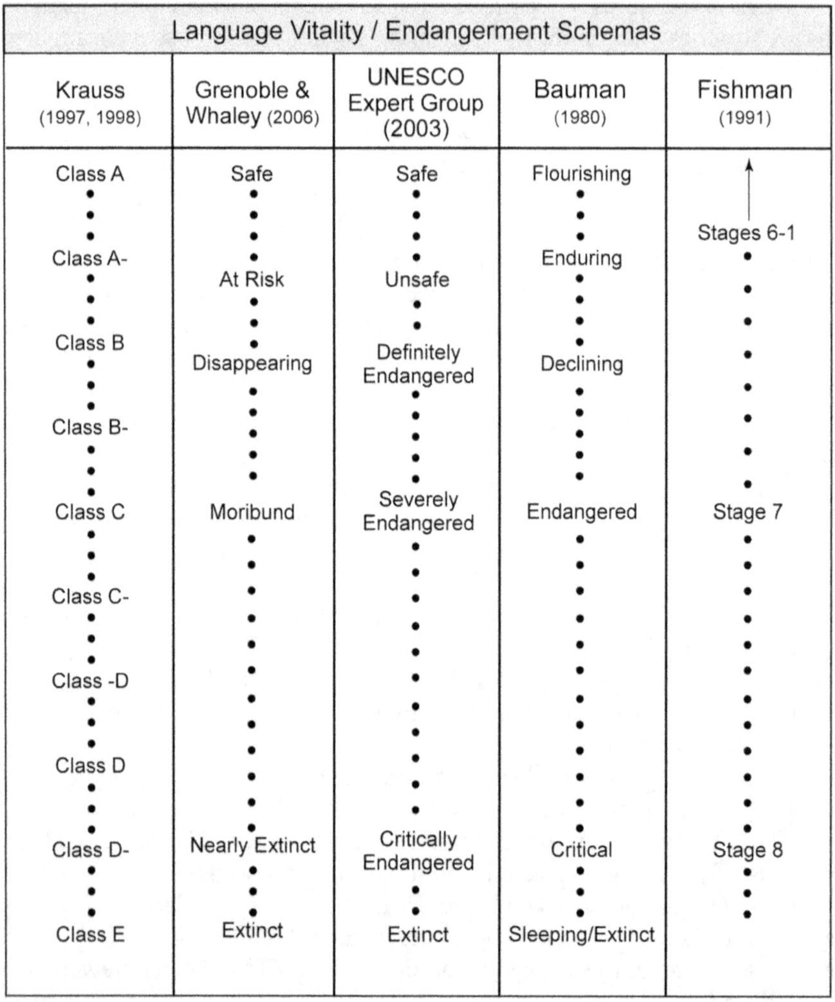

Language Vitality / Endangerment Schemas				
Krauss (1997, 1998)	Grenoble & Whaley (2006)	UNESCO Expert Group (2003)	Bauman (1980)	Fishman (1991)
Class A	Safe	Safe	Flourishing	Stages 6-1
Class A-	At Risk	Unsafe	Enduring	
Class B	Disappearing	Definitely Endangered	Declining	
Class B-				
Class C	Moribund	Severely Endangered	Endangered	Stage 7
Class C-				
Class -D				
Class D				
Class D-	Nearly Extinct	Critically Endangered	Critical	Stage 8
Class E	Extinct	Extinct	Sleeping/Extinct	

Figure 1.5 Comparison of language vitality/endangerment schemas (graphics by Shearon Vaughn)

reversal of language shift', by the year 2060, all but 20 Indigenous languages in the United States 'would be extinct' (Krauss, 1998: 11).

Grenoble and Whaley (2006) propose a six-way schema that, like Krauss's, indexes speakers' ages and the extent of intergenerational transmission:

- *Safe* languages are spoken by all generations in all or nearly all domains, and have a large number of speakers relative to others in the region. 'Many safe languages enjoy official status ... and as such tend to be held in higher prestige' (Grenoble & Whaley, 2006: 18).
- *At risk* languages retain a significant speaker base but have proportionately fewer speakers and use domains.
- *Disappearing* languages show an observable shift and decreasing intergenerational transmission.
- *Moribund* languages are no longer transmitted to children.
- *Nearly extinct* languages have only a handful of elderly speakers.
- *Extinct* languages have no remaining speakers.

The UNESCO Ad Hoc Expert Group on Endangered Languages (2003: 8) uses a very similar six-way framework of 'safe', 'vulnerable', 'definitely endangered', 'severely endangered', 'critically endangered' and 'extinct' categories (cf. Wurm, 2001; see Figure 1.5).

In his 1980 *Guide to Issues in Indian Language Retention*, Bauman also provides a six-way classification, ranking languages from 'flourishing' to 'extinct':

- *Flourishing* languages have speakers of all ages, and the language is supported in all parts of home and community life.
- *Enduring* languages are spoken by a significant proportion of the population, although some younger people have switched to the language of wider communication.
- *Declining* languages are spoken by as much as half the adult population, but most young people use the language of wider communication.
- *Endangered* languages are spoken by older generations but are little used by parents of childbearing age.
- *Critical* languages have only a handful of elderly speakers.
- *Extinct* or *sleeping* languages have no speakers who learn the language through natural intergenerational transmission. (Cited in Task Force on Aboriginal Languages and Cultures, 2005: 34.)

Finally, in his seminal treatise, *Reversing Language Shift*, Fishman outlines a graded intergenerational disruption scale or GIDS, in which 'the higher the GIDS rating the lower the intergenerational continuity and maintenance prospects of a language network or community' (Fishman, 1991: 87). Fishman's GIDS differs from the classification schemas above in that he posits the stages as predictive of language loss and recovery; that is, while the other schemas are largely descriptive, Fishman's is theoretical in scope. In particular, he argues that stage 6, which centers on the home–family–neighborhood–community nexus, constitutes 'the heart and soul' of intergenerational language transmission: *'One cannot jump across or dispense with stage 6'*, maintains Fishman (1991: 95; emphasis in original). Fishman's stages, from most to least disrupted language maintenance, are as follows:

- At *stage 8*, language users are socially isolated elders and the language 'needs to be re-assembled from their mouths and memories' (Fishman, 1991: 88).
- At *stage 7*, most users represent a socially integrated and ethnolinguistically active population beyond childbearing age.
- *Stage 6* represents the divide between languages considered 'healthy' or 'safe' and those 'at risk'. This is the stage at which the heritage language is transmitted intergenerationally and is a natural and regular part of family and community life. Accordingly, stages 5–1 support but do not replace stage 6 in Fishman's framework.
- *Stages 5 and 4* involve mother tongue literacy and the use of the heritage language in school.
- *Stages 3–1* involve heritage language use in the workplace, government, and media, respectively. (Fishman, 1991: 81–121)

Figure 1.5 provides a comparison of these language classification schemas. While the schemas provide a sense of language trajectories, as noted previously, they also mask dynamic processes of language use and change. Assessments of language vitality 'represent general trends, not hard-and-fast rules', cautions Grenoble (2011: 42). Moreover, the static nature of scaling and staging can discourage language revitalization efforts, especially for communities that the schemas position on the 'class D/E' or 'critical' end of the scale. 'No longer do we accept the 'e-word' (*extinct*) to describe *myaamia* [the Miami language]', Miami linguist Wesley Leonard asserts; 'we instead use the term sleeping to refer to its status during its period of dormancy, noting that this term is not only more socially appropriate but also more accurate in that our language was never irretrievably lost' (Leonard, 2011: 141–142). As Fishman himself stresses, language revitalization 'must not be approached in absolute terms ... but, rather, in functional, contextual, or situational terms [and] in terms of immediate vs. longer-range goals' (Fishman, 1991: 12; see also Romaine's [2006] perceptive discussion of the language revitalization 'journey' and what it might mean for a language to 'survive' without intergenerational transmission – issues also raised by Leonard (2008, 2011), and taken up in Chapter 5 of this book.)

In response to the problems of fixed and unitary language classifications, Leonard (2008) has proposed a 'revised view' of language vitality and

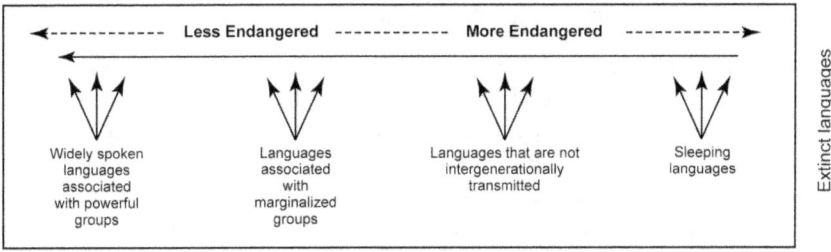

Figure 1.6 Leonard's 'revised view of the language endangerment continuum' (adapted from Leonard, 2008: 27; graphics by Shearon Vaughn)

endangerment, in which language varieties are viewed along a continuum of 'less' and 'more' endangered. Leonard's continuum is shown in Figure 1.6. As he points out (and as we will see in ensuing chapters), even 'formerly sleeping' languages, like the situation of Miami described by Leonard, can, when language-learning conditions are re-engineered, be reactivated within the 'sociolinguistic nexus' of their respective communities.

With this orientation in mind, the remainder of this chapter explores Indigenous language use in the public domains of tribal government, religion, print and digital media, and education. Although it is not possible to do justice to all Native American language communities in this discussion, these examples, I hope, provide a sense of the 'persistence of viable languages' (Medicine, 2001: 52) in contemporary Native American life.

Contemporary Native American Language Use in Public and Communal Spaces[8]

Historically, Native American languages had a strong public presence in all arenas of social life. During the Hawaiian monarchy, for instance, Hawaiian was the language of government, religion, business, the media, education and interethnic communication; even 'the children of immigrants ... spoke Hawaiian with native-speaker fluency' (Wilson, 1998: 127). This centrality of Indigenous languages to Native community life is well documented throughout the Americas.

Native American languages and speakers have played prominent roles in global affairs as well. During World War II, the Navajo, Choctaw, Comanche and Lakota Code Talkers in six US Marine divisions were responsible for transmitting thousands of military messages in their mother tongues via telegraphs and radios. It would be more than two decades before the US government declassified the Code Talkers' messages. Their contributions are widely credited with the Allied victories in the Pacific and with hastening the end of the war.

Native languages in tribal governance

In 1987, Diné sociolinguist Alyse Neundorf documented the significance of bilingualism within the Navajo Tribal Council, where, she argued, interpreting from Navajo into English served as a stepping-stone to power (Neundorf, 1987: vii; Spolsky, 2002: 152). Indicative of language hierarchies, Neundorf found that interpreting from English to Navajo held much less social currency. Today, proficiency among high-ranking tribal officials (e.g. the Navajo Nation president and vice president) is expected, and especially in the reservation interior, Navajo predominates at local chapter meetings (ofen compared with a Western-style town hall). At the same time, code-switching for lexicons associated with Anglo-American institutions and personnel is common, meeting minutes are recorded in English, and council delegates often use English to report to home communities (Benally & Viri, 2005). As Spolsky observes,

> Formal parliamentary statements [are] made in English ('Referring to section 5B of the bill tabled yesterday'), but many speeches ... then switch into culturally sensitive and rhetorically Navajo presentations, with full and appropriate kinship references ... [T]hose who do not speak Navajo ... must depend on the simultaneous interpretation into English now provided through headphones. (Spolsky, 2002: 154)

Native languages remain important resources in the Pueblos of New Mexico as well, where theocratic governments combine secular and traditional leadership forms. Writing of the Keres-speaking Pueblo of Cochiti, Benjamin *et al.* (1996: 119–120) note that, 'Critical to this form of government is the underlying commitment [leaders] have ... to the traditional lifestyle ... the more a person engages in [government-related] events, the more ... competent he or she becomes' in Keres. The interpenetration of tribal governance with Native religious systems in Pueblo societies creates unique opportunities for Native language use. Describing the Keres-speaking Pueblo of Acoma, Sims states that 'oral Acoma ... continues to be an important part of council deliberations and public meetings ..., as well as in conducting the internal affairs of the pueblo's socioreligious life' (Sims, 2001: 64).

These studies highlight what other LPP research and practice have shown: that the use of Indigenous languages in official governmental processes, coupled with concrete tribal-level support, can be a critical force for language maintenance and revitalization. As Lizette Peter observes for the Oklahoma Cherokee, official and unofficial tribal language policies and programs have not only resulted in the creation of new language-learning resources, but also 'help to raise the status of the Cherokee language as a marker of ethnicity and ... a way to exercise power as Cherokee people' (Peter, 2007: 335). She writes:

[T]he support of influential leaders not only promotes the use and learning of the language, but also an understanding of the role it plays in contemporary life. As a result, Cherokee language-revitalization efforts have a greater potential for long-lasting sustainability. (Peter, 2007: 335)

Native languages in community religious life

As suggested by the example of Pueblo theocratic societies above, the religious sphere remains a bastion of Native-language use among many Native communities. Traditional Navajo religion, for example, involves complex and 'carefully prescribed rituals conducted by highly trained singers or medicine men' who apprentice for years to learn the long poetic prayers and songs that constitute a vital core of Navajo life (Spolsky, 2002: 147). Among the Arizona Tewa, ceremonial leaders 'require and enforce an explicit proscription against the use of foreign words' during ritual performances, and talk in the kiva (a ritual chamber of great symbolic importance in Pueblo societies) 'would lose its integrity if it admitted expressions from other languages' (Kroskrity, 2000: 338). Benjamin *et al.* (1996), Romero (2003) and Sims (2001) describe similar linguistic practices at Cochiti and Acoma Pueblos. Hopi scholar Sheilah Nicholas (2008, 2009, 2011) explains that these practices promote the ideals of respect, obligation, reciprocity and humility, enabling young people to develop a sense of aesthetics for Hopi (Pueblo) culture and confirming the kiva as a stronghold for the Native language.

Christian sects have promoted Native-language literacy, although often in opposition to Indigenous values and beliefs. At the same time, literacy promulgated in the context of Anglo-American religion has been co-opted for Indigenous ends (see the discussion of this for Navajo in Chapter 4). In an ethnographic case study of Navajo literacy, Daniel McLaughlin reports that, 'one important way for ... churchgoers to act is to read and write Navajo for indigenous purposes in home settings unconnected to church ... and identified as ... crucial to the survival of Navajo language and culture' (McLaughlin, 1992: 152). In recent decades, Wayne Holm adds, 'a Navajo Christianity is emerging', led by Navajo ministers, and 'Navajo literacy is much more common in these Navajo-led churches' (personal communication, 4 July 2009).

Perhaps the most widespread religious context in which Native American languages are prominent is the Native American Church (NAC), a multitribal religion that emerged as a resistance movement during the late 19th century and whose origins are often attributed to the Comanche leader Quanah Parker. The NAC has spread throughout the United States, and ceremonial songs and prayers are given in Native languages appropriate to particular tribal contexts. (For more on the NAC, also called the peyote religion, see Aberle, 1966.)

Native languages in literature, public media, and the digital world

Print and audio-visual media are contentious domains for Native-language use, as mainstream media – Hollywood films as well as some ethnographic and documentary media – are rife with racist stereotypes and misrepresentations. Images of 'Tonto and the Lone Ranger' still appear in film and online media, and more subtle but equally dehumanizing portrayals populate multiple literary genres (McCarty, 2008c). Yet many culturally authentic Native-language media exist, often 'in contradistinction to ... non-Indian imaginings' (Deloria, 2011: 175). Historically, one example is the *Cherokee Phoenix*, which rolled off the presses on 28 February 1828 – eight years after Sequoyah published his syllabary – and is still published today (see Figure 1.4). The paper garnered international attention but had as its primary audience the diasporic Cherokee community spread across present-day Georgia, Alabama, Tennessee, North Carolina, Arkansas, Oklahoma and Texas. In 1834, the first Hawaiian-language newspaper, *Ka Lama Hawai'i*, was published, and by 1900, over 100 Hawaiian-language newspapers were in circulation (Wilson, 1998). The first newspaper in Navajo was *Ádahooníłígíí (Events)*, started by the BIA during World War II to inform tribal members of wartime events, and made possible by the partnership of Anglo linguist Robert Young and Navajo linguist William Morgan (see the discussion of this in Chapter 4). *Ádahooníłígíí* continued to be published until 1957.

Today, numerous Native American dailies, weeklies and monthlies exist. Nearly two centuries after its founding, the *Cherokee Phoenix* has a subscribership of nearly 30,000 readers and continues to publish via a monthly broadsheet, a website (http://www.cherokeephoenix.org/), a mobile application, and a weekly electronic newsletter (Cherokee Phoenix, 2011). Most Native American newspapers appear in English, but many include Native-language columns and sections. In addition, at least one scholarly journal, the *Journal of Navajo Education*, has included scholarly articles and poetry in a Native American language (Navajo). Unfortunately, the journal was discontinued in the 1990s owing to lack of resources for its publication and distribution, although it is still available in libraries and selected museum collections.

There is a growing Native-language print literature for readers of all ages, some of it originating in former federally funded bilingual-bicultural education programs. Native writers such as Ofelia Zepeda, Laura Tohe, Evangeline Parsons-Yazzie and Rex Lee Jim are just a few who publish in their mother tongue, contributing to a corpus of Native American poetry, storybooks, song texts and other literature published by academic and commercial presses (e.g. Evers *et al.*, 1983; Evers & Molina, 1987; Hinton & Watahomigie, 1984; Jim, 1998; Tohe, 2005; Zepeda, 1995b). Some have been translated and published internationally (Jim, 1998) and recorded in CD-ROM format, such as Zepeda's (1997) *Jewed 'I-Hoi: Earth Movements*. In 2008, New Mexico became the first state in the United States to officially adopt a Native American-language textbook, Parsons-Yazzie and Speas's (2008) *Diné Bizaad Bínáhoo'aah (Rediscovering the Navajo Language)*. As noted earlier, many Native American writers also claim various forms of English in their work, including Indigenous Englishes, which may be used in conjunction with autochthonous Native American languages (Webster & Peterson, 2011: 8).

While electronic media have, in the past, been regarded as an 'enemy' of lesser-used languages ('cultural nerve gas', says Krauss [1992]), television, radio and digital technologies have become important tools for language revitalization – again disrupting dominant, taken-for-granted assumptions about Indigenous language forms and practices (Deloria, 2011). Cherokee speakers with iPhones can text other speakers using Sequoyah's syllabary. An application called iSyllabary enables Cherokee users 'to check the pronunciation of less-familiar characters, and beginners can practice basic vocabulary with an [application] called iCherokee' (Biemiller, 2011: 3). Leonard writes of *myaamia* that, 'Many Miamis use Facebook and similar social-networking sites':

> In doing so, it is common for us to intersperse *myaamia* within our English when communicating with other tribal members ... Similarly for the main text of e-mail and instant messaging (or telephone texting), many Miamis incorporate quite a bit of *myaamia*, with some longer passages entirely in the language. (Leonard, 2011: 151–152)

Among the Ojibwe in Minnesota, a National Science Foundation-funded project, directed by Indigenous language scholar and educator Mary Hermes, is videotaping native speakers conversing in everyday settings to preserve and teach natural speech. The movies are then transcribed in consultation with native speakers and 'combined with vocabulary lists, pronunciations, and interactive games to create educational DVDs' (O'Brien & Walton, 2011: para. 7). As Eisenlohr writes of these types of sound and image recordings, '[They] can provide richer and more multidimensional records especially in the fields of phonology and prosody, as well as in the performative and interactional contexts of use as compared to print media' (Eisenlohr, 2004: 24).

Talking storybooks incorporating videos of community members and animated children's songs are part of the Arapaho Tribe's language revitalization efforts in Wyoming, which also have involved adapting Walt Disney's animated movie, *Bambi,* with voicing by Arapaho children and adults (Greymorning, 2001). Such productions demand new engagements with the cultural appropriateness of animated animals speaking the Indigenous language on screen, writes Leighton Peterson, even as they counter 'colonial language ideologies and practices' (Peterson, 2011: 112).

These are but a few examples; digital technology supports the production and dissemination of a host of Indigenous language resources, including online dictionaries and teaching materials (for examples see Baldwin &

Costa, 2005, on Miami; Mato Nunpa, 2006, on Dakota; and Penfield & Flores, 2006, on Mohave). Moreover, computer-assisted language learning (CALL), 'an established field' for dominant languages (Holton, 2011: 381), is available for some Native American languages. Rosetta Stone, a commercial language-learning software producer, has, as part of its recently launched Endangered Language Program, developed software in partnership with the Inupiaq, Unuktitut, Navajo, Mohawk, and Chitimacha in the United States and Canada (http://www.rosettastone.com/global/endangered/projects). 'This CD-ROM follows the standard template of other Rosetta Stone CALL products but makes use of locally sourced images, at least in part' (Holton, 2011: 382).

Websites and social media such as blogs, web forums and Facebook are increasingly popular LPP resources. As Moriarty writes, 'Perhaps the most significant of all digital platforms is the internet, the defining technology of globalization' (Moriarty, 2011: 453). 'All Things Cherokee' is one example: with 20,000 fans in 2012, the site includes resources for tracing family genealogies, links for the display and sale of contemporary art by Cherokee artists, an archive of articles and fact sheets, a monthly newsletter, and links to numerous historical, cultural, legal and linguistic resources (http://www.facebook.com/allthingscherokee). While this and other Native American media sites are typically in English, Indigenous-language resources can also be accessed. 'All Things Cherokee', for instance, includes links to the Cherokee syllabary and other language-learning resources, and Apple includes Cherokee in its computer operating system. These new communicative spaces not only provide speakers and language learners 'with opportunities to hear and maintain skills in the language', they also may achieve 'a transformation of ideological valuations of the language so that the lesser-used language is viewed as part of the contemporary world and as relevant for the future of a particular group' (Eisenlohr, 2004: 24).

Native American languages have a growing presence on television and in radio. In conjunction with electronic and hard copy distribution, the *Cherokee Phoenix* produces Cherokee Phoenix Radio, a Sunday morning radio news broadcast (Cherokee Phoenix, 2011). Radio stations with Native American programs, many in local Indigenous languages, operate throughout North America. A major media outlet is Canyon Records, headquartered in Phoenix, Arizona, which has produced traditional and contemporary Native American music for more than 50 years (http://www.canyonrecords.com).

Finally, in recent years there has been a significant increase in the number of films and videos directed and produced by Indigenous artists and organizations (including youth), and featuring Native actors. Peterson notes that these films 'are sometimes made as direct responses to dominant ideologies and expectations, as indigenous perspectives on marginalized or misrepresented histories, as documentation, or as entertainment for local and global audiences' (Peterson, 2011: 112). The Native American Film + Video Festival, founded in 1979 (and reachable on Facebook and Twitter), is the oldest media arts center for Native American film. Dedicated 'to indigenous production from throughout the Americas', it is 'designed to be a welcoming place for Native filmmakers and other participants in indigenous film' (Native Networks, 2011: para. 2). Organized by the Film and Video Center of the National Museum of the American Indian, recent festivals have featured long and short films, some scripted in Indigenous languages (http://www.nativenetworks.si.edu/eng/blue/nafvf_11.html).

These new cultural spaces and uses for Indigenous languages have many benefits, but are not without controversy or problems. The advantages include the assertion of linguistic self-determination in virtual space; the ability to create more precise, durable and authentic linguistic resources that access local Indigenous voices; less costly ways of disseminating language documentary and educational resources; the creation of new textual genres; the facilitation of networking among a community of language users; and the status-enhancing valorization of Indigenous languages through coeval temporal and spatial positioning in contemporary communicative domains (Eisenlohr, 2004). Many argue that these new digital spaces are essential for bringing youth to their heritage language and bringing the language to youth. As noted by Navajo language curriculum specialist Don Mose, a translator for Rosetta Stone's Level 1 Navajo language course, '[t]he whole idea is to use new media ... the kids are glued to computers today – why not use language and technology to help them learn their culture?' (Brossy, 2007: 2). Further, Mose adds, while there may be many good Native language teachers, 'we've been using old materials because there's nothing available that uses the current technology' (Brossy, 2007: 2). According to Indigenous Language Institute director Inée Slaughter, these new technologies take 'language where the kids are and ... social networking sites, texting, MySpace, YouTube ... is where they are' (cited in Nott, 2010: para. 8).

It would be disingenuous, though, 'to assume that the provision for endangered languages in media and pop-culture domains does not raise other language-revitalization issues' (Moriarty, 2011: 449). A prime issue is access to computer technology, which is a function of potential users' location and of the presence of financial resources to support such access. There are other issues of access as well; many communities are rightly concerned with the potential for illimitable appropriation, reproduction and exploitation of Indigenous-language resources by outsiders. Like print literacies, technology-mediated documentation and revitalization 'raise questions of access and power'; are these processes simply new forms of 'storage and display, such as the museum and the archive?', asks Eisenlohr (2004: 27). The use of electronic media can also give rise to conflicts among speakers about new language genres, varieties and standards, potentially alienating those whose participation in revitalization efforts is most vital to the efforts' success.

At the same time, these new language practices 'demonstrate how we continue to adapt to our environment and to the evolving communicative cultural needs of our population', emphasizes Leonard (2011: 153). All of this raises questions about the relationship between language, power and self-determination. Ultimately, Leonard (2011) suggests, these issues must be decided by Indigenous communities themselves as part of a necessary process of ideological clarification. 'Part of our reclamation process involves our recognition and legitimization of how we exist', Leonard says, 'which is as a diverse group of people who share a common history, language, and ... cultural values' (Leonard, 2011: 153).

Native languages in schools

The foregoing discussion highlights the fact that much of the media utilizing Native American languages is intended to serve local revitalization and education goals. Education represents the most extensive – if contested – public domain for contemporary Native American language use. Approximately 646,000 American Indian and Alaska Native students – 1% of the US student population – attend K–12 schools. In addition, there are an estimated 71,000 school-age Native Hawaiian children in the State of Hawai'i and more than 123,000 school-age Native Hawaiians nationwide (Ng-Osorio & Tibbetts, 2010: 1; Nielson, 2011: 4). Native students are served by schools operated by the federal Bureau of Indian Education (BIE), tribal or community controlled schools under BIE purview but operated by local Native school boards, state-supervised public schools, private schools, and mission or parochial schools. Nearly 90% of Native American students attend public schools, although students are likely to rotate through several school systems over their academic careers or even within a single school year (Brayboy *et al.*, 2013; Moran *et al.*, 2008; Grigg *et al.*, 2010). Although many of these schools are located within reservations or Alaska Native villages and have a majority Native enrollment, more than half of all Native American students attend schools in which they comprise less than 25% of the student body (Stancavage *et al.*, 2006). These schools are much less likely to have Native American teachers or teachers with proficiency in a Native American language. More than 60% of American Indian and Alaska Native students attend schools in which less than 5% of the teaching staff are Native American (Stancavage *et al.*, 2006).

Understanding the possibilities for language education policy and practice in this sociolinguistic and educational environment requires a brief introduction to how it came about. Well into the 20th century, Native American students were forbidden to use the Native language in school. It was not until the mid-1950s, with the passage of federal legislation to fund school construction on federal trust lands, that public schools became locally available to a significant number of American Indian students. Although Native languages were not necessarily prohibited in public schools, neither have they been well supported.

The first secular Native American-controlled school to provide systematic instruction through a Native American language was established in 1966 at Rough Rock, Arizona, on the Navajo Nation. The school created the first Native American publishing center, taught initial literacy in Navajo and implemented innovative programs to certify Native teachers. It also galvanized federal policy changes that enabled Rough Rock and other Native American communities to operate community-based bilingual–bicultural schools (McCarty, 2002b; see the discussion of Rough Rock in Chapter 4). Today there are 126 tribal/community-controlled schools, all of which offer some form of Native language and culture instruction.

Although they are locally controlled, these schools are subject to federal mandates under the BIE, the office within the US Department of Interior charged with overseeing federal Indian schools. In addition to tribal/community schools, the BIE oversees 183 elementary and secondary schools across 23 states enrolling 48,000 students (7% of all American Indian/Alaska Native students; DeVoe *et al.*, 2008: iv; US Department of the Interior, 2004). These schools tend to place much less emphasis, if any, on Native language and culture instruction. Charter schools – public schools linked through formal agreements to authorizing entities such as public school districts, and chartered by a distinctive mission – are an increasingly popular, if controversial, option for bringing Native linguistic and cultural content into the school. The controversial nature of these schools stems not from the fact that some are Indigenous-serving, but rather from more general concerns about the charter school movement as a tool for the privatization of public education. For many Native American communities, however, charter schools are viewed as an 'opportunity to create and offer curriculum geared toward local cultures' (Tirado, 2001: 14; see also Belgarde, 2004; Ewing & Ferrick, 2012). Thousands of American Indian, Alaska Native and Native Hawaiian students are enrolled in charter schools, examples of which are offered in the final chapter of this book.

As we will see in Chapter 5, many Native nations and Indigenous nonprofit organizations are operating schools outside of direct federal and state purview. In 2001, the Cherokee Nation opened a language immersion school that, at the time of this writing, enrolled over 100 students in grades K–5. Taking advantage of new electronic media, students work on laptops loaded with the Cherokee syllabary and a special keypad that fits over the regular computer keyboard (Fife, 2010). The idea for the school and its use of technology, according to Cherokee Chief Chad Smith, 'is to spread the use of the [Native] language among technology-savvy children in the digital age' (Sydney Morning Herald, 2010: para. 5).

Native-language programs also exist at the post-secondary level. In 1968, the Navajo Nation opened Navajo Community College (now called

Diné College), the first college established by Native Americans for Native Americans (http://www.dinecollege.edu). Diné College offers a variety of Navajo language courses, including Navajo-as-a-second-language, Navajo literacy and composition, Navajo linguistics, Navajo grammar and courses designed to endorse Navajo-language teachers (Slate, 2001). There are currently 35 tribal colleges and universities (TCUs), and two BIE-operated post-secondary institutions, including Haskell Indian Nations University, which enrolls approximately 1000 students from across the United States. There are also numerous examples of partnerships between TCUs, Native nations, and public and private post-secondary institutions, many of which support the preparation of Native-language teachers and the teaching of Native languages in K–12 schools (see Biemiller, 2011 on Cherokee; Baldwin & Olds, 2007, on Miami; Bear Nicholas, 2009, on Maliseet and Mi'kmaq in the Canadian Maritimes; and McCarty et al., 2001, on multiple Indigenous language groups).

Although schooling for Native Americans is complicated and compromised by federal mandates and purse strings, it remains a crucial arena for the exercise of tribal sovereignty and linguistic and educational self-determination. As this section suggests, much of this revolves around the right (and the fight) to teach and maintain Indigenous languages – a topic examined in greater detail in the chapters that follow.

This chapter has explored what Medicine called the 'sociolinguistic nexus' of diverse Native American communities, and the exercise of tribal sovereignty across multiple sociocultural, educational and public domains. How self-determination plays out in social practice is a function of individual community histories, aspirations, and human and material resources. Succeeding chapters illustrate these processes across a spectrum of languages and community contexts.

Notes

(1) I thank Professor William H. Wilson for pointing out the connections between Indigenous peoples in Alaska and the Russian Federation.
(2) This necessarily brief discussion of the complex legal, political and historical issues surrounding tribal sovereignty has important implications for citizenship. Native Hawaiians were granted US citizenship when Hawai'i was annexed as a US territory in 1898. It was not until 1924, however, that American Indians were officially declared US citizens, but the federal legislation through which this occurred – the Indian Citizenship Act of 1924 – did not guarantee suffrage rights, including the right to vote. The State of Maine, for example, did not extend voting rights to Native Americans until 1953; Arizona and Utah withheld voting rights from Native people until 1948 and 1957, respectively. Hence, even as thousands of Native Americans were serving in the US military during World War II, many were legally prohibited by their state of residence from voting. Eventually, as Native people became 'naturalized' as US citizens, state and federal citizenship 'were "layered" onto their tribal citizenship' (Wilkins & Lomawaima, 2001: 147). Native Americans therefore possess multiple, overlapping citizenships.

(3) The US Census, following the federal Office of Management and Budget, defines American Indian or Alaska Native as 'a person having origins in any of the original peoples of North and South America (including Central America) and who maintains tribal affiliation or community attachment' (Norris *et al.*, 2012: 2). The identification of Native Hawaiian or Other Pacific Islander 'refer[s] to a person having origins in any of the original peoples of Hawai'i, Guam, Samoa, or other Pacific Islands' (Hixson *et al.*, 2012: 2). Beginning with the 2000 census, the Census Bureau allowed respondents to report multiple racial identities. The figures cited here are for persons identifying as American Indian, Alaska Native, Native Hawaiian or Other Pacific Islander 'either alone or in combination with one or more other races' (Hixson *et al.*, 2012: 1).
(4) Hawaiian Homelands are 'public lands held in trust by the State of Hawai'i for the benefit of Native Hawaiians' (Hixson *et al.*, 2012: 19).
(5) See Thornton (2002) for a fascinating, illustrated account of a recently resurfaced 18th/19th century Lakota winter count on muslin consisting of 136 pictographs.
(6) Ten years after the *Cherokee Phoenix* began publication in New Echota, and following the Indian Removal Act of 1830, a federally sponsored militia took some 13,000 Cherokee citizens prisoner, burning their homes, plundering their property and forcing them into concentration camps in Tennessee. The Cherokee were then forcibly removed to what was then called Indian Territory and is now the State of Oklahoma. The Cherokee 'Trail of Tears' led to the deaths of hundreds of Cherokee people from starvation, disease, exposure to the elements and violence along the route. The present Cherokee capital, where the *Cherokee Phoenix* continues to be published, is Tahlequah, in northeastern Oklahoma.
(7) This notion of a literacy continuum incorporates elements of Hornberger's (2003) well-known continua of biliteracy, but broadens the scope to include oral and visual literacies and the unique qualities of Indigenous knowledge systems (see also Menezes de Souza, 2002).
(8) Parts of this section are adapted from McCarty (2010).

2 Conceptualizing Native American LPP: Critical Sociocultural Foundations

> [B]ecause human society is constituted of, by, and through language, all acts and actions mediated by language are opportunities for the implicit (or explicit) expression of language policies.
> Ricento and Hornberger, 1996: 420

In this chapter, I discuss the guiding conceptual, theoretical and methodological underpinnings for the treatment of Native American LPP in the chapters to come. Recognizing that readers may have more, or less, familiarity with LPP as a field of scholarship and practice, I begin with an overview of basic terms, recognizing that they are never truly 'basic' in the sense of being ideologically neutral. In contested arenas such as language education, 'words and concepts frame and construct the phenomena under discussion, making some persons and groups visible, others invisible; some the unmarked norm, others marked and negative ... Concepts also can be defined in ways that hide, expose, rationalise, or question power relations' (Skutnabb-Kangas & McCarty, 2008: 3). My position vis-à-vis these terms and concepts should become clear to readers in the pages that follow.

LPP Goals and Approaches[1]

As a social practice, language planning and policy is as old as humankind itself; people have devised ways of organizing and regulating talk and communication since time immemorial. 'As in all societies', the linguist William Leap writes, 'Indian Tribes have always had to face the task of transmitting to the next generation the "standards of behavior" appropriate for a variety of domains', and language is 'only one of the types of cultural information ... transmitted and reproduced through such efforts' (Leap, 1988: 285; see also Wright, 2004: 1). As a social scientific field, however, LPP is relatively young, having grown out of pragmatic concerns with solving language 'problems' in decolonizing, multilingual polities during the second half of the 20th century. LPP 'arose as an extension of sociolinguistics into the domain of social planning', write Luke *et al.* (1990: 25), 'and the job of describing and tracing patterns of language change thereby was tied to the normative task of prescribing such change'. Thus, the principal questions were which languages (colonial/Indigenous) to develop for which purposes in the context of nation building (Ricento, 2006: 13). In addressing those questions, there was an assumption of LPP as a technical, autonomous and value-free positivist social science that would describe, analyze and prescribe the development, use and status of languages in contact (Luke *et al.*, 1990: 26). As we will see in subsequent sections of this chapter, this top-down, technicist approach has been increasingly superseded by more dynamic, critical approaches.

In their comprehensive treatment of the subject, Kaplan and Baldauf define *language planning* as an 'attempt by someone to modify the linguistic behavior of some community for some reason' (Kaplan & Baldauf, 1997: 3). *Language policies*, they say, arise from these language intervention activities, and can be conceptualized as a 'body of ideas, laws, regulations, rules and practices intended to achieve the planned change in the society, group or system' (Kaplan & Baldauf, 1997: xi). Ricento distinguishes language planning as the 'development, implementation, and evaluation of specific language policies' (Ricento, 2006: 4), while also considering language planning and policy together as an integrated field. For Spolsky (2004: 5), language policy – which he characterizes as language practices, beliefs or ideologies, and interventions – encompasses language planning. These definitions provide good starting points, although they have not gone unchallenged (see, e.g. Hornberger's [2006b: 25] discussion of the debates surrounding the language planning–policy relationship), and I develop them further throughout the book.

LPP scholars have distinguished three primary types of language planning activities:

(1) *Status planning* is the planned use of particular languages for particular purposes in distinct domains – education, judicial proceedings, public services, the media, cultural activities, economic and social life, and the exchange of information, to name a few (Hornberger, 2006b: 28; Ó Riagáin, 2006: 2).
(2) *Corpus planning* concerns decisions about linguistic norms and forms (e.g. the creation of writing systems, questions of standardization, terminological modernization).
(3) *Acquisition planning* involves decisions about who will acquire the language and how (e.g. intergenerational transmission in the family and community, the promotion of a language in school and/or workplace, and so on; Cooper, 1989; Haugen, 1983; Hornberger, 1994, 1996, 2006b; Kaplan & Baldauf, 1997; Ó Riagáin, 2006).

In a framework that integrates the work of a number of LPP scholars, Hornberger (1994, 1996, 2006b) cross-indexes the three types of language planning above with the goals of policy planning, which focuses on language form (e.g. officialization), and cultivation planning, which focuses on function (e.g. revival, maintenance, reacquisition).

It is important to recognize that these processes are not discrete, but are interdependent, co-occurring and mutually constitutive. LPP is a 'multilayered construct', Ricento and Hornberger emphasize, involving multiple agents, levels, and processes that 'permeate and interact with each other in ... complex ways' (Ricento & Hornberger, 1996: 419). Moreover, these processes cannot be isolated from the broader social, political, economic and historical contexts in which they operate. Some LPP scholars use the metaphor of *linguistic ecology* (a construct introduced by Vogelin *et al.* in 1967) to represent this complexity, referring to the larger, heterogeneous environments in which languages and speech communities interact and in which, like living human beings, the 'modification of any part may have correlated effects (and causes) on any other part' (Spolsky, 2004: 6; see also Haugen, 1972; Hornberger, 2003; Mühlhäusler, 1996, 2003). This view of linguistic environments often advocates (re)building those environments to promote self-regulating linguistic diversity (Mühlhäusler, 2000: 306, 310). Schiffman has developed a related construct, *linguistic culture*, to describe 'the set of behaviours, assumptions, cultural forms, prejudices, folk belief systems, attitudes, stereotypes, ways of thinking about language, and religio-historical circumstances associated with a particular language' (Schiffman, 1996: 5) – what he calls the 'cultural 'baggage' that speakers bring to their dealings with language from their culture' (Schiffman, 2006: 113).

Language orientations, attitudes, and ideologies

Ruiz identifies three language orientations, defined as 'a *complex of dispositions toward language and its role, and toward languages and their role in society*' (Ruiz, 1988: 4, emphasis in original). Dispositions, Ruiz says, may be 'largely unconscious and prerational because they are at the most fundamental level of arguments about language' (Ruiz, 1988: 4); the job of the LPP theorist is to excavate the roots of these dispositions within a speech community, thereby making orientations visible. Dispositions 'constitute the framework in which [language] attitudes are formed' (Ruiz, 1988: 4).

According to Ruiz, a *language-as-a-problem* orientation reflects LPP's founding as a field. In the United States, this orientation was the defining feature of more than two centuries of federal policy for American Indians. It also is evident in decades of bilingual education legislation (a misnomer, as true bilingualism has never been a US policy goal, but rather linguistic assimilation). A *language-as-a-right* orientation, says Ruiz, is concerned with the basic human right to education in the mother tongue as well as the language of wider communication (LWC). In counterpoint to these two orientations, Ruiz proposes a *language-as-a-resource* orientation as a way of promoting bi-/multilingualism for all.

Two concepts related to language orientations are *language attitude* and *language ideology*. Language attitudes are the feelings individuals have about their own and others' language (Crystal, 1992). The seminal work on language attitudes was undertaken by Wallace Lambert and his associates, in which Canadian Francophone and Anglophone subjects were asked to rank different speakers on a variety of personality traits they thought they could detect from recorded speech (e.g. height, intelligence, dependability, sociability, likability; Lambert *et al.*, 1960). Both groups ranked English higher on these traits, while French was ranked higher on such traits as religiosity. In a subsequent study of teachers' ratings of African American and White children's videotaped speech, Fasold (1984) found that teachers rated White students' speech more highly. More recently, Baugh (2000) has linked findings such as these to linguistic (and racial) profiling and discrimination.

In her study of Quichua language revitalization, King notes that, while language attitudes are directed toward a specific object, language ideologies reference 'a broader system of beliefs, norms, or values' (King, 2000: 168). Woolard (1998: 3) defines language ideologies as culturally mediated 'ideas about language and about how communication works as a social process' (Woolard, 1998: 3). Ideologies about language are taken-for-granted beliefs and assumptions about language statuses, forms, users and uses that, by virtue of being naturalized as 'common sense', contribute to linguistic and social inequality (Tollefson, 2006: 47). Like orientations and attitudes, language ideologies are not about language *per se*, but rather about identity, power relations, and 'the very notion of the person and the social group' (Woolard, 1998: 3).

Kroskrity and Field (2009) examine how language ideologies operate across a range of Indigenous settings in the United States, Canada, and Latin America. Important in their examination are the linkages made between language ideologies, cultural renewal and tribal sovereignty. Native American languages are a crucial part of these processes, these researchers say, 'because they provide uniquely important cultural resources for allowing communities to ... recontextualize traditional practices to ever-changing socioeconomic patterns' (Field & Kroskrity, 2009: 3). Field and Kroskrity also remind us that language ideologies 'are inherently multiple', and that within and across Indigenous communities (as in all speech communities), those ideological processes are 'complex, heterogeneous, contradictory, and even contentious' (Field & Kroskrity, 2009: 7). In other words, there is no 'one-size-fits-all' LPP approach. Moreover, a single individual 'may hold conflicting attitudes regarding a language and its use' – an issue we will delve into more fully in a study of Native youth language practices discussed in Chapter 6.

LPP in practice: who 'does' it?

As noted above, LPP has historically been approached as a top-down process centered on official acts and government-authorized texts (see, e.g. Ricento & Burnaby, 1998: 33; Sallabank, 2011: 278). However, as we will see in the sections and chapters that follow, LPP is a practice each of us engages in every day. While we do not want to lose sight of the consequential nature of government-backed LPP – indeed, government policies loom large in the history of Native American language education and in current efforts to revitalize Indigenous languages – neither should we privilege *only* official language planning activities and policy documents (cf. Ball, 2006; Levinson & Sutton, 2001). LPP is both bottom-up and top-down (and, argues Mary Eunice Romero-Little [2012], 'inside out, and outside in'); much of what is taking place in the field today, particularly within Indigenous communities, operates at the dynamic macro–meso–micro interstices of official and unofficial or grass roots planning and policy. 'Anyone and everyone can do language planning', Leanne Hinton observes (2001b: 51). The important point is that language planning and policy-making can be and are carried out by families, communities and individuals each and every day. Each of us has the power to create, resist and transform language policies, and human agency is therefore a central factor in LPP.

Language regenesis as a core LPP goal

Language planning aimed at recovering, reclaiming and strengthening endangered Native American languages is the theme of this book. *Language regenesis, revitalization, renewal* and *reclamation* are overarching terms to describe these LPP goals and activities. To begin unpacking these terms, we can first consider what makes a language 'endangered'. An entire scholarly discourse has developed around these terms, as exemplified by a December 2002 exchange in the *Journal of Linguistic Anthropology* entitled, 'Examining the Language of Language Endangerment', and by numerous texts on the topic (for recent examples see Austin, 2008; Grenoble & Whaley, 1998, 2006; Harrison, 2007; Hornberger, 2008; Nettle & Romaine, 2000; Tsunoda, 2005; see also Kroskrity's [2011] critical analysis of the rhetoric of endangerment and case studies in Duchêne & Heller, 2007).

A language is said to be *moribund* when children no longer acquire it as a first language (Grenoble & Whaley, 2006; Krauss, 1992). A language is *dormant* or *sleeping* when it is no longer spoken but the potential for renewal exists by virtue of existing documentary resources and an ethnic heritage community, as in the cases of Miami and Wôpanâak discussed in Chapter 5 (Leonard, 2007: 23; see also Hinton, 2001d; Leonard, 2008, 2011). A language becomes *endangered* when it is likely that it will cease to be spoken *at all* within the next 50–100 years (Grenoble & Whaley, 1998: vii).

According to UNESCO's Ad-Hoc Expert Group on Endangered Languages (2003: 2):

> A language is *endangered* ... when its speakers cease to use it, use it in an increasingly reduced number of communicative domains, and cease to pass it on from one generation to the next. That is, there are no new speakers, adults or children. (See also Krauss, 1992; McCarty *et al.*, 2008.)

As discussed in Chapter 1, declining numbers of child language-learners and overall numbers of speakers are the two most frequently cited criteria for moribundity and endangerment. Other criteria include a reduced number of communicative domains and low social status (Skutnabb-Kangas & McCarty, 2008: 8).

Implicit in the concept of language endangerment are the dual notions of *language loss* and *language shift*. 'Shift generally refers to a collective or communal process, while "loss" refers to the reduction of specific linguistic competencies at the individual level' (Kouritzin, 1999: 12–13). These processes are, of course, interdependent. Language shift occurs when the transmission and acquisition of a language from one generation to the next breaks down, with fewer speakers, readers, writers, 'even understanders' each generation (Fishman, 1991: 1). Language shift is almost always associated with minoritized status and the displacement of a community language by a dominant one and its associated domina*ting* community of users. Community-wide language shift generally occurs over many years, although recent studies show shift occurring within the space of a single generation or less (see Wyman's [2012] account of this for Yup'ik). Language shift arises both within and outside a speech community in the context of cultural, economic and physical dislocations and social pressures. Internal change occurs through attrition of language forms (Hill, 1993: 68) and as speakers begin to shift their language allegiances, 'abandoning' their language in favor of the LWC because they believe it is more socially useful and beneficial. Eventually, productivity is lost as individuals come to believe that their heritage or community language has less utility and importance, 'tipping' language use away from that language in favor of the LWC (Dorian, 1989; Hill, 1993; Romero-Little & McCarty, 2006: 6).

Terms such as language abandonment, shift, tip and moribundity should be used carefully, then, as they can make shift and loss seem almost natural, obscuring the power relations that dispossess certain communities of their languages while empowering certain classes of speakers of the LWC. All linguistic systems change as the social contexts for their use also change. Language shift is different from language change, however, as shift typically arises as a consequence of colonization, genocide, territorial displacement and official policies of coercive linguistic assimilation. In the case of Indigenous peoples, colonial schooling has been a prime instrument of language shift. Skutnabb-Kangas describes this as *linguicide*; languages that have been exterminated, she states, 'have died ... *not* because this has been a "natural" development, but because they have been "helped" on their way. They have not "died" because of old age or lack of adaptability – they have been murdered' (Skutnabb-Kangas, 2000: 222; see also Crawford, 1995a, 2000).

Language regenesis represents an up-ending of these power relations and a reassertion of a community's inherent linguistic, cultural and educational rights. This is also referred to as *language regeneration*, which, as Māori scholar Margie Kahukura Hohepa notes, speaks 'more of ... growth and regrowth, development and redeveloping', acknowledging that '[n]othing regrows in exactly the same shape that it had previously, or in exactly the same direction' (Hohepa, 2006: 294). Leonard (2007: 2–3) offers the overarching term *language reclamation*, which connotes 'that the language was taken away by outside forces' (Hinton, 2011: 291). Leonard further divides reclamation into linguistic reconstitution, 'recreating a full language from the existing corpus of documentation', and language revitalization, creating new speakers and domains.

For present purposes, we can distill these various usages into three types of regenesis/regeneration activities:

(1) *Language revival* seeks to restore oral and/or written functions for a language with no native speakers, and for which there may or may not be a corpus of written documentation.
(2) *Language revitalization* refers to activities designed to engender 'newfound vigour of a language already in use' (Paulston *et al.*, 1992: 279). To revitalize a language is to cultivate new speakers: 'to find ways of helping people learn the language in situations where normal language transmission across generations no longer exists' (Hinton, 2003: 45).
(3) *Reversal of language shift* (RLS), a concept developed by Joshua Fishman (1991, 2001), connotes transforming the social mechanisms and contexts that promote transmission of a language from one generation to the next. As discussed in Chapter 1, the key to RLS, according to Fishman, is restoring and buttressing the family–neighborhood–community nexus in which intergenerational language transmission takes place. (See also King (2001: 23–27) for a helpful discussion of each of these terms.)

Hinton states that all of these processes involve two primary sets of activities: (1) teaching 'the language to those who do not know it', and motivating both learners and speakers 'to use the language in a broadening set of situations' (Hinton, 2011: 293). Like status, corpus and acquisition planning, these language regenesis/revitalization/RLS goals and activities intersect and conjoin. We can easily see, for instance, how activities designed to revitalize Native languages overlap with those intended to reverse language shift. All of these activities should be distinguished from *language maintenance*, which 'supports a language that is truly vital' by protecting 'current levels and domains of use' (Grenoble & Whaley, 2006: 13; see also Hinton 2011: 291).[2]

It is important to again emphasize the *human* dimensions of these activities. Languages are peopled symbolic systems, just as schools and communities are peopled social institutions. When we talk about the possibilities and limitations of language education planning and policy as a vehicle for language regeneration, we are talking about human-built systems and human agency. When we talk about reviving, revitalizing and strengthening Native languages, we are talking about families and communities whose lives, relationships, and well-being are constructed, legitimated and passed on to future generations through those linguistic and cultural resources. Years ago, a Navajo elder told me, 'If a child learns only English, you have lost your child'. This elder's statement problematizes the academic discourse around language loss, revitalization and identity, and is a powerful reminder that these are not mere abstractions, disconnected from human lives. At its root, language revitalization is about personal and communal identity, wholeness and the strengthening of intergenerational ties.

A Critical Sociocultural Perspective on Language Planning and Policy

With their focus on solving language 'problems', early approaches to LPP were, as we have seen, largely technocratic and linear (identify the problem, formulate the policy, implement and evaluate it, and revise accordingly). Einar Haugen, a Norwegian American linguist credited as the first to use the term 'language planning' in the scholarly literature (but see St Clair's [1982] discussion of this for the international language, Esperanto), described language planning as the 'exercise of judgment in the form of choices among available linguistic forms', and the 'evaluation of linguistic change' (Haugen, 1972: 512). Language planners, according to Haugen, were basically decision-makers. This framework was elaborated by Robert Cooper as a multifaceted question: 'What *actors* attempt to influence what *behaviors* of which *people* for what *ends* under what *conditions* by what *means* through what decision-making *process* with what *effect*?' (Cooper, 1989: 98). This approach can be described as *rationalistic,* its premise being that effective LPP involves the weighing of alternatives by rational agents. 'The agent commonly evaluates competing language plans within the framework of cost/benefit analysis', say Ricento and Hornberger (1996: 406) of this approach. Tollefson (1991) characterizes it as neoclassical, in that LPP is assumed to be ideologically neutral and the primary unit of analysis is the ahistoricized and decontextualized individual.

In contrast, a growing body of scholarship critically interrogates the ideological, social–structural and historical bases of LPP, emphasizing the relationships among language, power, and inequality (see, e.g. Fairclough, 2001; Luke *et al.,* 1990; May, 2012; Tollefson, 1991, 2002a, 2002b, 2012). Drawing on the work of critical theorists such as Michel Foucault, Pierre Bourdieu and Jürgen Habermas, *critical approaches* recognize the planning–policy-making process and the field of LPP itself as ideological and discursive, reflecting and (re)producing relations of class, race, language and power. From a critical perspective, Cooper's questions might be reframed as *who* is planning *for whom, whose language behavior* is taken as the controlling standard, and *with what overt and covert aims* (Luke et al., 1990: 29)? Tollefson (1991, 2002a, 2006, 2012) characterizes this as an 'historical–structural' approach, tying it to critical language studies and critical linguistics. The goal is to critically 'read' language planning–policy processes as a means of understanding their social, political and economic meanings and ramifications within particular historicized contexts (Tollefson, 2002b: 4). Critical LPP research also makes visible the researcher's subject position and relationship to those who are the focus of the research (Tollefson, 2006: 44). The critical perspective is committed to the ideals of equity and social justice, acknowledging that, even as LPP is a mechanism for majoritarian control, it can be a site of resistance and transformation (see, e.g. Phillipson & Skutnabb-Kangas, 1996; Skutnabb-Kangas, 2000; Skutnabb-Kangas et al., 2009; Tollefson, 1991, 2002b, 2006).

With the advent of this critical sociocultural 'turn' in LPP studies has come the privileging of popular, grassroots and 'bottom-up' planning and policy work. This is the focus of the present volume. The analytical framework applied throughout the book conceives of LPP as a *sociocultural and therefore political process* (McCarty, 2004: 72, 2011c). From this perspective, LPP includes public and official acts and documents – laws, formal rules and regulations – but equally important, LPP constitutes and is constituted by everyday social practices by which language uses, statuses and forms are regulated. Policy is not a disembodied 'thing', but is rather a situated sociocultural process – the complex of practices, ideologies, attitudes and formal and informal mechanisms that influence language practices and futures in profound and everyday ways (McCarty, 2011b: xii). 'When we fight in support of a community-based language program', Pennycook (2001: 215) writes, 'when we allow or disallow the use of one language or another in our classrooms, when we choose which language to use in Congress, conversations, conferences, or curricula', we are planning language and making language policy.

Schools are among the most dominating discursive sites in which tacit and official language policies are produced and legitimated. Throughout this book, I offer a critical sociocultural analysis of these enactments in the education sphere. This analysis assumes that language policies are neither historically nor socially neutral; they are not simply about 'the educational efficacy of one code over another' (Pennycook, 2001: 195). Rather, decisions about language, whether officially sanctioned or not, concern struggles for linguistic and educational sovereignty, democracy and human rights.

Critical ethnography and LPP interpretation and praxis

Much of the work presented herein grows out of my long-term collaborations and ethnographic research with Native American communities. With its overriding concern with cultural interpretation (Wolcott, 2008), ethnography is uniquely suited to critically examine these LPP processes. Ethnography provides a means of analyzing LPP holistically and systemically, through a situated sociohistorical and cultural lens; it reveals and (re)presents 'grounded, insider perspectives on linguistic needs and aspirations', while also showing the 'local realizations' of both tacit and official language policies (Canagarajah, 2006: 164; cf. Ramanathan, 2005). Participant observation, in-depth interviews and document analysis are the mainstays of the ethnographic toolkit. In the chapters that follow, these methods are sometimes complemented by sociolinguistic surveys and academic achievement data.

However, ethnography is more than a set of methods; it is also a way of 'seeing' and 'being' in the world (cf. Wolcott, 2008). What ethnographers do, Dell Hymes argued decades ago – 'learn the meanings, norms, and patterns of a way of life' – is precisely what humans do every day. Because ethnography is 'continuous with ordinary life [and] the knowledge that others already have' (Hymes, 1980: 98), it carries within it the seeds of transformation whereby hierarchies between the 'knower' and the 'known' can be dissolved. As Hymes emphasized, ethnography is a particularly appropriate form of inquiry for a democratic society (Hymes, 1980: 99; see also McCarty et al., 2011: 31).

In this sense this book furthers the ethnography of language policy (Hornberger & Johnson, 2007, 2011; McCarty, 2011a), an approach that has its origins in Hymes's (1964, 1974) and Gumperz and Hymes's (1972) ethnography of communication. This ethnographic tradition been continued in numerous studies of Indigenous language education, including Hornberger's (1988) research on Quechua bilingual education in Peru, May's (1991, 1994) study of language policy at the Richmond Road School in New Zealand, Aikman's (1999) study of intercultural education and mother tongue literacy among the Arakmbut of Peru, Davis's (1999) research on Native Hawaiian language planning, King's (2001) research on Quichua[3] language revitalization in Ecuador, House's (2002) study of language shift on the Navajo Nation, Patrick's (2003) ethnography of language use among the Inuit of Nunavik (Arctic Québec), Wyman's (2012) ethnography of language shift among Yup'ik youth in the Far North, and my own longitudinal study of Navajo bilingual–bicultural education at Rough Rock Community School in northern Arizona (McCarty, 2002b). Increasingly, Indigenous scholars are advancing this ethnographic work in their own communities. Notable examples include Adley-SantaMaria's (1999) study of language shift on the White Mountain Apache reservation in Arizona; Charles's (2005, 2011) work with Yup'ik language teaching and culturally based language assessment; Beth

Leonard's (2007) study of Deg Xinag oral traditions in language and education; Gegeo and Watson-Gegeo's (1999, 2012) and Watson-Gegeo and Gegeo's (1999, 2011) work on language education and Indigenous knowledges in the Solomon Islands; Hermes's (2005, 2007) study of Ojibwe language immersion; Kamanā's (2011) research on the practice of *ho'oponopono* or Hawaiian conflict resolution in an Hawaiian-medium school; Lee's (1999, 2007, 2009, 2013 [in press]) studies of Navajo and Pueblo youth's language attitudes and practices; Manuelito's (2004, 2005) analysis of educational self-determination in the Navajo community of Ramah; Nicholas's (2005, 2008, 2009, 2011) study of Hopi youth's language ideologies and practices; Romero's (2003) examination of language socialization at Cochiti Pueblo and of the role of Indigenous languages in early childhood education (Romero-Little, 2010); Wesley Leonard's (2007) case study of Miami language reclamation in the home; Sims's (2001, 2005, 2006, 2008) examinations of Keres language revitalization in the New Mexico Pueblos; and Warner's (1999a, 1999b, 2001) and Wong's (1999b, 2011) critical analyses of authenticity and identity in Hawaiian language revitalization.

The chapters in this book draw heavily on the ethnographic insights contained in this growing body of work. I am concerned not only with 'seeing' through the lens of ethnography (Wolcott, 2008), but also with applying ethnographic knowledge to a counter-hegemonic project of linguistic, social and educational justice. Scholarship, like language policy, 'is inseparable from both dialogue and domination, and often contains an admixture of the two' (Boyarin, 1992: 8). In Indigenous communities, research and scholarship have historically been tethered to a colonizing agenda (Smith, 1999). The goal here is to develop and share qualitative research that is critical, humanizing (Paris, 2011) responsible, respectful, and decolonizing (Lomawaima, 2000; Lomawaima & McCarty, 2002b; Matua & Swadener, 2004; Paris & Winn, 2013; Smith, 1999). Reflecting that stance, I have sought to position this work within a framework of co-participation, social action and Indigenous self-determination.

Safety Zone Theory

The critical sociocultural and ethnographic framework employed here expands on an earlier analysis of Native American education carried out with K. Tsianina Lomawaima (Lomawaima & McCarty, 2002a, 2006; see also Lomawaima, 2002, 2012). Specifically, we argue that struggles over Native American language rights can be conceptualized as contests over what constitutes 'safe' vs 'dangerous' difference in human social life. As early as the 1970s, the legal scholar Arnold Leibowitz argued that language is 'primarily a means of control' (Leibowitz, 1974: 1). Tracing the history of official language policies in the United States, Liebowitz posited that language restrictionist policies are implemented 'when an ethnic group [is] viewed as irreconcilably alien to a prevailing concept of American culture' (Leibowitz, 1974: abstract).

Similarly, Lomawaima and I argue that, when Indigenous linguistic and cultural difference have been viewed by dominant interests (in particular, federal authorities) as instrumental or non-threatening, those differences have been tolerated and even supported in official and unofficial ways. 'Dangerous' expressions of Native difference – manifest, for example, in the presence of thousands of Native-speaking children in 19th and early 20th century federal schools – has been systematically suppressed. We use the metaphor of a 'safety zone' to theorize these policy shifts. As illustrated in Figure 2.1, the safety zone is conceived as a physical, social, psychological and pedagogic space in which federal officials and other colonizing agents, through education policies and practices, have deliberately and systematically sought to distinguished 'safe' from 'dangerous' Indigenous beliefs and practices:

> Drawing the boundaries between safe and dangerous cultural difference and illuminating the safety zone of [US] national culture lie at the heart of [the] history of American Indian education ... Which Native beliefs and practices might be judged safe, innocuous, and tolerable? Which Native beliefs and practices are too dangerous, different, and subversive of mainstream values? How best to manage or eradicate dangerous cultural expression? (Lomawaima & McCarty, 2006: 5)

Figure 2.1 The metaphorical safety zone: A theoretical model for analyzing Indigenous language planning and policy (graphics by Shearon Vaughn)

To understand how the safety zone works in social practice, consider, for example, the contradiction between 'elite' and 'compensatory' forms of language education represented in the differential value placed on 'foreign' or 'world' language education vs 'bilingual' education in the United States. Who are the intended recipients of these two very different language policies? Whose interests are served by sorting language education in these ways? To take another example, if we assume a federal commitment to eradicate Indigenous languages, as articulated in more than two centuries of federal Indian policy (discussed in detail in Chapter 3), how do we explain the federally sponsored development and dissemination of Native-language textbooks during the 1940s? How do the 1975 Indian Self-Determination and Educational Assistance Act and the 1990/1992 Native American Languages Act square with the English-only requirements of the No Child Left Behind Act of 2001? (For further discussion, see Lomawaima & McCarty, 2002a: 282–283; 2006: chapters 5–7.)

Scholars of American Indian policy (and policy more generally) have likened these contradictory trends to the swings of a pendulum, in which federal policy oscillates from tolerance to containment and control. Lomawaima and I point out that, while the pendulum model *describes* policy changes over time, it is not capable of theorizing or *explaining* them (Lomawaima & McCarty, 2002a, 2006: 6; see also Fixico, 2002). From the perspective of safety zone theory, these policy oscillations can be traced to an ongoing struggle over cultural difference and its perceived threat or benefit to the larger society (Lomawaima & McCarty, 2006: 6).[4]

It would be a gross misrepresentation, however, to portray Native American language education solely from a colonialist, top-down perspective; this direction of influence is only part of the story. Native peoples have never been passive recipients of oppressive federal policies; like all social–political processes, the interactions between tribes and the federal government operate through complex, situated networks of agency, constraint and power, and individuals within institutional contexts interpret and enact policy in multifarious ways. As the case studies in this book show, Native individuals, families and communities have consistently and successfully contested safety zone boundaries, vigorously exercising tribal sovereignty and seizing political windows of opportunity to carve out new niches for linguistic and cultural self-determination. These agentive processes are depicted in Figure 2.1 by the fuzziness of safety zone boundaries, and by arrows signifying the push and pull of sovereign powers from within and without.

The chapters that follow interrogate the contours of the safety zone, focusing on the negotiation and impacts of tacit and official language education policies within Native American communities. Equally important, this work shows how Native educators, parents and communities have worked around and through these structurating forces, creating and improvising spaces for the expression of Indigenous identities and subverting or re-engineering coercive language policies. As Lomawaima and I have written, these efforts 'hold a promise for schools and a promise for a nation that can look cultural difference in the face, not as an enemy but as an ally' (Lomawaima & McCarty, 2006: 170). They also hold lessons for those who choose to resist the forces of homogenization and to fight for linguistic and cultural diversity as an inalienable human right. The next chapter examines these processes in greater detail.

Notes

(1) Parts of this section are adapted from a previous work by Teresa L. McCarty (2011c), Introducing ethnography and language policy in *Ethnography and Language Policy*, reproduced by permission of Taylor and Francis Group LLC, a division of Informa plc.
(2) Quichua and Quechua refer to the same ethnolinguistic group, the peoples who reside in several nation states in the Andean region of South America. Quichua is used exclusively in Ecuador.
(3) For a different view of language maintenance and renewal, see the work of William Leap; language renewal, says Leap, 'is only one of a series of variations' on the more inclusive project of language planning (Leap, 1988: 290).
(4) In this theoretical framing, Lomawaima and I use the notion of 'safety zone' in a very different way from the construct of a 'zone of safety' developed by Begay *et al.* (1995), Lipka and McCarty (1994), McCarty (2002b: ch. 11), and McCarty and Dick (2003). In the latter works, the 'zone of safety' describes a co-constructed social and intellectual space in which Native teachers, often working with elders, critically examine their personal language and literacy histories and mainstream pedagogies as a basis for indigenizing the curriculum. Lipka and his associates also refer to this as a 'zone of possibility' wherein cultural 'insiders and outsiders ferret out the meanings, conflicts, and confusions surrounding the practical question of how to negotiate [Native] cultural knowledge within a school context' (Lipka *et al.*, 1998: 26).

3 Native American Languages In and Out of the Safety Zone, 1492–2012

> *I grew up in a home where only Navajo was spoken ... At an early age I learned the values, beliefs, and traditions of my people.*
> Galena Sells Dick, Navajo bilingual educator, 1998: 23

> *I grew up speaking the Cree language and my parents did not speak a word of English at all – at least not around us ... And we spoke the [Cree] language all the time.*
> Soloman Ratt, Cree bilingual educator, interview, 22 June 2000

> *Yes, I grew up speaking the heritage language. When I was growing up, the whole community spoke just Mohawk.*
> Dorothy Lazore, Mohawk bilingual educator, interview, 14 July 2000[1]

Imagine the time and place as mid-20th century North America. We cannot know for certain, but there is strong evidence, from Indigenous and non-Indigenous accounts, that many (even most) Native American languages were still a regular part of daily life, actively transmitted by adults and naturally acquired by children. The linguist Wallace Chafe estimated in 1962 that, of 206 Native American languages spoken at the time, more than 150 had speakers representing multiple generations, including young children (Chafe, 1962, 1965). My late colleague and co-researcher, Galena Sells Dick, who grew up during this period and who taught and worked at the Rough Rock Community School for 36 years, wrote this about learning her native language:

> We lived in a one-room *hooghan* (an earth and log dwelling with sacred as well as practical significance), with no modern amenities. I learned to greet people by kinship. We never called each other by our English names, only by our Navajo names ... The passing on of these values and of history, ritual, and family traditions was done through oral tradition. (Dick, 1998: 23)

Although patterns of language socialization differed (and differ) among diverse Native peoples, account after account, like Galena Sells Dick's, emphasizes the importance of the spoken word. Acoma writer Simon Ortiz describes his childhood as 'the oral tradition of the Acoma people':

> It was the stories and songs which provided the knowledge that I was woven into the intricate web that was my Acoma life. In our garden and our cornfields I learned about the seasons, growth cycles of cultivated plants, and what one had to think and feel about the land; and at home I became aware of how we must care for each other: all of this was encompassed in an intricate relationship which had to be maintained in order that life continue. (Ortiz, 1993: 29, 38)

Speaking of his mother tongue, Ortiz further reflects, 'We have always had this language, and it is the language, spoken and unspoken, that determines our existence, that brought our grandmothers and grandfathers and ourselves into being in order that there be a continuing life' (Ortiz, 1993: 38). Similarly, referring to the stories and songs that compose her Diné heritage, poet Luci Tapahonso writes:

> Because I was born into and come out of an oral culture, I learned early that the use of words involves responsibility and respect for oneself. A person is known primarily by his [her] use of language and song ... and my sense of language, my awareness of words, becomes entangled with songs, memories, history and the land. (Tapahonso, 1987: 53–54)

Implicit in these statements are strongly held ideologies about language that valorize the spoken word – oral tradition – as the binding knot of a shared sense of place, community and self. The 'core foundation of tribal languages has been rooted in oral tradition', Acoma educator Christine Sims stresses, 'with their functions being to represent and recreate tribal sociocultural, socioreligious, and sociopolitical life' (Sims, 2005: 105). Oral traditions both describe and recreate the 'home places' of their narrators:

> It is the language that conveys a sense of places considered home. In its versatility and complexity, it is the language that is most capable of portraying events and places to children and grandchildren who have never experienced them ... [Oral traditions] remind their listeners that this is where they come from; these are their relatives; this is who they are ... the events, both recent and ancient, that are the shared history of a people. (McCarty & Zepeda, 1999: 205; see also Evers & Zepeda, 1995)

It was these concrete and ideological connections between language, people and place that Europeans systematically sought to destroy and replace with English and Christian values of individualism, industry and private property (Adams, 1995: 15). In this chapter, I sketch the sociohistorical context for these campaigns of planned linguistic and cultural transformation (Spring, 1996), drawing on written documents and the oral accounts of individuals whose lives and languages were the targets of these policies. Although I cover a wide historical horizon, it is not my intention to provide a comprehensive history of Native American language and education policy. For that, readers are referred to Archuleta *et al.* (2000), Lomawaima and McCarty (2006), Reyhner and Eder (2004) and Szasz (1974, 1988). Rather, my goal is to outline the key social, political and educational arenas in which tacit and official policies toward Native American languages and their speakers have been negotiated and contested, as successive generations of colonizers have sought to distinguish 'safe' from 'dangerous' cultural difference. In the past century, especially, those contests have been waged in classrooms and schools. I begin with what we know of these LPP processes from the first encounters between Native peoples and Europeans.

Print Literacy as a Colonizing Tool[2]

In the swirl of interests that engulfed the North American continent following the European invasion, multilingualism was common and necessary, a tool of trade and intertribal communication among Native peoples, and of the diffusion of Christianity and European ideals. Linguistic anthropologist Lisa Philips, for example, documents dozens of Indigenous languages spoken in the Northwest and Old Oregon Territories during the 18th and 19th centuries, including many from outside the region, such as Cree, Iroquois, Hawaiian and Plains Sign Language (Philips, 2011). The linguist Ives Goddard (1996a) documents 62 language families and more than 300 distinct languages indigenous to North America. To rephrase a metaphor proposed by Ofelia García (1992), this linguistic diversity made Native North America one of the hemisphere's most vibrant 'language gardens'. Although less diverse, colonial languages also flourished, with Spanish, French, English, Dutch, German and Russian being the most numerically significant. It is not surprising, then, that there was also widespread use of regional lingua francas, both among Indigenous peoples and between them and Europeans, as practical means of communication for specific purposes (Silverstein, 1996: 17).

Beginning with Christopher Columbus's 15th century expedition, and continuing into the 16th century with Ponce de Leon's colonization of Puerto Rico and Florida and the subsequent expeditions of Cabeza de Vaca, Cortés, de Soto, Alarcón and Oñate, 'Spaniards held a virtual [colonial] monopoly over the southern half of [the present-day United States] for one entire century before the arrival of other Europeans' (Castellanos, 1992: 14). In his comprehensive examination of overlapping 'cycles of conquest', the anthropologist Edward Spicer (1962: 281) asserts that the ruling principle of the Spanish Catholic Church was 'an obligation to civilize'. Native life, Spicer says, was to be reorganized around the missions, led by the Jesuits in the south (until their expulsion by the King of Spain in 1767 from what was called New Spain), and the Franciscans in the north. The fundamental change introduced by the missionaries 'was summed up in the conception of "reduction"': forced settlement in compact villages where Native people presumably would be more susceptible to social manipulation and ideological management (Spicer, 1962: 288).

Alphabetic literacy in both Spanish and Indigenous languages was a primary 'tool of conquest'. As Antonio de Nebrija, author of the first modern grammar of a European language, famously told Queen Isabella of Spain, 'language has always been the consort of empire and forever shall remain its mate' (quoted in Skutnabb-Kangas, 2000: 506). The indoctrination of children was a major focus of the missionaries' efforts, and in schools in or near the missions, they taught literacy and numeracy in Spanish. However, instruction in Native languages also was fundamental to the Spanish program. Particularly among the Jesuits (less so for the Franciscans, at least in northwest New Spain), there was an emphasis on the missionaries' acquisition of Native languages. Almost all Indigenous languages in what is now Sonora and Chihuahua, Mexico were committed to writing by Spanish Jesuits. The oldest surviving Native North American grammar, of Timucua (spoken in what is now Florida and Georgia), was completed by the Franciscan missionary Francisco Pareja. Goddard (1996b: 18) writes that, 'Many Timucuas, both men and women, learned to read and write using Pareja's books'. As early as 1688, there is evidence of Native literacy in Apalachee, a Muskogean language spoken in what is now the Florida Gulf Coast (Goddard, 1996b).

The policy of using Native languages as media of instruction, and of developing Indigenous writing systems to create religious texts, continued with the English and French Jesuits in Algonquian-speaking country, known by Europeans as New England and New France. Assisted by Native translators, the Congregationalist minister John Eliot completed a translation of the Bible into Massachusett in 1663.[3] Like other Puritan missionaries, Eliot espoused an ideology of White supremacy, deeming Native peoples to 'have no principles ... nor wisdom of their own' (Eliot, 1651, cited in Szasz, 1988: 106). One of his chief projects was the Indian 'praying town', small, self-governing villages where Native children were removed from their families and communities and instructed in Christianity, English and the 'civilized' arts. Paradoxically, Native languages were essential to the Europeans' goal of deculturation, and in the 18th century, 'Native literacy became widespread in the praying towns' (Goddard, 1996b: 23).

German Moravian, Russian Orthodox, Dutch Reformed, Presbyterian and Roman Catholic missionaries adopted similar practices. A primer in Delaware, an Eastern Algonquian language, was developed by Moravian missionary David Zeisberger and became 'the first school book used in the state of Ohio' (Goddard, 1996b: 23). In 1819, Cherokee speaker David Brown and Congregationalist missionary Daniel Buttrick produced a Cherokee spelling book (Buttrick & Brown, 1819, cited in Goddard, 1996b: 31; see also Noley, 1979). As discussed in Chapter 1, this was significantly enhanced by Sequoyah's Cherokee syllabary in 1821. In accordance with 18th century church policy, Russian Orthodox missionaries also developed alphabets, grammars, dictionaries, and primers in Aleut and Central Yup'ik (Goddard, 1996b).

Missionaries were not alone in the instrumental value they attached to Indigenous languages and literacies. Thomas Jefferson recorded vocabularies of Unquachog and Unami, spoken in what is now Long Island and New Jersey. William Anderson, a member of Captain James Cook's 18th century maritime expedition, and numerous other European traders and invaders, found it expedient to become knowledgeable in Indigenous languages.

Thus, from the initial invasion through the early 1800s, there was a striking consistency in the formal and informal policies of Europeans toward Native languages and speakers. These policies can be characterized as ones of *expedient tolerance* (cf. Kloss, 1998: ch. 3). Although the transmission of colonial languages was clearly a priority, this aim, and the larger ones of religious conversion and the seizure of Indigenous lands, could only be achieved through knowledge and use of Native languages.

It would be a misrepresentation of experience, however, to leave the analysis here, for early colonial policies toward Native languages cannot be decoupled from the larger colonizing agenda and its diffuse and deadly impacts. Two centuries of contact with Europeans decimated Native communities, leaving an estimated population of just 250,000 by 1890 (Adams, 1988; Lomawaima, 1995: 332–333). Native peoples often felt the impact of Europeans well before they saw a European, as European diseases spread more quickly than did Europeans themselves. Corruption and brutality among state and church officials was rampant (see Spicer's [1962] documentation of these crimes). Language policies were but one aspect of a much broader cultural transformation project carried out by multiple competing colonial regimes – all intent on asserting dominion over Native lands and lives.

Colonial Schooling: the 'Slow Match' of Forced Cultural Transformation

Following the American revolution, the new federal government turned its attention to 'pacifying' Native peoples, 'so that they would live on small farms and, therefore, make available their hunting grounds to White settlers' (Spring, 1996: 12). Toward that end, in 1819 Congress passed the Civilization Fund Act to support the work of missionary schooling. As is evident from the legislation's title, in the minds of federal policy-makers, education was synonymous with 'civilization' and the inexorable tide of 'progress'. The goal was the extermination of Indigenous languages and lifeways so as to literally clear the path for the takeover of Indian lands. The policy issue for the new national government, Adams (1995: 5) writes, 'could be reduced to this fact: Indians possessed the land, and whites wanted the land'. The mechanism for the divestiture of Indian lands would be schooling, justified ideologically by European notions of racial superiority and the triumph of civilization over savagism (Adams, 1995: 12–21; Spring, 1996). The words of a 19th century missionary to the Lakota capture this ideology:

> Uncle Sam [the federal government] is like a man setting a charge of powder. The school is the slow match. He lights it and ... in time it will blow up the old life, and of its shattered pieces will make good citizens. (Cited in Adams, 1988: 3)

Throughout the 19th century, the campaign for Indian removal and containment continued through a combined policy of military aggression, removal to Indian Territory (modern-day Oklahoma and Kansas) and to reservations, and formal schooling. Toward the end of the century, as treaty-making ended, the federal government assumed ever-greater authority over schooling in the quest to solve what it called the 'Indian problem' (i.e. 'Indians possessed the land, and whites wanted the land'). In 1887, Congress initiated a two-pronged policy designed to 'blow up the old life' once and for all. The General Allotment Act, also called the Dawes Act after its sponsor, Senator Henry Dawes of Massachusetts, called for the division of reservation lands into 160-acre family parcels, with the 'surplus' to be sold to Whites. The proceeds would be 'held by the government for the tribe's "education and civilization"' (Adams, 1995: 17) – an arrangement that exposes the policy link between the divestiture of Indian lands and schooling. At the same time, the federal government declared a policy of compulsory education for Indian children, with threats of imprisonment for parents who failed to comply. Adams (1988: 8) characterizes the federal goal as 'education for citizenship focused on [English] language instruction and political socialization'. English-only policies were instrumental to this project, with the real objective being 'the Indian's political socialization' (Adams, 1988: 9).

The chief vehicle for implementing this plan was the federal boarding school system. 'Schools ... could not only civilize, they could civilize quickly' (Adams, 1988: 12). That federal officials understood this is obvious in the historical record. 'Schools alone cannot make over a race', the Board of Indian Commissioners wrote in their 1902 annual report, 'but no one instrument is so powerful in producing desirable changes in a race as are schools for the young' (Annual Report of the Commissioner of Indian Affairs, 1901: 781, cited in Lomawaima & McCarty, 2006: 7). 'It is a mere waste of time to attempt to teach the average adult Indian the ways of the white man', a federal agent to the Lakota reflected; 'our main hope lies with the youthful generations who are still measurably plastic', another federal official stated at the time (cited in Adams, 1995: 18–19). The so-called civilization of American Indians, sometimes simply called Americanization, would require the transformation of Indigenous nations and individuals: 'Replace heritage languages with English; replace "paganism" with Christianity; replace economic, political, social, legal, and aesthetic institutions' (Lomawaima & McCarty, 2006: 4).

Over the next century, on- and off-reservation boarding schools proliferated as sites where Indian children could be isolated for years at a time, until their deculturation and re-ethnification were deemed to be complete. 'Federal educators envisioned the boarding school as a training ground', Lomawaima (1994: 112) writes, 'a controlled environment where behavior and belief would be shaped by example and instruction'. The following statement, recorded by Lomawaima at the Yakima Indian National Cultural Center in Toppenish, Washington, captures the goal of these schools from a Native perspective:

> The purpose of these schools was:
> To break down our family ties.
> To steal our children's hearts and minds.
> To train our children to a life of servitude and trade. (Lomawaima, 1994: 80)

Children's experiences in the boarding schools have been well documented and I will not repeat them here (see, e.g. Adams, 1995; Child, 1998; Ellis, 1996; Horne & McBeth, 1998; Lomawaima, 1993, 1994, 1996; Lomawaima & McCarty, 2006; McCarty, 2002b; Reyhner & Eder, 2004; Trennert, 1988). What is of interest for present purposes are the shifts in education policy that attended the boarding schools in the federal government's attempt to discern 'safe' or allowable cultural differences from those deemed to be so dangerously different as to be neutralized and suppressed.

For much of the 20th century, the boarding schools remained the bulwark of the government's assimilation campaign. Whereas earlier mission schools, with their overriding aim of Christianization by whatever means possible, often taught in the Native language, prohibitions against speaking Indigenous languages in federal boarding schools were strictly enforced. As Leibowitz notes, '[t]he language issue, which had received little [prior] attention, now was mentioned in almost every [federal] report concerned with Indian education' (Leibowitz, 1974: 17). 'The Indian child ... must be compelled to adopt the English language', Commissioner of Indian Affairs Hiram Price wrote in 1881, precipitating a boarding school rule of 'No Indian Talk' (Spack, 2002: 24). 'There is not an Indian pupil ... who is permitted to study any other language than our own', Commissioner of Indian Affairs John D.C. Atkins asserted in 1887, articulating a 'one nation–one language' policy that would remain in effect for more than six decades:

> No unity or community of feeling can be established among different peoples unless they are brought to speak the same language, and thus to become imbued with like ideas of duty. Deeming it for the very best interest of the Indian, both as an individual and as an embryo citizen, ... no school will be permitted on the reservation in which the English language is not exclusively taught (Cited in Crawford, 1992: 50–51)

The purpose of these policies is clear, Leibowitz writes: to separate Native children from their families and prepare them in such a way that they 'would never return to [their] people ... Language became a critical element in this policy [and] English-language instruction and abandonment of the native language became complementary means to the end' (Leibowitz, 1974: 17).

An appalling plentitude of accounts describe children being beaten, placed in solitary confinement, having their mouths 'washed' with yellow bar or lye soap, and being forced to stand for hours holding stacks of books over their heads as punishment for speaking the mother tongue (Archuleta *et al.*, 2000; Ellis, 1996; McCarty, 2002b; Spack, 2002). 'We were punished and pressured to learn English', Galena Sells Dick writes of the trauma she endured in BIA schools: 'It was confusing and difficult ... Students were punished and abused for speaking their native language' (Dick & McCarty, 1996: 72–73). Canadian residential schools followed the US model, including its violent English-only coercion. As one residential school survivor recounts,

> When little children first arrived at the school, we would see bruises on their throats and cheeks that told us that they have been caught speaking Mi'kmaw. Once we saw the bruises begin to fade, we knew they'd stopped talking. (Cited in Grant, 1996: 190)

The English-only curriculum fitted hand-in-glove with manual training intended to produce docile, low-wage laborers. Indian school textbooks in the 1950s, for example, featured titles such as *Shoe Repairing Dictionary* (Rhodes, 1953), *Please Fill the Tank* (Benton & Kinsland, 1953), *Be a Good Waitress* (Payne, Wallace, & Shorten, 1953) and *I Am a Good Citizen* (Williamson, 1954), with instructions to teachers that 'all pupils ... should understand the contents of this book' and that each page 'should be studied thoroughly and slowly' (Clark, cited in Williamson, 1954: ii; see Figures 3.1 and 3.2).

The abuses of the boarding schools came under public scrutiny in an independent survey of school conditions published in 1928. *The Problem of Indian Administration*, commonly referred to as the Meriam Report after the study's

Figure 3.1 Examples of BIA texts from the 1950s (photograph by Teresa L. McCarty)

A Good Citizen Obeys Rules

Rules tell me how to behave.

Rules tell me what I can do.

Rules tell me what I cannot do.

Good rules make a good school.

My school has good rules.

I will obey them.

I am a good citizen.

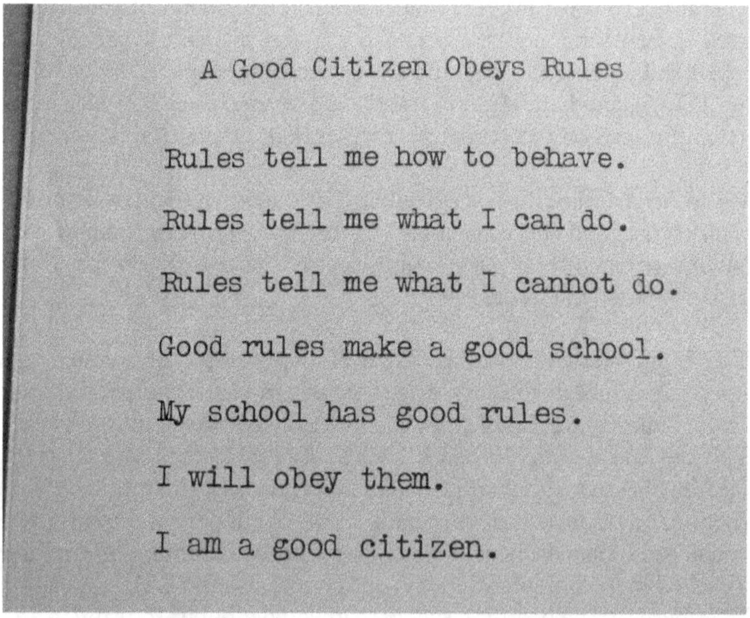

Figure 3.2 'A good citizen obeys rules', from the BIA-produced text, *I Am A Good Citizen* (Williamson, 1954: 20; photograph by Teresa L. McCarty)

director, Lewis Meriam, is a scathing indictment of federally controlled Indian education (Meriam *et al.*, 1928). 'The survey staff finds itself obligated to say frankly and unequivocally that the provisions for the care of the Indian children in boarding schools are grossly inadequate', Meriam and his associates wrote (Meriam *et al.*, 1928: 11). Moreover, the Meriam team took the then-unprecedented position of advocating the right of Indigenous education *choice*:

> The position taken ... is that the work with and for the Indians must give consideration to the desires of the individual Indians. He [sic] who wishes to merge into the social and economic life of the prevailing civilization of this country should be given all practicable aid and advice in making the necessary adjustments. He who wants to remain an Indian and live according to his old culture should be aided in doing so. (Meriam *et al.*, 1928: 86)

Looking beyond the gendered language and fallacious reference to an unchanging, monolithic 'old culture', the Meriam investigators (who included Winnebago educator Henry Roe Cloud) 'rightly grasped the principle of choice – the ability "to remain an Indian" as an essential human right' (Lomawaima & McCarty, 2006: xxii).

Over the next few decades, the BIA loosened its stranglehold on the use of Indigenous languages in schools, and in the context of the progressive education movement, authorized the development of some Native-language teaching materials. While most of these texts had a clear assimilationist agenda, there is evidence that they were appropriated by Native American children and teachers for Indigenous ends. (For a detailed analysis of Lakota and Navajo 'Life Readers', see Lomawaima & McCarty, 2006: 98–108.) Beatrice Medicine, for example, described her peers' and her own astonished but pleased reaction to the BIA Lakota readers published in the 1940s, considering them 'welcome additions to Christian hymnals and bibles' that 'may be evaluated in the historic record as the initial impact of bilingual and bicultural education for ... the Native population' (Medicine, 2001: 50).

Under Commissioner of Indian Affairs John Collier, who served President Franklin D. Roosevelt from 1933 to 1945, the Indian 'New Deal' included these corpus planning activities alongside policies for tribal economic development, self-government and 'civil and cultural freedom' (Szasz, 1974: 41). Although the Collier-era reforms represented a decided break with the past, they did not radically alter the status quo, and the safety zone of federal control remained firmly intact. Newly authorized tribal governments, for instance, were patterned after the US constitution, with BIA oversight. Newly created day schools – intended in theory to be schools from which children would return to their families at the end of the day – were in practice little more than local boarding schools. Although the edifices had changed, the ideologies held by BIA school personnel were not easily modified

(Szasz, 1974: 71–72). The assumption continued to be that children's use of the Native language and contact with family members had polluting effects and interfered with 'educational progress'. 'We weren't allowed to talk Navajo', one day school graduate recalls, '[a]nd our visitation from our parents was very limited – maybe 5 or 10 minutes, that was it' (cited in McCarty, 2002b: 49).

Thus, federal Indian education policy throughout the 19th and much of the 20th centuries was one of almost zero tolerance for linguistic and cultural difference. Although John Collier and his successors instigated important reforms, including the introduction of bilingual instruction at selected locales, the assimilationist goals and ideology of White superiority were never threatened. As late as 1953, BIA Education Director Willard Beatty – an architect, with Collier, of New Deal reforms – wrote that Indian education required 'a recognition that the richest future for Indians ... lies in a mastery of the material culture of the dominant race' (Beatty, 1953: 10–11).

Subverting the Safety Zone

The federal assimilationist agenda was not simply received by its intended targets. 'Indian people at boarding schools were not passive consumers of an ideology or lifestyle imparted from above by federal administrators', Lomawaima (1994: 167) points out:

> They actively created an ongoing educational and social process. They marshaled personal and shared skills and resources to create a world within the confines of boarding-school life, and ... [i]n the process, an institution founded and controlled by the federal government was inhabited and possessed by those whose identities the institution was committed to erase.

The testimony of Shoshone educator Esther Burnett Horne, who attended Haskell Indian Institute in Lawrence, Kansas during the 1920s, illustrates these educational and social processes. '[W]e created our own community at the school', she writes; '[w]e were proud that we had retained so much of our Indianness' (Horne & McBeth, 1998: 53). Galena Sells Dick, who attended the Chinle Boarding School in northern Arizona 30 years later, writes similarly that, 'Formal education did change my behaviors and attitudes. At the same time, I maintained a strong belief in my language and culture. Looking back, ... this foundation led me to become a bilingual teacher in my own community' (Dick, 1998: 24).

One unintended consequence of the boarding school policy was the coalescence of an alliance of Native people from diverse tribes who grew up together in the schools, and who shared the sentiments espoused by Galena

Sells Dick and Esther Burnett Horne. In the context of the Civil Rights Movement and liberal Democratic Party reforms, these experiences and sentiments found expression in a growing movement for Indigenous self-determination. Perhaps more than any other episode in the history of American Indian education, that movement lays bare the fault lines between perceptions of 'safe' and 'dangerous' difference as they were expressed in medium-of-instruction policies in Indian schools.

Prying open policy-making windows of opportunity

In 1970, President Richard M. Nixon delivered a historic message to Congress, promising Indian 'self-determination without termination'[4] and proclaiming that 'every Indian community wishing to do so should be able to control its own Indian schools' (Scheirbeck et al., 1976: 111). Later that year, Nixon's commissioner of Indian Affairs, Louis R. Bruce, outlined plans to implement the president's congressional message: 'For Indian educational programs to become truly responsive to the needs of Indian children and parents, ... control of those programs should be in the hands of the Indian communities' (cited in Scheirbeck et al., 1976: 117).

What happened to precipitate this about-face in federal Indian policy? In a revealing twist on interpretations of 'safe' vs 'dangerous' policies and practices, Nixon's statement followed a widely publicized and highly negative assessment of failed federal policies and BIA mismanagement as well as equally well-publicized Native efforts to assert tribal educational rights. Just months before, the Senate Special Subcommittee on Indian Education, chaired by Robert Kennedy and, after his death, by his brother Edward (Ted) Kennedy, had released a report on a two-year congressional investigation of Indian education. Condemning federal policy as 'one of coercive assimilation', the report cited dismal statistics of Indian student failure and the denigration of Native languages and identities in federal schools, all of which 'had disastrous effects on the education of Indian children' (US Congress, Senate Committee on Labor and Public Welfare, Special Subcommittee on Indian Education, 1969: 21).

Changes in federal Indian education policy also had been foreshadowed by the strong support for public education of Presidents John F. Kennedy and Lyndon B. Johnson. In 1954, *Brown v. Topeka, Kansas Board of Education* reversed a century-and-a-half of legal doctrine upholding 'separate but equal' racial segregation that had been sanctified in *Plessy v. Ferguson* in 1886.[5] In 1964, Congress passed both the Civil Rights Act and the Economic Opportunity Act, which, respectively, provided legal protection from discrimination and authorized community development programs for the poor. In 1968, Congress passed the Bilingual Education Act (authorized as Title VII of the 1965 Elementary and Secondary Education Act), calling for 'new and imaginative' programs that used children's native language while they learned English. Even some BIA personnel at the time embraced bilingual education as 'one of the most promising approaches' for educating Native American students (Bauer, 1970: 223).

At the same time, tribal leaders, educators, political activists and scholars continued to push for tribal sovereignty: 'self-government, self-determination, and self-education' (Lomawaima & McCarty, 2006: 116). A fledgling self-determination movement took root in several Native communities. On the Navajo reservation in northeastern Arizona, an experimental Navajo bilingual–bicultural project jointly funded by the Office of Economic Opportunity and the BIA was established at Lukachukai, Arizona in 1965. Relocated the following year to a new and as yet unstaffed BIA school facility at Rough Rock, Arizona, the Rough Rock Demonstration School quickly rose to international prominence as a model of American Indian educational leadership and self-determination (Johnson, 1968; McCarty, 2002b; Roessel, 1977). At Blackwater, an Akimel O'odham (Pima) community on the Gila River Indian reservation in central Arizona, a pre-K–1 BIA school was under the direction of a local board of trustees by 1968 (Cooper & Gregory, 1976). Other Native American communities watched these developments with great interest and, in time, 'activists within the [BIA] re-established procedures for contracting Bureau schools' (Holm & Holm, 1990: 173).

These developments led directly to the passage of two of the most significant federal Indian education policies of the 20th century. The first was the 1972 Indian Education Act, which provided funding for Native language instruction (acquisition planning), the development of Native-language teaching materials (corpus planning), and the preparation of Native American bilingual teachers (acquisition planning). Three years later Congress authorized P.L. 93-638, the Indian Self-Determination and Education Assistance Act, providing the legal mechanism for Native nations and individual Native communities to contract with the federal government to operate their own schools and other health and social services. Together with the Bilingual Education Act, this legislation laid the legal and financial framework for placing Native American education under community control. A 1976 report in the *Journal of American Indian Education* describes these policy developments in abundantly optimistic terms:

> We now stand on top of the mountain, about to walk down the other side into a valley of sunshine, with a new ray of hope called Indian self-determination. Hopefully, we will realize that our future as a people rests in a rediscovery of our Indian roots. We must accept the challenge of creating a well-ordered and meaningful school system in all our communities. (Cooper and Gregory, 1976: 2)

By the late 1970s, 34 American Indian communities had taken up the challenge to which Cooper and Gregory refer, and were running their own schools. During this period the 1978 Tribally Controlled College or University Assistance Act also was passed, supporting tribes in operating community colleges, and the Coalition of Indian Controlled School Boards, a lobbying force and clearinghouse on educational self-determination, emerged as 'the most important thrust in the education of Indian children today' (Scheirbeck et al., 1976: 257; see also Szasz, 1974: 162). The policy paradigm had shifted, as federal interests and those of Native communities appeared to be fortuitously (if momentarily) aligned. According to Wayne Holm, cofounder of the Navajo bilingual–bicultural program at Rock Point, Arizona, Native American communities 'had a window of opportunity ... where we were allowed to do our own thing, and communities were willing to try [bilingual–bicultural education], and ... the government was set up in a way that they weren't down on us so hard' (cited in McCarty, 2002b: 113). Within a short time, Holm reflected, 'if you were not attempting to have community-based curriculum, to use [the Native] language, if you did not have something dealing with culture, the question was, why not?' (interview, 31 January 1996).

Self-determination through bilingual–bicultural education

In 1974, Spolsky reviewed 74 American Indian and Alaska Native bilingual–bicultural programs – the majority in existence at the time (Spolsky, 1974). The programs reflected a wide diversity of American Indian and Alaska Native languages, including the following regions and language groups:

- Alaska (Aleut, Athabaskan, Haida, Inupiaq, Tlingit, and Yup'ik);
- Arizona (Navajo, Tohono O'odham (then called Papago));
- California (Pomo);
- Colorado (Southern Ute, Navajo);
- Florida (Miccosukee);
- Maine (Passamaquoddy);
- Montana (Cheyenne, Cree, Crow);
- Oklahoma (Cherokee, Choctaw, Seminole);
- New Mexico (Keresan, Navajo, Tewa, Zuni);
- South Dakota (Lakota); and
- Wisconsin (Chippewa, Menominee, Oneida, Potawatomi, Winnebago).

Spolsky's program descriptions provide a sense of Native-language repertoires across a wide spectrum of communities at the time. Some were situations of strong intergenerational language transmission (Miccosukee and Navajo). In other communities, the Native language was used primarily by adults (Seminole), and in others it was in serious decline, with only a few elderly speakers (Pomo). The goals, content and teaching approaches of these programs varied accordingly, from language maintenance to language regenesis and revival programs that were 'cultural rather than linguistic' in nature (Spolsky, 1974: 32).

Not one of these programs was part of the regularly funded school system (Spolsky, 1974: 56). Native American LPP must be understood in light of these circumstances; for the most part, corpus and acquisition planning have had to be carried out in the context of short-term, inconsistent federal funding. This has required schools and communities to grow their Native-language initiatives from the bottom up, including, in some cases, developing the first practical writing systems for their languages. Bilingual–bicultural education was nonetheless central to 'a movement for tribal or community [education] control' (Spolsky, 1974: 25). Legally sanctioned but financially constrained, these programs became a lightning rod for Native American self-determination, permanently altering the metaphorical safety zone boundaries. In subsequent chapters, we will explore these social transformations in detail.

Policy Turnabout: 'To Preserve, Protect, and Promote Native American Languages'

By the late 20th century, Native American bilingual–bicultural programs had been in operation for more than three decades. Yet even as these programs have been a force for promoting and maintaining Indigenous languages, they have not been sufficient, in and of themselves, to turn back the myriad social, political and economic forces that have led to language shift.

Certainly the boarding schools were instrumental in accelerating the shift. One does not simply 'get over' the federally sanctioned abuse children experienced for speaking their mother tongue (Krauss, 1998). 'I was not taught my language', a Hualapai youth relates, 'because when [my dad] was going through school he saw what difficulty *his* peers were having because they learned Hualapai first ... [a]nd so we were not taught, my brothers and I' (cited in Watahomigie & McCarty, 1996: 101). 'The era of the BIA, they took away our culture', a young O'odham parent told my colleagues and I in the context of a large-scale study of Native language shift and retention (McCarty *et al.*, 2006a, 2006b; Romero-Little *et al.*, 2007):

> they stripped us of who we were as a people, forcing the elders to forget their language, ... making them speak strictly English. And when they did come back to the reservation, they were afraid to pass the language on to their kids. And so, if it was passed on ..., it was minimal at most. (Interview, 8 December 2005)

An elder from the same community made this comment:

> [T]hey didn't allow us to talk our native language [at school]. If we did we got in trouble ... and I guess that is how we learned. We thought it

was a bad thing ... so when I grew up and had children, I didn't teach my children the language. (Interview, 8 December 2005)

This situation has given rise to a widespread language revitalization movement, represented in the grass roots projects explored in Chapter 5 and in two recent federal language policies. The first is the Native American Languages Act (NALA; see Appendix 1 for full text). Passed in 1990 and authorized for funding in 1992, NALA reverses more than two centuries of formal and informal federal language policy, vowing to 'preserve, protect, and promote the rights and freedom of Native Americans to use, practice, and develop Native American languages' (NALA, 1990, Sec. 104[1]). It further makes it federal policy to 'use the Native American languages as a medium of instruction in all schools funded by the Secretary of the Interior' (NALA, 1990, Sec. 104[5]). This stands in stark contrast to Commissioner of Indian Affairs Atkins' pronouncement, just a century before, that '[t]eaching an Indian youth in his own barbarous dialect is a positive detriment' (cited in Crawford, 1992: 51). To paraphrase the words of Joshua Fishman in a 2002 commentary on decades of sociolinguistic research (Fishman, 2002), what a difference 100 years make!

From the federal perspective, NALA might be considered merely symbolic; unlike their status as primary – hence 'dangerous' – languages in the 19th and early 20th centuries, Native American languages today are likely to be perceived by members of the dominant English-speaking class as well within metaphorical safety zone boundaries. In this regard, Schiffman (1996: 245) describes NALA as 'locking the barn door after the horse is stolen'. This interpretation is buttressed by the legislation's meager funding. Authorized two full years after the bill's passage and only after voluminous congressional testimony by Native linguists and educators and their allies (see Warhol, 2011, 2012, for a discussion), NALA allocations have averaged $2–3 million per year, an amount that, if distributed equally among 565 federally recognized tribes, would represent between $3500 and $5300 annually – hardly sufficient for the task at hand.

However, this analysis falls short for several reasons. NALA is more than empty symbolism (although symbolic expressions of language rights are not inconsequential); it is a formal articulation of Indigenous sovereignty and linguistic human rights. Written and propelled through Congress by Native American linguists, educators and their allies, NALA is 'the product of Indigenous vision, intent, and design' (Lomawaima & McCarty, 2006: 36; for further discussion of these LPP processes, see Hinton, 1991; Warhol, 2012).[6] Moreover, as the chapters that follow illustrate, NALA has supported some of the most ambitious and impressive Native American language revitalization initiatives to date.

In the years following NALA's passage, a sizable constituency of tribal representatives, language activists, and scholars sought to amend the law to provide additional measures for Native-language revitalization. Although not immediately successful, those efforts eventually came to fruition in December 2006 with the passage of the Esther Martinez Native American Languages Preservation Act (EM-NALPA), so named to honor the late Esther Martinez, a linguist, storyteller, language teacher and advocate for the Tewa Pueblo language. EM-NALPA provides for:

(1) Native American language nests (site-based Native-language immersion programs for children under age 7);
(2) language classes for parents;
(3) language survival schools for school-age children to promote fluency in the Native American language as well as academic proficiency in mathematics, reading/language arts and science; and
(4) Native American language restoration programs that offer training for teachers of Native American languages, develop instructional materials and 'work toward a goal of increasing proficiency and fluency in at least 1 Native American language' (EM-NALPA, Sec. 2[C][iv]; see Appendix 2 for the full text of this law).

In 2007, also through the efforts of a coalition of tribal representatives and language activists, Congress authorized an additional $3 million for the implementation of EM-NALPA and NALA. These new funds brought total federal funding for Native American language programs to an unprecedented $7 million – a tiny fraction of the federal budget, but a significant political and financial victory nonetheless. 'This day may well mark the turning point in our efforts to halt the dramatic decline in Native languages', Ryan Wilson, president of the National Alliance to Save Native Languages, stated in a press release at the time (National Alliance to Save Native Languages, 2007: 2). 'This is only the beginning', he continued; 'Indian Country has been united in this effort, [and] if we remain united, we shall succeed' (National Alliance to Save Native Languages, 2007: 2).

Repatriating the Spoken Word

In 2010, the National Indian Education Association's White House Native Languages Working Group delivered to President Barack Obama a discussion draft of an Executive Order for a White House Initiative on Native American Language Revitalization (White House Native Languages Working Group, 2010). The document reaffirms the federal policy 'to revitalize, and protect the rights and freedom of Native Americans to use, practice, and develop Native American languages to ensure their survival' (White House Native Languages Working Group, 2010: 1). It also calls on federal agencies to coordinate resources 'to revitalize and protect Native American languages', and for the federal government to establish within the US Department of Education a White House Initiative on Native American Language Revitalization (White House Native Languages Working Group, 2010: 1, 3). At the time of this writing, the draft Executive Order remained unsigned. It is, nonetheless, testimony to more than five centuries of Indigenous resistance and persistence. For many Native educators and language planners, the importance of these policy initiatives is the opportunity to repatriate the spoken word that has been the primary means of socializing new generations, and to advance the use and development of Indigenous languages in concrete new spaces and places, including schools (McCarty et al., 2012).

Subsequent chapters detail the ways in which Native American communities are creating new 'safety zones' for these LPP goals. It 'may sound trite', Richard Littlebear observes, but '[w]e seem to forget that we acquire fluency by speaking' (Littlebear, 2000: 18). According to Richard Littlebear and others, the most pressing charge is ensuring that Indigenous-community languages are remembered not only in the pages of books, but in the minds, hearts and tongues of younger generations. 'I believe our Cheyenne language is sacred and holy and came from the Great Spirit', Littlebear says—

> Did it come from Ma'heo'o as isolated words, in neatly written form? Was it intended to be stagnant and never grow? I think not. We are attempting to preserve our languages in a hostile environment, contemporary America. We must change many of our teaching practices if we are to succeed. (Littlebear, 2000: 20)

The following chapters explore how some of those changes have been seeded and the regenesis of Indigenous languages that has taken root in their wake.

Notes

(1) The interviews cited in the epigraph to this chapter were undertaken with Lucille J. Watahomigie during the summer of 2000.
(2) Portions of this section and the section that follows are adapted from McCarty (2004), and Lomawaima and McCarty (2006: chs 6 and 7).
(3) As discussed in Chapter 5, the Eliot Bible has become a primary resource for the revitalization of the Massachusett language by the Mashantucket Pequot, Mohegan and Wampanoag Nations in the northeastern United States.
(4) Another government attempt to find a 'final solution' for what it called the 'Indian problem', the termination policy was intended to hasten assimilation by 'freeing or emancipating' American Indians from the federal trust relationship and by abolishing reservations, thereby ostensibly placing Native Americans 'on an absolutely equal footing with white citizens' (Prucha, 1984: 341). Racial discrimination, inferior education and economic disparities made this premise ludicrous, but the policy nonetheless went into full effect through a series of federal laws passed in the early 1950s. Among the devastating consequences were the divesture of millions (more) acres of tribal lands, the displacement of families through forced relocation (disingenuously described as 'moving them from overcrowded reservations to urban areas, where employment possibilities might be better'), and the 'transfer' of tribal judicial

authority and of federal Indian education responsibility to states (Prucha, 1984: 346–351, 354). 'As the Indians moved out of the reservations, they presumably would disappear into the general population and no longer be of concern to the government' (Prucha, 1984: 356). Termination was disastrous to Native lives, languages, cultures and lands, and was subsequently rejected by President John F. Kennedy in the 1960s and repealed by President Nixon's 1970 proclamation, as formalized in the Indian Education Act of 1972.

(5) In *Plessy v. Ferguson*, the US Supreme Court in 1896 upheld a Louisiana law mandating the segregation of Blacks and Whites in railroad cars operating within the state. Distinguishing between 'political and social equality', the majority opinion stated that although Blacks and Whites had the same political rights under the Constitution, 'the Constitution ... cannot put them on the same [social] plane' (US Supreme Court, cited in Zimmerman, 1997: 2). This decision had the effect of legalizing racial segregation in the United States for the next 58 years. Although never legally tested, that precedent is also evident in the segregation of Native American children in BIA boarding schools.

(6) The original resolutions that led to NALA were developed by participants in the 8th Annual Native American Languages Issues Institute held in Tempe, Arizona in June 1988, and specifically opposed 'any movements, initiatives, policy, [or] practices ... to inhibit, restrict, damage, or in any manner eliminate Indian languages in the classroom, public and private places, throughout the United States and Canada' (Arizona Department of Education, 1988: 269). The template for NALA, the 'Resolution Regarding Indigenous American Cultural Survival Act', was based on the 1978 American Indian Religious Freedom Act (Public Law 95-341), which, the NALI participants noted, 'carries no funds but ... sets a policy' (Arizona Department of Education, 1988: 271).

4 Indigenous Literacies, Bilingual Education and Community Empowerment: The Case of Navajo

> *My first English literacy experiences were with the 'Dick and Jane' basal readers. I remember looking at the books and wondering where this fantasy place was. 'Will I ever get to see this place?' I wondered ... [Later, as] I worked on my degree and in my classroom, I began to learn to read and write my language along with my students. I had to pick up where I stopped when I entered boarding school, because my language and culture had been taken away from me.*
>
> Dick, 1998: 24–25

For the past 30 years, I have had the opportunity to collaborate with Native American educators, students, parents and elders on bilingual–bicultural education programs in a variety of settings. Over that time, definitions of and approaches to 'bilingual–bicultural' education have changed in response to changing sociolinguistic ecologies and larger political and educational processes. This chapter explores the shifting but critical role of bilingual–bicultural education as an expression of and a force for Indigenous self-determination, focusing on how those processes have played out within the Navajo Nation over the past century.

I focus on Navajo – in the Navajo language, Diné, The People (the terms are used interchangeably here) – not only because it is a situation with which I have long-term, first-hand involvement, but also because it offers an especially rich, multifaceted look into the ways in which status, corpus and acquisition planning are enacted and interact locally, 'on the ground', in conjunction with changing national and global conditions. 'Navajo has occupied a special place in bilingual education in the United States in the latter half of the 20th century', Hale observes, adding that, '[c]ommunity control has been the keystone, the sine qua non' of these remarkable programs and institutions (Hale, 2001b: 199–200). Further, Navajo has a relatively long history as a written language, presenting the additional opportunity to consider the role of print literacy in these processes. Navajo print literacy has also had a prominent role in the Navajo Nation's more recent efforts to reverse language shift – a topic introduced here and addressed in greater detail in Chapter 5.

In the examination that follows, I rely once again on my long-term ethnographic and collaborative work with Diné communities and schools, including participant observation, in-depth interviews, archival research and document analysis. I begin by outlining the physical, demographic, sociolinguistic and educational conditions for contemporary Navajo LPP activities. To situate those activities, I trace the history of print literacy in Navajo from the 19th century to present times. As we will see, in the Navajo case alphabetic literacy has been a prime mechanism for advancing Indigenous LPP goals. However, as noted earlier, the role of print or alphabetic literacy is not unproblematic; committing a traditionally oral language to writing produces new and sometimes fractious language ideologies, practices and uses. Drawing on safety zone theory, I then examine the intertwined rise of Navajo community-controlled schools and bilingual–bicultural education within a political landscape of possibility and constraint. Throughout this analysis, I show how LPP operates at the interface of 'bottom-up', meso-level, and 'top-down' initiatives enacted in social practice. 'What happened in Navajo', says Wayne Holm, a leading architect of Diné bilingual–bicultural education, 'was an interaction of what was happening worldwide, politically in the U.S., and in Navajo communities' (personal communication, 29 June 2009). I conclude by considering the current status of the Navajo language and the challenges and possibilities for Indigenous LPP that this case example represents.

Situating Navajo LPP

Geographic and demographic profile

Diné comprise the second-most populous Native American nation in the United States, with more than 330,000 enrolled members – nearly 7% of the total American Indian/Alaska Native population. More than half of Navajo Nation citizens (173,667) live on the Navajo reservation (Greyeyes, 2011), which occupies more than 27,000 square miles of high desert, forested mountains, and plateau and canyon lands in the US Southwest. Four sacred mountains in each of the cardinal directions mark the traditional boundaries of *Diné Bikeyah* (Navajoland or Navajo Country). 'Navajo people are close to the land', Slate explains, and Navajo discourses regularly refer to the sacred mountains as markers of the Navajo world (Slate, 2001: 391). Navajo origins are physically and cosmologically emplaced within this high, arid landscape, and the modern reservation lies within these cultural borders,

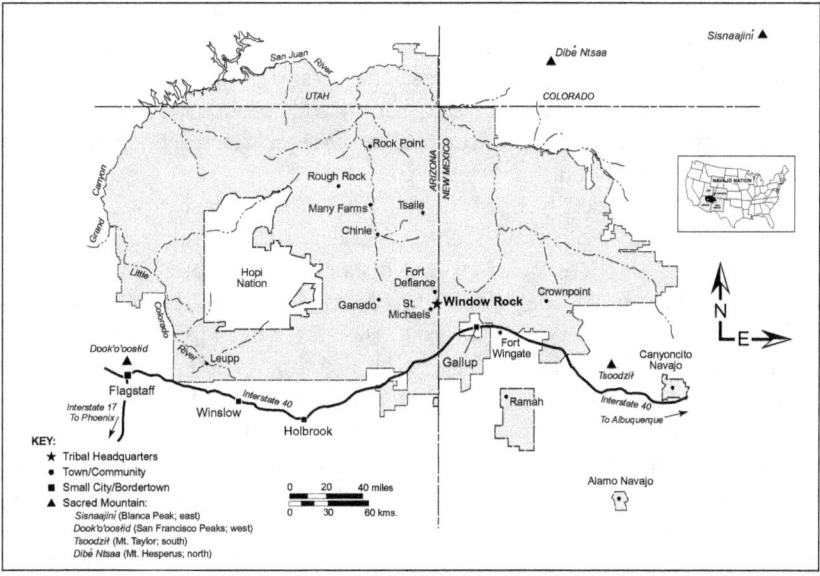

Figure 4.1 The Navajo Nation, showing key LPP sites discussed in the book (graphics by Shearon Vaughn)

stretching across parts of the US states of Arizona, New Mexico and Utah (see Figure 4.1).

Blessed with spectacular scenery and abundant natural resources, the Navajo Nation's economy includes the traditional subsistence pursuits of sheep and goat herding and cattle ranching; entrepreneurial activities associated with contemporary weaving and jewelry making; and newer industries brought in by outside interests such as coal and uranium mining, tribal and federal government services and administration, tourism and small businesses. In recent years, casino gaming has become an important element of the Navajo Nation's economic development activities. Despite the presence of these industries, economic injustice on the reservation is profound: 56.1% of tribal members live below the federal poverty line (per capita income in 2005 was $6217), the unemployment rate is more than 43%, and many homes lack basic amenities such as electricity and running water (Navajo Nation Washington Office, 2005; Slate, 2001: 391).

Education systems and language policies

In 2009–2010, approximately 39,000 Navajo children attended school within the Navajo Nation, and an additional 49,486 students attended off-reservation schools in reservation border towns (Greyeyes, 2011). Public, federal and private mission schools all serve Navajo students, and in the course of their school careers students often move among these education systems as well as on- and off-reservation schools – a situation described by historian Peter Iverson as resembling an educational 'crazy quilt' (2002: 255). Within the Navajo Nation there are 157 elementary and secondary schools; there are also 105 schools serving Diné students in off-reservation schools in Arizona, New Mexico, and Utah (Greyeyes, 2011).

The Navajo Nation has two higher education institutions: Diné College in Tsaile, Arizona, and Navajo Technical College in Crownpoint, New Mexico (see Figure 4.1 for these locations). As discussed in Chapter 1, Diné College, originally a two-year college located in Many Farms, Arizona, was the first tribally controlled college and played a crucial role in the authorization of the 1978 Tribally Controlled College or University Assistance Act (now the Tribally Controlled Colleges and Universities Assistance Act). Diné College has eight branches across the reservation and offers a four-year teacher education degree and a graduate degree in education administration, the latter in partnership with Arizona State University. Navajo Technical College is a two-year vocational technical school.

On the reservation, all but the mission schools depend heavily on federal funding, with each funding agency dictating 'its own organizational goals and philosophy' (Emerson, 1983: 659; see also McCarty, 2002b: ch. 10). These funding agencies 'co-exist uneasily', Diné educator Gloria Emerson notes, 'often competing for the same pot of monies, for public support for their goals, and inevitably, for children to justify their budgets' (Emerson, 1983: 659). Also co-existing somewhat uneasily are tribal, state and federal agencies charged with overseeing reservation schools. The state education agencies within each of three contiguous states are self-authorized to oversee and monitor reservation public schools. Federal agencies have authority over BIE and community-controlled grant and contract schools, which are in turn required to meet state subject-area standards. In 1971, the tribe established the Navajo Division of Education to oversee all reservation schools, but, Emerson says, tied its hands 'by not giving it sufficient powers to establish an authoritative Tribal governmental educational agency similar to a state education agency' (Emerson, 1983: 660).

This authority structure has changed substantially in recent decades. In 1984, the tribal council passed a resolution (codified into tribal law in 1986) mandating that all reservation schools provide Navajo language and culture instruction for every child at every grade level. The difficulty with this is that, because the tribe does not control funding for reservation schools, the mandate has been unenforceable (Slate, 2001: 392). In 2005, the tribal council expanded tribal authority over reservation schools with the passage of the Navajo Sovereignty in Education Act (NSIEA). Widely hailed as an historic assertion of tribal sovereignty, the NSIEA affirms the Navajo Nation's 'inherent right to exercise its responsibility to the Navajo people for their education by prescribing and implementing educational laws and policies applicable to all schools serving the Navajo Nation and all educational programs receiving significant funding for the education of Navajo youth or adults' (NSIEA, 2005: Sec. 3.1; see also Winstead *et al.*, 2008).

This new education policy: (1) elevates the former tribal education department to a department comparable to a state education agency (the Department of Diné Education) charged with overseeing all reservation schools, including establishing and monitoring curriculum, standards, assessment and 'criteria for endorsing Navajo language and culture knowledge programs' (NSIEA, 2005: Sec. 3: 106.G.3.a–d); (2) creates the position of Navajo superintendent of schools; and (3) establishes a reservation-wide, 11-member Navajo board of education to work in conjunction with the reorganized Department of Diné Education and superintendent to carry out its duties and responsibilities (NSIEA, 2005: Sec. 3: 106. G.3). 'We can never forget who we are', then-Navajo Nation President Joe Shirley, Jr, stated in signing the resolution into law. 'We are a sovereign nation and we need to conduct ourselves as such. These changes now head us in that direction, getting back to standing on our own two feet and being a true sovereign' (Norrell, 2005: 1).[1]

Spoken Navajo

Navajo is an Athabaskan language, a family of languages spoken from the circumpolar north to the US border with Mexico (see Figure 4.2). It is most closely related to Western Apache and Mescalero–Chiricahua Apache, and is included in the Apachean branch, the southernmost division of Athabaskan languages (Goddard, 1996a: 5; Young, 1983: 393). Consensus is lacking on numbers of Navajo speakers, with Hale, writing in 2001, using Robert Young's (1983: 399) figure of 100,000 (Hale, 2001a: 84); Slate (2001) citing 80,000 speakers within Arizona, New Mexico, and Utah; Crawford (1995a: 21) using a 1990 census figure of 105,649; the National Clearinghouse for English Language Acquisition (2002) reporting 148,530 speakers; and Benally and Viri (2005: 88) reporting 178,014 based on the 2000 census – significantly higher than the most recent US Census figure of 169,471 (Siebens & Julian, 2011: 2). While these differences illustrate the problems of linguistic enumeration discussed earlier in the book, they simultaneously obscure the variability in spoken-language proficiencies (Benally & Viri, 2005; Krauss, 1998). Benally and Viri, for example, estimate that, of the 178,014 speakers counted in 2000, fewer than 3000 are monolingual Navajo speakers and fewer than 12,000 can be considered 'true bilinguals ... proficient and fluent in both languages' (Benally & Viri, 2005: 94). These authors characterize the early-21st-century language situation as follows:

> Roughly speaking, those over [age] 40 are more likely to be fully fluent and proficient in the Navajo language. [Those] younger are likely to have less proficiency, with the majority of those 30 years and younger more

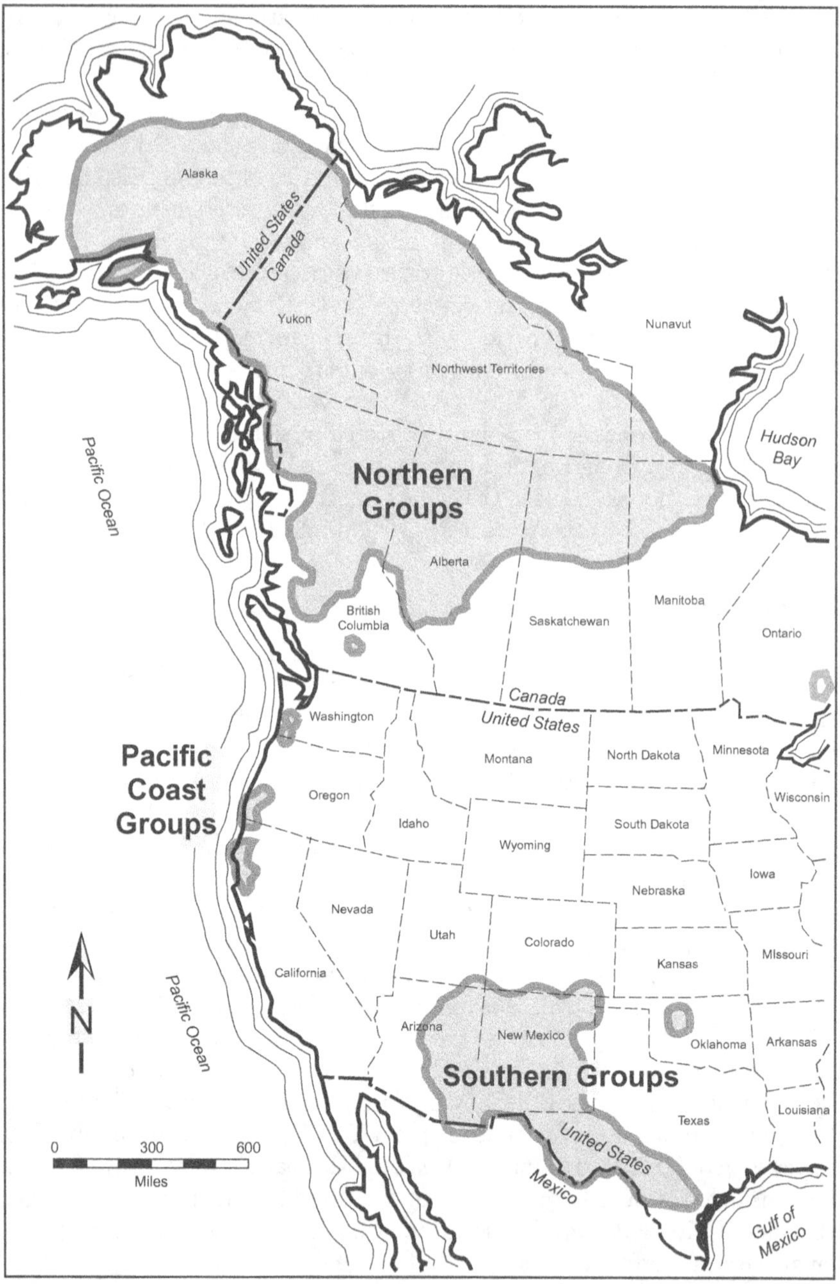

Figure 4.2 Distribution of Athabaskan languages (adapted from Institute of Social and Economic Research, University of Alaska Anchorage, 1998–2004; graphics by Shearon Vaughn)

likely to have no proficiency in Navajo ... And, incidentally, they are now the parent generation. (Benally & Viri, 2005: 94)

What there *is* consensus on is that the domains for Navajo are shrinking, along with the number of child speakers. A 1970 survey by Spolsky and his associates in the Navajo Reading Study showed this breakdown of language proficiencies among more than 3500 Navajo six-year-olds:

- 30% spoke 'no English at all';
- 40% 'knew a little English but not enough to do first grade work in it';
- 20% were 'equally at home in Navajo and English';
- 6% had English as a primary language and 'knew a little Navajo'; and
- 5% 'were monolingual in English'. (Spolsky, 1975: 348)

As Spolsky summarized the findings: '[O]ur survey showed that over two-thirds of the children would be in serious trouble faced, as nearly all were, with a monolingual English teacher' (Spolsky, 1975: 348).

A decade later, when I began working at the Rough Rock Demonstration School (see Figure 4.1 for Rough Rock's location), virtually all students at the school spoke Navajo as their primary language, a situation typical of reservation-interior communities at the time. The exceptions were the children of non-Navajo employees, and even they were learning Navajo in and out of school. Reporting on the nearby Rock Point bilingual education program in 1980, Paul Rosier and Wayne Holm – instructional leaders in that program – stated that, 'Navajo is still *the* language of two out of three homes' (Rosier & Holm, 1980: 5). In fact, they said, the number of Navajo speakers was increasing, stressing that, 'Navajo is not a dying language!' (Rosier & Holm, 1980: 5).[2]

Just 10 years after publishing those figures and 20 years after Spolsky's original survey data were published, Marie Arviso and Wayne Holm (1990) presented a very different sociolinguistic portrait of Fort Defiance, Arizona, an emerging on-reservation town located about 30 miles from a major off-reservation trading center on the Arizona–New Mexico border (see Figure 4.1 for location). Fort Defiance (discussed in more detail in Chapter 5) established a voluntary Diné immersion program in 1986. When the program began, 'there were fewer and fewer [local] Navajo speaking students ... We found roughly that only a third of the incoming kindergartners had *any* knowledge of Navajo', and that 'less than a tenth could be considered ... fluent speakers of five-year-old Navajo' (Arviso & Holm, 1990: 40). Diné linguist Paul Platero confirmed the growing shift toward English in a 1991–1992 Navajo Head Start language study: of 682 preschoolers in 39 Head Start preschools, more than half (54.3%) were deemed to be English monolinguals (Platero, 2001).[3] Perhaps even more sobering in the Fort Defiance case is the fact that, although most Fort Defiance elementary students 'were monolingual or dominant in

English, their English did not seem to be adequate for school purposes... they controlled "conversational" English but not "academic" English' (Arviso & Holm, 1990: 40; cf. Cummins, 1989: ch. 3).

Using Cummins's (1989) constructs of academic and conversational language proficiencies, Arviso and Holm (1990) illustrate students' linguistic repertoires with a typology of eight sociolinguistic profiles among children at Fort Defiance Elementary School. Emphasizing that their classification 'does not see bilingualism as a disadvantage or English monolingualism as an advantage', they point out that it is intended to heighten awareness of many kinds of bilingualism and 'mono'-lingualism (Arviso & Holm, 1990: 41). Arviso and Holm's point is that recognition of children's *specific and multiple* language repertoires makes their academic success more likely – a point taken up with regard to language revitalization in Chapter 6. Table 4.1 summarizes the Arviso–Holm typology, where AP represents academic proficiency and CP represents conversational proficiency:

(1) *(AP) Navajo/(AP) English* – students with strong academic Navajo and academic English abilities.
(2) *(AP) Navajo/(CP) English* – students with academic Navajo and conversational English proficiency.
(3) *(CP) Navajo/(AP)English* – students with academic English and conversational Navajo proficiency (according to Arviso and Holm, these students tend to lose their Navajo abilities over time).
(4) *(CP) Navajo/(CP) English* – students with conversational but not academic proficiency in Navajo and English.
(5) *(AP) Navajo* – students with academic Navajo proficiency.
(6) *(AP) English* – students with academic English proficiency.
(7) *(CP) Navajo* – students with conversational Navajo proficiency.
(8) *(CP) English* – students with conversational English proficiency. (Arviso & Holm, 1990: 40–41)

Cross-cutting each of these categories is an additional sociolinguistic community – users of Navajo English – a variety strongly influenced by the phonemic, syntactic, semantic and pragmatic conventions of the Diné language. Often stigmatized by mainstream educators, 'Navajo English is a rich

Table 4.1 Arviso–Holm typology of Navajo students' multilingual competencies (adapted from Arviso & Holm, 1990: 41)

Bilingual competencies	(AP)Navajo/ (AP)English	(AP)Navajo/ (CP)English	(CP)Navajo/ (AP)English	(CP)Navajo/ (CP)English
'Mono'-lingual competencies	(AP)Navajo	(AP)English	(CP)Navajo	(CP)English

AP, Academic proficiency; CP, conversational proficiency.

and effective form of expression that is shared throughout Navajo country', including among Navajo teachers and other school personnel (Benally & Viri, 2005: 103). Navajo English 'enjoys a great degree of functionality and use in the Navajo speech community', state Benally and Viri (2005: 103).

The heteroglossic nature of Navajo children's sociolinguistic repertoires illustrates Elana Shohamy's point that language is 'an open, free, dynamic, creative and constantly evolving process' – not a 'closed, stagnated, and rule-bound entity' – involving multi-modalities in what she calls 'languaging' (Shohamy, 2006: xvii). The concept of languaging highlights the fact that languages change, borrow, and mix constantly over time in the context of human interaction (Shohamy, 2006: 8). Ofelia García (2009) proposes an additional concept, 'translanguaging', to refer to these inventive discursive practices in multilingual classrooms and across multiple sociolinguistic codes (see also García et al., 2007; Williams, 1994). As we will see in Chapter 6, the concepts of languaging and translanguaging have particular relevance for understanding language practices in Native American communities where shift is advanced, but language regeneration efforts are under way.

Written Navajo

The number of persons with proficiency in written Navajo is less well known. The historical record of Navajo alphabetic literacy dates to the early 19th century, with a list of 'ten largely undecipherable words' attributed to Pedro Bautista Pino (a deputy to the Spanish *Cortes* or legislative body) in 1812, and compiled in an 1892 Athabaskan-language bibliography by James C. Pilling, a congressional transcriptionist who had joined ethnologist John Wesley Powell's US Geological Survey of the American West (Young & Morgan, 1987: iv). Beyond this early reckoning, the record that has not been lost to history is populated by a remarkable array of Navajo and non-Navajo linguists, anthropologists, missionaries and military personnel. The first systematic attempts to develop written Navajo can be traced to 1852, when Captain J. H. Eaton, stationed at what was then a military installation at Fort Defiance, Arizona, translated 425 English words into Navajo for Schoolcraft's word lists of American Indian languages (Lockard, 1996: 40). With no Navajos who spoke English, no English-speakers who knew Navajo, and lacking training in the transcription of unwritten languages, Eaton 'had to invent his own method for the graphic representation of Navajo, and he no doubt had to rely on two interpreters: one for English and Spanish, and one for Spanish and Navajo' (Young & Morgan, 1987: iv). In the late 1880s, Chee Dodge, a renowned Navajo interpreter who would go on to become the first tribal chairman, worked with Washington Matthews, the post surgeon at Fort Wingate, New Mexico (see Figure 4.1), to produce the first Navajo orthography, dictionary and grammar (Holm, 1996; Lockard, 1996; Young, 1972). However, the Matthews grammar and dictionary were never published (Young & Morgan, 1987: iv).

In 1898, Franciscan missionaries arrived at St Michaels, Arizona (see Figure 4.1), near Fort Defiance. As the historical discussion in Chapter 3 relates, the translation of Native American languages was a keystone of the early Spanish missionization project, and this did not change with Franciscans who came into the US Southwest at a much later date and from different origins.[4] In her history of Navajo print literacy, language educator Louise Lockard explains how the fathers at St Michael's went about this work:

> Three Franciscans began to learn Navajo by inviting Navajos to eat with them and recording the names of objects as their visitors pointed to them. They also asked their visitors to name objects in the Montgomery Ward [a retailer based in Chicago, Illinois] catalog. (Lockard, 1996: 42)

In 1900, Father Berard Haile arrived at St Michaels and joined this work, publishing the *Ethnologic Dictionary of the Navajo Language* (Franciscan Fathers, 1910) and *Vocabulary of the Navajo Language* (Haile, 1912). According to Young and Morgan (1987: iv), Haile was keenly interested in learning the language and also produced the *Manual of Navaho Grammar* (1929), the four-volume *Learning Navaho* (1942–1949) and *A Stem Vocabulary of the Navaho Language* (1951). During the 1920s Haile worked with Edward Sapir, a student of anthropologist Franz Boas, who was the first to identify Navajo (along with several other Athabaskan languages) as a tonal language. This set the stage for the development of an appropriate and practicable orthography (Holm, 1996: 5).

Meanwhile, Protestant missionaries also were developing Navajo in written form. In 1910, C.F. Mitchell 'assembled a small phrase book and collection of verb paradigms' entitled *Diné Bizáád* [Navajo Language] (Young & Morgan, 1987: iv). A decade later, the Tolchaco Presbyterian Mission near Leupp, Arizona, on the western edge of the Navajo reservation (see Figure 4.1), opened an Interpreter's Institute for Navajos to 'learn to preach the gospel in their own language and cultural context' (Dolaghan & Scates, 1978: 31, cited in Lockard, 1996: 43). Philip Johnston, the son of Tolchaco's founder and a World War I veteran, subsequently worked with Navajo Marines in World War II to create what would become the famed code used by Navajo Code Talkers to transmit messages in the Pacific (see the discussion of the Code Talkers in Chapter 1). As Iverson recounts, while Johnston came up with the idea of the code, 'its development rested with the Navajos [who] employed Diné words for military terms, foreign countries, and other subjects' (Iverson, 2002: 184).

Throughout the 1930s and 1940s, an extraordinary (if loosely coupled) partnership emerged between federal officials, linguists, anthropologists, missionaries and native speakers – all with overlapping yet distinct sets of interests in Navajo print literacy. The development of bilingual readers and other print materials was a central goal of Commissioner of Indian Affairs John Collier's 'Indian New Deal'. 'We intended that school life become bilingual',

Collier wrote in later years; '[w]e encouraged the literalization of [American] Indian languages and the publication of Indian–English literature' (Collier, 1963: 196, cited in Lockard, 1996: 44). Under Collier's administration and that of his education director, Willard Beatty, linguistic anthropologist Edward Sapir was commissioned to write an introductory Navajo-language workbook for BIA employees; social–cultural anthropologist Gladys Reichard was sponsored in setting up a summer institute and 'hogan school' (a reference to a Navajo dwelling or *hooghan*) in Ganado, Arizona (see Figure 4.1 for location) to teach her writing system to Navajo interpreters; and linguist John Harrington was commissioned to develop a standard writing system. Because he had limited experience with Navajo, Harrington enlisted the aid of Robert Young, who had been working on the Navajo language with his colleague, William Morgan (a native speaker), at a sheep-breeding laboratory near Fort Wingate. Young and Morgan accepted some elements of the Franciscans', the linguists' and the Protestants' orthographies, but, according to Holm, 'went further than they did: [They] were working towards an orthography that could be realized on a minimally-modified typewriter and type-font' (personal communication, 29 June 2009; see also Lockard, 1996: 45). The result was the standard-bearing system known today as the Young and Morgan orthography.

In 1943, Young and Morgan produced the first of several dictionaries, praised as 'the best dictionary of a native North American language at the time' (Hale, 2001b: 200). As Young and Morgan (1987) explain the impetus for this work, with the outbreak of World War II, many Navajos joined the military, and only a few spoke English. Their supervisors demanded a dictionary 'in the hope of learning enough Navajo to meet basic communication needs' (Young & Morgan, 1987: iv). Years later, Robert Young would reflect on the format and method for this linguistic work:

> [T]he Bureau [of Indian Affairs] wanted something as nearly like English as [the] Navajo [language] would permit: 1) in view of the fact that children will also be learning English; and 2) in view of the fact that they would want to write Navajo on ordinary typewriters ... and ... on the lino-type machine. So we developed a system that utilized letters that were either similar or somewhat alike between Navajo and English. (Cited in Silentman, 1996a: 16)

The result was an orthography that used only two non-English characters (in addition to accent diacritics to mark high tones): the slash-L (Ł) and reverse cedilla or nasal-tone hook (e.g. ą) (Holm, 1996).

The Bureau continued producing bilingual textbooks and other print materials into the 1950s, including Young and Morgan's Navajo-language newspaper, *Ádahooníłígíí* (*Events* or *Occurrences*), described as a 'jewel in the body of written literature in Native American languages' (Hale, 2001b: 200; see the discussion of Native-language media in Chapter 1). While these materials included the ground-breaking Young and Morgan dictionary and other texts developed by them, many of the Bureau's materials – particularly those produced after the departure of Collier (in 1945) and Beatty (in 1952) – seem, in retrospect, to have served a patently assimilationist agenda. For example, in the Navajo–English reader, *The Flag of My Country* (King, 1956), which chronicles a Navajo youth away at a distant boarding school, the 'English text is unrelenting, almost strident, in its essentialized ... one-to-one connections between national homeland and family, possessions, and personal identity' (Lomawaima & McCarty, 2006: 106). Interestingly, the Navajo text, positioned to follow the English text, lacks these connotations and includes language that is 'deeply evocative of a Navajo sense of identity and of sacred landscape as homeland' (Lomawaima & McCarty, 2006: 106). In an analysis of this text aided by Navajo linguist Mary Willie, Lomawaima and I contemplate the meaning of these differences in tone and style:

> We can only imagine how, why, and by whom these [Navajo] words were chosen but one wonders if there was a conscious translation of the Bureau's inculcation of [US nationalism] into a more locally and personally meaningful sense of 'Navajo-ness'. (Lomawaima & McCarty, 2006: 106)

With the advent of the Cold War and a new federal policy designed to terminate the tribal–federal relationship (see the discussion of termination in Chapter 3), the Bureau's forays into bilingual–bicultural education came to a halt. By this time, however, the seeds of transformation through written Navajo had been sown, laying the foundation for more sweeping LPP changes to come.

Between 1987 and 2000, Young and Morgan published four additional lexicographical works: *The Navajo Language: A Grammar and Colloquial Dictionary* (1980), a revised edition of the same in 1987 (both much different from the 1943 dictionary), *Analytical Lexicon of Navajo* (Young et al., 1991), and *The Navajo Verb System* (Young, 2000). The team of 'YounganMorgan', as they came to be known, 'not only created a writing system but ... also put that writing system to use' (Holm, 1996: 8). By the time the first Navajo bilingual–bicultural education programs were established in the 1960s, Holm reflects, 'it was reprints of [Young and Morgan's] first dictionary that we all relied upon':

> In the end, the important thing was that the dictionary was there. Its being there was proof that Navajo was a written language. The dictionary was more than just a collection of 'old words in an old language'. Being there, it could be used as a tool to enable people not just to read Navajo but also to write Navajo now, for their own purposes. (Holm 1996: 8–9)

Holm's assessment, published in a special issue of the *Journal of Navajo Education* dedicated to the work of Young and Morgan (Silentman, 1996b), perfectly summarizes the latent possibilities of Navajo print literacy, and the ways in which corpus, acquisition and status planning activities co-constructed those possibilities 'from the bottom up' (Hornberger, 1996). Holm's statement also hints at another outcome of these multifaceted processes: the cultivation of a generation of bilingual, biliterate Navajo students, many of whom would go on to become the bilingual teachers in the very programs to which he refers.

Lynda Teller, a former teacher at Rough Rock Community School, is just such an educator. In this excerpt from a life history interview I conducted with her in 1996, she describes her self-empowerment on first experiencing her language in print:

> What I remember about the language was that I was so amazed that our *bilagáana* [a Navajoization of the Spanish *Americano* or 'Americans', sometimes glossed as White/English-speaking] teacher could read something out of the Bible and it sounded very familiar.[5] It was in Navajo. She would read it for us, and then we would follow, repeating it after her again ... And I guess that's how I got interested in it. I thought, 'This is *my* language, and this is how *I* can talk'. (Cited in McCarty, 2002b: 51)

Lorinda Gray, also a former bilingual teacher at Rough Rock, learned to read and write Navajo at the local mission school. '[W]e were taught in English', she recalls, 'but there was a time when we did written Navajo, and we ... probably read the whole New Testament in Navajo!' (cited in McCarty, 2002b: 52).

Lynda Teller's and Lorinda Gray's literacy experiences, like those of many other mission school graduates, profoundly influenced their decision to become bilingual teachers. Stories such as theirs, Lockard writes, help us 'understand the possibilities of literacy in Navajo in our homes and classrooms' (Lockard, 1996: 47). In like manner, Daniel McLaughlin, in his ethnographic study of Navajo literacy in the pseudonymous Mesa Valley community, shows how both students and churchgoers 'read and write Navajo for indigenous purposes in home settings unconnected to church or school domains and identified as "useful," "crucial to the survival of Navajo language and culture," and "important for Navajos' self-awareness"' (McLaughlin, 1992: 152).

These accounts remind us that literacy is never neutral, ahistorical or context-free, but is social as well as personal, historical, 'fluid, multiple, and power-linked' (McCarty, 2005: xvii–xviii; Gee, 2012; Street, 2001, 2008). These accounts also illuminate the specific ways in which language planning and policy are enacted in everyday social practice. Although the origins of Navajo print literacy lay in the overlapping safety zones of church and state, print literacy was appropriated by Diné speakers for Diné purposes. This opened up new 'ideological and implementational spaces' (Hornberger, 2006a; Hornberger & Johnson, 2007) for indigenizing school pedagogy and curricula, as the following section shows.

In the remainder of this chapter, I examine these more recent Navajo LPP initiatives. It should be remembered that these activities and the education programs of which they are part are, like linguistic and cultural systems, fluid and dynamic. Some programs have withered away; others continue to grow and unfold. My goal is to portray them not as static models, but rather as examples of the ways in which LPP activity works within and against a field of possibilities and constraints. As is true in many Native America communities, the starting point for these activities has been the conjoined ascendancy of bilingual–bicultural education, Indigenous print literacies and local community-controlled schools.

Bilingual–bicultural education: Symbol and mechanism of self-determination

If we were to pinpoint a single 'taproot' within the 20th century fight for Native American self-determination, a sure candidate would be the demonstration school at Rough Rock. Founded in 1966, *Tsé Ch'izhí Diné Bi'ólta'* – Rough Rock The People's (Navajos') School – is a story of many firsts (see Figure 4.3). It was the first school to elect an all-Navajo governing board (although other Navajo schools had Navajo education committees), and the first to explicitly define its role as a conduit for community economic, social and political empowerment. 'Until the advent of the Rough Rock Demonstration School,' Agnes Holm and Wayne Holm write, 'no school had

Figure 4.3 Rough Rock Community Middle School and local environment, *ca* 2007 (photograph by Leroy Morgan)

formally empowered parents or the community to have a significant say in the education of their children' (Holm & Holm, 1990: 183).

An outgrowth of federal War on Poverty initiatives, the Rough Rock Demonstration School (now called Rough Rock Community School) came about through an unprecedented contract between a locally elected Navajo governing board, a tribal board of trustees, the BIA and the US Office of Economic Opportunity (see Figure 4.4; for more on the school's founding, see Collier, 1988; Johnson, 1968; McCarty, 2002b; and Roessel, 1977). From its inception, Rough Rock was positioned as an engine of economic and social change. In its early days, in addition to an innovative bilingual–bicultural and ESL program, the school sponsored a greenhouse, a poultry farm, a toy and furniture factory, an adobe home-building project, an arts and crafts enterprise, adult education, and a medicine man training project. These programs were designed to cultivate local talent and provide income to community members in what was then one of the most economically depressed parts of the country (McCarty, 2002b: 84). Parents and grandparents – many of whom had never had the opportunity to hold a paying job – served as dormitory assistants, sharing their knowledge of oral traditions during evening storytelling events. Teachers made regular home visits to inquire into

Figure 4.4 Historic agreement launches the first American Indian community-controlled school. *From left to right:* Rough Rock community member Todecheenie Singer, original school board members Ada Agnes Singer and John Dick, a BIA official, and original school board member Teddy McCurtain (photograph courtesy of Arizona State University Center for Indian Education Archives)

80 Language Planning and Policy in Native America

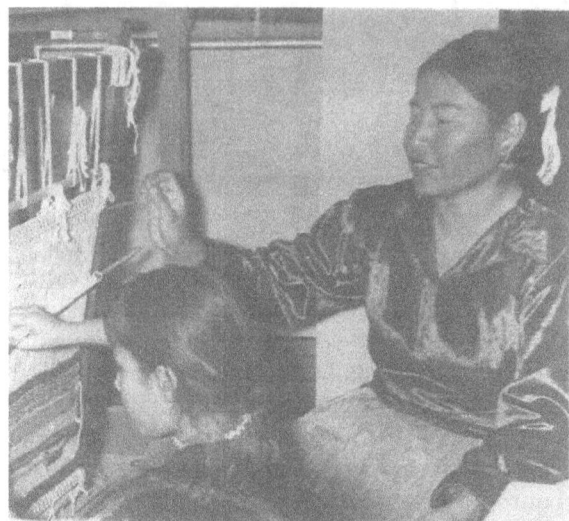

Figure 4.5 Rug weaving illustrates a Diné pedagogy of storytelling and cultural practice exemplified at Rough Rock School (photograph by John Collier Jr, ca 1970, from the archives of Robert A. Roessel Jr, courtesy of C. Monty Roessel)

local 'funds of knowledge' (González *et al.*, 2005) so that this could be incorporated into instruction (see Figures 4.5 and 4.6).

Activities such as these brought community members into the school and the school into the community. 'In the past, Indian schools have taken little interest in their communities', the school's cofounding director, the late

Figure 4.6 Nearly four decades after the photo in Figure 4.5 was taken, Ruth Roessel, as director of Rough Rock's Diné program, makes an offering to a piñon tree to protect students. Like the young piñon tree, students will 'grow and change' (Roessel, 2007: 121; photograph by C. Monty Roessel, 2007)

Robert A. Roessel, Jr, told a reporter in 1967; 'but here, we want to involve adults and teenagers, dropouts, and people who have never been to school' (Conklin, 1967: 8). Years later, in an informal interview with me, he stressed: 'It was *all* a Navajo program ... We brought the entire community into the school ... This was what the school was all about' (cited in McCarty, 2002b: 84; see Figure 4.7).

However, Rough Rock's taproot was not seeded in sterile ground, nor did it spring up alone. As the demonstration project got under way, educators at the Rock Point BIA school 40 miles away (see Figure 4.1 for location) were also testing the premise that teaching Navajo students to read in their primary language would have beneficial academic outcomes (Rosier & Farella, 1976: 380).[6] Using students' first language for initial literacy learning is, of course, standard practice for speakers of dominant languages. However, this tried-and-true method was 'radical ... and extraordinarily exciting' in Native American education at the time (Hale, 2001b: 199). At Rock Point, the approach was called coordinate bilingual instruction; Navajo language teachers communicated only in Navajo, and English language teachers only in English, dissolving traditional status boundaries between uncertified (mostly Navajo) and certified (mostly White) teachers (Holm & Holm, 1990: 176).

Within a few years, other Navajo communities, including Rock Point, 'went contract' (i.e. contracted with the federal government to run their own schools). In 1970, at Ramah, a Navajo community apart from the southern boundary of the New Mexico portion of the reservation (see Figure 4.1 for location), 'a few courageous, nonformally educated Navajo elders and a recent high school graduate traveled to Washington, D.C. to request funding for

Figure 4.7 Robert A. Roessel, Jr, co-founder and first director of Rough Rock Demonstration School, and an architect of the American Indian education self-determination movement, 1967 (photograph courtesy of C. Monty Roessel)

a school in their community' – a struggle they had been waging with the federal government for some time (Manuelito, 2005: 77). Kathryn Manuelito, a native of Ramah who taught in and directed Ramah's bilingual–bicultural program, describes what happened next:

> When their demands were ignored, Bertha Lorenzo, a frail elder, threw her blanket down in the doorway of the BIA building and said she wouldn't leave until they were granted aid. Thus, on April 20, 1970, Commissioner of Indian Affairs Louis Bruce approved funding for the Ramah Navajo High School, the first Navajo community-controlled secondary school. (Manuelito, 2005: 77)

The early Ramah program emphasized both oral and written Navajo, and 'all non-Navajo speakers on the school staff were required to study elementary Navajo' (Spolsky, 1974: 26–27). In 1972, Rock Point 'went contract', followed by Borrego Pass (Dibé Yázhi Habitiin Ólta') at Crownpoint, New Mexico (see Figure 4.1). By 1974, in addition to these four schools, five other Navajo BIA schools and three public school districts had established bilingual–bicultural programs (Spolsky, 1974).

These Indigenous community initiatives sparked a flurry of status, corpus and acquisition planning. Working with others at the national level, school leaders at Rough Rock and other community-controlled schools pushed successfully for passage of the 1972 Indian Education Act and the 1975 Indian Self-Determination and Education Assistance Act.[7] As discussed in Chapter 3, the Indian Education Act provided for the development and implementation of linguistically and culturally responsive curricula, the preparation of Native teachers, and the involvement of Native American parents in their children's education. The Indian Self-Determination Act provided the legal mechanism for tribes and Native American communities to operate their own schools. With this legislation in place, new 'implementational space' (Hornberger, 2002, 2006a) opened for other Native American communities to operate bilingual–bicultural education programs and establish community-based schools.

In every program, corpus and acquisition planning were primary concerns; 'there ... needed to be material and curriculum development and the use and training of ... native speakers', Spolsky writes (1974: 62). With the target of producing 1000 Navajo bilingual teachers in five years, the newly established Navajo Division of Education, under the leadership of Rough Rock's second director Dillon Platero, began a Navajo teacher education project, delivering university courses on-site at reservation schools and providing graduate training for Navajo school administrators (Read et al., 1975: 5). Navajo bilingual educators at Rough Rock established the Diné Bi'ólta' (Navajo School) Association, holding regular workshops to develop Navajo literacy materials and train bilingual teachers to read and write Navajo. 'Out of these workshops ... came many materials on Navajo language and culture and much refinement of Navajo-related curricula', writes Silentman (1995: 10). In 1967, Rough Rock founded the Navajo Curriculum Center, the first publishing house on Navajo and Native American language, culture and history. A few years later, a consortium of Navajo community-controlled schools established the Native American Materials Development Center (NAMDC). Under the direction of Gloria Emerson and with William Morgan (coauthor of the *Navajo Dictionary*) as language specialist, NAMDC produced an entire K–6 Navajo reading series and an integrated series of K–8 social studies and science materials. '[T]he really significant contribution of NAMDC', Wayne Holm notes, 'was not so much the quantity of materials they produced as the fact that they produced a whole program of K–6 materials. There was, after that, no excuse for schools not teaching (initial) literacy in Navajo' (personal communication, 29 June 2009). Altogether, NAMDC, the Navajo Curriculum Center and other school-based curriculum projects produced hundreds of high-quality language teaching materials during this period, many of which are still in use today (see Figure 4.8).

Throughout the next two decades, '[m]eetings were occurring constantly on the refinement of the Navajo language', Silentman recalls; '[s]peakers and experts (both traditional [i.e. elders] and academic) were brought in to help us decide on bilingual education concerns and issues' (Silentman, 1995: 10). The BIA, Teacher Corps, Center for Applied Linguistics, Massachusetts Institute of Technology, and numerous other universities all had programs to prepare bilingual teachers and Native linguists. At the University of New

Figure 4.8 Examples of corpus planning at Rough Rock Demonstration School, 1971–1983 (photograph by Teresa L. McCarty)

Mexico in Albuquerque (see Figure 4.1 for location), Bernard Spolsky launched the Navajo Reading Study, surveying child language use as a basis for developing Navajo reading materials (Spolsky, 1972: 11). On the assumption that these materials must be written first in Navajo rather than translated from English, Spolsky insisted that teacher education be a central component of the study (Spolsky, 1972: 16, 1975: 350). When the Navajo Reading Study ended in 1975, it had produced 50 children's books and 24 technical reports on Navajo and Native American education, and trained dozens of individuals in Navajo literacy and materials development, virtually all of whom went on to become language educators and activists. This was a period when 'Navajo bilingual programs were at their peak', Silentman notes, a time that produced a growing Indigenous literature hand-in-hand with a cadre of bilingual teachers:

> Many more Navajo teachers were certified and trained for bilingual programs, the state's public schools were implementing some form of bilingual instruction..., and everyone was developing sequential curricula for their schools. Support was coming from the local communities and school administrators... There was even support from the tribal headquarters. (Silentman, 1995: 12–13)

This testimony foregrounds the ways in which status, corpus and acquisition planning are braided, reciprocal, co-occurring processes. In the Navajo case, those processes were catalyzed by the appropriation of Indigenous literacies for Indigenous ends. 'We came to value our own language, particularly when we saw it in print', Silentman states; 'our language was just as valuable and was on equal status with, if not above, the English language' (Silentman, 1995: 16–17). Through these processes, Silentman adds, Navajo educators came to see themselves as 'equals with non-native teachers and administrators' (Silentman, 1995: 16).

Indigenous Community-controlled Schooling: Possibilities and Constraints

In an analysis of Native American bilingual–bicultural education, Read et al. (1975: 3) emphasize that these programs are integrally 'tied up with the question of who should control the schools'. In this section, I pause to take stock: what can we learn about Indigenous linguistic and educational self-determination from the ways in which Diné citizens and communities responded to that question?

First, let us take the students. Later in the book, I take up the problems associated with the most common (and misused) indicator of student progress – English standardized tests. For the moment, however, it is instructive to examine the test score performance of Navajo students in bilingual–bicultural programs, as this has been a pedagogic terrain of great contention that was equally of great concern to those charged with the programs' implementation.

When the Rock Point program began, students there ranked near the bottom of all Navajo BIA schools on standardized tests (Rosier & Farella, 1976: 379). In moving forward with a bilingual program, the Navajo school board insisted that its students would perform at least as well as BIA students on BIA-mandated tests. As a consequence, Rock Point compiled excellent longitudinal data on students' academic achievement (Holm & Holm, 1990). These data show unequivocally that children who learned to read first in Navajo not only outperformed comparable students in English-only programs, but they also surpassed their own previous annual growth rates, reinforcing the findings from international research on the cumulative benefits of well-designed and implemented bilingual education programs (Holm & Holm, 1990, 1995; Rosier & Farella, 1976; Rosier & Holm, 1980). 'More impressive', Holm and Holm (1990: 182–184) state, the students 'did so by a greater margin at each successive grade'. Rock Point students also had the advantage of becoming literate in their mother tongue (i.e. they experienced additive bilingualism), and they exhibited 'considerably more self-confidence and pride' (Holm & Holm, 1995: 148; see also Rosier & Farella, 1976: 388). Rosier and Holm sum up the academic effects of the Rock Point program after 12 years of implementation:

- By third grade, students who were taught to read first in Navajo read better in English than those who were taught to read in English only.
- By fourth grade, Navajo students who were initially taught mathematics in Navajo performed better in mathematics than those who were taught mathematics in English only.
- At each grade level, 'the bilingual students' scores diverge further from those of the EFL [English-as-a-foreign-language] ... students and converge closer toward national norms'. (Rosier & Holm, 1980: 28)

In short, 'a good bilingual program showed demonstrably better results' (Rosier & Holm, 1980: 28).

Rough Rock has more limited documentation on students' school performance from its early years, but there is a good database for the Rough Rock English–Navajo Language Arts Program (RRENLAP), begun in the mid-1980s. These data show that students who experienced sustained (i.e. cumulative and progressive over four to five years) initial literacy learning in Navajo made greater gains than their non-bilingual education peers on local and standardized measures of achievement. After four years in the program, RRENLAP students' mean scores on criterion-referenced tests of English comprehension rose from 58% to 91%. On standardized reading subtests, students' scores initially declined, then rose steadily, in some cases approaching or exceeding national norms. RRENLAP students were also assessed by their teachers as having stronger oral Navajo and Navajo literacy abilities than their non-bilingual education peers (McCarty, 1993, 2002b: ch. 11). These findings reinforce those of an earlier national survey of Indian community-controlled schools, which reported lower dropout rates, higher scores on standardized tests, and restored self-image and interest in learning among Native children in these schools (Scheirbeck et al., 1976).

Yet, as Spolsky (1974: 52) points out, student achievement is only one outcome of interest in assessing the impacts of bilingual–bicultural programs (see also Spolsky et al., 1974). By definition, these programs are anti-hegemonic – a rejection of colonial schooling and an assertion of Indigenous language and education rights. The radical challenge to safety zone boundaries represented by these projects cannot be overstated. 'People were shocked when we suggested using Navajo ... in the school to learn', said Agnes Holm, cofounder of the Rock Point bilingual program (cited in McCarty, 2002b: 113). Before Rough Rock, explained Wayne Holm, 'the notion that you have to have community-responsive curricula, or ... some form of [community] empowerment ... it was just literally unthinkable' (cited in McCarty, 2002b: 123). 'We planted the seeds ... of Indian self-determination', former Rough Rock school board president Ernest Dick explained in a 1997 interview (cited in McCarty, 2002b: 195). As the previous section shows, those seeds came to fruition in new forms of Indigenous leadership, a corps of Native teachers, and a corpus of Native language and culture teaching materials. Holm and Holm (1990) describe this as a 'four-fold empowerment' – of Indigenous school leaders, who acquired increasing credibility with community members, staff and students; of Indigenous educators, whose pedagogical vision and expertise were validated within and outside the community; of parents, who were positioned as equal partners in their children's schooling; and of students, who 'came to value their Navajo-ness and to see themselves as capable of succeeding because of, not despite that Navajo-ness' (Holm & Holm, 1990: 182–184).

Taken together, these emancipatory processes ruptured metaphorical safety zone boundaries even as they collided with monumental safety zone constraints. Chief among the latter is a federal bureaucracy and school funding system that, for years, has seemed to stifle self-determination at every turn. Unlike off-reservation public schools, Indigenous community schools must rely on congressional appropriations for virtually all their funding. This obligation is entailed by the federal trust relationship, but it is equally a consequence of the massive economic disparities facing reservation schools. Also, unlike more affluent, off-reservation school districts, Indigenous community-controlled schools operate as independent units, providing all education services – from transportation to paper and pens to employee salaries – from a single local budget. The costs of these largely rural schools are significantly higher, yet their material resources and infrastructure support are much more limited. Further, their budgets are highly volatile, dependent upon annual congressional appropriations, which change from year to year. Thus, a school's base budget also fluctuates from year to year.

For decades, community-controlled schools were enmeshed in protracted, time- and labor-intensive budget negotiations that, in one school director's words, 'would defeat the President of General Motors' (Scheirbeck et al., 1976: 311). It was typical for school budgets to be finalized months after the school year began, stalling staff hiring and even the purchase of school supplies, and keeping school leaders at distant budget meetings instead of at school when the academic year began. These realities forced community-controlled schools to cobble together instructional programs from disparate federal programs, resulting in chronic programmatic volatility and staff turnover, and contributing to academic disparities for Native American students (for an extended discussion, see McCarty, 2002b: ch. 5).

These volatile conditions were partially ameliorated by a forward-funding formula contained in the Elementary and Secondary School Improvement Amendments of 1988, commonly known as Public Law 100-297. While this has made community-controlled school budgets more predictable, it has not necessarily provided adequate funding. Moreover, the legislation contains a crucial 'catch': eligibility for forward funding (called 'grant status') requires Indigenous community-controlled schools to tailor instructional programs to externally imposed standards – a mandate that locks these schools into a system of federal constraint and control. These requirements have been dramatically intensified with the 2001 Elementary and Secondary Education Act reauthorization known as No Child Left Behind.

Thus, Indigenous community-controlled schools have been forced down the slippery slope of high-stakes, English-only 'accountability' – a situation discussed more fully in the final chapter of this book. The fact that many Native communities have managed to work around these constraints, continuing to implement robust bilingual–bicultural–biliteracy programs, is testimony to their imagination, perseverance and commitment to self-determination. Reflecting on these challenges at Rough Rock, Ernest Dick remarked in a 1995 interview, 'The way I look at it, it's how Indian education actually survived' (cited in McCarty, 2002b: 4).

Navajo Language 'at a Crossroads'

At the time of this writing, there are 122 American Indian community-controlled schools, of which 26 are Navajo. 'Navajo schools – of all types – now offer some kind of Navajo language and culture instruction', Holm states (personal communication, 20 June 2009). In some reservation public schools, Navajo is taught as a 'foreign' language, and a few schools, including Rough Rock, have full or partial Navajo-language immersion programs. Some schools publish Navajo-language materials, and the *Navajo Times* includes news stories in Navajo. In New Mexico, the state has officially adopted Parsons-Yazzie's *Diné Bizaad Bínáhoo'aah: Rediscovering the Navajo Language*, a 448-page textbook and correlated workbook that introduces students to the Navajo sound, verb and writing systems (Parsons-Yazzie & Speas, 2008; Parsons-Yazzie & Yazzie, 2008).

At the post-secondary level, Diné College offers 13 courses in Navajo that enroll approximately 600 students per semester, three-quarters of whom speak 'or at least understand' Navajo (Slate, 2001: 396). Diné College has partnerships with state universities to prepare Navajo teachers and school administrators, and Navajo is taught at several universities and their branches in Arizona, New Mexico, Utah, Colorado and the Navajo Nation.

As discussed in Chapter 1, Navajo can still be heard in the chapter houses and remains important in tribal government; the language can also be heard in trading posts, grocery stores, post offices and other public spaces. Navajo predominates in traditional healing ceremonies and the Native American Church. Regional radio stations broadcast in Navajo, including one that broadcasts solely in Navajo except for its country music (Slate, 2001: 393).

However, in the critical domains of family and home, Navajo is, as Benally and Viri (2005: 106) put it, 'at a crossroads. It is at a stage where it can be revived [and] strengthened in daily use, or it can continue to decline'. As early as 1986, former Rough Rock School director Dillon Platero observed that, while the Navajo Nation had 'the largest number of speakers of Navajo ever in its history, it also [had] the greatest number of nonspeakers' (cited in Brandt, 1988: 322). Ten years later, Parsons-Yazzie (1996/1997) described the creeping infiltration of English into all domains of family and community life as 'students see the Navajo employees in subservient positions and begin to see a glass ceiling placed over their own aspirations if they are Navajo speakers' (Parsons-Yazzie, 1996/1997: 63). Benally and Viri expand on this, noting that, for some young people, Navajo is viewed as 'a language only for the old, for the people who do not have the amenities of modern life such as electricity and indoor plumbing. It is the language of those who are powerless and possess little' (Benally & Viri, 2005: 93). Slate (2001: 394) sums up the early 21st century language situation this way: 'An ever-increasing portion of Navajos are monolingual in English, the power language for most settings and functions, and there are few communities where Navajo is spoken everywhere' (Slate, 2001: 394).

There is nonetheless a good deal of effort underway to restore the Navajo language within family homes, communities and schools (see, e.g. Holm, 2006; House, 2002; Manuelito, 2005; McCarty, 2002a, 2002b: ch. 13). As we will see in Chapter 6, these interventions are beginning to be guided by youth and young adults. 'After becoming cognizant of the language shift occurring in their families and ... communities', Tiffany Lee writes, 'these youth [express] a desire to intervene through their own research, language practices at home, and personal efforts to learn their heritage language' (Lee, 2009: 317). While these projects are yielding some impressive successes, language and culture renewal among younger generations continues to represent what some Diné scholars view as 'one of the greatest challenges the Navajo Nation and Diné people will have to face' (Lee & Lee, 2012: 124).

The most significant challenge for these renewal efforts may lie in transforming the long-term effects of policies and practices that have led to language shift in the first place, and that continue to condition language attitudes, ideologies and practices. How these transformations are being instantiated is the sequel to the LPP story told in this chapter, and yet another proactive and hopeful response to histories of linguistic repression and the larger question of 'who should control the schools'.

Notes

(1) Writing seven years after passage of the NSIEA, Lee and Lee (2012: 124) observe that the Act has not yet yielded the promise of these early prognostications by then-President Shirley largely because the underlying power structure has not changed: the states in which Navajo Nation public schools are located continue to exercise budgetary control over those schools, and the Department of Diné Education lacks sufficient financial resources to implement the Act (see also Winstead et al., 2008).
(2) Decades after this publication, Holm noted that subsequent analyses 'suggested that Navajo-language use may have peaked in the late [1970s], although it may have been a few years later in [reservation interior] communities like Rock Point and Rough Rock. Perhaps because it had become "normal" for children to go to school in Navajo by then, we felt that more people were continuing to talk Navajo in the home' (personal communication, 29 June 2009).
(3) Head Start is a federally funded program begun as part of the Johnson Administration's 'War on Poverty' initiatives in the 1960s. The program provides grants to public and private non-profit agencies for 'comprehensive child development services to economically disadvantaged children and families', with a focus on early reading (Administration for Children and Families, 2011: para. 4). At the time of Platero's study, the Navajo Department of Head Start had received funding for 3398 eligible children, who constituted less than a third of eligible Navajo children, 13.4% of all Navajo children of preschool age (Platero, 2001: 88).
(4) The Franciscans at St Michaels were from Cincinnati, Ohio, and most were of German descent (Wayne Holm, personal communication, 29 June 2009).
(5) I thank Wayne Holm (personal communication, 4 July 2009) for this translation of *bilagáana* (see also Young & Morgan, 1987: 221).
(6) The fortunes of the Rough Rock and Rock Point schools have long been intertwined. In the 1960s, both communities were seeking new BIA school facilities to replace their tiny local schools. The BIA agreed to expand the Rock Point School, later coming back to the school board to say 'that if Rock Point would wait, they [the BIA] would build a bigger school for 600+ students the following year' (Wayne Holm, personal communication, 29 June 2009). The latter was on the condition that the

Rough Rock community would send its children to Rock Point, thereby filling the additional school 'seats'. According to Wayne Holm, who was employed at Rock Point at the time, 'They [BIA] didn't ask Rough Rock ... That was what is disturbing in retrospect – that, at the time, no one thought this was something someone should ask Rough Rock parents about' (personal communication, 29 June 2009). The Rock Point education committee decided 'it really isn't right for the Rough Rock kids' to have to travel all the way to Rock Point (cited in McCarty, 2002b: 72). Rock Point kept its smaller three-teacher school for the time being, and the BIA built a new elementary school facility at Rough Rock that would eventually house the demonstration project (Wayne Holm, interview, 31 January 1996). 'I've always admired the then-Rock Point Board for that decision', Holm said, '[b]ecause that [having a bigger school] would have meant many more jobs in a very poor community' (personal communication, 29 June 2009).

(7) As an example of the influence of Indigenous leaders on national policy, Rough Rock's school board minutes refer repeatedly to congressional testimony by Navajo and other Native American educators and community members on the direction that policy should take (McCarty 2002a, 2002b). Following one Senate hearing, Robert Kennedy, then chair of the Special Subcommittee on Indian education, asked pointedly, 'Why *not* Indian parents enriching the curriculum ... Why *not* community development ... for every school?' (US Congress, Senate Committee on Labor and Public Welfare, Special Subcommittee on Indian Education, 1969: 1057). Within a year, President Nixon would deliver an historic message to Congress calling for American Indian self-determination and setting the stage for passage of the Indian Education and Indian Self-Determination Acts.

5 Language Regenesis in Practice

> *I think what we all need to do is look at our contemporary condition, and through our own experiences try to come up with what is going to work within our own communities ... I like to think that we don't know what the future holds and anything is still very possible. The only way to arrive at those possibilities is through our own empowerment as Myaamia people.*
>
> Daryl Baldwin, director, Myaamia Project, personal communication, 11 May 2009

What does language regenesis look like in social practice? How do regenesis efforts come about? Who are the stakeholders, and what are their goals? What approaches have been successful in what contexts – and what have been some of the challenges?

In recent years, there has been a proliferation of descriptive reports and scholarship on language revitalization around the world. My goal in this chapter is to put a human face on the project of Native American language revitalization by exploring a select number of cases in depth. The cases were chosen to illustrate language regenesis (revitalization) processes across a range of sociohistorical and sociolinguistic settings, from formerly sleeping languages (Leonard, 2008), to those considered moribund, to those in which intergenerational transmission still occurs but is rapidly losing ground to English. The cases also illustrate a cross-section of family-, community-, school- and university-based approaches.

Throughout the narrative, I highlight the voices and perspectives of local language planners, drawing on formal and informal interviews, participant and non-participant observation, public documents, digital and audiovisual sources, and personal communications with key project personnel. In one case – Miami – the back-and-forth with local language planners was so extensive that this section of the chapter came to represent a co-authorial voice, and I have indicated co-authorship of the section accordingly.[1]

For each case, I begin with a brief sociolinguistic profile and a sketch of the historical circumstances leading to language shift. I then explore how grass roots language planners are opening what Nancy Hornberger (2002, 2006a) calls 'ideological and implementational spaces' – windows of opportunity in which negative language trajectories can be re-envisioned and new language learning possibilities emplaced. As the epigraph that begins this chapter suggests, these language planning windows of opportunity emerge out of local conditions that have shaped historic language trajectories and that also shape contemporary language learning resources and scale-levels (Blommaert, 2010) – that is, language regeneration potentials. If there is a universal lesson to be drawn from the project of language revitalization, it is that it must be undertaken and evaluated in terms of locally available resources and locally meaningful goals. We begin our exploration of these issues with the examples of two formerly sleeping Algonquian languages, Miami and Wôpanâak.

neetawaapantamaanki iilinwiaanki meehkamaanki niiyoonaani: Searching for Our Talk and Finding Ourselves
Written with Daryl Baldwin, George M. Ironstrack and Julie Olds

The Miami people's traditional homelands, called *Myaamionki* or 'the place of the Myaamia [Miami people]', include what are today the states of Indiana and Illinois as well as parts of Ohio, Wisconsin and Michigan. The cultural core of their historic homelands remains in what is now known as the Wabash River Valley in present-day Indiana (Strack *et al.*, 2011b: 2). By the Miamis' own account, the Myaamia 'lived in this location from time immemorial until arrival of Europeans in North America' (Strack *et al.*, 2011b: 2). One of the major dialects of what linguists call Miami–Illinois, Miami is an Algonquian language originally spoken by peoples indigenous to this southern Great Lakes region (Baldwin, 2003; Baldwin & Costa, 2005; Leonard, 2007; Rinehart, 2006). The seeds of Miami language shift and reclamation were jointly sown in the 17th century, when French Jesuits entered Miami–Illinois territory and began documenting the language as part of their efforts to evangelize and translate religious texts into Miami–Illinois. By the late 1700s, at least three known Illinois–French dictionaries existed. Over the next century and a half, others would continue documenting the language, producing a very large volume of extant materials that would one day become key resources for language regeneration.

At the same time, the Miami people faced a severe and rapid fracturing of their collective way of being. The Miami population declined rapidly in the latter half of the 18th and the 19th centuries. This population decline, brought on by disease and war, was quickly followed by the intentional erosion of the Miami traditional land base through the American-dominated treaty process. These events produced a series of fault lines that crisscrossed the Miami community. Following the forced removals of 1846 and the 1870s, these fault lines ruptured and the community began to fragment into smaller and more isolated pieces.

The signing of the Treaty of the Forks of the Wabash in 1840 ceded all remaining tribal allotments in Indiana, and six years later, half the tribal community was forcibly removed to a reservation in Kansas Territory. '[C]lutching handfuls of earth from their ancestors' graves' (Wirtner, 1994: 122, cited in Rinehart, 2006: 98), the Miami were loaded onto canal boats in what is now Peru, Indiana, taken up the Wabash–Erie Canal to Fort Wayne and then down the Miami–Erie Canal in Ohio, and transferred onto steamships in Cincinnati, until they reached what is today Kansas City. From there, they made the last 50 miles of the trip by foot, horse and wagon (Baldwin, 2003: 5; Strack *et al.*, 2011b; see Figure 5.1). Nine years later, following Kansas statehood, the Miami were forcibly removed again, this time to what was then called Indian Territory and is today the State of Oklahoma. 'By the time our ancestors stepped onto Indian Territory after two removals', Miami linguist and language planner Daryl Baldwin writes, 'there were less than 80 individuals who made the final leg of the journey, leaving behind relatives in both Kansas and Indiana' (Baldwin, 2003: 7). Today, as

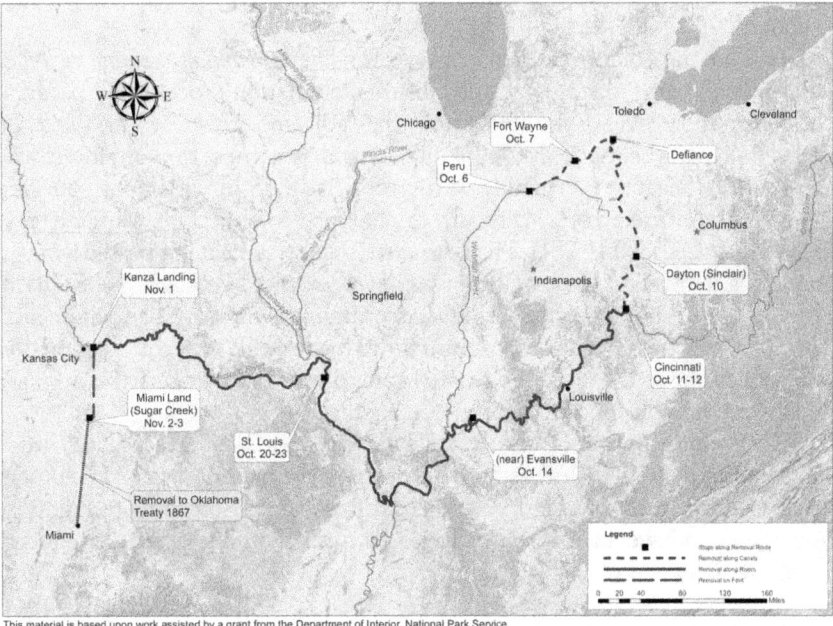

Figure 5.1 Miami removal route (map by Kristina Fox and Bradford Kasberg, courtesy of Myaamia Heritage Museum and Archive)

a result of forced removal, a quarter of the Miami tribal population resides in these three areas.

Removal to Indian Territory placed the Miami amongst tribal communities who were formerly from their homeland, some of whom were historical enemies, with English as the common language. At the same time, many Miami children were sent to federal boarding schools both near and far from home, and the Miami faced 'continued social and governmental pressures to suppress all aspects of being Miami' (Baldwin & Olds, 2007: 281). Meanwhile, the federal government refused to recognize the Indiana Miamis' treaty rights, and the Oklahoma Miamis were left to live on individual allotments as part of the federal government's allotment policy, a thinly disguised campaign to seize remaining Native American lands (see the discussion of allotment in Chapter 3). It was not until the 1970s that the Miami Tribe of Oklahoma – the only federally recognized Miami nation – was able to begin reacquiring communal lands (see Figure 5.3). The tribe now has about 1300 acres, but, Baldwin says, 'we have literally had to buy most of it back through our own economic ventures' (Baldwin, 2003: 7).

Today, Miami people live in 47 US states, including those who stayed behind during the Indiana and Kansas diasporas (Miami Tribe of Oklahoma, personal communication, 17 February 2012). There are approximately 4000 enrolled citizens of the Miami Tribe of Oklahoma, and an estimated 10,000 people who may be able to claim Miami or Illinois as a heritage language (Leonard, 2007: 28; see Figure 5.2).

This is the sociohistorical context for the *myaamiaki eemamwiciki* or Miami awakening, a language and culture reclamation process that began at the community level in the 1990s from the dedicated efforts of Julie Olds and Daryl Baldwin (Leonard, 2007: 23). 'This history is important', Baldwin and Olds write, 'because everything we do today as a nation, including our language and culture efforts, is in direct response to this oppressive history' (Baldwin & Olds, 2007: 281). The last native speakers of Miami passed away in the 1960s. However, the language was never 'extinct', Leonard (2008) maintains, as there is both a heritage-language community and language documentation spanning three centuries, beginning with the work by Jesuit missionaries and continuing to the present day (see Leonard's 'Revised view of the language endangerment continuum', Figure 1.6, Chapter 1).

Since the inception of this effort, Baldwin and Olds have used a garden metaphor to help them understand and describe the present historical moment and its significance for language and culture recovery. According to Baldwin, 'A garden can have a lot of weeds in it and it takes tilling it ... to encourage what we want to grow':

> And I think our history is such that if you look back at all of our ancestors' experiences, ... it's incredible the amount of weeds we've accumulated over the years because we have an untended garden. It is the

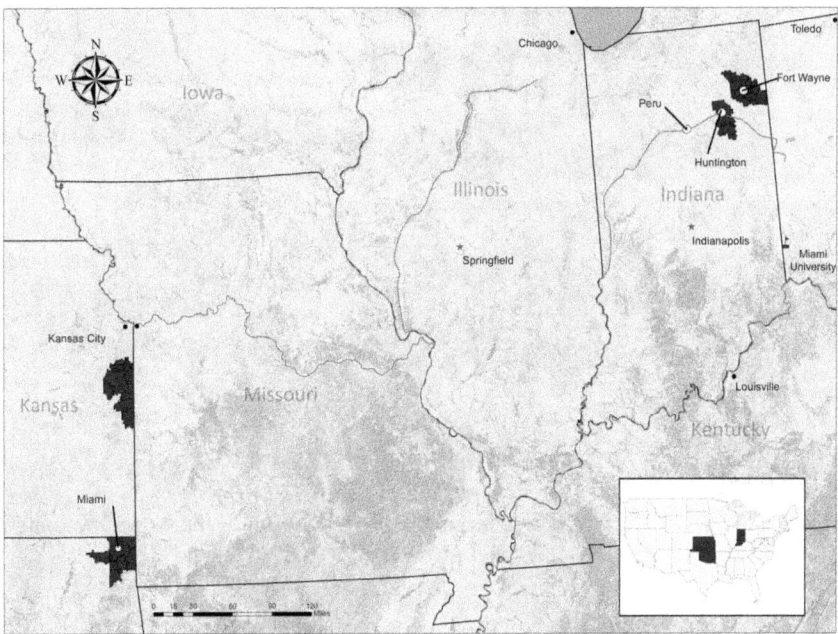

Figure 5.2 Contemporary Myaamia population centers (map by Kristina Fox and Bradford Kasberg; population data compiled by Aaron Lane; both courtesy of Myaamia Heritage Museum and Archive)

untended garden, over a long period of time, that leads to the many losses that we live with today. So you can't just go from a field of weeds to a beautiful garden in a day. It takes a lot of effort and a lot of work to build that back. And I really think that is the process for language and cultural revitalization ... It's more a matter of getting on with the work in a thoughtful way. We must be conscious gardeners if we are going to have a community harvest. (Personal communication, 11 May 2009)

Baldwin and Myaamia Project assistant director and education coordinator George Ironstrack use another metaphor – of legs – to describe the Myaamia awakening. The first 'leg', says Baldwin, was the breakthrough linguistic work undertaken in the 1980s and 1990s by David Costa (see Figure 5.3), who analyzed Miami historical documents and reconstructed Miami–Illinois phonology and morphology (Costa, 1994). As Costa explains in a tribal-developed documentary: it was the late-1980s and he had just completed a master's degree in linguistics. He was looking for a language to work on for his doctoral dissertation. 'There's this language, Miami, that we don't know ... what the language was like', he remembers an advisor saying; 'Why don't you start digging around and find out what's out there?' (Miami Tribe of Oklahoma, 2008). 'I'm not aware of any other [Native American] language ... where there's no

Figure 5.3 David J. Costa, the first 'leg' of the Miami awakening (photograph by Andrew J. Strack, courtesy of Myaamia Project Archives)

native speakers, no sound recordings, but massive written recordings', Costa relates (Miami Tribe of Oklahoma, 2008). Using that linguistic corpus, he completed a grammatical description of the language in 1994. Once he commenced on this project, Costa found that 'Miami language is not just this arcane subject of study but there was this whole community that was interested in getting this language back ... and to have it part of their culture again' (Miami Tribe of Oklahoma, 2008; see Figure 5.3).

This brings us to the next two 'legs'. According to Baldwin, the second 'leg' was his own. A descendant of a long line of Miami family members and leaders going 'back to the treaty that signed over the land that [Miami] University sits on', Daryl Baldwin 'knew the history of my family [and] how many generations fought to stay alive as Miami people' (personal communication, 11 May 2009). A student of wildlife biology at the University of Montana in the 1990s, he began working on the Miami language out of personal interest.

> Simply put, I wanted my children to have more of their heritage than I had growing up and I saw the language as the means to reconnect to my culture. With all the documentation I was looking at, I just simply didn't believe my language was extinct and I believe that more solidly today. (Personal communication, 22 February 2012)

Receiving encouragement from Miami elders and University of Montana linguistics professor Anthony Mattina, and using extant Miami texts and Costa's work, Baldwin began teaching himself the language, completing a master's degree in Arts with emphasis in Native American linguistics in

1999. He and his wife Karen (who is not Miami but who has also learned the language) are raising their four children as bilingual Miami–English speakers (see Leonard, 2007 for an ethnographic and linguistic case study of these family efforts). This personal commitment demonstrated what a dedicated household effort could achieve and helped to create a new possibility that many more Miami homes are choosing to follow.

The third 'leg', say Baldwin and Ironstrack, was Julie Olds, a Miami community member who wanted to expand the home efforts of the Baldwin family into the community. The Miami Tribe of Oklahoma had applied for and received a grant from the Administration of Native Americans (the federal agency charged with implementing the Native American Languages Act), to offer a community-based Miami language learning program beginning in 1996. Julie Olds was instrumental in serving as a catalyst for the community to begin their engagement in language revitalization. She had been elected to the tribe's governing body (the Business Committee) in 1996, serving until 2005, and her participation on the political level aided in gaining tribal support for the effort. She 'came in as the community leg', Baldwin said. 'She is the one that began to say, "Daryl, I like what you are doing. I believe in what you are doing. Can we start something at the community level?"'

> And so I think those three are the first legs of this effort and we learned very early on that because we did not have speakers to turn to, but we had a very large amount of documentation ... our effort was to spend an entire generation reconstructing the language and beginning to work with our community to change the way they think about their language. (Personal communication, 19 August 2009; see Figure 5.4)

There is yet a fourth 'leg' to the Miami story: Miami tribal leadership (Figure 5.5). As Baldwin reflected,

> [E]specially for groups like us [small, diasporized communities with few or no native speakers], tribal leadership has been critical to the progression of our work. We learned early on that even though self-motivated learning in the home may not require much in the way of financial resources, community based language learning does require a tremendous amount resources and tribal leadership has been critical towards supporting this need. (Personal communication, 19 August 2009)

The Miami Tribe of Oklahoma has had a long and remarkable relationship with its namesake university, which is located within the Miami historical homeland. The relationship was forged in the early 1970s in the context of negotiations over Miami University's (MU) then-'Redskin' mascot. In subsequent years those negotiations grew into a mutually beneficial exchange of personnel, projects and ideas (Bobbe Burke, personal communication, 12 May 2009). In the early 1990s – as Costa, Baldwin and Olds were

Figure 5.4 Daryl Baldwin and Julie Olds, the second and third 'legs' of the Miami awakening, at a community gathering in Miami, OK, 2004 (photograph by Karen Baldwin, courtesy of Myaamia Project Archives)

each engaged in their linguistic endeavors – an agreement was reached in which MU pledged 20 tuition waivers for Miami students each year. 'Twenty seemed very far away at the time', said Bobbe Burke, MU's coordinator of Miami Tribe Relations, 'but we now have family-like structures here, and relationships that have been built' (personal communication, 12 May 2009). MU's Miami Indian Heritage Award for [Miami] Tribe Students has enabled more than 80 tribal students to attend the university (Bobbe Burke, personal communication, 29 February 2012), including current Myaamia Project media specialist Andrew J. Strack. The combination of tribal youth and the Myaamia Project has created an environment of learning that has contributed to a 77% graduation rate among tribal students who attend MU (Bobbe Burke, personal communication, 29 February 2012).

These multiple 'legs' began to walk in unison when Julie Olds, the Miami Tribe's cultural resource officer, suggested to Baldwin that they approach MU with a proposal for a language revitalization project. As Baldwin describes the process that ensued,

> And I said, 'A university? Do you think it will go?' Fortunately we already had this relationship with the university. I had already been here because I did guest lectures on occasion ... So we identified two people on campus who were willing to help us put together a proposal and we put the proposal through and Miami University said, 'Sure, let's give it a try'. And I said, 'You've got to be kidding me!' (Personal communication, 11 May 2009)

Figure 5.5 Miami Tribal Business Committee, representing the fourth 'leg' of the Miami awakening, at a Miami Tribe of Oklahoma Annual Meeting in 2011. *Seated left to right*: Councilperson Scott Willard, Secretary-Treasurer John Kelly, Councilperson Donya Williams; *standing left to right*: Second Chief Douglas Lankford and Chief Thomas Gamble (photograph by Andrew J. Strack, courtesy of Myaamia Project Archives)

Jointly controlled and funded by the Miami Tribe of Oklahoma and Miami University, the Myaamia Project has been housed at MU since 2001. As stipulated in the memorandum of agreement between the tribe and the university, the project's dual mission is research and education: research to assist Miami language and culture preservation – a research agenda that, Wesley Leonard stresses, is 'directed by a sovereign Indigenous nation' (Miami Tribe of Oklahoma, 2008) – and the education of community members and MU students, respectively, through a summer program and 'visits to Oklahoma, direct involvement in research initiatives, class visitations by project staff, and access to Miami Tribe language and culture resources' (Myaamia Project, 2009).

This, then, has been the 'ideological and implementational space' (Hornberger, 2002, 2006a) for the Miami awakening. Creating and sustaining that space has been (and is) an ongoing 'multilegged' effort. 'We got lucky that Daryl Baldwin and his family were getting involved', Leonard states:

> The US government was changing its position on Native American languages [with passage of NALA in 1990]. And Dr David Costa was doing his research on the language. A lot of these things were happening at the

same time. But there was also a community need and community interest. (Miami Tribe of Oklahoma, 2008)

'And that is the bigger message that I would like to see come out of our story', says Baldwin; 'take your time and work with your people, work with institutions that believe in you and support you and collectively move with the community and tribal leadership in a direction that is positive' (personal communication, 19 August 2009).

The project today has three primary language planning activities: (1) summer youth programs that focus on contextualizing language as an expression of culture along with occasional adult workshops; (2) MU classes for tribal students required as part of their Heritage Award; and (3) home learning. Language documentation and corpus planning are central to all of these activities. 'This isn't a matter of settling on one way to do [language revitalization]', Baldwin maintains; 'it is to take advantage of all the different ways to capture [language and culture] and I think, for our case, documentation speaks pretty highly to what the possibilities are' (personal communication, 19 August 2009).

All of this involves what Ironstrack calls 'using the best of our knowledge and making strategic choices' that capitalize on Miami community-based knowledge, build family and community relationships through language, and raise consciousness about the place of the Miami language in a Miami sense of self (personal communication, 12 May 2009). For example, the workshops – which are primarily for adults – focus on developing a new community language ideology. Many adults want to know about the language, better understand its community value, and speak enough to support their children or grandchildren. The youth camps involve 20–35 student participants aged nine to 16, 'along with several camp counselors, staff and volunteers, all who have gathered to do myaamia things' (Leonard, 2011: 45). Games, field trips, traditional Miami sports such as lacrosse, puppetry, storytelling, singing and dancing are all contexts for learning language, culture, history and identity (see Leonard, 2011: 146–150 for details on some of these activities, and illustrations in Figures 5.6 and 5.7). The goals of these activities go beyond 'teaching words in a class', Baldwin emphasizes:

> Our hope is that [the youth] will be able to use the language, that they'll be able to create an identity around [the] language. When the kids go home, they teach their parents and family members ... If they return to camp next year, they build relationships through the language. (Miami Tribe of Oklahoma, 2008)

Wesley Leonard puts it this way: 'Teaching the language is not our goal, it's using the language as the articulation of our culture. And everybody has a right to claim it' (Miami Tribe of Oklahoma, 2008).

Figure 5.6 George Ironstrack building *wiikiaami* (house, lodge) at the Eewansaapita (Sunrise) Summer Educational Experience, Miami, OK, 2011 (photograph by Andrew J. Strack, courtesy of Myaamia Project Archives)

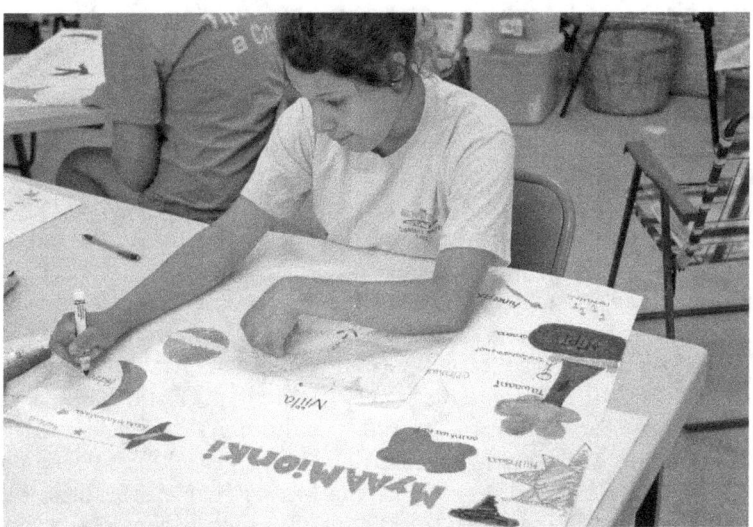

Figure 5.7 Student working on a poster project during the Eewansaapita Summer Educational Experience, Miami, OK, 2008 (photograph by Karen Baldwin, courtesy of Myaamia Project Archives)

That Miami citizens are exercising that right is evident in the project's educational efforts. Baldwin, for instance, related the story of a tribal member, Dr Timothy McCoy, who works at the Smithsonian Institution and on the Mars Rover team. 'He came to us one year and said, "I would like to be involved. I would like to help, and I'm interested in how our ancestors thought about the world – the sky, the stars, and those sorts of things"' (personal communication, 11 May 2009). With a grant from the National Aeronautics and Space Administration (NASA), the project worked with McCoy to develop a curriculum 'anchored in Myaamia ideology about earth and sky' (personal communication, 11 May 2009). Baldwin continued:

> And it [the NASA grant] was to develop a curriculum for use in the home and in the community to further develop these ideas and concepts. And in the course of putting that together ..., we have been able to explore traditional narratives ... that connect to sky ... [this] helped lead to the creation of our first lunar calendar ... So that's a project that has a context for what people do today. (Personal communication, 11 May 2009)

'It's not immersion', Baldwin added, 'but it's part of the awakening':

> Because even if we have [one] tribal member who wakes up tomorrow and thinks to themselves, 'You know what? Our language isn't gone, it's still here, and it's useful in my everyday life' – that didn't happen 15 or 20 years ago. So to us, that's success because you begin to change the attitudes around language. (Interview, 11 May 2009)

These types of community-linked efforts have enabled a relatively tiny project staff – Baldwin, Ironstrack, media specialist Andrew Strack (the latter two are also Miami citizens and MU graduates) and linguistic consultant David Costa – to construct an impressive curriculum for home- and community-based language and culture learning. In addition to the earth and sky curriculum – a beautifully illustrated collection of stories and activities designed to engage multigenerational learners (McCoy *et al.*, 2011) and supported by an interactive website (myaamiaproject.org/earthandsky/) – the project has produced a text that explores the Miami removal (Strack *et al.*, 2011b), a bilingual collection of Miami and Peoria narratives and winter stories (Costa, 2010), a Miami dictionary (Baldwin & Costa, 2005), a phrase book of greetings (Baldwin *et al.*, 2007), a children's language curriculum (Johnson, 2003), and a booklet and DVD based on the 2008 MU exhibition *myaamiaki isi meehtohseeniwiciki*/How the Miami People Live (Strack *et al.*, 2011a; see Figures 5.8 and 5.9). In collaboration with MU computer science professor Dr Douglas Troy and his students, computer-assisted language learning programs have been developed, and soon to be released iOS applications (e.g. iPhone) are available free of charge on the project's website

Language Regenesis in Practice 103

Figure 5.8 Myaamia Project publications (photograph by Kristina Fox, courtesy of Myaamia Project Archives)

Figure 5.9 Miami tribal youth playing with computer language learning games developed by the Myaamia Project (photograph by Andrew J. Strack, courtesy of Myaamia Project Archives)

(see, e.g. http://myaamiadictionary.org/files/csa/numbers/). (For all Myaamia Project publications, see http://www.myaamiaproject.org/publications.html). As Baldwin describes these types of efforts: 'The Miami language essentially began in the home, and I know that it will end there, but in the interim, we need to create the language learning environment and tools ... for youth and adults ... [These] materials ... support that' (Miami Tribe of Oklahoma, 2008).

There is one additional – and critical – 'strategic choice' underlying the project's endeavors: a long view of the language regenesis process. 'For us to reach a point where our language was no longer spoken, that was an intergenerational process of declining language and cultural use', Baldwin points out.

> Part of that process was the changing of people's minds – the way they think about themselves, their identity, their culture, their language, their community, their tribe – all of those things begin to transform. It ... took about three generations for that to reach a point where there were no speakers. The revitalization of [the language], the return of that, is also an intergenerational process. (Personal communication, 11 May 2009)

'I often get asked how we motivate our community', Baldwin adds, 'and my answer is always the same'—

> You don't motivate the community directly. Instead you create an environment around the use of language and culture that is motivating. You have to raise the prestige of the language before a larger segment of the community begins to realize that this effort is real and growing and they should be part of it. But they have to come to that conclusion on their own by what they see, hear and feel. We have learned that telling someone they should learn their language or culture almost never works. We have found that the language of guilt is rarely inspirational. And what we need, more than anything else, is a generation to be inspired. (Personal communication, 22 February 2012)

Baldwin notes,

> So early on, our effort was to spend an entire generation reconstructing the language and beginning to work with our community to change the way they think about their language. [Immersion will come later] ... The idea is that we are creating a generation of young people who ... think differently about their language and begin to value themselves as Myaamia people and begin to dream about the possibilities. (Personal communication, 19 August 2009; see Figure 5.10)

Extending the garden metaphor, George Ironstrack concurs: '[W]hat we need to accomplish is laying down lots of different seeds that will sprout later on

Figure 5.10 Tribal student (*right*) at Miami University discussing Miami morphology with Daryl Baldwin during language class, Oxford, OH, 2011 (photograph by Andrew J. Strack, courtesy of Myaamia Project Archives)

... That is a lengthy process – one that I don't expect to accomplish in my lifetime' (personal communication, 19 August 2009).

The Myaamia Project is very much a multigenerational one, with the goal of teaching 'as much of the language as we can', Baldwin says, 'but really to change the language ideology of our own people and slowly raise the prestige of the language and culture ... [T]his is the real work of language revitalization' (personal communication, 19 August 2009). From this perspective, fluency in Miami is the outcome of a longer, more complex process of ideological transformation and community building. As the late Chief Floyd Leonard expressed this goal for his people, 'Everybody has to feel they belong somewhere ..., and I think that's what we're doing ... we're recovering that' (Miami Tribe of Oklahoma, 2008).

'We're very much a nation rebuilding and reawakening', Baldwin notes. As the rebuilding moves forward, it is enabling hundreds of Miami people to claim 'some knowledge of the language', Leonard states, with perhaps 150 'actually speaking it on a regular basis' (Leonard, 2007: 29). This includes a few children, like the Baldwins, the Ironstracks and the Olds, who are being raised with the language. 'Our language reclamation work has forced us to look at ourselves and have a better understanding of our history and how we got to this point in time', Baldwin stresses. 'Language reclamation is about community building [and] healing from the past' (Baldwin, 2003: 15–16). According to Scott Shoemaker, a member of the Miami Nation of Indiana (a non-federally recognized group that consists of those who remained behind during the 1846 removal): 'Whenever you talk to Miami people, there's a kind of hole in our hearts, and I think that language ... is part of that healing of that hole in our hearts' (Miami Tribe of Oklahoma, 2008).

'Language Can Come Home Again': Wôpanâak Language Reclamation[2]

Wôpanâak – the Wampanoag language, also called Natick and Massachusett – is one of three-dozen Algonquian languages spoken by peoples indigenous to what is now southeastern New England (see Figure 1.1 and Table 1.4, Chapter 1).[3] The Algonquian language family extends from Canada to the southeastern United States; languages related to Wôpanâak include Narragansett, Mohegan–Pequot, and Western Abenaki (Goddard, 1996a: 5; Hale, 1997: 8).

The Wampanoag Nation once included 69 separate tribal groups whose territory encompassed 194 present-day towns from Provincetown, Massachusetts to Narragansett Bay on the northern side of Rhode Island Sound (Ash et al., 2001: 28). These communities were among the first to be impacted by the European invasion. 'We're the nation that helped the Pilgrims through that first winter', said Eva Blake, Assonet Wampanoag and a language teacher for the Wôpanâak Language Reclamation Project (WLRP) (Makepeace, 2011).

However, even before the Wampanoag encountered the Pilgrims at Plymouth Rock in 1620, the Native population in the region had been decimated by diseases introduced by European fishing and trading expeditions (Rees-Miller, 1998: 536). Following the Pequot War of 1637, the British massacred and enslaved large numbers of Wampanoag people, and by the latter part of the 17th century, they had become 'economically, politically, and militarily subject to the English' (Rees-Miller, 1998: 596). By the 19th century, a constellation of factors – including the movement of families from traditional multifamily homes to European-style nuclear family dwellings, the confiscation of tribal farming and fishing grounds by Whites, and schooling in English – had conspired to fragment the community and produce the 'first generation of children [who] no longer used the ancestral language among themselves as adults and did not speak it to their own children' (Rees-Miller, 1998: 547).

In 1908, the last native speaker of Mohegan–Pequot, Mrs Fidelia Fielding, passed away. According to Wampanoag linguist Jessie Little Doe Baird, Wôpanâak had ceased to be spoken well before that – as much as 170 years ago (Makepeace, 2011). Massachusetts Institute of Technology (MIT) linguist Kenneth Hale, who worked with the Wôpanâak language revitalization program until his death in 2001, described the late-20th century situation this way: 'The few people who know phrases and texts in the language have learned them from written sources or have learned to recite them from older relatives' (Hale, 1997: 8).

Wôpanâak, like Miami, has a large corpus of written documentation – indeed, 'the largest corpus of Native written documents on the continent' (Wôpanâak Language Reclamation Project, 2010a: para. 2). Wôpanâak was the first American Indian language to have an alphabetic writing system, the outcome of the efforts of Puritan missionary John Eliot to translate the King James Bible. Eliot could never have accomplished this feat, however, without the help of Wampanoag language teachers and translators, in particular bilingual–biliterate Wampanoag tribe members who were attending the newly formed Harvard Indian College. By 1663, Eliot and his Indigenous consultants had translated both the New and Old Testaments, and 1000 copies of the Eliot Bible had been printed by Harvard Indian College. 'It was the first Bible published in America, its title page reading *"Mamusse Wunneetupanatamwe up-Biblum God naneeswe Nukkone Testament kah wonk Wusku Testament"* – "Entire Holy his-Bible God both Old Testament and also New Testament"' (Mifflin, 2008: para. 5; see Figure 5.11). The Eliot Bible, claims Hale, is 'the undisputed treasure of Massachusett linguistics' (Hale, 1997: 9; see also Ash et al., 2001: 32).

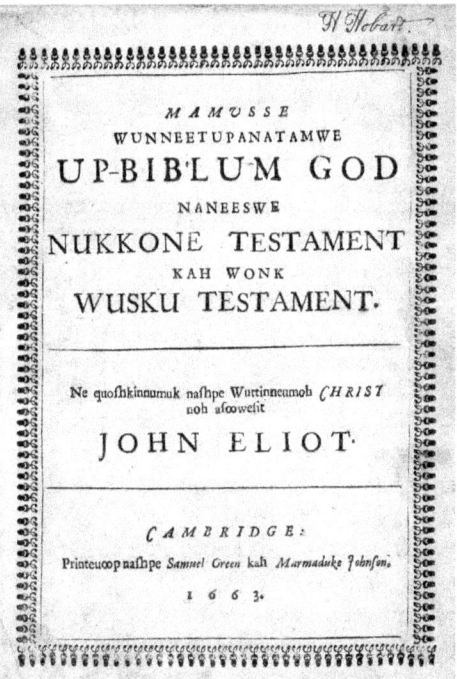

Figure 5.11 Cover of the Eliot Bible, the first Bible printed in North America and published in the Wampanoag language in 1663 (photograph courtesy of Rare Book and Manuscript Library, University of Pennsylvania)

Native-language literacy was common among Wôpanâak/Massachusett speakers throughout the 17th, 18th and 19th centuries. In fact, 'Wampanoag literacy would rival that of the English during the 18th century' (Wôpanâak Language Reclamation Project, 2010a: para. 2). Lexicons, personal letters and legal documents such as wills and deeds still exist, including a petition to the Massachusetts legislature to prevent White settlers from seizing Wampanoag land (Kageleiry, 2001: 19). In 1903, the Bureau of American Ethnology published a Natick dictionary (Trumbull, 1903), and in 1988, linguists Ives Goddard and Kathryn Bragdon assembled extant Massachusett texts in a 791-page book, *Native Writings in Massachusett* (Goddard & Bragdon, 1988). All of this is 'fortunate indeed', Hale writes, as it provided 'a foundation upon which the linguistic phase of the Wampanoag project [could] begin with dispatch' (Hale, 1997: 9).

After seven generations of silence, the reclamation of Wôpanâak began in 1992 with a series of visions or dreams by Jessie Little Doe Baird, a citizen of the Mashpee Wampanoag Tribe of Cape Cod, who was then working as a social worker. In those dreams, Little Doe Baird saw

> people who appeared to be her ancestors, speaking a language she couldn't understand. Then one day, she passed a Cape Cod road sign for the village of Sippewisset. Seeing the traditional Wampanoag writing on it, she suddenly realized that her visions were about Wôpanâak, the language that her ancestors had spoken when they encountered the Pilgrims at Plimoth Plantation. (Mifflin, 2008: para. 1)

As Little Doe Baird relates,

> '[W]e are here', They said to me. This is the sacred message I was gifted with ... given to me in Wôpanâak (Wampanoag).
> I knew nothing of my People's language at that time. For that matter, none of my People remembered the way in which we spoke about our lives and our ways ... This is what I am saying to you now. We are here. (little doe, 2000: 3)

Thus, proceeding 'as if by a calling' (Feldman, 2001: para. 3), Baird conducted a language survey among the Mashpee and Aquinnah Wampanoag Tribes to determine the extent of community interest in reviving the language. 'The task I was given by my ancestors', Little Doe Baird states, 'was to see if the people wanted this language reclamation project' (Feldman, 2001: para. 3). The response was overwhelmingly positive: 'Nobody said no', Little Doe Baird recalled years later. 'Nobody said, I'm not interested. Nobody said, don't do it' (PBS NewsHour, 2011: para. 8).

This became the 'ideological space' (Hornberger, 2002, 2006a) for language reclamation, as tribal members began to examine the vast corpus of Wôpanâak documentation. Spearheaded by Little Doe Baird, the Wôpanâak Language Reclamation Project began in 1993 as a collaborative effort between the councils of the Wampanoag Tribe of Gay Head/Aquinnah, the Mashpee Wampanoag Tribe, the Assonet Band of the Wampanoag Nation and the Herring Pond Band of Wampanoag (see Figure 5.12). Little Doe Baird worked with MIT linguist Norvin Richards, who had begun formulating a Wôpanâak dictionary; according to Richards, 'we've been working on it together ever since' (personal communication, 11 June 2012). Using the dictionary and a language curriculum developed by Little Doe Baird, in 1997 the first Wôpanâak classes were offered at Mashpee and Aquinnah, including an advanced immersion course (Feldman, 2001). 'It took us a full four years of ground work and training in order to begin our classes', Little Doe Baird explains. 'We had to sort through everything from primary source documentation and training in linguistics – to read the documents – to tribal politics and protocol' (little doe, 2000: 3).

It was during the initial stages of these efforts that Ken Hale was invited to a tribal meeting. As Jessie Little Doe Baird relates in a film documentary on Wôpanâak language recovery, *We Still Live Here – Âs Nutayuneân*:

> We showed up in Aquinnah ... and there was this elder White man standing there. 'This is our guest linguist from MIT. His name's Ken Hale'. And I'm sitting there listening to this White man tell us, maybe he could help us bring our language home. And that ... really bothered me ..., that the question wouldn't be, couldn't we do it ourselves, that we would have to depend on some White person to do the work. So then

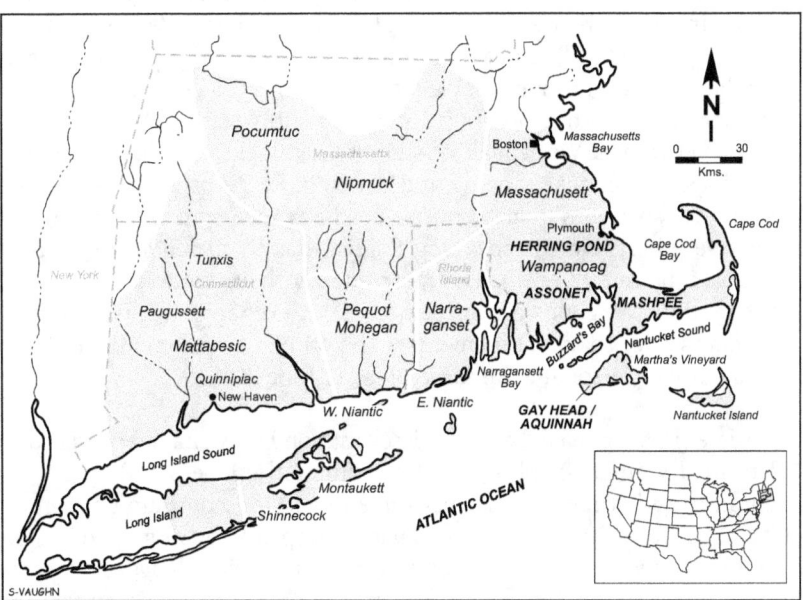

Figure 5.12 The contemporary Wampanoag Nation vis-à-vis other nearby Native peoples, and Wôpanâak language reclamation sites (graphics by Shearon Vaughn)

the next option was to take responsibility ourselves and get the training ourselves, and do the work ourselves. (Makepeace, 2011)

A few months later, at a tribal meeting, Little Doe Baird was given a fellowship application for a year's study at MIT. She was awarded the fellowship, and it was there that she re-encountered Hale. As she relates in the film documentary, she opened the door to Hale's office and he said: 'I remember you. You're Jessie Little Doe. Where have you been? I've been waiting for you' (Makepeace, 2011). 'We started working [on the language] that afternoon', Little Doe Baird says (Makepeace, 2011). Learning linguistics as she compiled language materials, Little Doe Baird also looked to experts and documentation in other living Eastern Algonquian languages as resources (Ash *et al.*, 2001: 32).

From these combined efforts have come individuals with sufficient proficiency to teach others at the introductory level. Wôpanâak classes continue at Mashpee, Boston College, and Aquinnah (Wôpanâak Language Reclamation Project, 2010b). The classes are free of charge and are offered for tribal and family members only. 'We have nothing we can claim as exclusively ours', Little Doe Baird explains; '[t]he only thing we truly have is our language' (cited in Kageleiry, 2001: 18). Immersion camps for all ages offer additional opportunities for intergenerational language learning through hands-on activities and classes. As Richards describes these activities:

> There are formal classes, taught monolingually with a lot of pictures and gesturing, that are organized around particular themes (e.g., giving directions, making food), and are generally intended to give practice in a particular area of grammar. People play cards (e.g., Go Fish) and Scrabble in Wôpanâak, and they team up to present short skits in Wôpanâak (one year there was a Wôpanâak version of Goldilocks). During breaks there is a lot of Wôpanâak singing and dancing. Every participant is given a string of 'wampum' (plastic purple beads) at the beginning of camp, and anyone who is caught speaking English has to surrender beads to the people who caught them. The camp ends with an auction in Wôpanâak, where donated goods are auctioned off in exchange for 'wampum' (so students have to at least remember the numbers well enough to bid, by this point). (Personal communication, 11 June 2012)

To date the Wôpanâak Language Reclamation Project has credentialed two MIT-trained Wampanoag linguists (including Little Doe Baird), 'produced a dozen advanced students' and 'instructed over 150 community members' (Cultural Survival, 2012: para. 3), and has developed an adult second-language acquisition curriculum and a 'no English curriculum for all ages' (Wôpanâak Language Reclamation Project, 2010a: para. 5). Phrase books, grammars and a dictionary begun by Richards and Little Doe Baird at MIT, which now contains some 11,500 items, have been developed (Wôpanâak Language

Reclamation Project, 2010a: para. 5). The language reclamation project has also galvanized the revitalization of Wampanoag songs, ceremonies and the stories that accompany them, and has served to strengthen kin and cultural bonds within the Wôpanâak-heritage language community. 'When I speak Wampanoag', Eva Blake reflects, 'how much I love this language ... I feel so much more connected to the person that I'm talking to, knowing that ... we're talking Wampanoag' (Makepeace, 2011).

At the time of this writing, Little Doe Baird, who was honored with a MacArthur Foundation 'genius' award for her language revitalization work in 2010, is writing a layperson's grammar to accompany the dictionary. A 2010 grant from the Administration of Native Americans (under the Native American Languages Act) is enabling Little Doe Baird to train three language apprentices – Nitana Hicks, Melanie Roderick and Tracey Kelly – in advanced Wôpanâak fluency so that they can begin to teach children (Wôpanâak Language Reclamation Project, 2010c: para. 2). 'Training more teachers', Little Doe Baird explains, 'will allow us a much broader reach in teaching Wampanoag tribal members and restoring fluency of our language more quickly' (Wôpanâak Language Reclamation Project, 2010c: para. 3). The longer-term goal is to establish a Wôpanâak-medium school, beginning with preschool and kindergarten and adding a grade a year (MacArthur Fellows Program, 2010), with the ultimate goal of 'return[ing] fluency to the Wampanoag Nation as a principal means of expression' (Wôpanâak Language Reclamation Project, 2010c: para. 6; see also Ash *et al.*, 2001: 32).

From a language that was sleeping seven generations ago, the Wôpanâak language now has its first native speaker, Jessie Little Doe Baird and Jason Baird's daughter, Mae Alice. 'She's the first', Little Doe Baird says, 'and there necessarily has to be a second, and a third, and a fourth. Language can come home again' (Makepeace, 2011).

Wôpanâak language reclamation illustrates what can be accomplished with determination, knowledge, and commitment, even for sleeping languages lacking native speakers (Hinton, 2001d). 'We are still here on our ancestral lands', Jessie Little Doe Baird points out: 'We have survived and gained enough strength once again to not only assert ourselves as a strong Wampanoag Nation, but more importantly, to reclaim what is ours by sacred privilege and right' (little doe, 2000: 3).

'We Wanted Language Learning to be Family Based': The California Master–Apprentice Language Learning Program[4]

Native peoples in what is now the State of California felt the presence of Europeans as early as the 16th and early 17th centuries, when Spanish and

British expeditions reached the Colorado River and Pacific Coast, bringing with them epidemic diseases (Bean & Vane, 1997: 333). Prior to European contact, this was one of the most linguistically and culturally diverse regions of the world, with 300,000 to 400,000 Native people who spoke some 100 languages (Hinton, 1998: 85; 2001c: 217). Successive waves of colonization – first by Spanish missionaries, then by Mexican ranchers, and finally by Anglo-Americans in the wake of the Gold Rush – brought devastating disease, indiscriminate carnage by miners and farmers, and legalized kidnapping and enslavement of children and young women, forcibly removing 'many survivors from their families and cultures forever' (Hinton, 1998: 85; 2001c: 217; see also Sims, 1998: 97).

By 1850, when California was incorporated as the 31st US state, fewer than 30,000 Native people had survived this holocaust. Those who had, had been dispossessed of their lands. Although some reservations had been established, Native people 'found little protection there, due to the corruption of government agents' (Hinton, 1998: 85). Many tribes remained unrecognized by treaty and hence ineligible to receive the aid inherent in the tribal–federal trust relationship. The federal boarding school system and campaigns to eradicate Native religious, social and economic systems further broke down traditional village life. By the early 20th century these disruptions had 'set the stage for an increasingly tenuous linguistic situation' (Sims, 1998: 99–100). As Leanne Hinton writes: 'It was not until the 1870s that the atrocities began to decline enough for Indian survivors to begin establishing settled families again, and by the end of the century their population was growing once more' (Hinton, 1998: 85).

According to Hinton, who has worked with Native California language revitalization since its inception, by the turn of the 21st century 50 Native California languages were being spoken, all by elders. Of these, Hinton states, only four had more than 100 speakers. Twelve had 10–60 speakers, 13 had 6–10 speakers, and 21 had fewer than five speakers (Hinton, 2001c: 217). 'Not a single Californian Indian language is being used now as the language of daily communication', she adds; even elders who were raised with the language may not speak it, but 'rather, they remember how to speak the language' (Hinton, 1998: 83). Since that time, many of the fluent speakers have passed away, 'and an increasing number of languages are down to semi-speakers' (Leanne Hinton, personal communication, 10 February 2012).

Unlike the situation for Miami and Wôpanâak discussed above, or for Navajo, discussed in Chapter 4, California languages encompass at least six major language 'root stocks' and some 18 different language families (Goddard, 1996a). Thus, each language must be dealt with individually (see Figure 5.13). Also unlike Miami, Wôpanâak and Navajo, there is not a large corpus of written materials (Hinton, 1998: 86, 2001c: 218). Under these conditions language revitalizers have looked to elder speakers as primary language and culture resources, and to inter-tribal networks and community–university partnerships as the means for organizing language and culture regenesis.

Figure 5.13 Native California 'root' language groups and tribal languages (adapted from Hinton, 1994: ii; graphics by Shearon Vaughn)

In this context, language recovery has involved 'counterpoised' top-down and bottom-up efforts (López, 2008). During the 1970s, the push for self-determination and federal recognition by California tribes opened new 'ideological spaces' for language reclamation (Hornberger, 2002, 2006a). Some tribes began buying back parcels of their traditional homelands, 'thus creating communities that could potentially form a protected environment in which an indigenous language might be spoken' (Hinton, 1998: 86). In the 1970s and 1980s, the federal Bilingual Education Act provided funding for up to 21 Native language and culture programs in California, most housed in public schools.

During this time, book author and publisher Malcolm Margolin founded *News from Native California*, a quarterly journal dedicated to Indigenous issues (http://www.heydaybooks.com/news/). This became a significant source of information for language activists (Hinton, 1998: 87). As Bilingual Education

Act funds dwindled owing to an increasing federal policy emphasis on English (only), the Native American Languages Act provided new sources of financial support for California tribes and tribal organizations (see the discussion of NALA in Chapter 3). In 1992, the Native California Network (NCN) was established, providing additional funds for Native language and culture programs. Together, these funds became 'a very important component of language revitalization in California', states Hinton (1998: 87), although many people were 'doing language-revitalization with no funding at all'.

These social–educational and communication networks came together in a conference organized by NCN in the early 1990s. Attended by 60 Native Californians interested in language, the conference was cosponsored by Margolin's firm, Heydey Books, 'with participation based on the mailing list for *News from Native California*' (Hinton, 1998: 88). Hinton describes the 'implementational space' (Hornberger, 2002, 2006a) opened up by this event:

> [A] committee was formed called Advocates for Indigenous California Language Survival (AICLS), consisting of seven California Indians who would oversee the development and implementation of language programs and advise NCN about language issues. The conference was also the first time most California language activists had met each other, and this direct contact allowed mutual encouragement and idea sharing that was extremely helpful ... The conference has since become a biannual event. (Hinton, 1998: 88)

This biannual event, called 'Language Is Life', continues to be held every odd year in September (Leanne Hinton, personal communication, 10 February 2012).

Out of the Language Is Life Conference and the NCN and AICLS grew the structure for training, administration and funding of one of the boldest and most ambitious language revitalization initiatives to date: the Master–Apprentice Language Learning Program (MALLP). The heart of the MALLP is the positioning of elders as language teachers in a close, long-term relationship with language learners. 'This is not a traditional classroom situation with a trained teacher who [decides] what the student is to learn', Hinton *et al.* (2002: xi–xii) explain in their highly accessible guidebook (which constitutes the AICLS training manual), *How To Keep Your Language Alive*. Instead, master speakers/teachers are paired with younger language learners in a one-on-one immersion setting, with the overall goal of teaching the tribal language to 'at least one younger member ... who is then encouraged to set up language training for children of that tribe' (McBroom, 1995: para. 8). Often the pairs are family members. The most important criteria for the selection of teams are fluency for the master and demonstrated interest in learning and teaching the Native language by the apprentice (Hinton, 2001c: 218).

The apprentice 'should be a proactive learner', Hinton explains, eliciting vocabulary in the Native language, suggesting activities, bringing props and taking correction positively; for their part, master teachers should 'learn to correct without criticizing' (Hinton, 2001c: 303).

Both master and apprentice must make a considerable investment of time, good will and effort. The teams work together for 10–20 hours per week and one to three years at a time – sometimes longer, depending on the team. 'This is very fragile work', Hinton notes:

> Oftentimes, the elder whose language was ignored for years must be convinced that this is a sincere effort, while the apprentice must dedicate a large portion of his [or her] life to the relationship, putting aside other career and educational goals. (Cited in McBroom, 1995: para. 10)

Each team member receives a small stipend and training in the following principles of Native-language immersion:

(1) Both master and apprentice use only the Native language (no English).
(2) Both master and apprentice are active communicators.
(3) Oral, not written, language is emphasized.
(4) Language learning occurs in everyday situations (e.g. gardening, taking walks together, participating in traditional cultural activities).
(5) Activities provide the context for language comprehension. (Hinton, 2001c: 218; see also Hinton, 2011: 303).

In contrast to some school-based language learning approaches that use formal study of linguistic structures (e.g. grammar exercises), the master–apprentice approach is entirely communication-based. In the context of everyday tasks and activities, both learner and master teacher interact in the language ('What is this?', 'What am I doing?'), using gestured and spoken commands and visual cues to aid comprehension. This is followed by a 'post-mortem' debriefing about the immersion set. 'There might have been things the apprentice couldn't understand ... You may also want to talk about improvements you could make', advise Hinton *et al.* (2002: 26–27), such as planning for the next session, and farewells. The California MALLP includes a periodic two-part assessment, although not in the form of a strict written test. Instead, the master teacher first asks questions and observes how the apprentice responds, then gives the apprentice a picture and asks her or him to say anything she or he can about it. Are there lapses into English? How conversant has the apprentice become? The assessment is usually videotaped and used as a tool for planning future learning activities (Hinton *et al.*, 2002: 99–101). The goal, Hinton states, is for apprentices to be 'at least conversationally proficient in their language' and ready to teach it to others within three years – a goal that many apprentices have achieved.

The teams' work is reinforced by a number of related activities and programs. Among the most important are immersion camps for children, parents and elders. 'We wanted language learning to be family based', Karuk language activists Terry and Sarah Supahan state (Supahan & Supahan, 2001: 197). In some places, public school classes are also offered (Sims, 1998; Supahan & Supahan, 2001: 197). In schools attended by Yurok youth in northern California, for example, introductory Yurok languages classes are being taught. As former MALLP apprentice and secondary Yurok language teacher Barbara McQuillen notes, learning Yurok in high school can enable young people to take the language 'out of the classroom and [back] into the community' (cited in Atherton, 2010: para. 52).

In addition, over the past 15 years, the AICLS and the University of California, Berkeley have sponsored the biannual 'Breath of Life/Silent No More' workshop for Native California communities with few or no fluent speakers (see Figure 5.14). The workshop's goal is for 'participants to access, understand, and do research on materials on their languages, and to use them for language revitalization' (The Regents of the University of California, 2009–2010: para. 2). The conference has been replicated elsewhere (see, e.g. the Oklahoma Breath of Life Workshop, http://ling.uta.edu/SWNAL/projects/OK-Breath/).

In the summer of 2011, the first national Breath of Life Archival Institute for Indigenous Languages was held in Washington, DC, with the goal

Figure 5.14 2012 Breath of Life/Silent No More workshop participants (photograph by Scott Braley)

of helping Native American language revitalizers identify and make use of materials on their languages housed in the National Anthropological Archives and Library of Congress (Endangered Language Fund, 2011: para. 1). The two-week institute:

> is specifically geared toward the task of finding, interpreting, and newly using the information from archival sources, such as written materials and audio recordings. For this reason, the Institute will be of particular interest for members of communities whose languages are not currently spoken, though communities with speakers can also benefit by discovering new vocabulary, uncovering old speech styles, and otherwise finding and learning language information held in archival form. (Endangered Language Fund, 2011: para. 12)

Organized by Hinton and Breath of Life mentor Lisa Conathan, the 2011 workshop brought together language learners, mentors and activists representing 24 Native American languages from California, Arizona and British Columbia, and multiple Algonquian communities throughout the United States. A second national Breath of Life Archival Institute is planned for 2013 (L. Hinton, personal communication, 10 February, 2012; for information see http://www.endangeredlanguagefund.org/BOL.php).

At the time of this writing, over 100 California MALLP teams had been trained, representing more than 30 different languages. In many cases, apprentices have achieved conversational proficiency and, in some cases, a delicate restoration of intergenerational transmission has been achieved. Among the Karuk of northern California, for instance, who had only 12 elderly speakers when the MALLP began, four younger Karuks have learned to speak the language fluently. In her book, *Bringing Our Languages Home*, Hinton (2013) presents the language revitalization journey of two young Karuk parents who were trained through the MALLP, and whose parents, Terry and Sarah Supahan (mentioned above), were also MALLP participants (and are now Karuk language teachers). Elaina Supahan Albers and her husband, Phil Albers Jr, are raising their children in the Karuk language. Although daunted by enormous motivation-sapping challenges, including the tragic sudden death of their beloved mentor and 'auntie', Violet Super, in 2006, Elaina and Phil 'have devoted their lives to Karuk language revitalization..., constantly working to stay one step ahead of their children' (Hinton, 2013 [in press]). As a community, the Karuks 'continue language revitalization on many fronts', Hinton states, including classes, community-based language documentation, work with academic linguistics, group meetings with elders, and family revitalization efforts such as those of the Supahan and Albers families (personal communication, 10 February 2012).

The MALLP has been adopted (and adapted) by endangered-language communities around the world, with applications in multiple US states (including a recent NALA grant to implement a master–apprentice program in the Wampanoag Nation described earlier in this chapter), and in Canada, Brazil, Spain and Australia (Hinton, 2011: 303). AICLS provides the training in most cases. In Australia, AICLS has initiated a 'trainer of trainers' approach so that Indigenous communities there can prepare their own master–apprentice teams. Hinton et al.'s (2002) guidebook has been translated into Brazilian Portuguese for distribution among Indigenous communities there. In at least one case – Yurok – which no longer has speakers who possess the fluency of elders 10 or 20 years ago, but which has individuals who used the language as children, a new revitalization process has been invented called 'language pods'. Hinton describes how the language pod concept works:

> These are meetings where small groups of people get together on a regular basis to speak the language. They have a topic that everyone knows of in advance, so that they can prepare, though going off-topic is fine so long as they stay in Yurok (the No-English rule is firm), and a facilitator that helps keep the conversation going. The point of the language pods is the development of habits of language *use*; and it is also based on the principle that a group collectively knows more than any individual in the group, so that people can bring each other up 'by each other's bootstraps'... We are looking into the idea of MALLP evolving into the Language Pod approach for those languages [that] might benefit by it. (Personal communication, 10 February 2012)

In addition to restoring conversational proficiency among younger generations of language learners, the MALLP has brought tribal members 'back in touch with their roots' (Hinton, 2001c: 225). The program is also an enormously hopeful and uplifting movement. As Phil Albers Jr relates his and Elaina's experiences learning Karuk through the MALLP and now teaching it to their children:

> Seeing them respond and understand their Native language, and hearing them comfortably speak in their Native language is the most rewarding feeling we could ever imagine. It is bigger than the first day of school or the first lost tooth. It is an experience that can happen every day of our lives as long as we continue to encourage it. Even after reaching the last step into complete surrender and then starting all over, it is worth every minute. (Cited in Hinton, 2013 [in press])

'The passion and dedication of those who are working with their languages is obvious and inspiring to others', Hinton reflects; it is 'a healthy movement... toward recovery from the devastating social and cultural wounds inflicted by the European incursion' (Hinton, 1998: 92).

'We Decided to Raise *Mohawk* Children': Kanienkeha Regenesis[5]

The Iroquois or Haudenosaunee – People of the Longhouse, also known as the Six Nations Iroquois Confederacy – have a political organization that is 'hundreds of years older than the United States' (Waterman & Arnold, 2010: 128). That polity is based on The Great Law of Peace, the oral constitution of the Iroquois Confederacy, represented in a belt made of wampum (long cylinder-shaped purple and white beads made of clamshell and whelk, respectively, and strung into belts with strings), which signifies 'the unity of the Confederacy' (White, 2009: 53) and 'forms the infrastructure of Iroquoian culture, politics, religion, and social [organization]' (Maracle *et al.*, 2011: 83). The belt, an exquisite example of non-alphabetic literacies, is 'read from right to left to symbolize the journey of Peacemaker [*Tekanawihta*, sent by the Creator to end warfare] throughout Haudenosaunee territory' (White, 2009: 53). The first square of the belt represents the Mohawk people, the Keepers of the Eastern Door; the other symbols (moving leftward) represent the Oneida, Onondaga, Cayuga and Seneca – the original five member-nations of the Iroquois Confederacy (also called the Iroquois League; see Figure 5.15).

Mohawk is a Northern Iroquoian language spoken by peoples indigenous to what is now upstate New York, southern Québec, and eastern Ontario. Related languages include Cayuga, Huron, Laurentian, Nottoway, Onandaga, Oneida and Susquehannock, of which Oneida is most closely related to Mohawk (Goddard, 1996c: 320). The term Mohawk is a Dutch

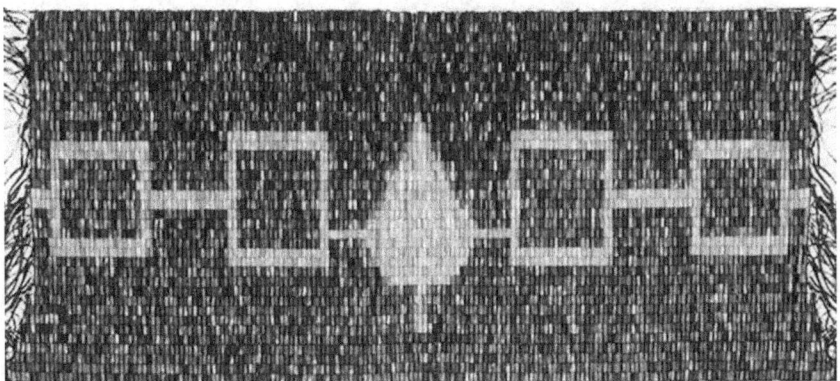

Figure 5.15 The Great Law of Peace or Hiawatha Belt, a classic example of multimodal literacies and their central role in Indigenous societies (photograph from Decolonize North America, http://decolonizenorthamerica.org/?page_id=87, accessed 31 December 2012)

barbarization of an Algonquian term, and although widely (and officially) used by both Natives and non-Natives, the term is not of Aboriginal origin. The Indigenous self-referential term is Kanienkehaka,[6] People of the Flint, a reference to the flint deposits used for tool-making in the Kanienkehaka homelands within present-day Mohawk Valley, New York. The Kanienkehaka were part of the five- and later six-nation Iroquois Confederacy (the Tuscarora joined the League as the sixth member nation in 1722). Historically, this was a 'distinctive group of people who were primarily dependent on agriculture' for subsistence but who also relied on hunting, gathering, and fishing, living in palisaded, multifamily dwellings known as longhouses (Bragdon, 1997: 122). As indicated above, the Confederacy long pre-dates the European invasion, having been formed to maintain peace and secure political and military cooperation among the six Indigenous nations (Mithun & Chafe, 1987: 5). When Europeans entered Iroquois territory in the 17th century, 'the League played a decisive role in Anglo-French relations' (Bragdon, 1997: 142).

Throughout this period, Haudenosaunee homelands were the site of ongoing encroachment by the Dutch, French and British, who introduced new sources of subsistence and political rivalry in the region (largely through the fur trade), missionization and ravaging disease that killed 75% of the Iroquois population by the early 17th century (Bragdon, 1997; Sutton, 2004). The American Revolution brought more turmoil, fragmenting the Confederacy, and, following failed efforts to maintain neutrality, most in the Confederacy sided with the British. 'At the close of the war', ethnologist Kathleen Bragdon relates, 'the Iroquois found their position with the new American government precarious, and some groups removed permanently to Canada' (Bragdon, 1997: 142–143).

Kanienkeha or Kanienke:ha (the term for the language) was committed to writing first by the Dutch (e.g. number and month names in 1624), and soon thereafter by Moravian, French and American Congregationalist missionaries (Goddard, 1996b: 21–30). Kanienkeha was also used as a diplomatic language.

Today, the Kanienkehaka reside in settlements in inland New York (Ganienkeh and Kanatsiohareke), along the St Lawrence River (Akwesasne, Kanesatake and Kahnawà:ke) and in southern Ontario (Tyendinaga, Wahta/Gibson and the Six Nations of the Grand River; see Figure 5.16). Most native speakers are older adults, although in some areas there are younger speakers (Gordon, 2005). Three such areas are Kahnawà:ke, a community of approximately 8000 on the south shore of the St Lawrence River 10 kilometers from Montréal, Québec; Akwesasne (also known as St Regis), a reserve of about 13,000 straddling the international boundary between Ontario and Québec in Canada and the State of New York; and Tyendinaga, with 7760 members, located 50 miles west of Kingston, Ontario. The remainder of this section considers LPP activities at each of these three reserves.

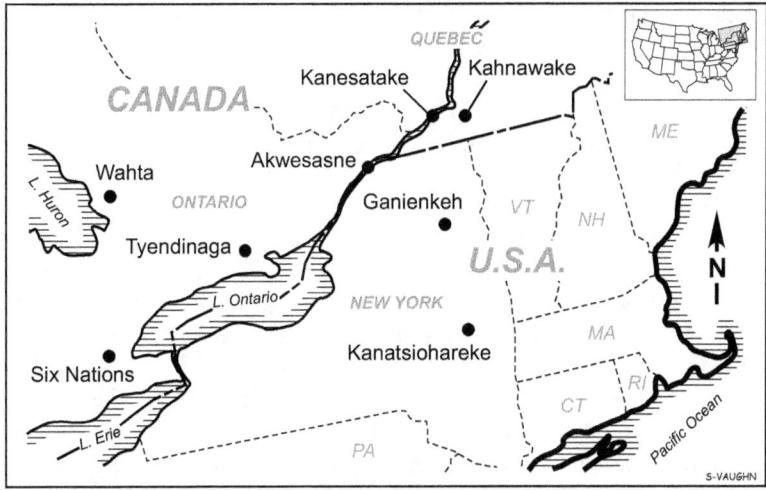

Figure 5.16 Map showing the location of primary sites within the Mohawk (Kanienkehaka) Nation today (graphics by Shearon Vaughn)

Kahnawà:ke Survival School

Through much of the 19th century, Kahnawà:ke was a bilingual French–Kanienkeha community. However, by the mid-20th century, 'English had grown to play such a large role both in the community ... and in job opportunities', that most Kahnawà:ke families 'were raising their children exclusively in English' (Hoover & Kanien'kehaka Raotitiohkwa Cultural Center (KRCC), 1992: 270). Kanienkeha regeneration began at Kahnawà:ke in 1970, when a small group of parents, aided by a non-Native elementary school principal, pushed for teaching Kanienkeha for 15 minutes each day (Arbuthnot, 1984; Hoover & Kanien'kehaka Raotitiohkwa Cultural Center, 1992: 270; Jacobs, 1998: 117). Prior to that time, 'the only thing native in our schools was the children', writes Kanienkehaka scholar-practitioner Kaia'titahkhe Annette Jacobs (1998: 117).[7] Over the next several years, 15 minutes grew to a half hour each day, and language revitalization was accelerated by a Native-language teacher preparation program established at the University of Québec in 1972. Mohawk student teachers taught by linguist Marianne Mithun created a standard orthography for use in the schools, and further teacher-directed corpus and acquisition planning followed (Jacobs, 1998: 118). As Mithun and Chafe describe this process of language reclamation:

> Over a period of several years, the Mohawk teachers devoted their entire summers, as well as their weekends during the winter to mastering Mohawk structure. They then began to construct a curriculum [that would enable children to acquire the language] naturally if Mohawk were

their first language ... Their goal is to teach children a way of thinking, not simply a translating skill. (Mithun & Chafe, 1987: 27–28)

At about the same time as these efforts got under way, the newly elected Parti Quebecois passed Bill 101, the French Language Charter, making French the sole official language of Québec and restricting education in other languages (Hoover & Kanien'kehaka Raotitiohkwa Cultural Center, 1992: 270). Protesting the Bill's violation of tribal sovereignty and historic treaty agreements, the Kahnawà:ke community established the Native-controlled Kahnawake Survival School and the KRCC, charged with ensuring that 'future Mohawk generations would continue to survive with their language, culture and traditions intact' (Hoover & Kanien'kehaka Raotitiohkwa Cultural Center, 1992: 270; Kahnawake Survival School, n.d.; Grenoble & Whaley, 2006: 87). The Center soon began the first Indigenous immersion program in Canada, which, with widespread community support, grew incrementally from a full-immersion preschool to a preschool through grade 4 immersion program followed by grade 5–6 maintenance and a middle school and senior program that teaches Kanienkeha as part of the regular curriculum (Grenoble & Whaley, 2006: 88; Hoover & Kanien'kehaka Raotitiohkwa Cultural Center, 1992: 271; Jacobs, 1998: 119).

Twelve years into the immersion effort, a community survey showed a dramatic reversal of language shift among young people in the 10–19 years age group. As Hoover and the KRCC relate, 'Through the control of its school system, which enabled the community to introduce a Mohawk immersion program ..., [t]he trend over the last 50 years of each succeeding generation speaking less Mohawk has been reversed' (Hoover & Kanien'kehaka Raotitiohkwa Cultural Center, 1992: 281; see also Mithun & Chafe, 1987).[8]

The Kahnawake Survival School continues as one of three community schools under the administration of the Kahnawà:ke Education Center. In 2012 the Survival School enrolled 100 middle school students (grades 7 and 8) and 170 students in grades 9–11, with a mission for students to 'achieve pride and self sufficiency through powerful curriculum based on Kaien'kehá:ka language, values, beliefs, and traditions along with sound academic [principles] and content, guided by innovative teaching methods' (Kahnawake Survival School, n.d.: para. 8).

Akwesasne Freedom School

The 41-square-mile Akwesasne/St Regis Reservation straddles the US–Canadian border (see Figure 5.16).[9] At Akwesasne ('Land Where the Partridge Drums'), Kanienkeha is the traditional language of the community, and the Mohawk Nation Council of Chiefs, the traditional governing body on the Canadian side, uses Mohawk as the official language (Metz, 2008; Louellyn White, personal communication, 8 May 2012). Mohawk scholar Louellyn

White, who, at the invitation of the Akwesasne Freedom School, conducted an ethnographic case study of the school, states that it was 'born out of the "ethnic reorganization" of the Akwesasne community' (White, 2009: 85). Like all Native North American communities, Akwesasne has been impacted by a history of assimilation policies, both in the United States and in Canada, designed to eradicate Native identities. As a consequence, according to an unofficial estimate of community members, only about 5% of those who live on the Akwesasne reservation are fluent speakers of Mohawk (White, 2009; but see Metz, 2008 for slightly higher estimates). Despite the pressures of assimilation, residents of Akwesasne, White maintains, 'have preserved their distinct ethnic identity as members of a once powerful Confederacy' (White, 2009: 67).

The Akwesasne Freedom School grew out of activist movements such as the American Indian (Red Power) Movement of the 1960s and 1970s (for a discussion of the movement, see Cobb & Fowler, 2007), although White dates the school's origins to even earlier activist efforts by Native teachers determined to prepare Kanienkehaka youth in the ways of their culture. The school began through a grass roots effort arising 'out of internal conflict on the reservation over jurisdictional issues and in response to public education systems in both [the United States and Canada] where Mohawk culture and language were desperately lacking' (White, 2009: 17). Margaret Peters, a long-time Akwesasne educator, describes the school's genesis this way:

> A struggle between the U.S. government who wanted control and the Mohawk people who simply wanted to maintain their culture and save their language gave birth to the Freedom School. Taking control of the children's education was the only alternative there was. (Cited in Stairs *et al.*, 1999: 45)

Thus, founded in 1979 by 'Mohawk parents who were interested in insuring that our children are able to acquire an education rich in their language and culture' (Mohawk Council of Akwesasne, 2007), the Akwesasne Freedom School began with 63 students; 'by 1981 the number had increased to 81 students, approximately half of whom came from the Canadian side of the reservation' (White, 2009: 88).

Situated in a facility built to resemble a longhouse and constructed by parents and other volunteers, the Akwesasne Freedom School today has 12 teachers and enrolls 60–65 students in a year-round, pre-K–8 program (Metz, 2008; Stairs *et al.*, 1999; White, 2009; see Figures 5.17 and 5.18). For many years, Kanienkeha was the sole language of instruction until the end of sixth grade, when English was introduced as students prepared to enter the public high school. In 2011, the school began to implement immersion in grade 7; at the time of this writing, grades 7 and 8 are to become immersion grades, this being 'therefore a transition year,' as White reports.

Figure 5.17 Akwesasne Freedom School, built to resemble a traditional Mohawk longhouse (photograph by Louellyn White)

The Haudenosaunee Thanksgiving Address or *Ohonten Kariwahtekwa,* which teaches gratitude to the earth and all it provides, and the *Kaianere:kowa* (the Great Law of Peace) anchor the school curriculum. Holistic and experiential learning, including participation in Mohawk songs, dances and other religious and cultural ceremonies, are key pedagogic practices (White, 2009).

Figure 5.18 Akwesasne Freedom School (photograph by Louellyn White)

Stairs *et al.* (1999: 45) describe this as the practice of '*making*, the most powerful way to find oneself in relating to the world'. White uses a tree metaphor to represent the curriculum:

> Students learn about the *Kaianere:kowa* ... and become empowered when they learn their own history [the roots of the tree] ... The [Mohawk] language acts as the trunk of the tree which is a vital lifeline to all of the branches of the tree [i.e. to content knowledge and pedagogy] ... At the top of the tree model positive identity formation is depicted as being *fully Mohawk* or a whole human being. (White, 2009: 116).

Each day opens and closes with a student delivering the *Ohonten Kariwahtekwa* from memory. The cultural knowledge and values embedded in this oral narrative are 'to be understood and lived, not merely recited', White stresses, with the Thanksgiving Address providing 'structure to the curriculum and allow[ing] students to explore ... botany, fisheries, astronomy, and planting' (White, 2009: 116).

At the Freedom School, '*Kanienke:ha* is heard almost everywhere', White observes, and 'English is rarely heard or seen'; all content is taught through the Native language (White, 2009: 175–176). At the same time, White's research suggests that the school is the primary and even the only place where young people are likely to hear the Kanienkeha language spoken. 'The only place that taught me the language was the Freedom School', an alumnus told White (2009: 175–176).

Like Kahnawà:ke and other school-based language regeneration efforts, a major challenge at Akwesasne has been corpus planning – specifically, the development of Native-language materials for all subject areas. As Dorothy Lazore, a leader in the movement and a native of Akwesasne, explains, '[T]eachers who get involved in immersion, they're doing teacher training, methodology, curriculum development, ... and also developing evaluations for all the subject areas ... So that's the amount of the work that has to be done, the load that has to be created' (interview, 14 July 2000).

The Akwesasne Freedom School is funded primarily by parents, grants, donations, tuition and fundraisers such as a renowned annual quilt fair; handmade quilts are donated by every parent, note Stairs *et al.* (1999: 47), 'an obligation even for those who are not quilters.' The school includes adult immersion classes as well. The school 'has never received direct funding from state, provincial, or federal governments', White states; 'to do so would undermine [parents'] sovereign rights to decide the type of education their children would receive' (White, 2009: 91). Although the school struggles with limited fiscal resources, parents see in this situation a certain strategic value. As a parent told White: 'It helped to keep the school united. We were required to do so much more ... you had to do it' (Stairs *et al.*, 2009: 97).

As with the other examples of school-based language regenesis discussed in this chapter, the Akwesasne Freedom School has impacted out-of-school language learning opportunities as well. Dorothy Lazore, for example, has 'taught a three-year teacher training program at the [school] to prepare adults for language teaching positions' (Louellyn White, personal communication, 28 April 2012). White (2009) also reports at least three families – all Freedom School alumni – who are raising their children as primary speakers of Kanienkeha.

Moreover, the community has established the Akwesáhsne Mohawk Board of Education with three additional schools under its charge in the community districts that fall within the geographic boundaries of Québec and Ontario (http://www.akwesasne.ca/PDF/SupplyTeacherInfo.pdf), as well as singing societies and summer language classes for adults (Louellyn White, personal communication, 28 April 2012). All of these efforts are designed to repatriate Kanienkeha, or, as White puts it, to help Mohawk people 'find our talk' (White, 2009: 177). Sheree Bonaparte, one of the first teachers at the Freedom School, sums up these intergenerational efforts this way:

> We saw what happened to one generation that lost their culture, ... their history, ... their language. We decided that we didn't want to raise American children or Canadian children. We wanted to raise *Mohawk* children. (Cited in Metz, 2008: 1; emphasis added)

Adult–child language learning at Tyendinaga

According to Iehnhotonkwas (Bonnie Jane) Maracle and her colleagues in the *Tsi Tyonnheht Onkwawenna* (TTO) Language Circle, 'adult language immersion programming is prevalent throughout the Mohawk Nation' (Maracle *et al.*, 2011: 93). Maracle *et al.* (2011) report on a unique effort combining adult and child language learning in Tyendinaga – the place name meaning 'Placing the Wood Together' and connoting strength in unity. With only a few elderly speakers remaining in Tyendinaga Mohawk Territory, the TTO was begun by six community members (including Maracle and her colleagues) out of concern for 'the crisis state of the Mohawk language in Tyendinaga today' (Maracle *et al.*, 2011: 84). Establishing themselves as a non-profit educational organization in 2001, TTO's mission is to keep 'Kenhte'kéha words and way of life alive as a community by promoting and revitalizing our Kanyen'kehaka language and culture' (Maracle *et al.*, 2011: 84).

The TTO group has concentrated on developing the language abilities of adult community members 'who in turn could potentially become language teachers' for a planned immersion school (Maracle *et al.*, 2001: 85). The TTO began by developing a one-year Mohawk Language Certificate Program in collaboration with Brock University in Ontario. 'From the Brock program', Maracle explains, 'two cohorts of Mohawk language learners [28 students in total] successfully graduated' (Maracle *et al.*, 2011: 86). In 2006, TTO began working with the Indigenous Studies Department at Trent University – a primarily undergraduate university in Ontario – on a two-year Adult Mohawk Language Diploma Program that would incorporate Mohawk culture. Students in the program do not need a high school degree or a Mohawk language background, although course credits are transferable to a bachelor's degree in Indigenous Studies at Trent (Maracle *et al.*, 2011: 87–88). Students attend class five days a week from September to May over two years, earning eight credits toward a diploma in Mohawk language (Anishinaabek Mushkegowuk Onkwehonwe (AMO) Language Commission of Ontario, 2012: para. 2). As Maracle *et al.* describe the coursework:

> ... [S]tudents ... experience daily language-learning in oral, written, and listening formats delivered through various activities and field trips such as fishing, apple picking, museums, grocery shopping, and tree tapping. Students are also required to complete a 20-hour practicum placement within the community. (Maracle *et al.*, 2011: 88; see pp. 89–90 for details on the curriculum.)

What is unique about the TTO program is the recent addition of a Mohawk-language immersion preschool, *Totahne*, which began in fall 2008 as a new cohort entered the two-year language program. Children eligible for the Totahne are the young (age two to six) offspring of cohort members; the idea is that, while their parents attend daily classes, the children also have the opportunity to learn the language, creating new opportunities for language learning at home (Maracle *et al.*, 2011: 91). With funding from the Province of Ontario and the Tyendinaga Band Council, and a facility donated by the First Nations Technical Institute, the project enlisted two fluent *tota* (grandmothers) from the nearby community of Kanehsatake (see Figure 5.16) to provide an immersion language-learning environment. 'The parents are the driving force of the program operating it much like a co-op where they help with meals, supplies and assisting with lunch-time supervision' (AMO Commission of Ontario, 2012: para. 3). According to Maracle *et al.* (2011: 92):

> Children who have regularly attended the Totahne program are now able to understand the Tota's and are using the language in their homes and with their extended families. The two-year-old ... not only understands everything the Tota's say ... in the Mohawk language but his first words were in Mohawk.

Together, these adult and child language-learning efforts are producing 'speakers with varying degrees of fluency', Maracle *et al.* state, with some adult learners going on to become language instructors and the 'celebrated outcome' of a '"mother tongue" Mohawk-speaking toddler in the community'

(Maracle *et al.*, 2011: 93). Moreover, the AMO Language Commission of Ontario (2012: para. 4) reports that, since the adult secondary program began, 'Mohawk language can once again be seen and heard throughout the community; at local restaurants, coffee shops and at community events'. With the long-term goal of establishing an elementary Mohawk immersion school in Tyendinaga, these twin adult–child initiatives illustrate the creative ways in which individual change agents, through organic, grass roots revitalization movements, can reclaim, in Maracle *et al.*'s (2011: 93) words, 'their Original' mother tongues.

'The Hawaiian Language Shall Take Its Rightful Place among the Languages of the World': Hawaiian-medium Education[10]

A continent and an ocean away, Hawaiian-medium schooling has followed a parallel path to Kanienkeha school-based immersion, including corpus planning assistance and policy advocacy from Kanienkehaka educator Dorothy Lazore (discussed above and later in this section). A Polynesian language closely related to Māori and Samoan, Hawaiian has been described as a 'vowel-rich language' (Wilson, 1999: 95). Hawaiian is advantaged by a large corpus of written materials, a long-standing history of teaching Hawaiian as a 'foreign' language at the secondary and post-secondary levels, and a 'traditional identification of the general population of the state with the language' (W.H. Wilson, personal communication, 19 July 2009).

'Hawai'i's primordial base', write William H. Wilson and Kauanoe Kamanā (2001: 148), 'is that of an isolated island chain distinguished and united by a unique Polynesian language and culture'. Migrating to these islands sometime in the eighth century C.E., the 'Hawaiian people thrived [there] for 1,000 years' (Warner, 2001: 133). From that time until the Hawaiians' first encounter with the British in 1778, Hawaiian was the only language used in the Hawaiian archipelago, and for generations, it developed with little outside influence (Wilson, 1998: 126). As described by Sam No'eau Warner:

> Although unwritten, Hawaiian at that time was a sophisticated language with a long and rich tradition of oral literature. This orature included chants of various kinds (e.g. cosmogonic, genealogical, migrational, and procreational), religious prayers, oratory, histories, myths, and traditional sayings and teachings created and passed down from generation to generation. (Warner, 2001: 134)

With the arrival of Captain James Cook in 1778, Hawai'i was drawn into an international trade and political system, and the years that followed saw the emergence of the Hawaiian Kingdom under an Indigenous monarchy, 'a multiracial nation using Hawaiian both as a lingua franca and as an official language of government' (Wilson & Kamanā, 2001: 148). During this time, 'Hawaiian was spoken by hundreds of thousands of people, perhaps even approaching one million' (Grenoble & Whaley, 2006: 95). Hawaiian was the language of business, government, religion, education and intercultural communication, as well as – importantly – the home and peer group (Wilson & Kamanā, 2006: 155). A missionary-introduced orthography had been in use since the early 19th century, and 90% of the Hawaiian population was reported to be literate in Hawaiian – the highest print literacy rate recorded in the world at the time (Grenoble & Whaley, 2006: 95). As discussed in Chapter 1, newspapers were published in Hawaiian, and even the children of immigrants 'spoke Hawaiian with native-speaker fluency' (Wilson, 1998: 127).

At the same time, however, like other Native Americans, Native Hawaiians faced the ravage of European-introduced diseases, and the population of 800,000 at the time of Cook's arrival plummeted to just 47,500 within the space of 100 years (Warner, 2001: 134). Foreign influence transformed traditional land use and subsistence, and in 1848 a law was passed called *māhele*, or division of land (i.e. individual/private ownership). In the growing cash economy, 'more than 98% of the *maka'āinana* or common Hawaiian people were disenfranchised' from their traditional lands, Warner states; many migrated to urban areas or foreign-owned sugar plantations (Warner, 2001: 134).

In 1893, backed by a group of sugar planters and other powerful American businessmen, the US military mounted an illegal takeover of the sovereign Kingdom of Hawai'i. Although protested by a significant number of US citizens and initially blocked by Democratic President Grover Cleveland, annexationists in the US Senate succeeded in establishing 'what [they] set out to establish', namely that 'no illegalities had been committed by US representatives or armed forces in Hawai'i' (Langer, 2008: 20).[11] Five years later, Hawai'i was 'annexed' as a US territory 'not by treaty but by ... Congressional resolution' (Langer, 2008: 15).

Although Native Hawaiians were incorporated into the US political system relatively recently, their experiences with that system bear the same imprint as those of other Native peoples in the United States. Following the US takeover, a ban ensued on Hawaiian-medium instruction in both public and private territorial schools. The 'resulting stigma' attached to speaking Hawaiian 'dramatically accelerated the process of language shift' (Wong, 2011: 4). There is good evidence, however, that Hawaiians strongly resisted that forced linguistic assimilation. 'There was considerable effort to maintain Hawaiian ... in the home, in church, in Sunday school, and in Hawaiian organizations', Wilson and Kamanā (2006: 156) observe. 'Hawaiian was used extensively in lower-level government and economic interaction with the Native Hawaiian population and plantation-derived immigrant population who spoke Hawaiian but not English':

> Hawaiian was also used extensively by politicians of all ethnicities to win seats in the territorial legislature as Hawaiian was the language spoken by the majority of voters for several decades into the territorial period. The territorial legislature even used Hawaiian as its operating language, contrary to federal law, during the initial ... years under United States rule. (W.H. Wilson, personal communication, 19 July 2009)

Ultimately, these efforts succumbed under the weight of English-only colonial rule (Wilson & Kamanā, 2006: 156). 'Very few domains of language use were able to fend off the pressure of this shift and today not one has been left unaffected', says K. Laiana Wong (2011: 4). By 1920, most Hawaiian children had begun speaking a local variety of English called Hawaiian Creole English, developed from the pidgin that arose from the importation of foreign workers (Warner, 2001: 133–135). Hawaiian Creole English served as both a peer language and 'a lingua franca among [N]ative Hawaiians, white Hawaiians, and the influx of immigrants from Asia' (Grenoble & Whaley, 2006: 95). By the mid-20th century, Hawaiian was spoken by only a few hundred inhabitants of the tiny island of Ni'ihau. At the same time, the Hawaiian Creole English that had replaced Hawaiian was 'used as a marker for socioeconomic discrimination against its speakers – Hawaiians and immigrants' (Warner, 2001: 135).

In 1959, Hawai'i was incorporated as the 50th US state. Over the next two decades, against the backdrop of the Civil Rights Movement, an 'Hawaiian renaissance' took root, with a strong language revitalization component. 'From this renaissance came a new group of second-language Hawaiian speakers who would become Hawaiian language educators', states Warner (2001: 135). In 1978, Hawaiian and English were designated co-official languages in the new state constitution, which also mandated the promotion of Hawaiian language, culture and history. University Hawaiian-language teaching expanded to focus on revitalization. By this time the language situation had become grave, as the 'number of children speaking Hawaiian was less than 50 statewide' (Wilson et al., 2006: 42).

Strengthened by contacts with Māori language activists in Aotearoa/New Zealand, in 1983 a small group of parents and language activists established the 'Aha Pūnana Leo (Hawaiian language nest) non-profit organization and then its preschools (a parallel to the Māori Kōhanga Reo [language nest] preschools). According to Noelani Iokepa-Guerrero, a former teacher assistant and an administrator in the program, the vision of 'Aha Pānana Leo is E ola ka 'olelo Hawai'i, 'that the Hawaiian language shall live and take its rightful place among the languages of the world and ... as the prominent language of Hawai'i' (Iokepa-Guerrero, 2008: 30).

So began the Pūnana Leo preschools, the name connoting 'the dominant learning method in which students are "fed" solely in their native language and culture much like the way young birds are cared for in their own nests' ('Aha Pūnana Leo, n.d.: para. 3). The family-run preschools enable children to interact with fluent speakers entirely in Hawaiian with the goal of cultivating fluency and knowledge of Hawaiian language and culture in 'much the same way that they were in the home in earlier generations' (Wilson & Kamanā, 2001: 151). With the first preschool established in Kauai'i in 1984, two additional centers opened the next year in Hilo on the island of Hawai'i, and in Kalihi on O'ahu. From there, the preschools 'spread to other islands' ('Aha Pūnana Leo, n.d.: para. 3).

At this same time, a state statute remained in effect based on an 1896 law closing all public Hawaiian-medium schools. As their children prepared to enter Hawaiian public elementary schools, Pūnana Leo parents lobbied for a change in the law, and were met with success in 1986. However, says 'Aha Pūnana Leo cofounder William H. Wilson, the state had not opened any schools taught through Hawaiian:

> When the state did not open a kindergarten in Hawaiian for our children here in Hilo, we held the children back and declared that we were opening up a public kindergarten through Hawaiian ... at the Pūnana Leo O Hilo. We declared it free of charge ... and ran it for a whole year. There were only four students, all from the Pūnana Leo, including our son Hulilau. We taught them reading and writing using the old Hawaiian syllabary method that we were also beginning to use in the preschool. All four could read Hawaiian pretty well at the end. (Personal communication, 24 July 2008)

The 'boycott kindergarten' was called Ke Kula Kauapuni Hawai'i (the Hawaiian Surrounding Environment School, or Hawaiian Immersion School).

It was during this time, Wilson relates, that '[w]e brought [Dorothy] Lazore to Hawai'i as we prepared to move our unofficial 'public' protest kindergarten ... onto a state public school campus for a combined K–1 class:

> This was four years after our founding the 'Aha Pūnana Leo. Lazore joined us in our creation of curriculum materials and then we took her before the State Board of Education (of our single state public education system) to testify on the existence of a Mohawk immersion program at Kahnewa:ke and the positive academic and English (and also Mohawk) outcomes. She was then a nun, and this added to her credibility before the DOE. (Personal communication, 19 July 2009)

The parents were ultimately successful in their efforts and, in 1987, the first Pūnana Leo children entered Hawaiian-medium public schools, 'taking the name Kula Kaiapuni Hawai'i ... with them' (Wilson & Kamanā, 2001: 150).

Hawaiian immersion then spread horizontally to other communities and vertically grade by grade through the public school system until the first students graduated from high school educated totally in Hawaiian in 1999. At present, Hawaiian remains the only Native American immersion program that extends through grade 12 (W.H. Wilson, personal communication, 19 July 2009).

As is evident from this brief history of the Hawaiian 'renaissance', all of this has required a great deal of political activism on the part of parents and other supporters, at both the state and national levels. The Hawaiians were instrumental, for instance, in crafting and passing the 1990/1992 Native American Languages Act and the Esther Martinez Native American Languages Preservation Act of 2006 (discussed in Chapter 3). As the connection with Dorothy Lazore and the Mohawk project shows, Hawaiian regenesis – like all the revitalization projects profiled here – has also benefited from a growing professional network of language planners (see Hinton & Hale, 2001; Reyhner, 2004; and Romero-Little *et al.*, 2011, for examples of these grass roots LPP efforts). This work has required extensive acquisition and corpus planning – most notably preparing certified Native-language teachers and developing teaching materials in all content areas that meet state curriculum standards. Cultivating those human and material resources has become an ongoing project undertaken in both university and community settings.

In example of this, Wilson and Kamanā (2001, 2006) report on the Nāwahīokalaniʻōpuʻu (Nāwahī) Laboratory School in Hilo, a full-immersion, early childhood through high school program affiliated with the University of Hawaiʻi Hilo's College of Hawaiian Language and the ʻAha Pūnana Leo (see Figure 5.19). The school teaches all subjects through Hawaiian language and values, offering a college preparatory curriculum and 'an explicit understanding that use of the Hawaiian language has priority over ... English' (Wilson & Kamanā, 2001: 158). Students also learn a useful third language such as Japanese, which, in light of Hawaiʻi's multiracial history, is for some students a heritage language as well. Reflecting the Pūnana Leo philosophy, the curriculum has 'a strong focus on Hawaiian music, traditions, and community values', and parents must commit to weekly language classes and monthly meetings (Wilson & Kamanā, 2008: para. 5).

Of special interest in the Nāwahī case is its role as part of an integrated system of Hawaiian-medium structures 'that can develop, protect, nurture and enrich young adult and child fluency in Hawaiian along with the crucial disposition to use Hawaiian with Hawaiian speaking peers' (Wilson & Kawaiʻaeʻa, 2007: 38). These structures and systems are captured by the Hawaiian term *honua*: 'places, circumstances, [and] structures where use of Hawaiian is dominant' (Wilson & Kawaiʻaeʻa, 2007: 38). As Pūnana Leo and Nāwahī co-founders William Wilson and Kauanoe Kamanā describe this learning environment:

> [Nāwahī's] unique ten-acre school site ... includes gardens of traditional Hawaiian crops such as taro, sweet potatoes and breadfruit. In these

Figure 5.19 Kauanoe Kamanā, cofounder of the 'Aha Pūnana Leo preschools and Nāwahī Laboratory School, teaching Nāwahī kindergartners the Hawaiian syllabary (photograph courtesy of Nāwahī Laboratory School)

gardens students connect to traditional Hawaiian practices and the natural environment that has nurtured their culture for generations. (Wilson & Kamanā, 2008: para. 2; see Figure 5.20)

Nāwahī's pedagogical goal is for learners to achieve Hawaiian dominance alongside high levels of English fluency and literacy, and simultaneously to produce students who 'psychologically identify Hawaiian as their dominant language and the one that they will speak with peers and their own children when they have them' (Wilson & Kawai'ae'a, 2007: 39).

A critical component in achieving these goals is Ka Haka 'Ula O Ke'elikōlani College. This fully Hawaiian self-governing unit provides curriculum support to pre-kindergarten through grade 12 laboratory schools (including Nāwahī) in partnership with the 'Aha Pūnana Leo. The college's 43-credit bachelor's degree program includes an additional 28 hours of language study, and is conducted entirely in Hawaiian after the first year. As Wilson and Kawai'ae'a describe the curriculum:

Students first experience sole use of Hawaiian when they enter the second year course. By the third year, they are expected to use only

Figure 5.20 Learning in Nāwahī's garden (photograph courtesy of Nāwahī Laboratory School)

Hawaiian among themselves. By the fourth year, students are expected to take leadership roles in moving lower level students to full use of Hawaiian. (Wilson & Kawaiʻaeʻa, 2007: 41)

An extension of this curriculum is the college's Kahuawaiola Indigenous Teacher Education Program, officially accredited in 2001. The teacher preparation curriculum is based on traditional Hawaiian beliefs that 'knowledge comes from direct experience' (Wilson & Kawaiʻaeʻa, 2007: 45). Entering students must have had eight semesters of Hawaiian language, a course on Hawaiian culture, and have volunteered for at least 75 hours in a Hawaiian-medium school; they must also pass a rigorous Hawaiian language fluency exam and are expected to be able to transcribe elders speaking on cultural topics and translate a contemporary newspaper article from English to Hawaiian 'from a Hawaiian cultural perspective... a skill important for teachers developing classroom curriculum ... in a language with an educational materials resource base thousands of times smaller than that of English' (Wilson & Kawaiʻaeʻa, 2007: 46).

Kahuawaiola students begin with intensive immersion in a six-week summer residency at Nāwahī during which they 'live their lives entirely in

Hawaiian' (Wilson & Kawaiʻaeʻa, 2007: 46). This is followed by a year of student teaching in which they work with master teachers in Hawaiian-medium schools and participate in weekly seminars and special workshops through distance education. As part of their coursework, preservice teachers design lesson plans aligned with state standards and Hawaiian *Nā Honua Mauli Ola Hawaiʻi Guidelines for Culturally Healthy and Responsive Learning Environments* (Native Hawaiian Education Council & Ka Haka ʻUla O Keʻelikōlani College of Hawaiian Language, 2002). The guidelines, written in Hawaiian and English and 'developed with the belief that continued learning and practicing of the Hawaiian language and culture is a fundamental prerequisite for nurturing culturally healthy ... citizens and contributes to the growth and harmony of the community', address the roles of learners, educators, schools, families and communities in sustaining positive learning environments to achieve these goals (Native Hawaiian Education Council & Ka Haka ʻUla O Keʻelikōlani College of Hawaiian Language, 2002: 11). A *Nā Honua Mauli* Action Plan provides further guidelines for establishing language proficiency levels, expanding inter-agency and community partnerships, and disseminating the guidelines statewide (Native Hawaiian Education Council & Ka Haka ʻUla O Keʻelikōlani College of Hawaiian Language, 2002: 77–78).

Additional supports to Hawaiian-medium schooling in which Ka Haka ʻUla O Keʻelikōlani College has been instrumental are three Hawaiian teacher content licenses, an Hawaiian Teacher Standards Board, a new PhD in Hawaiian and Indigenous Language and Culture Revitalization, and a new master's degree in Indigenous Language and Culture Education that provides 'the next layer of professional development' for teacher education candidates (Wilson & Kawaiʻaeʻa, 2007: 49; see Figure 5.21).

In their fight to establish a preschool through high school system of Hawaiian-medium education, Hawaiian language planners have focused on the civil rights issue of protecting children from forced loss of Hawaiian language (linguicide) and *mauli* (ethnicide) in the context of public schooling (Wilson & Kamanā, 2001: 149–150, 153–163). Although revitalization has been the LPP priority, Hawaiian-medium instruction has yielded impressive academic results. Nāwahī students, many of whom come from poor and working-class backgrounds, not only surpass their non-immersion peers on English standardized tests, but they also outperform the state average for all ethnic groups on high school graduation, college attendance and academic honors (W.H. Wilson, personal communication, 24 July 2008; Wilson, 2008, 2013; see Figure 5.22). Many are concurrently enrolled in university classes and have won prestigious college scholarships, and the school has a '100% high school graduation rate and a college attendance rate of approximately 80%' (Wilson *et al.*, 2006: 42). According to Wilson, the school has succeeded because 'we judge the school on Hawaiian language and culture achievement and holding Hawaiian language and culture high through the hard work so

Figure 5.21 Nāwahī teachers earn their master's degrees (photograph courtesy of Nāwahī Laboratory School)

highly valued by Hawaiian elders' (personal communication, 6 January 2007 and 24 July 2008). 'Most gratifying to us', Wilson adds, 'is the trend among graduates of Nāwahī and Ka Haka 'Ula O Ke'elikōlani College to raise their children speaking Hawaiian as a first language' (personal communication, 19 July 2009).

Hawaiian-medium education now serves approximately 2000 students of Hawaiian and non-Hawaiian ancestry in a coordinated set of schools, beginning with the preschools and moving through full Hawaiian-medium elementary and secondary education (Wilson *et al.*, 2006). Hawaiian is widely taught in Hawaiian universities. As noted above, the University of Hawai'i–Hilo offers a doctorate in Hawaiian language and culture revitalization as well as the Hawaiian immersion teacher preparation program. The University of Hawai'i Mānoa (on the island of O'ahu) also offers a teacher preparation program for Kula Kaiapuni teachers conducted in partnership with the Ke Kula Kaiapuni `o Ānuenue School, which serves children from birth through grade 12 (Warner, 2001: 140; see Figure 5.23). Hawaiian revitalization has extended into other, non-school domains, such as Hawaiian-speaking softball teams and the production of Hawaiian language-only plays 'written by Hawaiians about Hawaiians' (Warner, 2001: 141–142;

Figure 5.22 Nāwahī high school students working on a class project in Hawaiian (photograph courtesy of Nāwahī Laboratory School)

Figure 5.23 Students and faculty at Ke Kula Kaiapuni `o Ānuenue School greeting visitors with traditional Native songs, 2007 (photograph by Teresa L. McCarty)

see also Warner, 1999b). As many as 15,000 Hawaiians use or understand Hawaiian, the vast majority of whom are the products of the university, community and advanced high school classes that the Hawaiian revitalization movement has generated (W.H. Wilson, personal communication, 6 January 2007). Wilson and Kamanā cite two other outcomes of these efforts: the development of an interconnected group of young parents who are increasing their proficiency in Hawaiian, and the creation of a more general social climate of Native-language support (Wilson & Kamanā, 2001: 153).

None of this has been achieved without setbacks or strife, but the more important lesson is the sustained and determined quest for linguistic, cultural and educational self-determination made by those who began and have enjoined the movement. Laiana Wong, for example, who, with his wife enrolled their first-born child in the Pūnana Leo in 1987, describes 'the constant tension that attends the choice between Hawaiian and English in our communicative interactions [that] persists for me even as my communicative competence increases' (Wong, 2011: 5). William Wilson notes the challenges for parents to 'not only develop higher personal fluency ..., but also [to] develop words and usages for contemporary life that can then be used with children'. Furthermore, he notes:

> unless there are other children with whom [one's own children] can interact in the language, there can be challenges in maintaining at least equal fluency in the Indigenous language and the surrounding dominant language for the child, with it highly likely that the dominant language will overcome the home language as it does in many cases of immigrant children who speak a non-dominant language at home with their parents. (Personal communication, 17 July 2009)

The case of Hawaiian sheds light on the ways in which new 'ideological and implementational spaces' (Hornberger, 2002, 2006a) have been pried open as individual family language planning efforts such as these interact with wider social, cultural, educational and political processes. 'There is really no way to ensure the intergenerational transmission of the zeal that drives this type of movement', maintains Wong (2011: 9). It has nonetheless been one of the most lasting and effective Indigenous language regenesis movements in the world (Hinton, 2001a: 8). As Iokepa-Guerrero writes, Hawaiian-medium education has enabled the Hawaiian language to 'live and take its rightful place among the languages of the world' (Iokepa-Guerrero, 2008: 30). As the movement matures into its second quarter century, it continues to capture the public imagination and to serve as an exemplar of the counter-hegemonic possibilities of conjoined family-, community-, school- and university-based LPP.

'Harmonizing without Homogenizing': Navajo Immersion and Academic Success[12]

As discussed in Chapter 4, despite a relatively large number of native speakers and a robust print literacy history, the Navajo language faces an uncertain future. In this context, the Navajo Nation and individual Diné communities have launched a number of language revitalization efforts, including immersion preschools and K–12 schools. Two of the most long-lived and successful school-based revitalization efforts operate on either side of the reservation: Tséhootsooí Diné Bi'ólta' – The Navajo School at the Meadow Between the Rocks – situated in the border town of Fort Defiance, Arizona on the eastern side of the reservation, and Puente de Hózhǫ́ Trilingual Magnet School, an off-reservation public school near the reservation's western border in Flagstaff, Arizona (see Figure 4.1, Chapter 4, for locations of these sites). We begin at Fort Defiance.

Tséhootsooí Diné Bi'ólta'

A century-and-a-half ago, Fort Defiance, Arizona was the epicenter of Anglo-American violence perpetrated against Navajo people. Prior to Anglo intrusion, this place, which Navajos call *Tséhootsooí* – Meadow Between the Rocks – was a popular grazing area for Navajo horses and sheep. By 1851 it had become the first US military post in what is now the State of Arizona (Lapahie, 2001). For the next decade, Navajo families and US troops co-existed there uneasily. Then, in the fall of 1863, Colonel Kit Carson and his companies occupied the fort as a base for carrying out a scorched earth campaign, destroying Navajo corn and wheat fields, inciting other tribes to raid Navajo livestock, and forcing Navajo families to flee their homes. By the following spring, starvation and desperate circumstances had led thousands of Navajos to give themselves up to the troops at Fort Defiance, and from there to trek by foot and ox cart to a concentration camp 300 miles eastward at Fort Sumner, New Mexico (Lapahie, 2011; Underhill, 1956). Hundreds of people died on what came to be known as the Long Walk to Fort Sumner (the place called *Hwéeldi* by Navajos). During their incarceration there, thousands more succumbed to starvation and foreign-borne diseases. To speak of this place still brings tears to people's eyes. (For personal accounts of the Long Walk period, see Johnson & Roessel, 1973.) Finally, in 1868, a treaty was signed, promising, among other things, a schoolhouse and teacher for every 30 Navajo children between the ages of 6 and 16 (Link, 1968: 7). Four years later, the first federal boarding school for Navajos opened at the original Fort Defiance military base (Link, 1968: 19).

Fort Defiance is both a physical site and a symbol of genocide – quite literally the center of the federal safety zone. It is also 'crushing proof' of the federal abrogation of the trust relationship (Wilkins & Lomawaima, 2001: 87). The historic significance of this place makes contemporary language reclamation efforts there equally symbolic and momentous.

By the mid-1980s – just a few generations after the treaty signing – Fort Defiance had grown into a small town whose location adjacent to the tribal headquarters at Window Rock, Arizona and just 30 miles from the reservation border town of Gallup, New Mexico regularized contact with English speakers. These social and physical transformations, alongside the legacy of compulsory English-only schooling, are reflected in children's linguistic repertoires; increasingly, children growing up in border town situations such as Fort Defiance speak English as a primary (and sometimes only) language.

In response to the decline in Navajo speaking ability among younger generations, in 1986 the Window Rock Unified School District launched a voluntary Navajo language immersion program at Fort Defiance Elementary School. At the time, fewer than 1 in 20 kindergarten and first-grade students were considered 'reasonably fluent' in Navajo; a third were judged to have some passive knowledge of the language (Arviso & Holm, 2001: 204; Holm & Holm, 1995: 148). According to program cofounders Marie Arviso (the school principal) and Wayne Holm (the English language teacher), 'Despite a very supportive Navajo principal and a Navajo-majority teaching staff, it was obvious that even those children who spoke some Navajo were reluctant to do so in public' (Arviso & Holm, 2001: 204–205). At the same time, many Fort Defiance students had been labeled 'limited English proficient' on the basis of their performance on English standardized tests. 'But these children were not alingual or semilngual', Arviso and Holm emphasize; [t]hey were quite fluent in English and could interact well enough to get whatever they wanted in English' (Arviso & Holm, 2001: 205).

The Fort Defiance Elementary School had, in the past, run a 'relatively successful transitional bilingual program' (Arviso & Holm, 2001: 205). However, this type of program, it was clear, was not appropriate given students' linguistic repertoires. In this 'changed and changing language situation', Arviso and Holm write, it 'was becoming increasingly obvious that ... something more like the Māori immersion programs might be the only type of program with some chance of success' (Arviso & Holm, 2001: 205). Approaching the school district with a proposal for a voluntary immersion program, Arviso and Holm identified 48 kindergartners 'who had at least some passive knowledge of Navajo', and, '[t]o our great surprise, 46 of the 48 parents signed up their children' for the newly developed Navajo immersion track (Arviso & Holm, 2001: 205). As Arviso and Holm describe the program's initial goals:

We did not feel that we could claim ... that these children would necessarily do better academically. We were more concerned that the children come to identify and value themselves *as Navajos*. We said that in an environment which tended to devalue Navajoness, we wanted to help these children experience success in school *through* Navajo. We said that by the end of the 5th grade, these students not only would be doing as well academically as those children instructed only in English, but they would also have come to talk, understand, read, and write Navajo. (Arviso & Holm, 2001: 205)

The program began as a K–5 Diné immersion track in an otherwise all-English public elementary school. Participation was voluntary and, with the exception of two 20-minute periods in English each day, all instruction was in Navajo; teachers used Navajo on the playground and in the cafeteria. 'Remember', Arviso and Holm state, 'most of these children spoke little or no Navajo. We taught them, when they were not able to communicate with the teacher, to say, 'Shikáa anilyeed!' – 'Help me' (Arviso & Holm, 2001: 206). After the first few 'scary months' of program implementation, 'we noticed students beginning to use "survival Navajo" phrases with relative freedom' (Arviso & Holm, 2001: 205).

The initial curriculum was kept simple: developmental Navajo, reading and writing first in Navajo, then English, and math in both languages, with other subjects included as content for speaking or writing (Holm & Holm, 1995: 149–150). The program placed a heavy emphasis on language and critical thinking, and on process writing and cooperative learning. As children moved up through the grades, they received progressively less instruction in Navajo: by the second and third grades, the program included a half-day in Navajo and a half-day in English; fourth and fifth graders received at least one hour each day of Navajo instruction. In addition, program leaders insisted that an adult caretaker or relative 'spend some time talking with the child in Navajo each evening after school' (Arviso & Holm, 2001: 210).

In a retrospective analysis of the Fort Defiance immersion program after nearly a decade of operation, Holm and Holm (1995) summarize student achievement data from the project's first seven years (see Table 5.1). By the fourth grade, Navajo immersion students performed as well on local tests of English as comparable non-immersion students at the school. Immersion students performed better on local assessments of English writing, and were 'way ahead' in mathematics. On standardized tests of English reading, students were slightly behind, but closing the gap (Holm & Holm, 1995: 150). 'Thus it would appear', Arviso and Holm write, 'that Navajo immersion had not hurt these students. They were doing almost as well as, or better than, the [monolingual English] students' (Arviso & Holm, 2001: 211).

Looking at the third column in the second row of Table 5.1, an additional finding is worthy of note. By fourth grade, not only did Navajo immersion students outperform non-immersion students on assessments in Navajo – a finding we would expect – but non-immersion students actually scored *lower* on these assessments than they had in kindergarten. The Fort Defiance data

Table 5.1 Comparison of Fort Defiance Navajo immersion (NI) and monolingual English (ME) student performance after 7 years of program implementation (adapted from Holm & Holm, 1995: 150; McCarty, 2003: 156)

Assessment type	NI students	ME students
Local oral English assessment	Same as ME students	Same as NI students
Local Navajo language assessment	Higher than ME students	Lower than NI students and lower than their own kindergarten performance
Local English writing assessment	Higher than ME students	Substantially lower than NI students
Standardized mathematics assessment	Substantially higher than ME students	Substantially lower than NI students
Standardized English reading assessment	Slightly lower than ME students but closing the gap	Slightly higher than NI students

thus demonstrate the powerful negative effect of the *absence* of immersion schooling and, conversely, its positive effect on the recovery and maintenance of the Indigenous language as well as on students' acquisition of English and mathematics.

In 1999 – the same year that the first cohort of Pūnana Leo students graduated from high school – the Fort Defiance immersion program saw some of its first students graduate from high school. In the interim, the program was divided into primary and intermediate learning centers on separate campuses, and in 2003, all of the district's Diné immersion classes were consolidated at a single school, Tséhootsooí Diné Bi'ólta' (hereafter TDB). As with the initial program, in kindergarten and first grade, all instruction at TDB, including initial literacy, takes place in Navajo. English is introduced in second grade and gradually increased until a 50–50 distribution is attained by grade 6. Florian Tom Johnson and Jennifer Legatz, who were instrumental to the program's expansion, explain that it affords 'maximum exposure to the Diné language ... to provide for the greatest effect on acquiring (and instilling) the Diné language (heritage language) as a second language' (Johnson & Legatz, 2006: 27). TDB's curriculum integrates Navajo tribal standards for language and culture with those required by the state, and the school as a whole emphasizes a 'Diné language and culture rich environment ... including lunch room, playground, hallways and the bus' (Johnson & Legatz, 2006: 30). Parents enroll their children at TDB, Johnson and Legatz say, 'in hopes that the Diné language could be revitalized within their families through these children' (Johnson & Legatz, 2006: 30).

Longitudinal data from TDB continue to show that the benefits to language revitalization have not come at the cost of children's English language learning or academic achievement. To the contrary, Navajo immersion students consistently outperform their peers in English-only classrooms on local and standardized assessments of English reading, writing and mathematics, while also developing strong Navajo oral language and literacy skills (Johnson & Legatz, 2006). Moreover, adds Wayne Holm, 'What the children and their parents taught us was that Navajo immersion gave students Navajo pride in an urbanizing situation in which many students were not proud to be Navajo':

> [P]erhaps the most important thing that effective [immersion] programs can do today is to give students access to meaning in their lives and the lives of those about them ... Schools cannot save a language or a culture. But schools can serve as catalysts to help parents and grandparents make life more meaningful. In so doing, they may make it possible for students to find new and more meaningful ways of being Navajo ... We have to find ways of giving students access to the goodness of being and speaking Navajo. (Holm, 2006: 33, 35–36)

Puente de Hózhǫ́ Trilingual Magnet School

In the fall of 2009, with Arizona State University Professor Bryan M.J. Brayboy, I began a two-year ethnographic study of a trilingual K–6 (now K–5) public magnet school in northern Arizona.[13] Part of a larger national study investigating the role of Native languages and cultures in Native American students' academic achievement (McCarty, 2013b), we were drawn to this school because of its unique Diné–Spanish–English program and its successful record of meeting state and federal standardized testing mandates. Called Puente de Hózhǫ́, the school's name combines the Spanish *puente de* ('bridge of') and the Navajo *hózhǫ́*, meaning beauty or harmony. In English, this is Bridge of Beauty School. According to school cofounder Michael Fillerup, the name mirrors the vision of a 'school striving to connect and celebrate the three predominant languages and cultures' of the local community (Fillerup, 2011: 150).

To do this, the school offers a conventional two-way immersion program in which native Spanish-speaking and native English-speaking students are taught jointly for a half-day in each language, and 'one-way' Navajo immersion in which English-dominant Navajo students are taught in their heritage language. In the latter program, kindergartners receive approximately 80% of their instruction in Navajo, with English instructional time gradually increased until a 50–50 balance is attained in grades 4 and 5. All required state standards are taught in either Navajo and English or Spanish and English. In a school district in which 26% of students are American Indian (mostly Diné) and 21% are Latino/a, 'local educators were searching for innovative ways to bridge the seemingly unbridgeable gap between the academic achievement of language minority and language majority children', explains Fillerup (2005: 15). The goal is to create an environment in which children from diverse language and culture backgrounds can 'learn harmoniously together', while acquiring the ability to speak, read, and write proficiently in two languages (Fillerup, 2011: 164).

Most of the school's 122 Native American students (about 27% of the school's 2010 enrollment of 449) are Diné, although many come from racially and ethnically mixed family backgrounds. Virtually all the Native students speak English as a primary language. While many Diné students come from nearby reservation border areas, Diné teachers noted that some come from the 'heart of the [Navajo] reservation' to obtain the kind of 'language rich, Navajo–English instruction' provided at the school (interview, 3 November 2009). All the Diné teachers at the time of the study ($n = 4$) came from strong Diné cultural backgrounds and had Navajo as a first language.

Like other language revitalization cases examined here, Puente de Hózhǫ́ (hereafter, PdH) grows out of a larger Indigenous revitalization movement. In 1998, Fillerup – an Anglo bilingual/English as a Second Language educator with many years of experience working in Diné education – met Timati Reedy, the former chief executive of the Department of Māori Affairs and an architect of Māori immersion, who had also influenced the start of the Hawaiian Pūnana Leo. At the time, Fillerup was guiding a Diné immersion program in the Flagatsff Unified School District's only reservation school at Leupp, Arizona (see Figure 4.1, Chapter 4). According to Fillerup (2000, 2002), the program had demonstrated remarkable success, showing that Navajo immersion *accelerated* children's English language development.

With a five-year federal Bilingual Education Act grant in 1999, Fillerup and his colleagues began planning PdH School. The goal, he relates, was to develop an instructional program that would 'harmonize without homogenizing':

> On a grander scale, the vision was to create a school where each child's language and culture was regarded not as a problem to be solved but as an indispensable resource, the very heart and soul of the school itself... English speakers would learn Spanish, Spanish speakers would learn English, Navajo children would acquire their tribal language, and all students would interact harmoniously and achieve academically. (Fillerup, 2008: para. 3)

There was great interest among a 'small but enthusiastic' group of local educators. At community meetings, Fillerup and others presented the idea for a trilingual school to teachers, administrators and parents. Receiving a positive response, the founding group formed an exploratory committee that included the former city mayor and a professor from the local state university, and met with Native American and Mexican American organizations.

An advertisement was placed in the local newspaper with the question, 'Would you like your child to have the Power of Two':

> the ability to speak, read, and write in two languages? We determined that all students attending *Puente de Hózhǫ́* would be enrolled in either the Spanish/English or the Diné/English bilingual programs with the goal of becoming proficient speakers, readers, and writers of English and either Spanish or Diné. (Fillerup, 2011: 150; see Figure 5.24)

The committee then began developing the curriculum and, '[o]nce we had ... a concrete plan, we surveyed the community to gauge the level of interest', explains Fillerup (2011: 152). Receiving an overwhelmingly positive response – 'We quickly realized that one of our biggest challenges would be turning students away because we could not accommodate all who were interested' (Fillerup, 2011: 152) – the PdH program was launched in the autumn of 2001 with 58 kindergarten students. Ironically, this was just a year after Arizona voters approved Proposition 203, 'English for the Children', which effectively outlawed bilingual education in Arizona public schools. As a voluntary magnet school with an enrichment focus and a research-based language instructional program, PdH was nonetheless able to proceed. (It remains one of a handful of bilingual schools in the state.)

'No one thought this was real', Fillerup recalls of the school's first weeks. No physical site for the program had been identified (the program was eventually housed in three available classrooms at a local high school), and such logistics as lowering drinking fountains and urinals to accommodate younger

Figure 5.24 Entrance to Puente de Hózhǫ́ School displaying the school's motto, 'The Power of Two' (photograph by Teresa L. McCarty)

children had to be worked out. 'It was a blitzkrieg effort' (Fillerup, 2011: 154), and for the first three weeks of school, Fillerup and other staff members personally transported students from throughout the city to and from school, as no bus transportation was yet available. Lacking a full-time administrator, Fillerup 'doubled up' as school director and bilingual/English as a Second Language director for the district.

By its second year, the PdH program had expanded to three kindergarten classes and first grade, serving 120 students in total. The next year, three additional kindergarten classes were added along with a second-grade class. Eventually, PdH was relocated to a public elementary school with declining enrollments. A full-time principal, Dawn Trubakoff (a former teacher at the same elementary school) was hired, and a phase out/phase in plan was put into place to build the PdH program 'until all the students in [all] grades ... would be participating in the full bilingual programs' (Fillerup, 2011: 157).

On our first visit to the school early in 2009, Diné teachers explained their view of the school this way: 'We're fighting for our kids to have the right to learn their language and culture!' (field notes, 13 January 2009; see Figure 5.25). Over the two-year study, we witnessed how this was accomplished through small and large acts of educational and linguistic self-determination. Those acts begin with a stunning visual statement that greets all who enter the school: expansive exterior wall murals created by the 'artists of Puente de Hózhǫ́' – students and renowned Diné artist Shonto Begay – depicting the

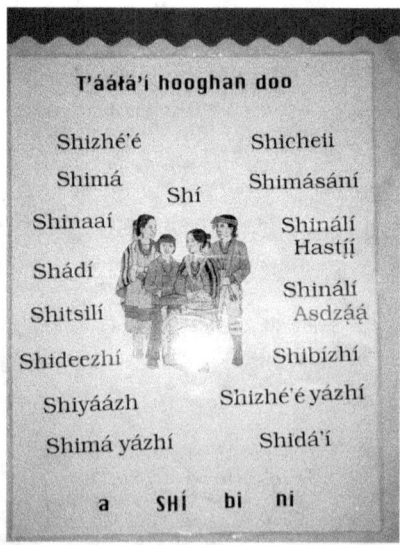

Figure 5.25 Using teacher-created materials such as this kinship chart, Diné teachers explain their pedagogic goal: 'We're fighting for our kids to have the right to learn their language and culture!' (photograph by Teresa L. McCarty)

Navajo girls' puberty ceremony (*Kinaaldá*) and the multihued topography of *Diné Bikeyah* (Navajo Country or Navajoland; see Figures 5.26 and 5.27). Throughout the school, the print environment displays vivid images of academic content in Navajo, Spanish and English.

PdH educators explicitly reject the remedial labels historically associated with bilingual and Indigenous education in the United States. According to these educators, the way to ameliorate long-standing academic disparities is to create a school culture in which 'diverse languages and cultures [are] regarded as assets rather than deficits, as things to be desired and augmented rather than eliminated or suppressed' (Fillerup, 2011: 149). Instruction in Navajo language and culture shares equal status with English and academic content in English. 'This school is predicated on [the assumption] that learning more than one language is a *good thing*', an administrator emphasized during one of our site visits; [t]here is a belief in this school that all three languages should be treated equally' (field notes, 12 January 2010). 'We have to tell the parents, this is not what they were used to in their own schooling', a Diné teacher pointed out (field notes, 12 January 2010). Explicit in these pedagogic practices is the 'shedding [of] the remedial label that has dogged American Indian ... children for over a century':

> Students in the Navajo immersion program are viewed not as problems to be solved but as an educational elite – the ones who are learning

Figure 5.26 Exterior wall mural created by Puente de Hózhǫ́ students and Diné artist Shonto Begay, depicting the morning run in the Navajo girls' puberty ceremony or *Kinaaldá* (photograph by Teresa L. McCarty)

Figure 5.27 Puente de Hózhǫ́ external wall mural depicting *Diné Bikeyah* or Navajoland (photograph by Teresa L. McCarty)

Navajo, that most difficult language [used by the Navajo Code Talkers] during World War II. It is *their* [the students'] language, program, school, culture, and heritage. (Fillerup, 2005: 16)

During the period of our research, every Diné-language classroom displayed a poster-size song script, *Shí Naashá* (literally, 'I Walk About' but translated culturally and historically by teachers as 'I'm Alive'). The song is a reminder and commemoration of the Navajo people's survival and return to *Diné Bikéyah* from Hwéeldi, the federal concentration camp at Fort Sumner, New Mexico. Teachers speak of their work as a reversal of past pedagogic practices, including their own. As one Diné teacher acknowledged when we asked if her children spoke Navajo:

When I was a young parent, I really didn't know what it meant ... to value the language that you were raised in ... we were just barely getting over the shame of being Native American ... that we were minorities and we were not of value – we were just healing from that ... I think working as a bilingual teacher here at Puente de Hózhǫ́ really opened my eyes to how important my language and culture are. (Interview, 12 January 2010).

Like immersion at TDB and Nāwahī, this is a school community that, in its everyday practice, aims to conquer what Luis Enrique López (2008) calls the 'subaltern condition' of bilingualism, indigeneity and difference.

How well have students done in PdH's Diné language and culture program? In terms of their academic development in English, with the exception of one year early in the program, PdH students have consistently met or exceeded federal and state benchmarks for 'adequate yearly progress'. 'This became our unofficial goal', Fillerup writes – 'to score high enough on [standardized tests] to appease the powers that be' (Fillerup, 2005: 15). In 2008, Native students at PdH surpassed their Native American peers in English-only programs by 14% and 21% in grades 3 and 4, respectively (see Tables 5.2 and 5.3). While 2008 math scores were lower, in 2009, fifth-grade Native students outperformed their English-only peers in mathematics by 12%. In math, sixth-grade Native students outperformed their English-only peers by 17%, and PdH students 'outperformed their English-only peers across all grade levels in writing' (Fillerup, 2011: 163). Importantly, and reflective of international research on bilingual education, the students who performed the best on English assessments had the longest experience in the Diné language and culture program (i.e. those who began in kindergarten) – and, of course, they were also becoming fluent and literate in a second language – Navajo.

However, the program's impacts extend beyond well beyond the scores on English-language tests. As one teacher noted, '[H]earing parents comment

Table 5.2 Percentage of PdH Native students meeting or exceeding state standards in reading, 2008 (Fillerup, 2011: 161)

Grade	District percentage	Puente de Hózhǫ́ percentage
3	57%	71%
4	54%	75%
5	48%	43%
6	53%	44%

Table 5.3 Percentage of PdH Native students meeting or exceeding state standards in mathematics, 2008 (Fillerup, 2011: 161)

Grade	District percentage	Puente de Hózhǫ́ percentage
3	68%	76%
4	61%	63%
5	60%	43%
6	55%	44%

on how much their kids have learned, or that their child may be the only one of all the cousins that [is] speaking to their grandparents – this tells us that we are doing something [worthwhile]' (interview, 3 November 2009). These are the unquantifiable but highly consequential outcomes of immersion programs such as that at PdH. As Fillerup describes the concrete reality of this unique, strengths-based, multilingual school culture:

> If you walk down the halls, you will hear students and teachers speaking in Spanish, Diné, or English, depending on the classroom. You will see student work featured on the walls in three languages. You may see students learning a traditional dance in the gym or working with local Diné artist Shonto Begay to create a cultural mural ... You may see students giving PowerPoint presentations ... in Spanish, English, or Diné. You will see a lot of smiles ..., and not just on the faces of the students. You will see living proof that children of diverse language and cultural backgrounds can learn harmoniously together. (Fillerup, 2011: 163–164)

Reimagining Possibilities for Indigenous Mother Tongues

The foregoing cases all foreground the *persons* and *communities* who are creating new niches for Indigenous mother tongues. In some cases, such as Miami and Wôpanâak, these efforts have begun from 'ground zero' (Baldwin, 2003) – quite literally from the bottom up. These grass roots efforts exemplify the power of human agency to pry open windows of language planning and policymaking opportunity via individual and collective reimaginings of the possible (Hornberger, 2006a: 233).

Wôpanâak and Miami are perhaps the most dramatic illustrations of these processes. Despite being silenced for more than a century, the Wôpanâak language has been repositioned from the pages of history to the tongues, minds and hearts of 21st century speakers. Despite two forced removals that destroyed their land base and livelihood, Miami tribal members are learning and speaking their heritage language in family homes and communities. These remarkable language revival efforts have occurred through a combination of Native vision and leadership, community support, partnerships with external allies and language documentation. For Native California peoples, a statewide Indigenous-language infrastructure has emerged alongside a network of master–apprentice language learning teams. That infrastructure now supports Indigenous-language regeneration efforts in other US states and is being applied by Indigenous communities around the world.

Kanienkeha and Hawaiian language revitalization began with a few activist parents who envisioned a different future for their children and their ancestral mother tongue 'in a way never dreamed possible' (Mithun & Chafe,

1987: 28). According to Kanerahtahere Michelle A. Davis – and as we see in the data presented here – these successes are directly attributable to high levels of parent involvement, Indigenized teacher pedagogy and curriculum implementation (Davis, 2008: 4). Hawaiian-medium education is now available from preschool to graduate school and has produced a new generation of speakers, many of whom are raising their own children as Hawaiian first-language speakers (Wilson, 2013). At Tséhootsooí Diné Bí'ólta' and Puente de Hózhǫ́, human and material resources, including a substantial number of literacy materials as well as bilingual teachers, are being marshaled to strengthen the Diné language and enhance student achievement. The salutary academic benefits have been ideological resources for program expansion.

These local efforts have spurred and been helped by 'counterpoised' top-down LPP initiatives (López, 2008). For example, in 1997, just a little more than a decade after the founding of Pūnana Leo, the Hawaiian legislature passed a law establishing the University of Hawai'i–Hilo's Hawaiian Language College, enabling programs to be operated through Hawaiian, including the teacher-training program discussed earlier in this chapter (Wilson *et al.*, 2006). Another new policy being piloted at Nāwahī establishes a 'Hawaiian medium mirror image of English medium instruction', whereby all administration and testing can be conducted through Hawaiian 'with a unique curriculum and ... policies relative to the circumstances of Hawaiian' (William H. Wilson, personal communication, 24 July 2008). On the Navajo Nation, local language regeneration initiatives have been helped by the 2005 Navajo Sovereignty in Education Act (NSIEA), which places supervision of reservation schools, including curriculum and assessment, under tribal authority (see the discussion of the NSIEA in Chapter 4).

Although they differ in their social–linguistic circumstances, strategies and goals, all of the cases profiled here exemplify the possibilities for Native American language regeneration. Many, many more examples could be cited, and before leaving this comparative analysis, it is instructive to briefly consider a few.

In Alaska, a region marked by vast distances and remote Native villages, community–university collaborations have been a key LPP strategy. Yup'ik scholar-practitioner Walkie Charles (2005) reports on the Yup'ik Language Institute at the University of Alaska Fairbanks that has enabled extensive corpus planning, teacher preparation and a summer intensive-language program for youth. Dementi-Leonard and Gilmore (1999) examine a grass roots, dialogic language planning effort among 20 Athabaskan communities in western interior Alaska that helped launch a mentor–apprentice program, a university-accredited Athabaskan Language Development Institute, and a career ladder program for language teachers (see also Marlow, 2006). As Dementi-Leonard and Gilmore (1999: 52) write, the dialogue sessions themselves 'seemed to create a free and public space for many of these transformations to occur, a place for affirmation, a place for action'.

Within the Cherokee Nation in northeastern Oklahoma, where most native speakers are over age 40, a comprehensive language plan has been developed with specific activities designed to shore up each of Fishman's stages 6–1 (Cherokee Nation Language Planning Committees, 2008). Lizette Peter (2007), a linguistic anthropologist who has worked closely with the Cherokee Nation's LPP efforts, examines one component, a Cherokee immersion preschool, *Tsalagi Ageyui* (Our Beloved Cherokee). Key to successful language regeneration in this case, she observes, is widespread community recognition that 'teaching the language to children in school [is] central to its survival', and elevation of the status of Cherokee by tribal leaders, who show, by their example, that 'language revitalization [is] a way to exercise power as Cherokee people' (Peter, 2007: 332, 335).

Also in Oklahoma, the Euchee (Yuchi) Language Project is working with a small group of Native-speaking elders – 'our living encyclopedia', says project director Richard Grounds – to create new Euchee language-learning opportunities. Adapting the California MALLP, language learning takes place in the Euchee House and garden, where project participants gather for such activities as after-school classes for children, sewing classes and immersion classes with elders (Grounds, 2011: 103–104). 'As long as we speak Yuchi', says Renée Grounds, Richard Grounds's daughter and the youngest fluent speaker of her language, 'the Yuchi people are still here. Today I am proud to report that we, the Yuchi people, are still here' (Grounds, 2011: 105).

In the foothills of the Rocky Mountains, the 15,000-member Blackfeet Nation of Montana offers a nationally recognized immersion program, *Nizipuhwahsin* (Real Speak). The program is operated by the Piegan Institute, a community-based nonprofit organization founded in 1987 by Blackfeet educators and language activists Darrell Kipp and Dorothy Still Smoking. With guidance from Pūnana Leo personnel, the Piegan Institute has established three K–8 Piegan (Blackfeet) immersion schools, 'cocoons where young children grow as Blackfeet' while also excelling in the English-based public schools they enter upon graduation (Kehoe, 2001: 4; see also Briggeman, 2007). 'You teach the children and they will show your success,' says Kipp (Kipp, 2000: 13).

In an Ojibwe reservation of 3000 in Minnesota, there were, in 2007, 10 fluent speakers – all elderly (Hermes, 2007). There, an Ojibwe immersion school, Waadookodaading, was started in 2000. Reminiscent of Dorothy Lazore's reflections on Akwesasne, Mary Hermes, an Indigenous scholar, teacher and language planner who helped found the school, writes that, 'we were creating the curriculum with nothing but a dictionary, a few grammar books, and a few elders ... the entire curriculum needed to be newly created' (Hermes, 2007: 59). According to Hermes, Waadookodaading has been 'heralded as a success'; it has grown from a few families to many, and children are learning Ojibwe while keeping up with the standard curriculum (Hermes, 2007: 59).

The nine Potawatomi tribes, diasporized through forced relocation from Oklahoma to Wisconsin to Michigan to Kansas to Ontario, count only 52 elderly speakers among 47,000 tribal members in the United States (Wetzel, 2006). Like other language regenesis projects discussed here, the Potawatomi are tackling language regeneration on multiple fronts, including language enrichment classes in Oklahoma with plans for a preschool, adult language classes and a tribal school in Michigan, a summer youth program in a second Michigan community, and a Potawatomi Language Scholars College convened at multiple locations throughout Potawatomi Country (Wetzel, 2006). These various projects 'are inextricably situated in the matrix of tribal life', sociologist Christopher Wetzel observes, but taken together, they create 'new prospects for imagining the [Potawatomi] nation':

> In these efforts there is no agenda to homogenize approaches to revitalization, to promote a unified national language over local vernaculars, or to preempt tribal linguistic pedagogies. National programs encourage and sustain tribal endeavors. (Wetzel, 2006: 80–81)

Wetzel's observation can be applied to all of the cases explored here. All are exemplars of grass roots, bottom-up language planning undertaken in response to particular sociocultural and sociohistorical contexts, and to contemporary local needs and desires. These projects are, as Messing and Rockwell (2006: 249) note for Mexicano (Nahuatl) in Mexico, opening new 'discursive space for the discussion of language shift and revitalization'. At the same time, they are elevating the scale of community languages (Blommaert, 2010) by creating new language genres and uses in public and private spaces. This social–cultural and linguistic–pedagogic work undergirds and is reinforced by a network of activists and organizations who are part of a more widespread language rights movement that has found expression in official policies such as NALA and EM-NALPA (see Appendices 1 and 2), and in such organizations as the American Indian Language Development Institute (McCarty *et al.*, 2001), the Indigenous Language Institute, the Foundation for Endangered Languages, the Breath of Life Workshops and the Stabilizing Indigenous Languages Symposium. These local, tribal and national efforts in turn have both benefited from and galvanized international language rights endeavors, reflected in the 2007 United Nations *Declaration on the Rights of Indigenous Peoples*, UNESCO's initiatives on language vitality and endangerment (e.g. UNESCO Ad Hoc Expert Group on Endangered Languages, 2003) and the UN Permanent Forum on Indigenous Issues (for more on these international efforts, see McCarty *et al.*, 2008; Skutnabb-Kangas, 2000, 2008; Skutnabb-Kangas *et al.*, forthcoming).

This LPP activity represents social practice *and* praxis – a powerful force for linguistic self-determination and *choice* that embraces a shared communal identification (Meyer, 2012). 'Learning the language of one's people does not force you to live your life in one and only one way', Wayne Holm points out; '[a]s a young adult, you can choose *whether* to use your language, *who* to use your language with, and *what* things you will talk about in your language' (Holm, 2006: 41–42). The language regeneration cases examined here have, as Dementi-Leonard and Gilmore observe, carved out space 'for the freedom to resist and challenge oppressive obstacles', to refute hegemonic attitudes, and to 'envision the unseen' (Dementi-Leonard & Gilmore, 1999: 53). Fundamental expressions of tribal sovereignty, these efforts demonstrate the human potential to reclaim local languages and the cultural systems they represent for Indigenous young people of today and tomorrow – the focus of the next chapter.

Notes

(1) In the section on Miami, 'personal communication' refers to Teresa McCarty's personal communications with Myaamia Project personnel, some of whom are also coauthors on the Miami section of this chapter. For autobiographical accounts by many of the language planners discussed in this chapter, see Hinton (2013).
(2) I thank Dr Norvin Richards of the Department of Linguistics and Philosophy at Massachusetts Institute of Technology for invaluable feedback on the Wôpanâak language revitalization initiatives discussed in this section.
(3) Wôpanâak is the spelling of the Wampanoag language used in most tribal documents and by the Wôpanâak Language Reclamation Project. Wampanoag is the official name of the tribes that comprise the Wampanoag Nation (Ash *et al.*, 2001: 28). Here, Wôpanâak is used with reference to the language, and Wampanoag for the tribal nation.
(4) I thank Dr Leanne Hinton, Linguistics Professor Emerita at the University of California Berkeley and cofounder of the California Master–Apprentice Language Learning Program, for providing generous and extremely valuable feedback on the language revitalization initiatives explored in this section. Parts of this section are adapted from Coronel-Molina and McCarty (2011).
(5) I thank Dr Louellyn White, Assistant Professor of First Peoples Studies in the School of Community and Public Affairs at Concordia University, for reviewing and providing expert commentary on the Mohawk section of this chapter, and in particular, for her very helpful insights on the Akwesasne Freedom School.
(6) There are various spellings for Kanienkehaka, Kanienkeha/Kanienke:ha, and Kahnawà:ke/Kahnawake. I use those found most commonly in the literature and online, and/or those used by specific communities and schools (e.g. Kahnawake Survival School but Mohawk Council of Kahnawà:ke).
(7) Leonard (2007) uses the term 'scholar–practitioner' to counter discourses that differentiate 'scholarly' from 'applied' work, pointing out that the two are not mutually exclusive. 'In particular, many people involved in language reclamation ... make a concerted effort to blend the two' (Leonard, 2007: 2). I have also adopted the use of this term in the discussion of cases presented here.
(8) According to Hoover and the KRCC, an unforeseen effect of Kanienkeha immersion was the creation of a generation of adult tribal citizens 'who were not given the opportunity to learn to speak Mohawk, and find themselves surrounded by [younger] Mohawk speakers' (Hoover & Kanien'kehaka Raotitiohkwa Cultural Center, 1992: 271). Adult immersion classes such as those discussed later in this chapter are one effort to provide these language-learning opportunities.

(9) According to Louellyn White, the size of the Akwesasne reservation land and water may be confusing because it is controlled both by the Mohawk Council of Akwesasne (within Canada) and the St Regis Mohawk Tribe (within the United States). White points out that 'Many services are duplicated, reporting is separate, and sometimes acres are reported that do not include water along the St. Lawrence'. Akwesasne's official website (www.akwesasne.ca) includes both sides of the reserve and both land and water (Louellyn White, personal communication, 8 May 2012).
(10) I am deeply grateful to Dr William H. Wilson for extensive commentary on the section on Hawaiian-medium schooling, and to Drs Wilson and Kauanoe Kamanā for their generous contribution of photographs illustrating the Nāwahī Laboratory School.
(11) The illegality of the Hawaiian takeover was formally acknowledged 100 years later in the Hawai'i Apology Act, whereby Congress noted that 'the United States Minister assigned to the sovereign and independent Kingdom of Hawaii conspired with a small group of non-Hawaiian residents ... to overthrow the indigenous and lawful Government of Hawaii' (Hawaii Apology Act, Preamble, Sect. I[1]).
(12) I thank Dr Wayne Holm, former director of the Navajo Nation Language Project and of the bilingual/immersion programs at Fort Defiance and Rock Point, Arizona, and Dr Michael Fillerup, director of bilingual/English as a Second Language education in the Flagstaff Unified School District, for extremely valuable feedback on the Navajo section of this chapter.
(13) Magnet schools are public schools with specialized programs and curricula – in this case, two parallel language immersion programs. The term 'magnet' refers to the fact that these schools draw their enrollments from throughout the school district (i.e. not necessarily from the surrounding neighborhood or local feeder schools).

6 Language in the Lives of Indigenous Youth

Teresa L. McCarty with Mary Eunice Romero-Little, Larisa Warhol and Ofelia Zepeda

> *Parents did not teach the [Native] language because they loved us and they didn't want us to suffer, to be abused, or to have a tough life ... they tried to protect us from the humiliation and suffering that they went through.*
> Darrell R. Kipp, Blackfeet language educator and activist, 2000: 7

> *I just want to learn [my Native language] real bad ... because I think it is a big important part of my life if I am going to be a Native.*
> 'Damen', youth interview, 1 June 2004

The statements above – the first by Darrell R. Kipp, cofounder of the Piegan Institute discussed in Chapter 5, and the second by a 14-year-old Native youth who we interviewed in 2004 – illuminate the intergenerational dynamics of language shift and reclamation, situating those processes within the metaphorical safety zone and the legacy of colonial schooling. The excerpts also suggest young people's desires to be full participants in their cultural communities – desires they explicitly link to learning their heritage mother tongue.

In this chapter, authored with my co-investigators on a large-scale study of Native language shift and retention – Mary Eunice Romero-Little, Larisa Warhol and Ofelia Zepeda – we examine the language practices, repertoires and ideologies of Native American youth, arguably the most crucial stakeholders in Indigenous language futures. As Euchee youth language activist Renée Grounds writes, 'My generation is the most important because we are the last ones who have the chance to learn the language from our elders and speak it to our children as their first language' (Grounds, 2011: 97). How are members of this generation responding to dynamic situations of language shift? How is language use situated in the 'here and now' (Bucholtz, 2002) of young people's everyday lives? What is the nature of youth's communicative repertoires? What ideologies about language do youth hold, and how do those ideologies influence their language practices and their ethnic, linguistic and academic identities? What can we learn from a closer look at youth language practices to inform community-based language reclamation?

We begin by reviewing the relatively limited but growing literature on Indigenous youth and bi/multilingualism, focusing on Native North America. We then discuss findings from the five-year (2001–2006) Native Language Shift and Retention Study, which we undertook with seven American Indian school-community sites in the US Southwest. Within that discussion, we present narrative portraits crafted from in-depth interviews with youth that illuminate facets of the questions above. As we will show, the portraits counter stereotypes of youth as disinterested in their heritage languages, even as they foreground the highly complex and ideologically fraught cultural and sociolinguistic environments in which youth are growing up. The youth accounts lead us to consider another group of stakeholders – young adults – many of whom are parents beginning to establish family language policies of their own. In the final part of the chapter, we relate the youth and young adult accounts to Simon Ortiz's (1992, 1994) notion of *cultural continuance* (see also Dunsmore, 2009) – a notion that pushes us to think beyond survival and 'saving' Indigenous languages, to (re)value the hybridity of youth communicative repertoires, and to build language regenesis efforts around that hybridity rather than to deny or negate it, thereby fostering youth self-empowerment.

Research on Native American Youth Language Practices[1]

Although much has been written on language shift and revitalization, studies from the perspectives of speakers themselves are still relatively rare (King & Ganuza, 2005; for counter-examples, see Kouritzin, 1999; Todeva & Cenoz, 2009). As King and Ganuza (2005) point out in their analysis of linguistic identification among Chilean–Swedish transmigrant adolescents, and as Meek (2007, 2010) also notes in her study of Kaska revitalization in the Yukon territory, even rarer are studies that privilege the voices of children and youth.

One of the first published studies to document the processes underlying language shift among Native North American youth was undertaken by Clifford Pye (1992) among the Chilcotin of central British Columbia. Pye argues that any analysis of language loss must also look closely at language acquisition – specifically the ways in which children 'learn to speak only one language even though two languages are present in their environment' (Pye, 1992: 75). At the time of Pye's research, Chilcotin children were being raised 'within earshot' of the Indigenous language (Pye, 1992: 80). A combination of English-only schooling, the importation of television reception into the community and the colonialist positioning of Chilcotin as subordinate to English all served to tip 'the scales against the maintenance of the

Chilcotin language' (Pye, 1992: 77). Importantly, Pye's research also showed that the English that children acquired in these contexts was significantly modified by the structure and use patterns of the Indigenous language – a finding reinforced in our own research, and which has been documented for Indigenous communities around the world (see, e.g. Warner [1999a] on Hawaiian and Kulick [1992] on Taiap in Papua New Guinea). Thus, says Pye, 'Rather than assimilating into the mainstream culture, the Chilcotin encounter as much discrimination based on their [creolized English] as ever' (Pye, 1992: 84).

Evangeline Parsons-Yazzie (1996/1997) found similar processes at work in her examination of the interruption of intergenerational transmission among rural Navajo families. As she writes in a translation of eloquent oral testimony by her mother, a gifted Navajo rug weaver:

> Our children are the rugs that we parents are weaving, but the yarns (warp) were cut before we could finish our teachings of the language, the culture, the beliefs and the traditions. The schools, the missionaries, we parents, ... and our own fears were what cut the yarns. Now our children will not be complete, because we did not place all the designs on our children that let other people know that our children are Navajo. (Parsons-Yazzie, 1996/1997: 60)[2]

Parsons-Yazzie interviewed Navajo-speaking parents and elders from two reservation communities whose children attended a nearby boarding school and did not speak Navajo, focusing on 10 children in grades 1–8 for in-depth case studies. Although all the children had access to Navajo-speaking family members and most had receptive abilities in Navajo, virtually all – like the Chilcotin youth in Pye's study – chose English to respond to adults' initiations in Navajo. Parsons-Yazzie attributes this to the influence of modern technology, enhanced mobility via automobiles, television – 'The television is robbing our children of language', one elder said – and schooling – 'When [my children] came back [from school] they came back not remembering their language', another parent reported (Parsons-Yazzie, 1996: 55–56). In short, children and youth 'just preferred to speak English and the adults were not persistent in responding in Navajo'– a factor Parsons-Yazzie relates, as reflected in the epigraph that begins this chapter, to parents' feelings of linguistic ambivalence bred in the boarding schools (Parsons-Yazzie, 1996/1997: 60, 64). Writing about these findings 10 years later, Wayne Holm adds that, 'In these and many other ways, young children set the language policy of the home; they train the adults around them to speak only English' (Holm, 2006: 7).[3]

Children 'setting the language policy of the home' is a common theme in discussions of language shift; under duress or social pressure, the decision to abandon the ancestral language is often made by the youngest speakers, who in turn influence the language practices of adults. Harrison writes in *When Languages Die*:

> The youngest speakers – acting as tiny social barometers – are acutely sensitive to the disfavored status of their elders' language and may choose to speak the more dominant tongue. Once this happens, the decision tends to be irreversible. (Harrison, 2007: 8)

However, as more recent research (including our own) shows, even as young people may be agents of language endangerment, when 'their circumstances and language-learning opportunities change, youth ... may still activate their heritage languages to productive levels and become the authorizing agents moving their languages forward in the future' (McCarty & Wyman, 2009: 286).

Tiffany Lee (2007, 2009, 2013), for example, explores youth negotiations of 'mixed messages' among Navajo and Pueblo adolescents and young adults. In Lee's first study, undertaken with 215 Navajo students in five reservation high schools, she found that, while Navajo language courses had a 'direct and positive influence' on students' Navajo abilities, including their 'commitment' to the language, school was so strongly associated with English that even Navajo-speaking students rarely used Navajo at school (Lee, 2007). Further, while all of the youth affirmed the value of the Navajo language, they were also acutely aware of demeaning stereotypes that associate speaking Navajo with 'backwardness' and lack of education – findings supported by our research as well.

In the second study, Lee (2009, 2013) documented ethnographically the competing ideologies of Native-language respect, stigmatization and shame expressed by Navajo and Pueblo young adults and present in their home-community environments. However, she also observed a 'critical Indigenous consciousness' and agency among these young adults, manifest in youth-initiated community language advocacy, conscious changes in family language policies, and the development of language-learning materials for younger relatives. In other words, Lee explains, 'these youth expressed a desire to intervene through their own research, language practices at home, and personal efforts to learn their heritage language' (Lee, 2009: 317). 'These young people are trying to make a difference', Lee maintains; 'reflecting a critical Indigenous consciousness, they are asserting their agency in reversing language shift' (Lee, 2009: 318). Wilson and Kamanā (2009: 374) note similar counter-trends by Native Hawaiian youth, who 'are becoming leaders in the Hawaiian language revitalization movement'.

Bielenberg (2002) and Nicholas (2005, 2009, 2011) studied the family-, community- and school-based dynamics that influence Hopi youth's language learning and language practices. In both studies, youth expressed a desire to learn their heritage language, but they also expressed fear of being ridiculed for linguistic errors: 'People sometimes laugh at you', one youth reported, 'and you don't want to speak it anymore' (quoted in Bielenberg, 2002, p. 250). Nonetheless, like Lee's findings for Navajo youth, Nicholas argues that Hopi youth possess a deep respect for the Hopi language, as embodied in oral tradition – 'song words, prayer, teachings, ritual performances, religious ceremonies, and cultural institutions' – which Nicholas calls the 'total communicative framework' (Nicholas, 2009: 333). She theorizes this as a process of 'affective enculturation' played out in the context of still-vital Hopi cultural practices that reinforce a strong Hopi identity among youth, including the desire to learn the Hopi language. While the youth in Nicholas's study yearned for the 'missing pieces' – the meanings of cultural practices embedded in the language – they nonetheless 'hold tightly to the Hopi way of life; they are bound to it by habit, intellect, and choice' (Nicholas, 2009: 332, 333).

Working in Alaska, Wyman (2004, 2009, 2012) followed two consecutive groups of Yup'ik Alaskan adolescents riding the cusp of linguistic tip: those known locally as the 'last real speakers' and a younger group identified within the community as those just 'getting by' (GB) in Yup'ik. Tracing ethnographically the GB group's 'strategic moment-to-moment emphasis or erasure of language boundaries', Wyman (2004: iv) reveals the complicated and contradictory workings of language ideology within youth peer culture, showing how youth '... broker language maintenance, shift, endangerment and/or ... revitalization ... [as they] navigate and transform the sociolinguistic worlds around them' (Wyman 2012: 1–2). Wyman finds that, 'Although Yup'ik was in the process of disappearing as a peer language among the GB group', Yup'ik 'remained one of a set of markers of local belonging' used to create a distinct peer culture (Wyman, 2004: 255, 256).

Also in the Far North, Tulloch (2004) examined Inuit youth language attitudes in three Nunavut Baffin Island communities where Inuktitut is the first official language and enjoys explicit government protection. There, Inuktitut is the mother tongue of the majority of youth, who not only speak and understand the language well, but read and write it. Yet Inuit youth express insecurity in speaking their mother tongue; 'they recognize language loss in their own lives and attribute it to the encroaching presence of English' (Tulloch, 2004: 5). Arguing that language attitudes are key to understanding language choices, Tulloch documents ethnographically the complex interaction of youth's perceived linguistic competence, language use and language attitudes. While Inuktitut is the language of access to family, community and Inuit history, English is perceived by youth as both 'cool' and necessary for life opportunities in Nunavut and beyond. The future of Inuktitut 'is hopeful, but uncertain', Tulloch concludes, as youth 'witness language loss first-hand in their own lives as they transfer to English as their dominant language' (Tulloch, 2004: 415).

Leonard (2007) presents a different but complementary portrait of the acquisition of Miami as a first language alongside English by Daryl and Karen Baldwin's youngest children (see the discussion of Miami in Chapter 5). In this sociolinguistic case study, Leonard illuminates the interplay of an explicit family language policy ('speak Miami whenever possible') with wider tribal and supratribal LPP efforts. In this case, the Baldwin children were increasingly immersed in situations inside and outside the home in which the 'Miami language and Miaminess are valued and esteemed', facilitating their bilingual development and social–psychological identification as Miami (Leonard, 2007: 223).

Finally, an emerging literature explores the ways in which Native American youth take up elements of popular culture – global hip-hop, for example – to create new heritage language uses and forms. In a case study of 'Jay', a Navajo underground hip-hop artist, O'Connor and Brown examine the ways in which he employs multiple semiotic resources to negotiate 'what it means to be an Indigenous person within the postmodern nation-state' (O'Connor & Brown, 2013 [in press]). Jay's innovative language practices, O'Connor and Brown argue, reappropriate conventional notions of Navajo/Indigenous identity, highlighting 'the dilemmas of identity' many Native youth encounter 'in everday life', and the ways in which their participation in translocal style communities open new pathways for linguistic and cultural expression (O'Connor & Brown, 2013 [in press]; see also Hornberger & Swinehart, 2012, for an analysis of similar processes among Quechua and Aymara young adults in the Andes).

Each of these studies reveals interlaced micro, macro and meso forces that serve to accelerate, divert or interrupt language shift among younger generations. In the remainder of this chapter we explore these processes in greater depth, drawing on findings from a multi-site study of American Indian youth language competencies, ideologies and practices.

Youth Language Practices, Ideologies, and Desires

About the study

In the spring of 2001, with funding from the US Department of Education, we embarked on a multi-year study of the impact of Native language shift and retention on American Indian student's language learning, identity formation and academic achievement.[4] The project responded to a 1998 Executive (Presidential) Order calling for research to 'evaluate the role of native language and culture in the development of educational strategies' for Native American students (Executive Order 13096, 1998, Section 2, [f][3]). Given the limited research on Indigenous youth language attitudes, ideologies and practices, our goal was to investigate how language loss and revitalization are experienced 'on the ground' by Native youth – and with what consequences for their language practices, identities and school achievement.

We did not 'recruit' research participants in the conventional sense, but instead worked with Indigenous communities with whom we had developed long-standing relationships through our work in Indigenous education. Seven school-community sites participated in the study, representing a cross-section of linguistic ecologies – from those in which intergenerational transmission of the Native language was still taking place (albeit at a diminishing rate), to those in which nearly all heritage language speakers were beyond childbearing age, to cases in which there were only a few elderly Native-language speakers. Rural reservation and urban settings were represented among the seven schools serving these communities, which together enrolled 2039 Native students in grades pre-K–12.

Over half of the families represented in the study were living below federal poverty levels; in some cases, median household incomes fell far below median per capita income for the US population as a whole. Unemployment was extremely high – as much as 80% – at the project sites. These profound economic disparities mirrored local educational disparities. The high school completion rate among community members at project sites ranged from 33% to 51% – as much as half the national average and slightly lower than the percentage for the American Indian/Alaska Native population as a whole. All but two of the seven schools faced some form of 'corrective action' under the federal No Child Left Behind Act of 2001.

At each site, we worked closely with teams of Indigenous educators identified as community research collaborators (CRCs). The CRCs facilitated entrée and access, validated the cultural and linguistic appropriateness of our research protocols, assisted with data collection, and participated in university-accredited coursework on language planning and ethnographic and sociolinguistic research methods. They were the critical change agents positioned to apply the study's findings when the project grant ended.

We employed an ethnographic case study approach, making 80 site visits over five years to collect data, debrief and plan with the CRCs, and report back to tribal councils, school boards and other stakeholders. Our data included demographic records, one- to three-hour audiotaped interviews with 168 adults and 62 children and youth in grades 3–12, sociolinguistic questionnaires (500) designed to elicit participants' language practices and attitudes, observation of language use and teaching, documents (lesson plans, school mission statements, etc.) and student achievement data collected by individual districts and the state education agency. The qualitative data alone produced more than 3300 pages of single-spaced text. Of those data, the ethnographic interviews constitute the largest corpus, and that is the data corpus we examine here.

In structuring interviews, we adapted Seidman's (2006) three-interview sequence, condensing his tripartite format into single 60- to 120-minute interviews that included:

(1) a focused life history, concentrating on home and school language learning experiences;
(2) details and observations of language use at home, at school, and within the community; and

(3) normative assessments of the role of families, community members, tribal governments, and the school in language education planning.

Interview and other qualitative data were coded using NVivo 7, a software tool for organizing, retrieving, analyzing and interpreting detailed text data. We first generated codes inductively in whole-day data analysis workshops involving the university-based research team. NVivo 7 was then used to search, retrieve, and display data in a condensed, organized framework (see, e.g. Weitzman, 2000: 805–806). Coded data were grouped into smaller sets of recurrent themes. (For more on the study's methodology, see McCarty et al., 2006a, 2009b; Romero-Little et al., 2007.) Initial findings and interpretations were shared and discussed in consultation with the CRCs. The data were then used to craft qualitative case studies for each site (McCarty et al., 2007). Within each case study, the narrative profiles of youth language practices, competencies and beliefs or ideologies about language became focal points of the analysis.

As we have reported elsewhere (McCarty et al., 2006a, 2006b, 2009a, 2009b), a key finding from this study was a pronounced difference between the perspectives on youth's language abilities, practices and beliefs held by adults, and those expressed and manifested by the youth themselves. Figure 6.1 compares educators' and youth's characterizations of students' home-community language environments. With the exception of one site where Navajo is spoken (site 3), most educators reported that very few (0–20%) of their students were likely to hear the Indigenous language spoken at home or in their communities. In contrast, many youth (47–90%) reported hearing the Indigenous language spoken at home, at tribal events, and in various other contexts within their communities. Similarly, when we asked adults and youth to characterize youth's linguistic abilities, the majority of educators reported that very few (0–20%) of their students spoke an Indigenous language 'fluently', while youth described more hybrid, varied language abilities (see Figure 6.2).

The same differences were reflected in the interview data, with educators characterizing local Indigenous languages as largely absent from young people's lives and youth as often indifferent to learning their heritage language. At the same time, students were likely to be labeled as 'limited English proficient' or 'language delayed' because they spoke a variety of English influenced by the local Indigenous language, and because of their performance on English standardized tests. These labeling practices found their way into school curricula and other official documents, where, at several school sites, their certification in print served to cement the notion that students' language practices constituted a problem in need of remediation – what Meek (2011) calls a logic of linguistic incompetence or 'dysfluency'. The state-prescribed remediation was to intensify scripted English reading instruction, leading to the reduction or elimination of Indigenous language and culture

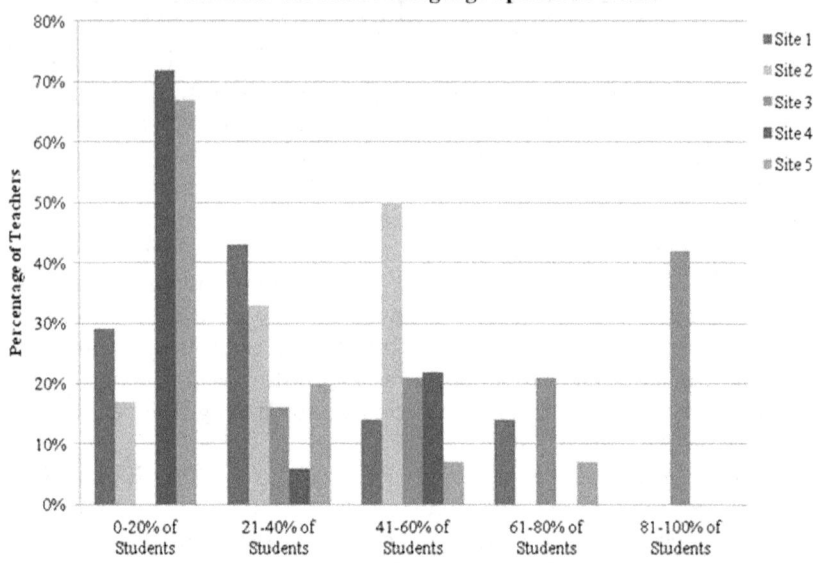

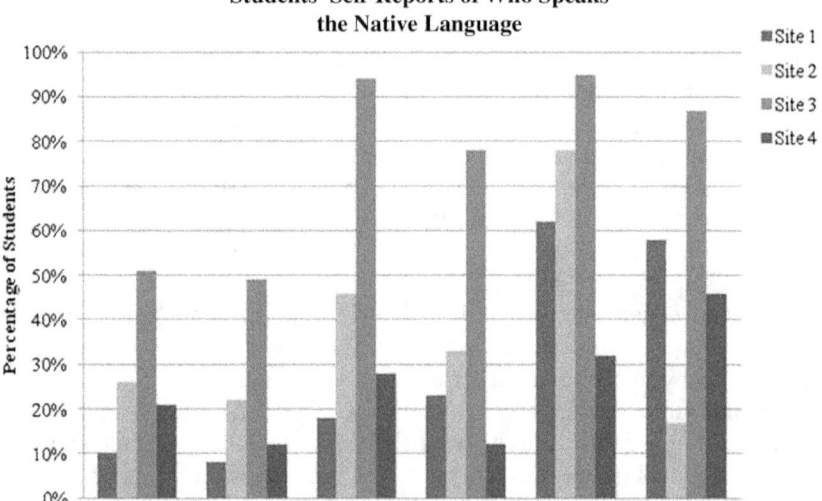

Figure 6.1 Comparison of educators' assessments and students' self-reports of students' home-community language environments (NL = Native language)

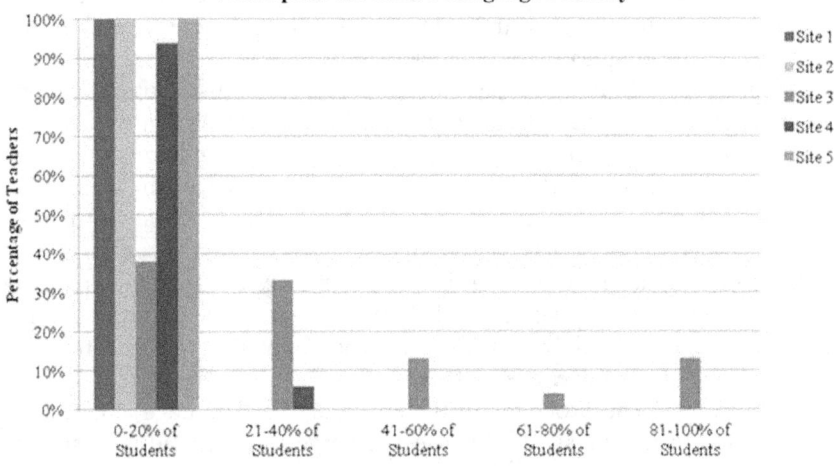

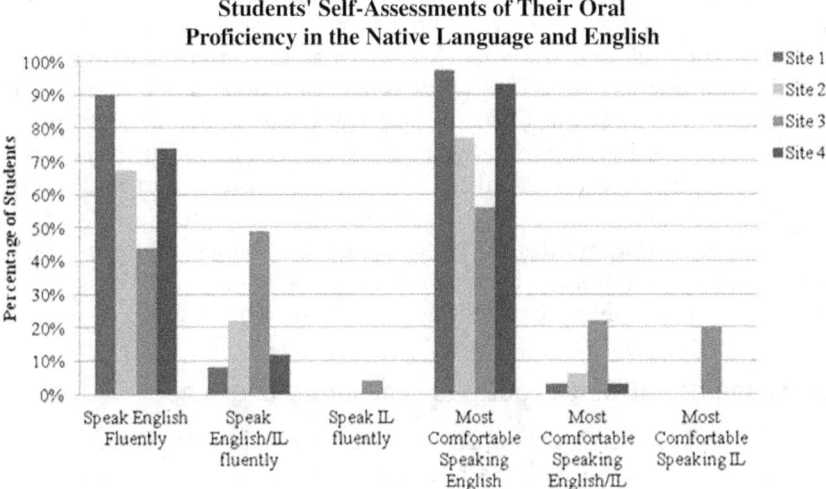

Figure 6.2 Comparison of educators' assessments and students' self-assessments of students' oral proficiency in the local Indigenous language (IL)

instruction. As one teacher noted, 'All the [bilingual–bicultural] curriculum we developed went out the door' (field notes, 17 February 2004). This fueled what Ajit Mohanty and his associates describe as 'the vicious cycle of language disadvantage' whereby Indigenous languages are pushed out of significant public domains (e.g. school), 'restricting their scope and development' (Mohanty et al., 2009: 283).

Yet, even as their language practices and communicative repertoires were often constructed as limited and a hindrance to school-defined 'success', youth testified to complex and dynamic sociolinguistic environments in which multiple languages and language varieties – one or more Indigenous languages, English and Spanish – were present but distributed unevenly among members of different age groups and households. As Figure 6.2 shows, most youth reported feeling 'most comfortable' speaking English, but they also described being 'overhearers' of some variety/ies of an Indigenous language – at home, at cultural events and in some cases on local radio broadcasts. Further, some youth had entered school as primary speakers of an Indigenous language and/or Spanish, and some were learning to read and write their heritage language as well. As we will see in the narrative profiles, youth also expressed deep yearnings for the opportunity to become more capable users of their heritage mother tongue.

Recognizing the problems with self-reports of language abilities and desires (see, e.g. Krauss, 1998), these divergent youth–adult responses nevertheless raise questions about the reasons underlying the differences. Were the adults simply unaware of what was occurring with regard to language in youth's lives (even though many adults were community members themselves)? Were youth 'closeting' their Indigenous-language abilities and desires – and if so, why? What was happening in these social contexts to influence young people's language practices and the perceptions of those practices by adults?[5] Answering these questions, we believed, could shed new light on ways to enhance language pedagogy and Indigenous-language recovery. With these goals in mind, we now present a sample of the youth narrative profiles. Although space prohibits a full exposition of our database, each profile illuminates facets of a larger case. We go first to the pseudonymous Black Foothills Unified School District.

Language use at Black Foothills community and school

The Black Foothills School District (all names are pseudonyms) ranks among the largest urban public school districts in the United States, with 113 schools and more than 60,000 students and 3700 teachers at the time of the study. When we began research at Black Foothills in 2003, the district had been under a federal desegregation order for more than two decades – a period punctuated by lawsuits filed by African American and Mexican American parents alleging racial segregation, and by Native American parents citing unstocked libraries, the absence of a science curriculum, and open mine shafts and contaminated water and soil just outside the schools their children attended.

Within this school district one of our sites was Cactus High. Located in a working class Latino and Native American neighborhood in a large metropolitan area, Cactus High enrolled over 1600 students, of whom 11% (168) were Native American, 67% (1131) were Hispanic, 4% (69) were African

American and 17% (287) were White. At Cactus High we heard from educators (who, in this case, were mostly non-Native) that:

> English is [students'] first language and everyone speaks English in the home ... there is just no [Indigenous language] in the family. (Interview, 10 May 2004)

> [W]hen I have spoken to the families they have never mentioned that [the Indigenous language] is their native language ... so I don't believe that the kids ... are very familiar with or influenced by ... [the Indigenous language] – mostly ... well, mostly English. (Interview, 10 May 2004)

Introducing Nora

Nora Valenzuela was an 18-year-old senior and softball star at Cactus High when we interviewed her in 2004. Nora's grandparents were survivors of the diaspora of Indigenous people who had fled northern Mexico in the wake of a scorched earth campaign that preceded the Mexican Revolution. (At the request of the tribe and to protect its privacy, we do not use the tribe's name or the name of its language.) Nora's grandparents' family had settled near an emerging urban area in the US Southwest. Nora grew up hearing the stories of hardship endured in the diaspora, and through tribal summer programs she had visited the original villages in Mexico where many of her relatives still lived.

Nora's father worked in landscaping at the tribal casino on the edge of town; her mother was a teaching assistant at the tribal preschool. As Nora was growing up, her mother 'spoke [the Indigenous language] to us ... almost all the time, everyday', she said. Her father grew up with Spanish as a primary language and 'just spoke to us in Spanish', Nora added. However, having been married to Nora's mother for many years, 'he's starting to understand the [Indigenous] language'.

Nora entered elementary school bilingual in the Indigenous language and Spanish, and understanding some English, 'but I couldn't speak it well. So I had to go to some kind of tutoring ... It was ... difficult for me'. At the same time, she related, 'I started forgetting how to speak [the Indigenous language], because my dad's family [speaks Spanish] and they were there most of the time'.

At home, at school and in her cultural community, Nora moved fluently between multiple linguistic systems; she was an adept 'translanguager' (García, 2009; García *et al.*, 2007; Williams, 1994). This interview excerpt illustrates Nora's interfamilial and intergenerational linguistic border-crossing:

> To my brothers I use Spanish [but] my youngest [brother], he doesn't really understand Spanish, so I speak English with him, and with my mom and grandmother, it would be [the Indigenous language]. (Interview, 11 May 2004)

Moreover, Nora articulated a clear understanding of the language pragmatics of her household and community, as this response to our interview question illustrates:

Interviewer: Your parents – when they visit with people their own age, do you notice if they have a preference [for the languages they use]?

Nora: My dad speaks English when he is working landscaping at the casino, and my mom speaks both languages, English and [the Indigenous language], 'cause her co-workers ... all speak the [Indigenous] language. But if they were to go outside [the community], like to conferences, they would speak English. (Interview, 11 May 2004)

Introducing Vaida

Vaida King was Nora's close friend. Vaida was a member of the same cultural community and a trumpeter in a well-known mariachi band. The two girls had gone to school together since elementary school. Vaida's father also worked in landscaping; her mother stayed at home, caring for the children of Vaida's older sister while their mother was at work.

Vaida reported that her 'first language is Spanish and ... that was the main language spoken around the house ... except for English when we would use it from time to time, but overall Spanish ... was the main language'. Her maternal grandmother and her father's family spoke the Indigenous language but 'overall', Vaida reiterated, 'I've never really heard it [at home]' (interview, 11 May 2004).

Vaida entered elementary school bilingual in Spanish and English; English 'was not difficult for me', she said, 'because I pretty much really knew it'. With her peers she spoke Spanish, although, as she said, 'English or Spanish, no difference'. Like Nora, Vaida articulated a clear understanding of the tacit language policies within her community: 'Yeah, ... some people, they will communicate in Spanish, but if they have to go somewhere, say for an interview or to meet someone, they would speak English' (interview, 11 May 2004).

Prior to the implementation of No Child Left Behind (NCLB), the feeder schools for Cactus High offered instructional programs in the Indigenous language taught by teaching assistants from the Native American community. Vaida and Nora had participated in these programs, and both expressed frustration and disappointment that the classes had been canceled when their language teachers were determined to lack NCLB 'highly qualified' credentials – an associate's degree or equivalent. Although they were esteemed elders in their community – among an elite group of trilingual culture-bearers – they did not possess the NCLB-required degree and were therefore dismissed from the school district's employ or reassigned to low-level clerical positions.

Asked whether schools with significant Native American enrollments should offer Native language and culture instruction, Vaida insisted that, 'It is something of our own that we should know'. Recalling the hardships of the diaspora, she added: 'Our ancestors had to sacrifice to get us here ... [This is] our entire history and culture ... we appreciate what our people had to deal with' (interview, 11 May 2004).

Both Vaida and Nora worried that their heritage language was in danger of falling silent; according to census data, a little over 100 individuals within their cultural community reported speaking the Indigenous language at home, and most were beyond child-bearing age. '[There are] only certain people who know the language', Vaida pointed out:

> What would happen if those people become deceased? I think [the Indigenous language] is a very precious thing, and that they [tribal citizens] should know – I should know. (Interview, 11 May 2004)

Vaida and Nora were not alone in expressing a yearning for their heritage language, or in the sociolinguistic dexterity they evidenced. We go now to another school community in our study, which we call Ak Wijid.

Language use at Ak Wijid community and school

The K–8 Ak Wijid School is located just outside another major metropolitan area, within a 16,000-member Native American nation that includes two distinct Indigenous-language groups. Flanked by low-lying desert mountains, the community is bisected by an expansive floodplain. Once a primary source of livelihood for the Native peoples of the region, the river was diverted for irrigation by White farmers in the early 20th century. This had life-altering ramifications for Native families, as they were forced to relocate near irrigable land or to seek off-reservation wage labor. As individuals were pulled into a cash economy, traditional village structures dissolved, setting the stage for the breakdown of intergenerational language transmission. Although a water settlement was reached in the 1990s, these historical experiences and the imposition of English-only mission schools a century earlier served to 'tip' (Dorian, 1981) community language use. As one community member stated:

> My mother grew up and saw the bad things that were done by the [missionaries] over at the school ..., punishing them for speaking their own language, trying to convert them ... She didn't want us to go through that ... She spoke to us in English. (Interview, 9 August 2006)

Introducing Damen

Damen Johns was a 14-year-old eighth grader attending Ak Wijid Middle School at the time of the interview. A class president and star three-point shooter, he had recently been named Most Valuable Player of his school's basketball team. Damen aspired to go to the nearby state university and one day to play for the National Basketball Association.

Damen was from a family of well-known Indigenous artisans. Damen's mother had grown up hearing her parents' language (one of the two Indigenous languages spoken in the community) but her parents, who were mission school survivors, had raised their children primarily in English, and Damen's mother rarely used the Indigenous language with her own children at home. 'I really don't hear her [speak the language]', Damen said, adding that his mother was attentive to and appreciative of his and his sisters' language learning at school: '[S]he will listen to us, what we are saying, or I will go home and tell her what I learned and she will ask me what certain words mean, ... and I tell her' (interview, 1 June 2004).

Damen's mother was raising Damen and his two sisters as a single parent, and because she worked full-time outside the home, Damen had spent his early years going 'back and forth', in his words, between his mother's and his maternal grandparents' households. There, he was exposed to the Indigenous language. Damen's maternal grandfather, who had passed away some years before, had been a great influence on him: he was 'the one that told me about Native stuff', Damen recalled; '[h]e was pretty cool and he was always part of the tradition, and I thank him for that' (interview, 1 June 2004).

Damen was growing up in an environment that included his maternal grandparents' native language as well as a linguistically unrelated Indigenous language that was the heritage language of his father. The community's agricultural base had drawn farmworkers from Mexico, and northern Mexican Spanish was part of Damen's sociolinguistic environment. In addition, because the community bordered a sprawling metropolitan area and had been the object of extended missionization, English had a prominent if conflicted role in the community's sociolinguistic ecology as well.

Damen's primary language was English, but he was growing up 'within earshot' (Pye, 1992) of multiple languages and language varieties. Although his Indigenous-language abilities were admittedly weak, he insisted repeatedly that:

> I want to learn it real bad ... I just want to learn my language because I think it is a big important part of my life if I am going to be a Native. (Interview, 1 June 2004)

Damen, Nora and Vaida were raised in Indigenous communities situated near or within large urban areas. In the next ethnographic vignette, we go to a very different setting – a Native American community we call Beautiful Mountain.

Language use at Beautiful Mountain community and school

The pre-K–12 Beautiful Mountain Community School is situated on a high plateau in the southwestern US. A two-lane highway leads into the community, cutting through red sandstone outcroppings and sage- and juniper-covered foothills that abut the pseudonymous Beautiful Mountain. On a typical weekday morning the road to Beautiful Mountain is busy with school buses, pick-up trucks and cars on their way to work and school. A network of dirt roads leads off the main highway to extended family households beyond. At the time of the study, this included 89 families and 113 households. As late as the 2003 school year – the middle period of our work at Beautiful Mountain – almost a third of these families lacked running water and 20% lacked electricity. This is 'traditional' Beautiful Mountain, a stronghold of Diné intergenerational language transmission. Nearer the school lies a complex of school facilities and dormitories, clusters of modern housing, rodeo grounds, a store and a church.

According to census data gathered at the time of our study, more than three-quarters of Beautiful Mountain community members spoke Navajo at home. However, according to the adults we interviewed, most speakers were older adults and elders. As educators described their students' communicative repertoires:

> I would say about half of my [students] understand [Navajo] but are not able to speak it. Then I would say that about ... 20 to 30 percent are just now learning the Navajo language and ... do not understand it, don't speak it. (Interview, 19 September 2002)

> [I]n thinking about [Navajo youth], they have all taken up English. There is no Navajo flickering in them ... this new generation of students will respond to you in English. Navajo is set on the side. That's the way it is now. (Interview, 13 December 2002)

> No one speaks Navajo. They only speak English now. (Interview, 23 January 2003)

Introducing Jonathan

At Beautiful Mountain we met Jonathan Nez, a 16-year-old ninth grader when we interviewed him in the spring of 2004. Jonathan had grown up in a 'traditional' extended family home, caring for livestock and the family homestead. His first language was Navajo, and he entered school having had little exposure to English.

Interviewer: So you were saying that your early school experiences with a Native-speaking teacher didn't instill in you a good feeling about your language –

Jonathan: No they didn't ... That [teacher] didn't know how to ... bring out that kind of – I don't know, that kind of pride and the continuation of the language in a positive sense ... And she was mainly forcing us to learn English ... I don't know, it was a real confusing time, I guess. (Interview, 6 May 2004)

Jonathan related these early language-learning experiences to 'what I like to call the Long Walk Syndrome', a reference to the Navajos' Long Walk to Fort Sumner, New Mexico, in the winter of 1863. Jonathan spoke of the 'inherited trauma' of that historic time, which 'has to do with the psyche' and 'goes from generation to generation', leading some contemporary youth to deny their Indigeneity. 'You forsake who you are to accommodate the mainstream life', Jonathan declared (interview, 6 May 2004).

Not long after the Navajos' release from federal imprisonment, a different kind of Long Walk ensued, as children were forcibly removed from their families and taken to distant boarding schools. 'Having all this boarding school stuff and the government trying to force English upon them', Jonathan explained. 'And a lot of people are still recovering from that' –

They [government officials] took the children away from their families at a young age and they instilled this image that is still alive – this image of self-hate. To be ashamed of who you are ... It's all about survival since 1492 ... It's all about how far will you go to – to survive. (Interview, 6 May 2004)

Although the interview questions asked about language, for Jonathan and many youth in our study, questions about language could not be divorced from issues of race, history, land and cultural survival. 'I just, it's just a meaning of survival', Jonathan reiterated when asked about his memories of learning English, 'having to learn how to cope and adjust in this colonial world that we live in. Both sides, no? So mainly I was forced into that out of my own will' (interview, 6 May 2004).

Jonathan's account brings into sharp focus the rebounding impacts of oppressive language policies within contemporary youth language practices and trajectories. 'It's being told that [the Indigenous language] is stupid', Jonathan said; 'to speak Indian is the way of the devil'. At the same time, Jonathan expressed a strong attachment to his native language. Asked whether he felt knowing Navajo was helpful to him now, Jonathan replied:

Yes, it helps me, having that as my first language ... Like y'know, it helps not lose the identity of who I am, of where I come from, of how – that's all linked with survival, y'know. (Interview, 6 May 2004)

Finally, asked whether he believed that 'people will still be speaking Navajo' 20 or 30 years from now, Jonathan replied:

> A part of myself likes to think there would be, but you never know ... Yeah, I have some hope, that is all I can say, I have hope. ... Hope that ... we can go back to living with the sacredness a little longer ... to continue, carrying on longer who we are, as a people. (Interview, 6 May 2004)

Lessons on language from Native American youth

There is much in these youth accounts to help us understand youth's language ideologies and practices, and the sociolinguistic environments they negotiate each day. Certainly the accounts counter popular notions of youth as disinterested or as simply abandoning their heritage languages and cultures in favor of 'powerful' English. The accounts also challenge the binaries that continue to populate the scholarly and popular discourse on language loss and revitalization:

- 'Speaker' vs 'non-speaker' – what constitutes 'speakerhood' in these settings?
- 'Fluent' vs 'non-fluent' – what does it mean to say an individual speaks a language 'fluently', and how do perceptions of fluency hinder or help language recovery?
- 'Extinct' vs 'living' with reference to languages – when is an allegedly 'dying' or 'extinct' language really only 'sleeping' (Leonard, 2008), and what can be done to 'awaken' sleeping languages among younger generations?

The youth accounts also provide a nuanced understanding of the often 'closeted' multilingual abilities of youth, and the on-the-ground, minute-by-minute pressures influencing their language choices. Most importantly, the data attest to significant, if latent, resources for language reclamation – resources that may go undetected, unappreciated and even stigmatized by the schools in which youth spend so much of their lives.

In all the youth accounts, there are implicit and explicit identity connections across a web of extended kin networks, including older siblings and out-of-school young adults. It was well into the data analysis that we realized that, in order to understand language in the lives of youth, we needed to look more closely at the accounts of their older siblings and family members – that is, young adults. The next section considers those data.

Young adults 'in the middle'

There are 33 interviews with Native American young adults in our database. In terms of chronological age, these are individuals who, at the time of the research, were in their 20s and early 30s. Some held staff positions in the schools attended by the adolescents we interviewed (thus, their survey responses are embedded in Figures 6.1 and 6.2). Some were attending college, and many were young parents beginning to raise children of their own. Like the adolescents, the language profiles of these young adults reflect the histories and circumstances of their respective communities; the accounts from our Navajo site, for example, differ in important respects from those of the other communities. However, across all young adult accounts there are two readily discernible themes:

(1) an expressed feeling of being 'in the middle', between generations of older 'speakers' and adolescents with less Native-language exposure and ability; and
(2) an expressed feeling of responsibility for helping to secure the linguistic and cultural futures of their communities.

As one 32-year-old educator and mother-to-be put it,

> I see our language as our guide, ... our bridge to our history ... Well, I want to encourage my community, I want to encourage all [Native] families to perpetuate that ... I want to do all that I can so that they [youth] at least have something and can identify themselves as [Native]. (Interview, 19 September 2002)

Introducing Darrell

Darrell Tsosie was 25 and a fourth-grade teacher assistant at Beautiful Mountain when we interviewed him in 2002. Darrell grew up in what he described as a traditional family, 'herding sheep and taking care of animals [livestock]' and being 'taught by my grandparents, because my grandma ... had a *hooghan* [a traditional Navajo home] we all lived in'. Darrell described his early language socialization this way:

Interviewer: And you were raised in [the] Navajo language?
Darrell: Yes, I was raised in Navajo language ... I had a lot of cousins and my grandma ... and we all used to communicate in Navajo ... [F]rom my grandparents [I learned] to respect myself, my culture, and my language ... Like right now, I'm still speaking Navajo. (Interview, 17 October 2002)

Exposed to English for the first time when he entered kindergarten, Darrell nonetheless remembered it being 'easy' to learn: 'I think it was easy for me to learn both languages, English and Navajo', he said.

Darrell had two young sons, the oldest of whom attended Beautiful Mountain preschool. 'I'm going to teach him the way I was taught to speak

Navajo', Darrell told us. With this as his goal, and to enhance his classroom teaching, Darrell was taking classes to improve his Navajo reading and writing abilities. 'I'm not ashamed to speak my language', he insisted:

> I love my language and I love to be around my language and ... that's why I'm taking Navajo [to] upgrade my language, my writing, my reading, and also storytelling. (Interview, 17 October 2002)

Yet, Darrell admitted to struggling with 'which way to go' in working out a family language policy at home. '[R]ight now I'm just ... right in the middle – right in the middle', he reiterated:

> And I don't know which way to go ... So I'm just like caught in the middle .... Because ... what if my son just learns nothing but Navajo? And if they gave him a paper like this [holding up a worksheet], he's not going to [be able to] read it ... So I hate to say it, but it's there ... Like I said, it's just really confusing to me. I mean I'm just right in the middle. (Interview, 17 October 2002)

Asked to project the future of his mother tongue, Darrell worried that 'it's gradually fading away' – an expression echoed throughout the young adult interviews. At the same time, he implied that the responsibility for language continuity 'is upon us' – his generation, he said.

Introducing Naysa

Naysa Begay was Darrell's contemporary, 28 years old and the mother of twin eight-year-old girls when we interviewed her in 2003. Naysa, who worked as a program assistant at Beautiful Mountain School, came from a prominent family of bilingual educators. Her grandparents on both sides were esteemed community elders and strong (even monolingual) Navajo speakers. Naysa had been raised in a largely English-speaking household, however, as her stepfather did not speak the Navajo language. As Naysa explained in this interview excerpt:

> [M]y mom just didn't think it was appropriate with my step-dad, you know, [to] speak Navajo in the home ... [W]e just got used to not speaking Navajo at home. (Interview, 12 December 2003)

Fortunately, Naysa had the opportunity to study Navajo in her school's bilingual education program and was surrounded by the language within her larger network of kin. At 28, she considered herself a proficient speaker, reader and writer of the language. Indeed, her colleague, one of the CRCs, remarked that Naysa was 'our Navajo speaking assistant that can go to the homes ... and translate [students' learning plans] into Navajo so that the parent understands' (interview, 12 December 2003).

Naysa recognized that many of her students hid their Navajo-speaking ability for the very reasons that Jonathan had suggested, noting that as a young adult her high school-age students had been 'really surprised to hear me talk Navajo'. She used her position to encourage students to 'open up' in Navajo, telling them: 'What's embarrassing about it? ... [B]e proud that you speak Navajo! Wear your turquoise!' (interview, 12 December 2003).

In contrast to Darrell, Naysa felt 'caught in the middle' in a different way; she worried that her own daughters 'are not knowing as much [Navajo] and I'm afraid that it's just going to get, like, it's going down with each generation ... That kind of scares me'. She was determined to establish a 'mostly Navajo' language policy at home:

> I always talk to [my daughters] in Navajo ... That's what I do with them because I just don't want to *not* do anything at all ... I feel proud when I speak Navajo, especially at my age, a lot of girls don't know how to speak Navajo ... I'm going to make sure my kids pick it up. (Interview, 12 December 2003)

However, Naysa admitted, it was an uphill struggle: 'I always tell my girls that when they get about my age, that they're going to wish they knew Navajo' (interview, 12 December 2003).

Introducing Sabrina

Sabrina López was 25 when we interviewed her in 2003. A member of Nora's and Vaida's cultural community, Sabrina lived an hour's drive from that community, working as a teacher at Damen's school. Sabrina's first language was Spanish. She recalled feeling 'caught between the two – English, all English, or bilingual and ESL [English as a Second Language] – as a child growing up'. Entering kindergarten, 'it was either swim or drown inside the classroom', she said; '[t]hat's how I felt' (interview, 14 May 2003).

Sabrina came from a family of educators; both her parents were teachers, as were her aunts. Her father spoke the Indigenous language, and her mother 'I think knows a little bit, not as much as my dad', but 'for some reason they [her parents and grandparents] never taught us', she said.

> I know they talked amongst each other and the elders in our home ... in our Native language, but never to us. My parents and my grandparents, within their school, were hit if they spoke any other language besides English. So I have cousins and uncles who never taught their kids even Spanish because of what happened to them in school. (Interview, 14 May 2003)

Sabrina was an active participant in her tribe's cultural and religious ceremonies, which she believed required knowledge of the Indigenous language.

> I think what are all of these young people – including my children and even my peers – what are they understanding of the ceremony if they don't understand the language we're talking or the prayers we're saying? If they're [spoken] in [the Indigenous language], ... what are they comprehending? (Interview, 14 May 2003)

To be a 'full participant' in her cultural community, Sabrina had 'gone back to school to learn my [Indigenous] language'. Her own family language policy was to use Spanish and the Indigenous language at home:

> I'm very confident that my kids will all learn English in school, and I don't have to worry about that part. My daughter's first language was Spanish, and when she went to school she did not know a word of English. Not one word ... But by the end of that school year, she didn't speak [Spanish] any more ... She'd answer me in English. So I force my kids to respond to me in Spanish, or to speak it, or to ask for something in Spanish or [the Indigenous language] before they get what they want. (Interview, 14 May 2003)

With her grandparents, she added, 'It's hard for them ... just to speak to us in Spanish, and ... I have to remind them to talk to me in [the Indigenous language] because we need that practice. Well, I need that practice'.

Introducing Gabriela

The final profile we will present is that of Gabriela Ramírez, aged 30 when we interviewed her in 2003. Like Sabrina, Gabriela was a member of Nora's and Vaida's cultural community but was teaching at Damen's school. Her maternal grandmother had been part of the diaspora; her father had relocated voluntarily and more recently from Sonora, Mexico.

As a child, Gabriela had begun to learn the Indigenous language from her maternal grandmother, who died when Gabriela was 10. 'And there's just a few words that I remember', Gabriela said, 'but after my *nana* died, there was nobody around [to teach the language]'. Her parents, she explained, 'speak a little, ... but they can't hold a conversation or anything'. Gabriela's first language was Spanish: '[I]n the home we always spoke Spanish, ... and when we were out with friends or playing outside ... what we always spoke was Spanish ... I don't remember hearing [the Indigenous language] when I was a kid, other than my *nana*' (interview, 28 May 2003).

At the time of our interview, Gabriela had three children, aged three, four and nine. What she desired for her children, as well as her students 'is for them not to lose their culture and ... help them, ... help them value it, keep it, never want to lose it'. For that to happen, she admitted, 'we [young adults] also need to be taught'. Gabriela felt 'caught in the middle' in yet another way; she desperately longed for the support of elder speakers so that she and her contemporaries could fulfill what she perceived as their responsibility to future generations. 'We haven't really been taught', Gabriela said. She closed her interview with this reflection on her position in a larger cultural community:

> Our elders [are the primary speakers of the Indigenous language]. And we have ... a growing [age group] – well, I'm 30 – that are interested now in learning the language. And hopefully we could – you know, I'm thinking of us that went to school around the same time and have kids – you know, we have an interest and we now have our kids [to teach]. I think our language would flourish again, you know, because I see the interest coming, being here again. (Interview, 28 May 2003)

Toward Linguistic and Cultural Continuance

We began this study with a central question: what can we learn about language loss and reclamation by attending closely to the experiences and perspectives of Indigenous youth? We believed it was important to focus on youth and young adults because their voices have been noticeably absent from scholarly inquiry into language loss and revitalization, and often from the language planning process itself. This 'tender excavation' into young people's lives led inescapably to their and their communities' linguistic genealogies. The stories underlying these genealogies are not easy, as they interweave with rebounding legacies of colonization, genocide, and racial and linguistic discrimination.

In our attempts to understand the meaning of these young people's accounts for language recovery, we have been inspired by Simon Ortiz's notion of *continuance*. As he writes in the introduction to his book, *Woven Stone* – a reference to his father's craft as a stone mason but also a metaphor for the crisscrossing connections between generations within Indigenous communities – continuance is 'something more than memory or remembering' and also more than an abstract or 'romanticized future that is impractical': 'We must not forsake the present reality of our continuing lives', Ortiz says, '[our] families, communities, cultures, languages, ... and ... struggles for ... self sufficiency' (Ortiz, 1992: 9, 32; see also Brill de Ramírez & Zuni Lucero, 2009; Dunsmore, 2009).

Applied to the project of language reclamation, continuance, as we understand it, is not so much about bringing a language 'back' as bringing it 'forward' into the vital, ever changing, everyday of people's lives (Hornberger & King, 1996). The data reported here strongly indicate that this needs to be a whole-community effort that acknowledges the dysjuncts as well as the bonds across and within generations, the sources of the dysjuncts within oppressive culture histories, and the 'present reality' and 'continuing lives' of all community members – including, especially, youth and young adults. This means simultaneously acknowledging the hybridity of young people's communicative repertoires, the heteroglossic qualities of their sociolinguistic environments (Deloria, 2011; García, 2009), and the pressures and 'mixed messages' (Lee, 2009) they encounter as they construct their self-identifications and their own family language policies. As linguistic anthropologist Jacqueline Messing points out, 'This knowledge is key for language revitalization, because if ideological orientations can change over time, then young [people] may reactivate their passive linguistic knowledge' (Messing, 2009: 361). The cases in Chapter 5 demonstrate that this can indeed occur: the mixed messages can be reframed and even erased when hybridity and heteroglossia are constructed as *resources* for language reclamation, rather than as markers of limitation, hindrance and shame (McCarty *et al.*, 2009a: 303).

These ideological and pedagogic transformations are being effected by the CRCs in some of our school-community study sites, where Native language immersion and family language classes are being vigorously implemented. These efforts recognize, as Lee (2007) points out, that if language regenesis is to occur, it must connect directly with the contemporary lives of Native American youth (see also Hill, 1993: 89). Such transformations are also represented by a larger youth movement for linguistic and cultural continuance. We close with a few illustrations of that movement.

In the Far North, the Inuit Circumpolar Youth Council, an initiative within the Inuit Circumpolar Council, is a youth-led non-governmental organization in which Inuit youth are positioned as 'deliberate agents of Inuit language preservation' (Tulloch, 2013 [in press]; see also http://www.inuit.org). Representing Inuit communities in Alaska, Canada, Greenland and Chukotka, Russia, the Inuit Circumpolar Youth Council has organized youth language symposia and numerous other efforts intended to build a social network of Inuit youth, increase youth agency through information-sharing and participation in international forums, and 'expand youth understanding of Inuit language issues across the Arctic' (Tulloch, 2013 [in press]). The participating youth disseminate this information 'naturally ... back to the local communities', a process, Tulloch *et al.* note (citing Cangarajah, 2005: xvii) of 'grassroots knowledge making' that is essential to language planning.

On the Fort Berthold reservation in North Dakota, a group of young adults is creating 'a community of hope' dedicated to reviving the Arikara language (Kroupa, 2013). Adapting a name used for the Arikara in the 18th and 19th centuries – 'Arikarees' – these young adults describe themselves as 'language warriors' and 'social and cultural Ree-volutionaries' (Kroupa,

2013). According to Standing Bear (K.T.) Kroupa, a leader in the group, the term Ree-volution signifies

> a contemporary cultural revitalization movement among the Arikara; a language revival and spiritual (ceremonial) resurgence; a reorganization of the Arikara people; and a new development of an evolved belief of Arikara thought, tradition, and ceremony. (Kroupa, 2013 [in press])

In collaboration with University of Indiana linguist Douglas Parks, who has studied the Arikara language for more than three decades, Kroupa and his colleagues Jasper Young Bear and Loren Yellow Bird have 'worked intensively on the language', including investigating an extensive collection of Arikara songs archived at Indiana University (Kroupa, 2013 [in press]). The group now includes other young adults of Arikara and non-Arikara heritage who have organized language summits designed to develop everyday conversational skills and to transcribe ceremonial songs. 'We have become leaders who will promote language learning and culture preservation for old and young alike', Kroupa (2013 [in press]) writes – and the Ree-volution continues.

For more than a decade, as many as 800 Native American students from several US states have gathered each summer for a two-day Native American Youth Language Fair at the University of Oklahoma. Hosted by the Sam Noble Museum Department of Native American Languages at the University of Oklahoma, the fair provides a public forum for youth to use their Native languages. According to linguist Mary Linn, curator of Native American languages at the museum, the fair gives an incentive 'for the students to work toward through the year as they learn their languages', encouraging them and their teachers as they have the opportunity 'to interact with so many others who are learning their Native languages':

> They can see how important it is to Native people all across the country and how many people are working together to help prevent languages from being lost. (Linn, cited in *Indian Country Today*, 2011: para. 4)

Each summer since 2009, 10 Shoshone/Goshute high school students from Idaho, Utah and Nevada – the self-described 'future guardians' of the mutually intelligible Shoshone and Goshute dialects – have participated in a six-week residential internship with Shoshone master teachers and elders at the University of Utah's Center for American Indian Languages (Brunden, 2009: para. 1). The Shoshone effort is noteworthy because youth, assisted by elder speakers, are involved in language documentation and the creation of language learning materials, including books, a Shoshone/Goshute and English talking dictionary, and films. They then 'share these materials with elementary-aged learners of the language when they return home' (Center for American Indian Languages, 2011: para. 5).

On the Fort Mojave reservation in Needles, California, a group of Mojave teens is working with adult language learners and a core group of elders to document Mojave bird songs – social songs that are integral to Mojave orature, and which are traditionally sung by males and accompanied by female singers or *hapuk*. The single fluent male Mojave bird song singer, Mr Hubert McCord, is 84 years old. '[W]hat we are fighting to preserve and revitalize [is] our Mojave identity', says Natalie Diaz, director of the Mojave Language Recovery Program (cited in Zrioka, 2012: para. 22). In addition to documenting the bird songs, summer camps and after-school activities aim to provide youth with basic conversational abilities in the language. 'We want to let young people ... write it, ... text in it, ... Facebook in it', says Diaz, who is a young Mojave language apprentice and teacher herself. 'The main goal is to not only speak and think in it, but to begin to live by it', she adds (cited in Zrioka, 2012: para. 20).

In Santa Fe, New Mexico, a group known as the 'young ancestors' – Pueblo high school students attending Santa Fe Preparatory School – is working on a project co-sponsored by their school and the Santa Fe-based Indigenous Language Institute to 'integrate the way we live with the way we talk and think' (Camino Vérité Films, 2012). Using a self-taught course for which they (ironically) receive foreign language credit, this group of Native students and their mentor, reading teacher Laura Jogles, have 'established a little community where it [is] safe to learn the language' (Camino Vérité Films, 2012). 'This isn't something where we dress up for a day or two ... and play Indian for a day', says Jeremy Montoya, a senior in the class of 2012. 'This program shows ... we're serious about it' (Camino Vérité Films, 2012).[6]

All of these are significant acts of youth self-empowerment and choice aimed at repatriating languages of heritage in their lives, their families and their communities. These acts of language reclamation, while important locally, are also part of a global movement in which youth 'are transforming their visibility by engaging in new forms of cultural production' (Kral, 2011: 5). Writing of these efforts for an Aboriginal youth media movement in Australia, Inge Kral notes that youth 'take on the role of "expert"', constructing identities not simply as learners, but as knowledgeable, capable citizens of mobile local, national, and global communities (Kral, 2011: 6, 11).

The research examined here, along with that of Kral and many others, shows Indigenous youth to be informed, thoughtful, critically conscious and vested stakeholders in Native-language futures. Moreover, they are, in fact, 'making' language policy in everyday social practice. We argue, then, that youth should be at the center of our LPP research, and, even more importantly, at the heart of the activism informed by that research. 'I want to share my language with little kids', a high school senior told us, because '[t]heir family probably [doesn't speak the Native language] to them, and it would be best for them to know how to speak it' (interview, 5 May 2004).

To fulfill these goals, we believe it is necessary to 'recalibrate' expectations for youth language practices and competencies (Meek, 2011: 56), making room for a wide range of varieties and fluencies. It is also important for youth and young adults (including young parents) to have the support of more powerful 'authorizing' agents – their elders, especially – as well as their Indigenous nations, communities and schools. This positions youth to build on their total communicative repertoires and to construct linguistic identities in terms of success and accomplishment rather than limits and attrition. Such an approach also positions youth as both language learners and language planners – a forward-looking orientation that bodes well for the prospect of cultural continuance.

Notes

(1) Parts of this section are adapted from McCarty (2012), and McCarty and Wyman (2009).
(2) Parsons-Yazzie explains that 'design' in this case refers to the Navajo language and culture: 'Just as a rug design depicts what area of the reservation a rug weaver is from, the Navajo language and culture place a design on our children to be identified with being Navajo' (Parsons-Yazzie, 1996/1997: 60).
(3) Holm analyzes this further as a culturally specific norm that 'one is expected to respect the integrity of the individual, even if that individual is a child', and for many parents, 'it is difficult if not unthinkable to force a child to speak Navajo' (Holm, 2006: 8).
(4) We express sincere gratitude to the Native-serving schools, tribal communities, youth and community research collaborators (CRCs) who participated in this study. At the request of the Internal Review Board (IRB) that sanctioned the Native Language Shift and Retention Study from 2005 to 2007, we include this disclaimer: all data, statements, opinions, and conclusions or implications in this discussion of the study solely reflect the view of the authors and research participants, and do not necessarily reflect the views of the funding agency, tribes or their tribal councils, the Arizona Board of Regents or Arizona State University (ASU), under whose auspices the project operated. This information is presented in the pursuit of academic research and is published in this volume solely for educational and research purposes. Pursuant to our agreement with ASU's IRB, this chapter may not be reproduced in any medium, transmitted or distributed, in whole or in part, without the authors' prior written consent.
(5) We thank Julie Weise of California State University Long Beach, for raising these important questions following a presentation by Teresa McCarty at the School for Advanced Research in Santa Fe, New Mexico, in October 2011. Dr Weise's questions caused us to revisit and rethink our data in ways that greatly expanded the analysis and its implications for language renewal.
(6) We thank Inée Slaughter of the Indigenous Language Institute and Rebecca Allahyari of the School for Advanced Research, both in Santa Fe, New Mexico, for calling the Young Ancestors project to our attention.

7 Planning Language for the Seventh Generation

> *What we do will affect the future of our children, our young people. What we do with our language will affect the rest of our generations.*
> Task Force on Aboriginal Languages and Cultures, 2005: 39

> *[I]t is vital to remember it is the youth of today and tomorrow who are the bearers of the language of today and yesterday.*
> Miali-Elise Coley, chair, Inuit Circumpolar Youth Council, 2005: 3

Many Native American oral traditions tell of the importance of the seventh generation. For the Anishinaabe (Ojibwe), the Seven Fires 'is a set of predictions about the Anishinaabe future' in which the language loss and cultural disruption that occurred over the course of six generations are redeemed by a new generation of young people, who, guided by the wisdom of elders, lead a process of cultural and spiritual regeneration (Bergstrom *et al.*, 2003: 1–3). According to this tradition, 'we are in the time of the seventh generation and ... the youth who will lead may be the children and grandchildren in current villages' (Bergstrom *et al.*, 2003: 2). In other Native American traditions, the lessons of three generations past provide a vision for three generations forward, with the current (seventh) generation positioned between them and poised to act (K. Tsianina Lomawaima, personal communication, 3 January 2009). Applying these teachings to LPP, Ash *et al.* write that, for the Wampanoag, who, prior to the regenesis activities described in Chapter 5, had not spoken their language for six generations, 'whatever they [the current generation] do will have an effect on the seventh generation of as-yet-unborn Wampanoag':

> In using the early documents written by Wampanoag families six generations ago, the people have a chance to close this circle during the seventh generation. They will be the grandchildren of the current generation. (Ash *et al.*, 2001: 31)

I began this book by quoting Roseanna Thompson of the Mississippi Band of Choctaw Indians, who refers to the Native language as providing 'the complete circle'. In this statement, as in the reference to Wôpanâak language revitalization above, the metaphorical circle indexes language as the strengthening bond for intergenerational ties and cultural continuance (Ortiz, 1992); the restoration of these ties, she implies, fosters communal and personal well-being and wholeness. In this final chapter, I attempt to come 'full circle', returning to the linkages Roseanna Thompson describes, which are apparent in the sociocultural and political processes underlying the LPP initiatives analyzed in previous chapters. Drawing on safety zone theory, I reflect on the radical transformations engendered through these processes as well as ongoing policy dilemmas and challenges. Specifically, I address the paramount challenge of twin movements for standardization and language restrictionism, which, I argue, are designed to defend White, English-(only)-speaking, dominant-class interests. I then examine Indigenous counter-movements and offer a pedagogic framework for 'strong' language and culture education initiatives. I conclude with the possibilities these initiatives hold for the seventh generation – the present generation of language learners and planners, and the future generations to come.

From Ideologies of Contempt to Ideologies of Valor: The Victories of Native American LPP

Since the first encounters between Native Americans and Anglo-Europeans, colonial policies have positioned Indigenous languages both inside and outside a zone of perceived tolerable or 'safe' cultural difference. This linguistic positioning has been proxy for the intended social, political and economic subordination of Native peoples within particular sociohistorical contexts. As Nancy Dorian observes,

> languages have the standing that their speakers have. If people who speak a language have power and prestige, the language they speak will enjoy high prestige as well. If the people who speak a language have little power..., their language is unlikely to be well thought of. (Dorian, 1998: 3–4)

To this it should be added that, in the case of Indigenous peoples, it has not been simply a matter of Indigenous languages not being 'well thought of'; as perceived embodiments of 'dangerous difference' and threats to White English-speaking supremacy, Indigenous languages have been targets for extinction.

Embedded in this LPP matrix is what Dorian (citing Grillo, 1989) calls an 'ideology of contempt' – the belief in a 'linguistic survival of the fittest' and the 'onerousness' of bi-/multilingualism (Dorian, 1998: 9–12). As we have seen, early church-promulgated policies were appropriated by federal authorities intent on 'blotting out barbarous tongues' (Atkins, 1887, cited in Crawford, 1992: 48). Shonerd writes that these policies have 'been part of the designs of [nation-states] to expand and consolidate their power geographically, politically, and socially' and have been 'rationalized as means to ameliorate deficient language abilities' (Shonerd, 1990: 193).

Within these broad social–historical parameters, compulsory English-only schooling has been the engine for intended linguicide and ethnicide, with the ultimate goal of clearing the path (literally, through the plundering of Indigenous lands) for Anglo-American rule (Adams, 1988, 1995; Spring, 1996). Although federally controlled English-only schooling was not entirely successful in its aims, it did take a heavy toll. The narrative accounts from the Native Language Shift and Retention Study described in Chapter 6 are replete with references to the costs of symbolic and physical violence borne by Native children and families.

However, as I have stressed, the power of the state is not totalizing, and the colonial domination represented by the safety zone has been resisted, challenged and transformed. In many Native American communities, schools have been appropriated as strongholds for 'grow (y)our own' teacher preparation programs (acquisition planning), the development of Indigenous literatures and literacies (corpus planning) and the creation of a network of language planners who, individually and collectively, have mobilized new national, state and local language education policies (status planning). Increasingly these LPP processes are being organized by youth and young adults. These Indigenous interventions are mending the metaphorical circle to which Roseanna Thompson refers. By 'reducing the generation gap felt by so many Native [people] who have struggled with enormous cultural changes in the last century', these initiatives bring 'people back in touch with their roots', observes Hinton (2001c: 225).

Yet the 'ideology of contempt' and views of bi/multilingualism as pathological continue to hold sway in public discourse and in federal and state policy. More than half of all US states now have English-only statutes. In the education realm these state policies are buttressed by federal high-stakes accountability regimes, which, by virtue of their reliance on English standardized tests to measure student achievement, serve as *de facto* language policies (Menken, 2008). To return to the epigraph that introduces this chapter, these policy processes profoundly affect the futures of Indigenous children, constricting LPP 'ideological and implemental spaces' (Hornberger, 2006a), particularly within schools. I turn now to a closer examination of these language education policies and their impacts.

Standardization and Language Restrictionism[1]

Federal education policy: leaving language and culture behind?

On 8 January 2002, then-President George W. Bush signed into law the No Child Left Behind (NCLB) Act of 2001, which simultaneously reauthorized and renamed the Elementary and Secondary Education Act (ESEA) of 1965. The premise behind NCLB is that holding schools accountable to English standardized tests will increase educational outputs or, as education researchers Julian Vasquez Heilig and Linda Darling-Hammond describe it, that '[p]ressure to improve test scores will produce genuine gains in student achievement' (Vasquez Heilig & Darling-Hammond, 2008: 75).

NCLB ushered in unprecedented levels of testing aimed at making schools, students and educators 'accountable' for results. On the positive side, NCLB directs schools to disaggregate achievement data by race/ethnicity, socioeconomic status, gender, ability and English proficiency, thereby motivating schools to focus greater attention on students who have historically been 'left behind'. All students are expected to demonstrate '100 percent proficiency' by 2014. As former BIE director Keith Moore noted in federal testimony in 2010, NCLB 'brought additional requirements to the schools by holding them accountable for improving their students' academic performance' (Moore, 2011: 9).

The problem lies in the law's high-stakes accountability system, which relies almost solely on a single achievement measure – English standardized tests – and metes out draconian penalties for low performance without regard for school funding inequities, students' primary language or long-term school improvement (see, e.g. Crawford, 2004a). Under NCLB, all K–12 schools, including BIE and tribally controlled schools, must administer assessments tied to state standards in reading/language arts, mathematics and science. For BIE-funded schools this creates staggering logistical challenges, as the BIE system is 'accountable' to the assessments of 23 states in which BIE schools are located (Moore, 2011). Moreover, the tests severely disadvantage students in these and other Indigenous-serving schools (and English learners more generally) because their students are significantly under-represented from the norming populations (Fox, 2012; Solórzano, 2008).

Schools that fail to demonstrate 'adequate yearly progress' (AYP, defined primarily on the basis of test scores) are subject to increasing levels of state surveillance and foreboding labels that escalate from 'alert' to 'school improvement' to 'corrective action' to 'restructuring' status. The latter two categories entail the replacement of all or most school staff and potential takeover by an outside agency or management firm (US Department of Education, n.d.). These statuses are made public in state 'report cards' disseminated by the news media – a form of public shaming (Cochran-Smith, 2005). Schools placed in remedial categories are required to implement highly scripted, phonics-based reading programs that consume huge parts of the school day. These programs, Reyhner and Hurtado note, are 'one-size-fits-all approaches targeted toward a "standard" dialect of English and a White, middle-class knowledge of the world that American Indian and other ethnic minority students often do not share' (Reyhner & Hurtado, 2008: 88).

What have been NCLB's impacts on Native American learners and schools? As Hornberger observes, 'With enactment of [NCLB] ..., bilingualism and bilingual education vanished' (Hornberger, 2006a: 230): federal funding for bilingual education was eliminated; the former Bilingual Education Act was renamed the English Language Acquisition, Language Enhancement, and Academic Achievement Act; and the former Office of Bilingual Education and Minority Languages Affairs was renamed the Office of English Language Acquisition, Language Enhancement, and Academic Achievement for Limited English Proficient Students (Wiley & Wright, 2004). Although NCLB includes provisions for Native American 'culturally related activities' (NCLB Act of 2001, Title VII, Sec. 7115 [a][1][1]), in practice these activities have been highly constrained, as funds under this provision have 'been diverted to preparing children for standardized tests and to provide remedial education' (Lee, 2012a: para. 11). Further, NCLB's single provision for Native language programs states that their goal 'shall be increased English proficiency' (NCLB Act of 2001, Title III, Sec. 3.216).

Because NCLB's stated goal is to eliminate achievement disparities between low-income African American, Latino/a and Native American students and their more affluent White peers, a key question in assessing the policy's impacts is whether achievement disparities have, in fact, been ameliorated. The National Indian Education Study (NIES) provides a large data set within which to address this question. Mandated by a 2004 Executive Order to 'assist [American Indian and Alaska Native] students in meeting the challenging standards' of NCLB (Grigg et al., 2010: 4), the NIES has been implemented every two years since 2005. Part I of the study uses National Assessment of Education Progress (NAEP) scores in fourth- and eighth-grade reading and mathematics to assess student outcomes. In 2003, one year after NCLB implementation, NAEP scores 'showed a continuation of negative trends among minority students that had been evident for years' (Lee, 2012a: para. 2). In subsequent NIES cycles mean NAEP reading and mathematics scores for American Indian/Alaska Native fourth- and eighth-graders have not changed significantly, and in some cases the negative trends have worsened (Grigg et al., 2010; Moran et al., 2008). According to a recent report, the fourth-grade reading scores of American Indian and Alaska Native students were identical in 2011 and 2003, and the gap between American Indian/Alaska Native and White fourth- and eighth-grade students' mathematics scores in 2011 was 24 and 28 points, respectively – larger than it was in 2003. 'In short', reports a panel of experts commissioned by the American Educational Research Association, 'the current state of [American Indian/Alaska Native] academic achievement, as measured by NAEP scores, is dismal' (Brayboy et al., 2013 [in press]).

The NIES data also indicate that the emphasis on high-stakes testing leads schools to curtail or eliminate Native language and culture instruction. Part II of the 2005 study surveyed 5600 students, 1300 teachers and 470 principals in 480 schools serving Native students (Stancavage et al., 2006: 2–3). A key component of the survey was the extent to which students' Native language and culture were incorporated into classroom instruction. In grade 4, only 21% of fourth-grade students and 16% of eighth-grade students had teachers who reported daily or regular use of an Indigenous perspective in instruction. At the same time, the large majority of teachers (81–90%) reported relying primarily on state content standards for instruction. Of all students queried, only 4% were learning how to speak and read their heritage language in school (Stancavage et al., 2006).

These trends are amplified in more recent NIES data. In 2009, 12,000 American Indian/Alaska Native fourth graders and 10,000 American Indian/Alaska Native eighth graders from 4400 schools participated in the study, along with 4200 school administrators and 8400 fourth- and eighth-grade teachers. According to the NIES researchers, most of these students were receiving instruction entirely in English (Mead et al., 2010). While many school administrators reported the presence of Native culture programs, these were fairly minimal and outside the 'regular' school curriculum: arts and crafts demonstrations, music and dance performances, and teachers 'talking about native culture in their classrooms at least once a month' (Mead et al., 2010: 18). Of all students queried, 77% of fourth-graders and 82% of eighth graders reported 'never or hardly ever' hearing their Native language spoken in school (Mead et al., 2010: 19).

In 2004–2005, the National Indian Education Association (NIEA) held 11 hearings throughout the United States to 'gather information on the impact of [NCLB] on American Indian, Alaska Native, and Native Hawaiian students' (Beaulieu et al., 2005: 1). Those testifying at the hearings included 120 Native and non-Native educators, tribal and state officials, school board members, tribal leaders, students and parents. 'These are the principal constituents of the National Indian Education Association and also the specific constituent focus of [the Indian education provisions] of NCLB', the study's principal investigators note (Beaulieu et al., 2005: 3). While welcoming the renewed emphasis on school accountability, the NIEA study found no evidence of student achievement gains as a result of NCLB. Further, the report expressed concern that the policy negatively impacts schools' ability to provide culturally based instruction – including Native-language instruction – and compromises tribal sovereignty (Beaulieu et al., 2005: 4).

In summarizing this national testimony, the investigators, led by then-NIEA president David Beaulieu, stated that there was an overall sense 'that profound changes are underfoot in Native education and that the Native education community has only just begun to sense the impacts and dangers incumbent in both the intended and unintended consequences of the No Child Left Behind Statute upon the future of Native education'. Moreover, Beaulieu et al. added, 'It is clear from the testimony that these changes to date have not included the Native voice' (Beaulieu et al., 2005: 4). Five years later this testimony was echoed by then-BIE director Keith Moore, in hearings on NCLB before the US Senate Committee on Indian Affairs. 'NCLB has diminished American Indian cultures and languages', Moore declared, 'and ... does not address the unique needs of tribal communities, especially in rural areas' (Moore, 2011: 10; see also Beaulieu, 2011: 49).

Research on NCLB implementation at the state and local levels is limited but growing, with a 2008 special issue of the *Journal of American Indian Education* devoted to this topic (McCarty, 2008d).[2] At the state level, David Garcia (2008) examined the academic achievement of Arizona Indian students from 2000 (pre-NCLB) to 2006 (four years after NCLB was signed into law). The Arizona data are significant because the state is home to 22 Native nations (a total Native population of 284,264, or 4.5% of the state population), and at the time of the study, some 42,000 Native American students were enrolled in the state's public elementary schools. This represents 6% of the state-wide public elementary school population and 11% of American Indian/Alaska Native elementary school enrollments nationwide (Garcia, 2008).

Garcia's initial analysis of statewide student achievement data showed that American Indian students made post-NCLB progress in most subjects and grades. However, on closer inspection, he found that the greatest gains occurred in 2005 when Arizona policy-makers lowered the bar for passing scores. When the 2005 test score spike was omitted, the achievement rates of American Indian students dropped sharply, in some cases by 10 or more points. In light of these findings, Garcia dismissed the gains as illusory, cautioning that, 'the manipulation of passing scores could deny American Indian/Alaska Native students the very academic assistance that NCLB is intended to provide' (Garcia, 2008: 150).

Between 2001 and 2004, Robert Patrick, an award-winning teacher–researcher, undertook a qualitative study to examine post-NCLB reforms at Warrior Elementary School (a pseudonym). Warrior Elementary enrolled 359 students in kindergarten through grade 5, the majority of whom were Navajo. Because the school had not met AYP, it faced imminent closure. As a result of personnel and curricular restructuring, Warrior Elementary was able to show test score gains. However, as Patrick (2008) describes, those gains came at the cost of disinvestment in culturally relevant pedagogy, test administration improprieties, and community alienation. At this school, Patrick concluded, 'a new era emerged under pressures [of] NCLB: achieving standardization' (2008: 78; see also Balter's [2006] and Balter & Grossman's [2009] similar findings in their examination of the effects of NCLB in Navajo Nation public schools).

In research among schools serving Yup'ik students in southwestern Alaska, Wyman *et al.* (2010a, b, 2011) have documented the ways in which high-stakes English testing pressures 'are intersecting with language shift in one of the few areas of the United States ... where an Indigenous language is still spoken by children' (Wyman *et al.*, 2010a: 29). As this team of university-, school- and community-based researchers shows, the majority of the schools in the Lower Kuskokwim School District that are meeting NCLB progress goals have Native language and culture programs that can be characterized as 'strong' – that is, that include culturally based Indigenous language instruction as a core element of the school curriculum (Beaulieu, 2006; Castagno & Brayboy, 2008; Demmert, 2011). Yet NCLB 'has created an atmosphere of overhanging anxiety about high-stakes testing', state Wyman *et al.*, leading parents to shift from Yup'ik to English at home, promoting an ideology that '"Yup'ik holds children back" from achieving in English', and causing reductions in Yup'ik language instruction (Wyman *et al.* 2010a: 40). 'Ironically', these subtractive language practices are intensifying 'in spite of direct evidence that most ... schools making AYP ... have used Yup'ik consistently as a primary language of instruction' (Wyman *et al.* 2010a: 40).

Finally, in the Native Language Shift and Retention Study discussed in Chapter 6, we found that NCLB pressures led all but one school in the seven-school study to curtail or eliminate their Native language and culture programs. At two schools, already-limited (one-hour-per-week) Native language and culture programs were reduced to a half-hour each week. With such abbreviated time, teachers could do little more than focus on vocabulary drills. At two other schools, the Native language teachers were either dismissed or reassigned to clerical positions because they lacked NCLB-mandated 'highly qualified' credentials (an associate degree or equivalent). At another school, Native language and culture instruction succumbed to the pressures of state standards and NCLB: '[W]e are driven by standards at this point', an administrator said; '[i]t is not like we can do our own plan ... English takes a front seat and [the Native language] takes a back seat' (interview, 22 October 2003). 'We are part of a Reading First program', another administrator pointed out:

> Teaching [English] reading all day long, prescriptive and formulated curriculum of 'Do this and say it exactly with these words, all in English'. It gets in the way of [Native language instruction]. (Field notes, 2 September 2005)

Youth were keenly aware of these pressures. As a ninth-grader told us: 'English is ... everything ... That's always taking over the priority of learning the [Native] language' (interview, 6 May 2004).

In summary, a decade of post-NCLB research shows that high-stakes accountability regimes force severely labeled schools to teach to the test, artificially manipulate test scores and eliminate or curtail 'low-stakes' subjects, including Native language and culture instruction. These findings are borne out by a wide array of studies among ethnically and linguistically diverse student populations (e.g. Amrein & Berliner, 2002; Nichols & Berliner, 2007; Nichols *et al.*, 2006; US Commission on Civil Rights, 2004; Wright, 2002).

'English(-only) for the children'

As the pressures for standardization and accountability have accelerated, the English-only movement has also continued to grow. The movement had its beginnings in 1981, when the late Senator S.I. Hayakawa introduced an amendment to the US constitution that would make English the nation's official language. Two years later, Hayakawa and John Tanton, a physician who had earlier founded the Federation for American Immigration Reform (an organization whose mission is to curtail immigration to the United States, particularly from the South), started US English, a group determined to end what it called 'the mindless drift toward a bilingual society' (Crawford, 2004b: 65; see also Combs, 1999; Ovando & Combs, 2012: 51–58).

Over the next decade and a half, 14 Official English bills – an average of one per year – were introduced in the US Congress (Chen, 2001). To date, none has been approved. Although still working at the national level, English-only activists have taken their message, and their dollars, to the state level. In 1986, with financial support from US English, California – the state with the fastest growing Latino population – declared English the state's official language. Within two years, nine additional states adopted official English statutes (Piatt, 1990: 22; for comprehensive examinations of English-only legislation vis-à-vis research on bilingualism and bilingual education, including Indigenous bilingual education, see Cazden & Snow, 1990; and González & Melis, 2001a, b).

In 1998 and 2000, with the passage of almost identical 'English-for-the-Children' statutes in California and Arizona (Proposition 227 and 203, respectively), the movement to officialize English was taken to the classroom. Initiated and financed by California software multi-millionaire Ron Unz, both statutes require public schools to replace multi-year bilingual education programs with one-year structured English immersion for English language learners (see Arias & Faltis, 2012, for a comprehensive analysis of structured English immersion implementation in Arizona). In California, Proposition 227 was followed by the adoption of an English-only school accountability program that presaged NCLB (Gutiérrez *et al.*, 2002). Arizona's Proposition 203 states that, 'All children in Arizona public schools shall be taught English by being taught in English and all children shall be placed in English language classrooms' (Sec. 3.1: 752). The Arizona law is more punitive than California's, threatening to rescind state licensure for educators who fail to use English (only) in instructing English language learners.

With the advent of Proposition 203, as education researchers Mary Carol Combs and Sheilah Nicholas point out, 'enrollment in Indigenous language programs became, if not illegal, certainly more complicated' (Combs & Nicholas, 2012: 103). Together with NCLB, language-restrictive policies such as Proposition 203 compromise tribal efforts to revitalize their languages, as well as rights to sovereignty and self-determination (Combs & Nicholas, 2012). Moreover, as Patricia Gándara, Gary Orfield and their associates in the University of California Los Angeles Civil Rights Project have shown in extensive research, the policies 'have not delivered on their promise'; the students subjected to them receive 'demonstrably weaker education' and their segregation in structured English immersion programs 'contributes to their depressed achievement' (Gándara & Orfield, 2010: 222–223).

Domesticating Dangerous Diversity

As I have written elsewhere (McCarty, 2004), high-stakes accountability and English-only regimes cannot be decoupled from larger sociopolitical, economic and demographic forces (see also the discussion in Lomawaima & McCarty, 2006: 157–158). It is not coincidental that NCLB and English-for-the-Children come at a time when the United States is experiencing an unprecedented demographic shift. Much of this stems from post-1965 immigration, when the US Congress relaxed national-origin immigration quotas. Unlike earlier waves of immigration, which originated in Europe and were largely White, more recent immigrants have arrived in the United States primarily from Latin America, Southeast Asia and the Caribbean (Qin-Hilliard *et al.*, 2001; Suárez-Orozco, 2001). Difference in the United States has taken on not only new languages, but also new colors. In the 2010 Census, children of color comprised the majority (50.4%) of US births. According to William Frey, the demographer who analyzed these Census data, this shift in birth rates represents a 'tipping point', marking a 'transformation from a mostly white ... culture to the more globalized multiethnic country that we are becoming' (cited in Chew, 2012: para. 30). People of color now make up 28% of the national population, with the numbers expected to grow to 38% in 2024 and 45% in 2050 (Banks, 2006). A significant proportion are English language learners who, in addition to Native Americans, speak more than 450 languages.

Between 1999 and 2009, the number of English-language learners in US public schools grew from 3.5 million to 5.4 million, or 51% (US Department of Education, 2011). During these same years, the general student population grew by less than 5% (US Department of Education, 2011; see also Gándara & Hopkins, 2010: 7). In the 500 largest public school districts in the United States – New York, Los Angeles, Chicago, Houston and Detroit, for instance – more than half of the student population are ethnic minority students, and in the 100 largest school districts, more than 60% of all students enrolled are minority students from low-income families (Moll, 2004: 126). In light of these demographics, current state-prescribed pedagogies and testing regimes can be seen as regulatory mechanisms aimed at domesticating 'dangerous' diversity – linguistic and cultural practices deemed to fall outside a narrowly circumscribed zone of tolerable linguistic and cultural difference (Lomawaima, 2012). 'Consider that the dominant response to these radical demographic changes has been to develop educational policies that obviate diversity in favor of practices that seek to control the student population', Luis Moll observes (2004: 126).

We are witness to this in the backlash politics being waged in US states with high minority/English language learner populations. In the border state of Arizona, for example, the Arizona legislature in 2010 approved Senate Bill (SB) 1070 (the 'Support Our Law Enforcement and Safe Neighborhoods Act'), an anti-immigrant measure that a federal judge ruled encourages racial profiling, key parts of which were subsequently struck down by the US Supreme Court. On the same day that SB 1070 passed, the Arizona legislature approved House Bill (HB) 2281, a ban on ethnic studies in the state's public schools – specifically, the Mexican American Studies program in the border city of Tucson – on the grounds that such programs 'promote resentment toward a race or class of people' and 'promote the overthrow of the United States government' (Hull, 2010: para. 8). The latter claim was made by then-state superintendent of public instruction Tom Horne and is cited in section 1.15–112 of the bill. The same week that SB 1070 and HB 2281 were approved, Horne instructed school districts to remove teachers with 'accents' from teaching English, threatening the loss of their jobs for noncompliance. Meanwhile, under an earlier policy enacted by Horne's office, English learners in Arizona public schools are segregated for four hours each day in mandated 'English language development' classes where they are prohibited from using their mother tongue. Horne subsequently ran a successful campaign for state attorney general on a 'Defending Arizona!' platform that discursively bonded the banning of bilingual education, ethnic (Mexican American) studies and (Mexican-origin) immigration.

Issues involving Native American LPP must be viewed within this larger sociopolitical context. Despite federal assurances of Indigenous language rights contained in the hard-won Native American Languages Act and the Esther Martinez Native American Languages Preservation Act, Native peoples 'are nonetheless affected by the harsh language and educational policies aimed at immigrant groups in the society' (Wong Fillmore 2011: 28). As Leibowitz observed, such language-restrictive policies function to 'control by exclusion and limitation' those deemed to be 'irreconcilably alien' and linguistically 'dissident' (Leibowitz 1974: 3). Even within American Indian and Alaska Native lands, public schools are required to abide by state and federal language-related regulations (see discussions by Balter, 2006; Balter & Grossman, 2009; Combs & Nicholas, 2012). Nor are tribal- and community-controlled schools immune from the pressures of English-only standardization. Both the BIE and US Office of Indian Education are required to use state standards as default benchmarks, with school funding contingent upon schools meeting AYP.[3]

Counter-Possibilities for Native Languages and Cultures in School

NCLB, English-only, Arizona's Mexican American Studies ban and other language- and culture-restrictive policies differ only in name from those designed to secure federal safety zone boundaries in centuries past. These policies, says bilingual education scholar Lily Wong Fillmore (2011: 28), 'stem from the same language policy that dictated how Native American children were to be schooled in reservation and off-reservation boarding schools.' However, the history of Native American LPP demonstrates the ability of individuals and groups to work around and through safety zone constraints, including in the domain of education. 'Indigenous intellectuals have surely become aware of the decisive role schools and education have played in the construction of the nation', López (2008: 60) writes, and they are using those institutions for their own nation-building. In this section, I offer a few final illustrations of the anti-colonial possibilities inherent in this work.

In Arizona, Tséhootsooí Diné Bi'ólta' (discussed in Chapter 5) has effectively contested the state's English-only law that would undermine its Navajo immersion program. In support of its position, the district has cited NCLB's goal of preparing students for meaningful citizenship. 'If students do not speak Navajo, they cannot be a meaningful participant in Navajo society', school officials point out (Johnson & Wilson, 2004). School officials have also cited NALA's protection of the right of Native communities to teach their language and culture in school (Combs & Nicholas, 2012), and the Navajo Sovereignty in Education Act's affirmation of the Navajo Nation's 'inherent right to exercise its responsibility to the Navajo people for their education', including teaching Diné language and culture (NSIEA, 2005, Sec. 3.1; see also Winstead et al., 2008). At Puente de Hózhǫ́ Trilingual Magnet School (also discussed in Chapter 5), while educators are concerned that test scores remain 'respectable enough to keep the NCLB wolves from the door', they also emphasize that 'standardized tests are only one piece in a very complex jigsaw puzzle we call education' (Fillerup, 2005: 15). At Hawai'i's Nāwahī Laboratory School, parents have boycotted English-only testing (Wilson, 2012), but school leaders note that Hawaiian-medium education often means 'applying oneself in academics to outperform those in mainstream schools to move the Hawaiian people forward' (William H. Wilson, personal communication, 23 November 2008).

Elsewhere, Native communities have looked to alternative institutional arrangements to exert local control over the content and medium of instruction their children receive. Bahidaj High (a pseudonym), an urban charter school and one of the participating schools in the Native Language Shift and Retention Study, is one such example. Founded in 1998 by a small group of Native and non-Native educators and parents dissatisfied with the BIE and public schools available for Native youth, Bahidaj High identifies itself as an academically rigorous, bicultural, community-based secondary school (Reeves, 2006). 'By infusing all aspects of the educational experience with elements of [Native] language and Native history, the school [nurtures] individual students, helping them become strong and responsible contributors to their communities' (cited in Lomawaima & McCarty, 2006: 159). Students learn their tribal language alongside Spanish as part of the 'foreign' language curriculum – a policy-making opportunity seized in a state that requires (safe) foreign-language education but bans (dangerous) bilingual education. At the time of the study, English classes emphasized the work of poets and writers of color, including Native authors. The US history text was Howard Zinn's *A People's History of the United States*, a radical critique of 'the telling of history from the standpoint of the conquerors' (Zinn, 2003: 22). Other curricular foci included Native basket weaving, ethnobotany and permaculture.

Like Puente de Hózhǫ́, TDB and Nāwahī, Bahidaj students have consistently performed on par with or better than their non-Indigenous peers in mainstream schools. Perhaps most impressive are students' responses to these language- and culture-rich learning experiences: 'I choose to learn about my culture', a graduate states, 'so I can know where I come from, and know who I am ... [and] that I won't get lost' (Juan, 2003, p. 29).[4]

In Alaska, a statewide initiative has created Indigenous cultural and linguistic standards that parallel those of the state (see Figure 7.1). These counter-standards 'are predicated on the belief that a firm grounding in the heritage language and culture indigenous to a particular place is a fundamental prerequisite for the development of culturally-healthy students and communities associated with that place' (Assembly of Alaska Native Educators, 1998: 2). The standards grew out of a collaboration between the University of Alaska Fairbanks and the Alaska Federation of Natives, who established the Alaska Native Rural Systemic Initiative, a network of 20 partner school districts representing 176 rural schools and 20,000 primarily Alaska Native students. According to Ray Barnhardt and A. Oscar Kawagley, the Alaska Native Rural Systemic Initiative promotes 'research-based initiatives to systematically document the Indigenous knowledge systems of Alaska Native people and to develop pedagogical practices and school curricula that

Figure 7.1 Alaska Native language and education guidelines and standards (photograph by Teresa L. McCarty)

appropriately incorporate Indigenous knowledge and ways of knowing into the formal education system' (Barnhardt & Kawagley, 2005: 15; see also Lomawaima & McCarty, 2006: 163).

The Alaska *Guidelines for Strengthening Indigenous Languages* call for schools, in consultation with local language advisory committees, to provide 'appropriate language immersion programs that strengthen the language in the community' and validate elders as key repositories of cultural and linguistic knowledge (Assembly of Alaska Native Educators, 2001: 2). The cultural and linguistic standards 'are not intended to produce standardization', the Assembly of Alaska Native Educators stresses, 'but rather to encourage schools to nurture and build upon the rich and varied cultural traditions that continue to be practiced in communities throughout Alaska' (Assembly of Alaska Native Educators, 1998: 3–4). In 2012, the Alaska legislature buttressed these standards with SB 130, which establishes an Alaska Native Language Preservation and Advisory Council 'to assess the state of Alaska Native [l]anguages, reevaluate the programs within the state, and make recommendations to the Governor and Legislature to establish new programs or reorganize the current programs' (NEA-Alaska, 2012: para. 1).

In the Yup'ik villages served by the Lower Kuskokwim School District discussed earlier in this chapter, Yup'ik teacher-researchers are reclaiming an Indigenous space despite NCLB pressures by identifying local human and material resources to reverse language loss. As Wyman and her colleagues describe those resources:

> All 11 [village] sites ... have Yup'ik-speaking adults, and vibrant spaces and activities in which most adult members of the community use Yup'ik. Sites have elementary-level Yup'ik language and content materials, and Yup'ik educators trained in language pedagogies and curriculum development. All village sites have at least some Yup'ik speaking children, and ... [a]n immersion school ... is additionally demonstrating how strong bilingual education models ... might foster language revitalization. (Wyman *et al.*, 2010a: 45).

Wyman *et al.* note the importance of collaboration among local Indigenous educators in marshaling local resources to resist the loss of local language and culture resources. Through their own action research, these educators are documenting children's language use and proactively 'focusing communities on language maintenance, highlighting the local possibilities for bilingualism' (Wyman *et al.*, 2010a: 45). In so doing, they are opening new 'implementational and ideological spaces' (Hornberger, 2006a) for language, culture, and education planning 'in challenging times' (Wyman *et al.*, 2010a: 46).

Finally, at Rough Rock, after having been nearly silenced by NCLB-mandated 'school improvement' dictates, the Diné language and culture are once again prominent in the school curriculum. According to former Rough Rock School superintendent Monty Roessel, under whose leadership the changes were instituted, while other schools 'were focused on AYP, we decided to create a Navajo language immersion program ... aligning our Navajo curriculum to our traditional ways of thought' (Roessel, 2011: 20). Not unlike the ways in which educators at other Indigenous-serving schools have created innovative curricula incorporating community languages and knowledges, Rough Rock educators identified six stages associated with *dzill* (*dzil*), 'meaning strength but also translated as sacred mountains' (Roessel, 2011: 20). 'With this', Roessel explains, 'as students develop through these six stages, ... they ... have a strong foundation of knowledge to plan and live their lives' (Roessel, 2011: 20–21). Although the school in 2011 had yet to 'make AYP', Roessel stresses that, 'We are creating students who know their place in the world – as a Navajo and as an American' (Roessel, 2011: 21).

Table 7.1 Comparison of 'strong' vs 'weak' Native language and culture programs (adapted from Baker, 2006: 215)

Program type	Strong (additive or full bilingualism/biculturalism)			Weak (subtractive or limited bilingualism/biculturalism)		
	Child's language status	Language of classroom	Program goals	Child's language status	Language of classroom	Program goals
Indigenous-language and culture immersion	Indigenous language as child's heritage/community language	Indigenous language	Indigenous-language and culture revitalization/maintenance; full bilingualism, biculturalism, biliteracy*	N/A	N/A	N/A
Indigenous-language and culture maintenance	Indigenous language as L1	Bilingual with emphasis on Indigenous language	Indigenous-language and culture maintenance; bilingualism, biculturalism, biliteracy	N/A	N/A	N/A
Two-way bilingual/dual-language immersion	Indigenous language as child's L1 or as heritage/community language	Mixed Indigenous language/English (90/10%; 50/50%, etc.)	Indigenous-language and culture revitalization/maintenance; bilingualism, biculturalism, biliteracy	N/A	N/A	N/A

Program type			Student characteristics	Language of instruction	Expected outcomes
Transitional	N/A	N/A	N/A	Indigenous language as child's L1	Indigenous language used for first years of schooling, then replaced with English	Strong English dominance/monolingualism, may include some Indigenous-language and culture enrichment
Mainstream with Indigenous-language and culture pull-out classes	N/A	N/A	N/A	Children enter school with mixed communicative repertoires (Indigenous language as L1, English as L1, or some combination)	English as primary language of instruction, with Indigenous language vocabulary drills and activities	Strong English dominance/monolingualism, with some Native-language and culture enrichment
Mainstream with foreign language instruction	N/A	N/A	N/A	Children enter school with varied communicative repertoires	English with Indigenous language taught as a 'foreign' language	Strong English dominance; limited bilingualism; little or no cultural emphasis
Structured English immersion**	N/A	N/A	N/A	Indigenous language as L1	English only	English monolingualism/monoculturalism (assimilation)

* A primary goal of some Indigenous-language programs is oral proficiency (i.e. not print literacy).

** Structured English immersion programs are best characterized as 'non-forms' of bilingual/multicultural education, also known as "submersion" or "sink-or-swim" (see Skutnabb-Kangas & McCarty, 2008).

Completing the Circle – Native American Linguistic and Educational Sovereignty

The examples above and those explored throughout this book illuminate the ways in which Indigenous communities have reconfigured safety zone borders to claim an Indigenous space (Smith, 2007). School-based programs are by no means the only tool by which this has been achieved, but where they are desired and controlled by Native communities, such programs constitute an 'instrument to conquer the bastions of the hegemonic society' and 'to recreate knowledge and local wisdom, to revitalize or even recover a vulnerable language' (López, 2008: 60). These are triumphs of voice and choice: not the manufactured either/or choice of colonial and neoliberal schooling, but Indigenous self-determinant choice about the content and medium of children's education (McCarty, 2006).

As the research literature and the language and culture reclamation projects examined here testify, the evidence is clear that strong, additive, academically rigorous Native language and culture programs produce beneficial academic *and* revitalization outcomes. Table 7.1 provides a framework for such programs, which include Native language and culture immersion (e.g. Nāwahī, TDB), maintenance (e.g. the early Rock Point and Rough Rock programs) and two-way bilingual or dual-language immersion programs (e.g. Puente de Hózhǫ́). In contrast, weaker transitional, pull-out, and add-on programs lead to subtractive bilingualism (monolingualism in the dominant language) and are not correlated with high levels of academic success (see, e.g. Hermes, 2005; McCarty, 2009, 2013b). As we have seen, strong Native language and culture programs also enhance student motivation, self-esteem and ethnic pride, as evidenced in improved school attendance and college-going rates, lower attrition and positive teacher–student and school–community relations. Finally, strong programs offer unique and varied opportunities to involve parents and elders in their children's schooling – a factor universally associated with academic success.

Evidence from these programs and an abundance of international data argue for strong bi-/multilingual education for *all* learners (García, 2009; García *et al*., 2006; Holm, 2006; López, 2008; McCarty, 2008b; Mohanty *et al*., 2009; Heugh & Skutnabb-Kangas, 2009). At one level this requires community-wide ideological clarification and 'intense conviction that this is the right thing to do' (Dauenhauer & Dauenhauer, 1998: 98). The diverse revitalization initiatives explored herein provide examples of this type of commitment in action. At another level, finding a 'safe harbor' for a minoritized language – what Nora Marks Dauenhauer and Richard Dauenhauer (1998: 97) call 'a safe place for language in daily life...where it can expand and grow' – entails power-sharing and dialogic engagement across multiple social sectors, including local schools. This is a formidable proposition, but myriad community-based language reclamation projects, in the United States and elsewhere, constitute living proof that this can be and is being achieved (see, e.g. Fishman, 2012; García & Fishman, 2012; Lee & Lee, 2012).

As this book was being written, the citizens of the United States of America elected their first African American president, Barack Obama. Among Obama's *Principles for Stronger Tribal Communities* was an affirmation of their sovereign, self-governing political status and recognition 'that instruction in tribal language increases Native American academic performance' (Obama, 2008: para 10). The fulfillment of these promises has been uneven; in particular, the wisdom and effectiveness of the Obama administration's education policies have been seriously questioned (see, e.g. US Senate Committee on Indian Affairs, 2011). More than 10 years into NCLB implementation, the law has been characterized as 'a bust in Indian Country' (Lee, 2012), and as a 21st century reincarnation of the late 19th and early 20th century BIA 'Uniform Course of Study' (Beaulieu, 2012: para. 22). According to Beaulieu, in terms of 'achievement levels, dropout rates, ... and [the] generally poor wellbeing of Indian children and youth', NCLB's long-term results 'beg attention to find a better way' (Beaulieu, 2012: para. 27).

At the same time, the Obama administration's Tribal Nations Summits, its reversal of the US government's earlier opposition to the 2007 United Nations *Declaration on the Rights of Indigenous Peoples,* and its widely heralded 2 December 2011 Executive Order, *Improving American Indian and Alaska Native Educational Opportunities and Strengthening Tribal Colleges and Universities* (The White House, 2011; see Appendix 3) have all offered hope for a new era of tribal–federal relations and of Native American educational and linguistic sovereignty. As Obama stated in the 2011 Executive Order:

> It is the policy of my Administration to support activities that will [expand] educational opportunities and ... outcomes for all AI/AN [American Indian/Alaska Native] students in order to fulfill our commitment to ... tribal self-determination and to help ensure that AI/AN students have an opportunity to learn their Native languages and histories and receive complete and competitive educations that prepare them for college, careers, and productive and satisfying lives. (The White House, 2011: Section 1, para. 2)

Certainly Obama's ascendancy to the presidency was itself a potent rupture of the safety zone. Yet it is entirely possible that all of this will be turned back in subsequent federal elections and policy initiatives. As the so-called 'birther' movement challenging Obama's US citizenship has persisted despite documentary evidence of the fallaciousness of the claims, and as the heated debate surrounding Mexican-origin immigration bleeds into school curricula through Anglo(phone) Studies-only laws such as those in Arizona, there can be no doubt of subterranean racial fears and the ferociousness of dominant-class interests in protecting a highly circumscribed and racialized safety zone.

I have argued that Native American LPP cannot be viewed separately from this larger power matrix, nor can we allow the appearance that Native languages and cultures no longer constitute a 'threat' to dominant interests to minimize the injustices or obscure the truly dangerous ideological mechanisms through which domination is exercised. Language policy is one of the most consequential of those mechanisms. However, if the past and present are any indication, Native American communities will continue to vigorously engage these unequal relations of power from an Indigenous vision of sovereignty and trust. That vision has already radically reshaped expectations for Indigenous languages – from loss and extinction to reclamation and empowerment. These human achievements constitute the storyline of this book, and they direct us toward ever-evolving strategies for dismantling the inequities and conveying diverse Native linguistic and cultural knowledge to the seventh generation and beyond.

Notes

(1) Parts of this section are adapted from McCarty (2009, 2013b) and Lomawaima and McCarty (2006: ch 8).
(2) Numerous other scholarly journals have published theme issues on NCLB implementation and impacts, although most do not specifically address Native American students. See, for example, Chrismer *et al.* (2006); Hollingsworth *et al.* (2007); and Valenzuela *et al.* (2007).
(3) At the time of this writing, this situation is changing, as the BIE has pressed Congress for a single set of standards for all BIE schools 'that will better meet the unique educational needs of Indian students' and that will be developed in 'consultation with tribes and educators, and ... accommodate those tribes wishing to develop their own standards and assessments' (Moore, 2011: 10). While some, including BIE officials, regard this as a positive step forward, others express strong concerns that it will, in reality, further distance control of Indigenous education from tribal governments and jurisdictions (see, e.g. Beaulieu, 2012).
(4) For other Native American charter school examples, see Belgarde (2004), Brayboy *et al.* (2013: ch. 4), Ewing and Ferrick (2012) and Manuelito *et al.* (2011).

Appendix 1

NATIVE AMERICAN LANGUAGES ACT OF 1990 (P.L. 101-477)

SHORT TITLE

SEC. 101. This title may be cited as the `Native American Languages Act'.

FINDINGS

SEC. 102. The Congress finds that--

(1) the status of the cultures and languages of Native Americans is unique and the United States has the responsibility to act together with Native Americans to ensure the survival of these unique cultures and languages;

(2) special status is accorded Native Americans in the United States, a status that recognizes distinct cultural and political rights, including the right to continue separate identities;

(3) the traditional languages of Native Americans are an integral part of their cultures and identities and form the basic medium for the transmission, and thus survival, of Native American cultures, literatures, histories, religions, political institutions, and values;

(4) there is a widespread practice of treating Native Americans languages as if they were anachronisms;

(5) there is a lack of clear, comprehensive, and consistent Federal policy on treatment of Native American languages which has often resulted in acts of suppression and extermination of Native American languages and cultures;

(6) there is convincing evidence that student achievement and performance, community and school pride, and educational opportunity is clearly and directly tied to respect for, and support of, the first language of the child or student;

(7) it is clearly in the interests of the United States, individual States, and territories to encourage the full academic and human potential achievements of all students and citizens and to take steps to realize these ends;

(8) acts of suppression and extermination directed against Native American languages and cultures are in conflict with the United States policy of self-determination for Native

Americans;

(9) languages are the means of communication for the full range of human experiences and are critical to the survival of cultural and political integrity of any people; and

(10) language provides a direct and powerful means of promoting international communication by people who share languages.

DEFINITIONS

SEC. 103. For purposes of this title--

(1) The term `Native American' means an Indian, Native Hawaiian, or Native American Pacific Islander.

(2) The term `Indian' has the meaning given to such term under section 5351(4) of the Indian Education Act of 1988 (25 U.S.C. 2651(4)).

(3) The term `Native Hawaiian' has the meaning given to such term by section 4009 of Public Law 100-297 (20 U.S.C. 4909).

(4) The term `Native American Pacific Islander' means any descendent of the aboriginal people of any island in the Pacific Ocean that is a territory or possession of the United States.

(5) The terms `Indian tribe' and `tribal organization' have the respective meaning given to each of such terms under section 4 of the Indian Self-Determination and Education Assistance Act (25 U.S.C. 450b).

(6) The term `Native American language' means the historical, traditional languages spoken by Native Americans.

(7) The term `traditional leaders' includes Native Americans who have special expertise in Native American culture and Native American languages.

(8) The term `Indian reservation' has the same meaning given to the term `reservation' under section 3 of the Indian Financing Act of 1974 (25 U.S.C. 1452).

DECLARATION OF POLICY

SEC. 104. It is the policy of the United States to--

(1) preserve, protect, and promote the rights and freedom of Native Americans to use, practice, and develop Native American languages;

(2) allow exceptions to teacher certification requirements for Federal programs, and programs funded in whole or in part by the Federal Government, for instruction in Native American languages when such teacher certification requirements hinder the employment of qualified teachers who teach in Native American languages, and to encourage State and territorial governments to make similar exceptions;

(3) encourage and support the use of Native American languages as a medium of instruction in order to encourage and support--

    (A) Native American language survival,

    (B) educational opportunity,

    (C) increased student success and performance,

    (D) increased student awareness and knowledge of their culture and history, and

    (E) increased student and community pride;

(4) encourage State and local education programs to work with Native American parents, educators, Indian tribes, and other Native American governing bodies in the implementation of programs to put this policy into effect;

(5) recognize the right of Indian tribes and other Native American governing bodies to use the Native American languages as a medium of instruction in all schools funded by the Secretary of the Interior;

(6) fully recognize the inherent right of Indian tribes and other Native American governing bodies, States, territories, and possessions of the United States to take action on, and give official status to, their Native American languages for the purpose of conducting their own business;

(7) support the granting of comparable proficiency achieved through course work in a Native American language the same academic credit as comparable proficiency achieved through course work in a foreign language, with recognition of such Native American language proficiency by institutions of higher education as fulfilling foreign language entrance or degree requirements; and

(8) encourage all institutions of elementary, secondary and higher education, where appropriate, to include Native American languages in the curriculum in the same manner as foreign languages and to grant proficiency in Native American languages the same full academic credit as proficiency in foreign languages.

NO RESTRICTIONS

SEC. 105. The right of Native Americans to express themselves through the use of Native American languages shall not be restricted in any public proceeding, including publicly supported education programs.

EVALUATIONS

SEC. 106. (a) The President shall direct the heads of the various Federal departments, agencies, and instrumentalities to--

(1) evaluate their policies and procedures in consultation with Indian tribes and other Native American governing bodies as well as traditional leaders and educators in order to determine and implement changes needed to bring the policies and procedures into compliance with the provisions of this title;

(2) give the greatest effect possible in making such evaluations, absent a clear specific Federal statutory requirement to the contrary, to the policies and procedures which will give the broadest effect to the provisions of this title; and

(3) evaluate the laws which they administer and make recommendations to the President on amendments needed to bring such laws into compliance with the provisions of this title.

(b) By no later than the date that is 1 year after the date of enactment of this title, the President shall submit to the Congress a report containing recommendations for amendments to Federal laws that are needed to bring such laws into compliance with the provisions of this title.

USE OF ENGLISH

SEC. 107. Nothing in this title shall be construed as precluding the use of Federal funds to teach English to Native Americans.

NATIVE AMERICAN LANGUAGES ACT OF 1992 (P.L. 102-524)

AN ACT

To assist Native Americans in assuring the survival and continuing vitality of their languages.

Be it enacted by the Senate and House of Representatives of the United States of America in Congress assembled,

SECTION 1. SHORT TITLE.

This Act, other than section 3, may be cited as the `Native American Languages Act of 1992'.

SEC. 2. GRANT PROGRAM.

The Native American Programs Act of 1974 (42 U.S.C. 2991 et seq.) is amended by adding after section 803A the following new section:

`SEC. 803B. GRANT PROGRAM TO ASSURE THE SURVIVAL AND CONTINUING VITALITY OF NATIVE AMERICAN LANGUAGES.

`(a) IN GENERAL- The Secretary shall award grants to any organization that is--

`(1) eligible for financial assistance under section 803(a); and

`(2) selected pursuant to subsection (c) of this section;

for the purposes of assisting Native Americans in assuring the survival and continuing vitality of their languages.

`(b) IN PARTICULAR- The specific purposes for which grants awarded under subsection (a) may be used include, but are not limited to--

`(1) the establishment and support of community language programs to bring older and younger Native Americans together to facilitate and encourage the transfer of language skills from one generation to another;

`(2) the establishment of programs to train Native Americans to teach native languages to others or to enable them to serve as interpreters or translators;

`(3) the development, printing, and dissemination of materials to be used for the teaching and enhancement of Native American languages;

`(4) the establishment or support of programs to train Native Americans to produce or participate in television or radio programs to be broadcast in their native languages;

`(5) the compilation, transcription, and analysis of oral testimony to record and preserve Native American languages;

`(6) the purchase of equipment (including audio and video recording equipment, computers, and software) required for the conducting of language programs; and

`(7) if no suitable facility is available, conversion of an existing facility for use in a language program.

`(c) APPLICATIONS- Grants shall be awarded on the basis of applications that are submitted by any of the entities described in subsection (a) to the Secretary in such form as the Secretary shall prescribe, but the applications shall, at a minimum, include--

`(1) a detailed description of the current status of the language to be addressed, including a description of any existing programs in support of that language;

`(2) a detailed description of the project for which a grant is sought;

`(3) a statement of objectives that are consonant with the purposes of this section; and

`(4) a plan to preserve the products of the language program for the benefit of future generations and other interested persons.

`(d) COLLABORATING ORGANIZATIONS-

`(1) IN GENERAL- If a tribal government or other eligible applicant determines that the objectives of its proposed Native American language program would be accomplished more effectively through a partnership with a school, college or university, the applicant may designate such an institution as a collaborating organization.

`(2) BENEFITS- As a collaborating organization, an institution may become a co-beneficiary of a grant under this Act.

`(3) MATCHING REQUIREMENTS- Matching requirements may be met by either, or both, the applicant and its collaborating institution.

`(e) LIMITATIONS ON FUNDING-

`(1) SHARE- Notwithstanding any other provision of this Act, a grant under this section shall cover not more than 90 percent of the cost of the program that is assisted by the grant. The remaining 10 percent contribution--

`(A) may be in cash or in kind, fairly evaluated, including plant, equipment, or services; and

`(B) may originate from any source (including any Federal agency) other than a program, contract, or grant authorized under this Act.

`(2) DURATION- A grant under this section may be for up to 3 years.

`(f) ADMINISTRATION- The Secretary shall administer grants under this section through the Administration for Native Americans.'.

SEC. 3. NATIVE AMERICANS EDUCATIONAL ASSISTANCE ACT.

(a) SHORT TITLE- This section may be cited as the `Native Americans Educational Assistance Act'.

(b) AGREEMENT TO CARRY OUT DEMONSTRATION PROJECT- The Secretary of the Interior is authorized to enter into an agreement with the National Captioning Institute, Inc., for the purpose of carrying out a demonstration project to determine the effectiveness of captioned educational materials as an educational tool in schools operated by the Bureau of Indian Affairs.

(c) REPORT- Prior to the expiration of the 12-month period following the date of the agreement entered into pursuant to subsection (b), the Secretary of the Interior shall report to the Congress the results of the demonstration project carried out pursuant to such agreement, together with his recommendations.

(d) AUTHORIZATION- There are authorized to be appropriated such amounts as may be necessary to carry out this section.

SEC. 4. AUTHORIZATION OF APPROPRIATIONS.

Section 816 of the Native American Programs Act of 1974 (42 U.S.C. 2992d) is amended--

(1) by striking out `sections 803(d) and 803A' each place it appears and inserting in lieu thereof `sections 803(d), 803A, and 803B'; and

(2) by adding at the end the following new subsection:

`(e) There are authorized to be appropriated to carry out the purposes of section 803B, $5,000,000 for fiscal year 1993, and such sums as are necessary for fiscal years 1994, 1995, 1996, and 1997.'

Appendix 2

H. R. 4766

One Hundred Ninth Congress
of the
United States of America

AT THE SECOND SESSION

Begun and held at the City of Washington on Tuesday, the third day of January, two thousand and six

An Act

To amend the Native American Programs Act of 1974 to provide for the revitalization of Native American languages through Native American language immersion programs; and for other purposes.

Be it enacted by the Senate and House of Representatives of the United States of America in Congress assembled,

SECTION 1. SHORT TITLE.

This Act may be cited as the "Esther Martinez Native American Languages Preservation Act of 2006".

SEC. 2. EXPANSION OF PROGRAM TO ENSURE THE SURVIVAL AND CONTINUING VITALITY OF NATIVE AMERICAN LANGUAGES.

Section 803C of the Native American Programs Act of 1974 (42 U.S.C. 2991b–3) is amended—

(1) in subsection (b)—

(A) in paragraph (5) by striking "and" at the end,

(B) in paragraph (6) by striking the period at the end and inserting "; and", and

(C) by adding at the end the following:

"(7)(A) Native American language nests, which are site-based educational programs that—

"(i) provide instruction and child care through the use of a Native American language for at least 10 children under the age of 7 for an average of at least 500 hours per year per student;

"(ii) provide classes in a Native American language for parents (or legal guardians) of students enrolled in a Native American language nest (including Native American language-speaking parents); and

"(iii) ensure that a Native American language is the dominant medium of instruction in the Native American language nest;

"(B) Native American language survival schools, which are site-based educational programs for school-age students that—

"(i) provide an average of at least 500 hours of instruction through the use of 1 or more Native American languages for at least 15 students for whom a Native American language survival school is their principal place of instruction;

"(ii) develop instructional courses and materials for learning Native American languages and for instruction through the use of Native American languages;

H. R. 4766—2

"(iii) provide for teacher training;
"(iv) work toward a goal of all students achieving—
"(I) fluency in a Native American language; and
"(II) academic proficiency in mathematics, reading (or language arts), and science; and
"(v) are located in areas that have high numbers or percentages of Native American students; and
"(C) Native American language restoration programs, which are educational programs that—
"(i) operate at least 1 Native American language program for the community in which it serves;
"(ii) provide training programs for teachers of Native American languages;
"(iii) develop instructional materials for the programs;
"(iv) work toward a goal of increasing proficiency and fluency in at least 1 Native American language;
"(v) provide instruction in at least 1 Native American language; and
"(vi) may use funds received under this section for—
"(I) Native American language programs, such as Native American language immersion programs, Native American language and culture camps, Native American language programs provided in coordination and cooperation with educational entities, Native American language programs provided in coordination and cooperation with local universities and colleges, Native American language programs that use a master-apprentice model of learning languages, and Native American language programs provided through a regional program to better serve geographically dispersed students;
"(II) Native American language teacher training programs, such as training programs in Native American language translation for fluent speakers, training programs for Native American language teachers, training programs for teachers in schools to utilize Native American language materials, tools, and interactive media to teach Native American language; and
"(III) the development of Native American language materials, such as books, audio and visual tools, and interactive media programs.",
(2) in subsection (c)—
(A) in paragraph (5) by striking "and" at the end,
(B) in paragraph (6) by striking the period at the end and inserting "; and", and
(C) by adding at the end the following:
"(7) in the case of an application for a grant to carry out any purpose specified in subsection (b)(7)(B), a certification by the applicant that the applicant has not less than 3 years of experience in operating and administering a Native American language survival school, a Native American language nest,

H. R. 4766—3

or any other educational program in which instruction is conducted in a Native American language.", and

(3) in subsection (e)(2) by inserting before the period the following: ", except that grants made under such subsection for any purpose specified in subsection (b)(7) may be made only on a 3-year basis".

SEC. 3. DEFINITION.

Section 815 of the Native American Programs Act of 1974 (42 U.S.C. 2992c) is amended—

(1) by redesignating paragraphs (1) through (6) as paragraphs (2) through (7), respectively, and

(2) by inserting before paragraph (2), as so redesignated, the following:

"(1) 'average' means the aggregate number of hours of instruction through the use of a Native American language to all students enrolled in a native language immersion program during a school year divided by the total number of students enrolled in the immersion program;".

SEC. 4. AUTHORIZATION OF APPROPRIATIONS FOR PROGRAM TO ENSURE THE SURVIVAL AND CONTINUING VITALITY OF NATIVE AMERICAN LANGUAGES.

Section 816(e) of the Native American Programs Act of 1974 (42 U.S.C. 2992d(e)) is amended by striking "1999, 2000, 2001, and 2002" and inserting "2008, 2009, 2010, 2011, and 2012".

Speaker of the House of Representatives.

Vice President of the United States and
President of the Senate.

Appendix 3

THE WHITE HOUSE

Office of the Press Secretary

For Immediate Release   December 2, 2011

EXECUTIVE ORDER

- - - - - - -

IMPROVING AMERICAN INDIAN AND ALASKA NATIVE EDUCATIONAL
OPPORTUNITIES AND STRENGTHENING TRIBAL COLLEGES AND UNIVERSITIES

By the authority vested in me as President by the Constitution and the laws of the United States of America, I hereby order as follows:

Section 1. Policy. The United States has a unique political and legal relationship with the federally recognized American Indian and Alaska Native (AI/AN) tribes across the country, as set forth in the Constitution of the United States, treaties, Executive Orders, and court decisions. For centuries, the Federal Government's relationship with these tribes has been guided by a trust responsibility -- a long-standing commitment on the part of our Government to protect the unique rights and ensure the well-being of our Nation's tribes, while respecting their tribal sovereignty. In recognition of that special commitment -- and in fulfillment of the solemn obligations it entails -- Federal agencies must help improve educational opportunities provided to all AI/AN students, including students attending public schools in cities and in rural areas, students attending schools operated and funded by the Department of the Interior's Bureau of Indian Education (BIE), and students attending postsecondary institutions, including Tribal Colleges and Universities (TCUs). This is an urgent need. Recent studies show that AI/AN students are dropping out of school at an alarming rate, that our Nation has made little or no progress in closing the achievement gap between AI/AN students and their non-AI/AN student counterparts, and that many Native languages are on the verge of extinction.

It is the policy of my Administration to support activities that will strengthen the Nation by expanding educational opportunities and improving educational outcomes for all AI/AN students in order to fulfill our commitment to furthering tribal self-determination and to help ensure that AI/AN students have an opportunity to learn their Native languages and histories and receive complete and competitive educations that prepare them for college, careers, and productive and satisfying lives.

My Administration is also committed to improving educational opportunities for students attending TCUs. TCUs maintain, preserve, and restore Native languages and cultural traditions; offer a high-quality college education; provide career and technical education, job training, and other career-building programs; and often serve as anchors in some of the country's poorest and most remote areas.

Sec. 2. Definitions. (a) "Agency" means any executive department or agency designated by the Secretary of Education and the Secretary of the Interior to participate in this order.

(b) "Indian tribe" means an Indian or Alaska Native tribe, band, nation, pueblo, village, or community that the Secretary of the Interior acknowledges to exist as an Indian tribe pursuant to the Federally Recognized Indian Tribe List Act of 1994, 25 U.S.C. 479a.

(c) "American Indian and Alaska Native" means a member of an Indian tribe, as membership is defined by the tribe.

(d) "Public school" means a Head Start center or a pre-kindergarten, elementary, or secondary school that is predominantly funded by public means through the Federal Government, a State, a local educational agency, or an Indian tribal government, including a school operated directly by or through contract or grant with the BIE, an Indian tribe, or a State, county, or local government.

(e) "Tribal Colleges and Universities" are those institutions that are chartered by their respective Indian tribes through the sovereign authority of the tribes or by the Federal Government, and defined in section 316 of the Higher Education Act of 1965 (20 U.S.C. 1059c).

Sec. 3. White House Initiative on American Indian and Alaska Native Education.

(a) Establishment. There is hereby established the White House Initiative on American Indian and Alaska Native Education (Initiative). The Secretary of Education and the Secretary of the Interior will co-chair the Initiative. The Secretary of Education shall appoint an Executive Director who shall be responsible for overseeing implementation of the Initiative. This individual shall be a senior-level, Department of Education official who shall serve as the Secretary of Education's senior policy advisor on Federal policies affecting AI/AN education.

The Executive Director shall work closely with the BIE Director and shall provide periodic reports to the Secretaries of Education and the Interior regarding progress achieved under the Initiative. The Executive Director shall coordinate frequent consultations with tribal officials and shall provide staff support for the National Advisory Council on Indian Education (NACIE), authorized by section 7141 of the Elementary and Secondary Education Act of 1965 (ESEA) (20 U.S.C. 7471).

(b) Mission and Functions. (1) The Initiative shall help expand educational opportunities and improve educational outcomes for all AI/AN students, including opportunities to learn their Native languages, cultures, and histories and receive complete and competitive educations that prepare them for college, careers, and productive and satisfying lives, by:

> (i) working closely with the Executive Office of the President to help ensure AI/AN participation in the development and implementation of key Administration priorities;

3

(ii)   strengthening the relationship between the Department of Education, which has substantial expertise and resources to help improve Indian education, and the Department of the Interior and its BIE, which directly operates or provides grants to tribes to operate an extensive primary, secondary, and college level school system for AI/AN children and young adults;

(iii)   coordinating, in consultation with the Department of Education's Director of Indian Education, programs administered by the Department of Education and other executive branch agencies regarding AI/AN education;

(iv)   serving as a liaison with other executive branch agencies on AI/AN issues and advising those agencies on how they might help to promote AI/AN educational opportunities;

(v)   reporting on the development, implementation, and coordination of education policy and programs that affect AI/AN students;

(vi)   furthering tribal sovereignty by supporting efforts, consistent with applicable law, to build the capacity of tribal educational agencies and TCUs to provide high-quality education services to AI/AN children;

(vii)   developing in partnership with tribal educational agencies a more routine and streamlined process for entering into agreements for educational studies conducted on tribal lands;

(viii)   developing sufficient data resources to inform progress on Federal performance indicators, in close collaboration with the Department of Education's National Center for Educational Statistics;

(ix)   encouraging and coordinating Federal partnerships with public, private, philanthropic, and nonprofit entities to help increase the readiness of AI/AN students for school, college, and careers, and to help increase the number and percentage of AI/AN students completing college; and

(x)   developing a national network of individuals, organizations, and communities to share best practices in AI/AN education and encouraging them to implement these practices.

(2) In order to help expand educational opportunities and improve education outcomes for AI/AN students, the Initiative shall promote, encourage, and undertake efforts, consistent with applicable law, to meet the following objectives:

(i) increasing the number and percentage of AI/AN children who enter kindergarten ready for success through improved access to high-quality early learning programs and services, including Native language immersion programs, that encourage the learning and development of AI/AN children from birth through age five;

(ii) supporting the expanded implementation of education reform strategies that have shown evidence of success in enabling AI/AN students to acquire a rigorous and well-rounded education and increasing their access to the support services that prepare them for college, careers, and civic involvement;

(iii) increasing the number and percentage of AI/AN students who have access to excellent teachers and school leaders, including effective science, technology, engineering, and mathematics (STEM), language, and special education teachers, in part by supporting efforts to improve the recruitment, development, and retention of effective AI/AN teachers and other effective teachers and school leaders, particularly through TCUs;

(iv) reducing the AI/AN student dropout rate and helping a greater number and percentage of those students who stay in high school to be ready for college and careers by the time of their graduation and college completion, in part by promoting a positive school climate and supporting successful and innovative dropout-prevention and recovery strategies that better engage AI/AN youths in their learning and help them catch up academically;

(v) providing pathways that enable those who have dropped out to reenter educational or training programs and acquire degrees, certificates, or industry-recognized credentials and obtain quality jobs, and expanding access to high-quality education programs leading to career advancement, especially in the STEM fields, by supporting adult, career, and technical education;

(vi) increasing college access and completion for AI/AN students through strategies to strengthen the capacity of postsecondary institutions, particularly TCUs; and

(vii) helping to ensure that the unique cultural, educational, and language needs of AI/AN students are met.

(3) To facilitate a new partnership between the Department of Education and the Department of the Interior, to improve AI/AN education, the Executive Director shall work with the BIE Director and develop

a Memorandum of Understanding (MOU) between the two Departments that will take advantage of both Departments' expertise, resources, and facilities. The MOU shall be completed within 120 days of the date of this order. Among other things, the MOU shall address how the Departments will collaborate in carrying out the policy set out in section 1 of this order.

(c) Funding and Administrative Support. Subject to the availability of appropriations, the Department of Education shall fund the Initiative, including NACIE. The Department shall also provide administrative support for the Initiative to the extent permitted by law and within existing appropriations.

(d) Interagency Working Group. There is established the Interagency Working Group on AI/AN education and TCUs, which shall be convened by the Initiative's Executive Director. The Working Group shall consist of senior officials from the Department of Education and the Department of the Interior and officials from the Departments of Justice, Agriculture, Labor, Health and Human Services, and Energy, the Environmental Protection Agency, and the White House Domestic Policy Council, as well as such additional agencies and offices as the Secretaries of Education and the Interior may designate. Senior officials shall be designated by the heads of their respective agencies and offices. The Secretaries of Education and the Interior shall serve as the co-chairs of the Interagency Working Group.

(e) Federal Agency Plans. (1) Each agency designated by the co-chairs as a member of the Interagency Working Group shall develop and implement a two-part, 4-year plan of the agency's efforts to fulfill the purposes of this order, with part one of the plan focusing on all AI/AN students except for those attending TCUs, and part two focusing on AI/AN students attending TCUs. Each agency plan shall include:

(i) annual performance indicators and appropriate measurable objectives with which the agency will measure its success in meeting the goals of this order;

(ii) information on how the agency intends to increase the capacity of educational agencies and institutions, including our Nation's public schools and TCUs, to deliver high-quality education and related social services to all AI/AN students; and

(iii) agency efforts to enhance the ability of these educational agencies and institutions serving AI/AN students to compete effectively for grants, contracts, cooperative agreements, and other Federal resources with which to serve the education needs of AI/AN students, and to encourage eligible schools and colleges serving those students to apply for Federal grants and participate in Federal education programs, as appropriate. Agency plans may also emphasize access to high-quality educational opportunities for AI/AN students, consistent with requirements of the ESEA, the Individuals with Disabilities Education Act, and other applicable Federal education statutes; the preservation and revitalization of tribal languages and cultural traditions; and innovative approaches to more seamlessly align early learning, elementary, and secondary education programs with the work of TCUs.

(2) Submission. Each agency shall submit its plan to the Initiative by a deadline established by the co-chairs. In consultation with NACIE, the Initiative shall then review agency plans and develop, for submission to the President, a synthesized interagency plan to achieve the aims of this order.

(3) Annual Performance Reports. Each agency shall submit to the Initiative an Annual Performance Report that measures the agency's performance against the objectives set forth in its plan. In consultation with NACIE, the Initiative shall review and combine Annual Performance Reports from the various agencies into one annual report, which shall be submitted to the Secretaries of Education and the Interior for review.

(f) Private Sector. In consultation with NACIE, and consistent with applicable law, the Interagency Working Group, led by the Executive Director, shall encourage the private sector to assist State- and locally-operated public schools that serve large numbers of AI/AN students, including those attending our Nation's public schools, publicly-funded preschools, and TCUs, through increased use of such strategies as:

(1) Providing funds to support the preservation and revitalization of Native languages and cultures;

(2) Providing funds to support increased institutional endowments;

(3) Helping these schools develop expertise in financial and facilities management, information systems, and curricula; and

(4) Providing resources for the hiring and training of effective teachers and administrators.

Sec. 4. Study. In carrying out this order, the Secretaries of Education and the Interior shall study and collect information on the education of AI/AN students.

Sec. 5. General Provisions. (a) NACIE shall serve as the Initiative's advisory committee.

(b) Insofar as the Federal Advisory Committee Act, as amended (5 U.S.C. App.), may apply to the Initiative, any functions of the President under that Act, except for those of reporting to the Congress, shall be performed by the Secretary of Education, in consultation with the Secretary of the Interior, in accordance with the guidelines issued by the Administrator of General Services.

(c) This order revokes Executive Order 13270 of July 3, 2002, Executive Order 13336 of April 30, 2004, and section 1(n) of Executive Order 13585 of September 30, 2011.

(d) The heads of agencies shall assist and provide such information to the Initiative as may be necessary to carry out its functions, consistent with applicable law.

(e) Nothing in this order shall be construed to impair or otherwise affect:

> (1) authority granted by law to an executive department, agency, or the head thereof; or
>
> (2) functions of the Director of the Office of Management and Budget relating to budgetary, administrative, or legislative proposals.

(f) This order is not intended to, and does not, create any right or benefit, substantive or procedural, enforceable at law or in equity by any party against the United States, its departments, agencies, or entities, its officers, employees, or agents, or any other person.

BARACK OBAMA

THE WHITE HOUSE
December 2, 2011.

# # #

References

Aberle, D.F. (1966) *The Peyote Religion among the Navajo*. Chicago, IL: Aldine.

Adams, D.W. (1988) Fundamental considerations: The deep meaning of Native American schooling, 1880–1900. *Harvard Educational Review* 58 (1), 1–28.

Adams, D.W. (1995) *Education for Extinction: American Indians and the Boarding School Experience*. Lawrence, KS: University Press of Kansas.

Adley-SantaMaria, B. (1999) Interrupting White Mountain Apache language shift: An insider's view. *Practicing Anthropology* 20 (2), 16–19.

Administration for Children and Families (2011) *About the Office of Head Start*. Washington, DC: US Office of Health and Human Services, Administration for Children and Families. Online at http://www.acf.hhs.gov/programs/ohs/about/index.html, accessed 6 July 2012.

'Aha Pūnana Leo (n.d.) History. Online at http://www.ahapunanaleo.org/index.php?/about/history/, accessed 6 June 2012.

Aikman, S. (1999) *Intercultural Education and Literacy: An Ethnographic Study of Indigenous Knowledge and Learning in the Peruvian Amazon*. Amsterdam: John Benjamins.

Amrein, A.L. and Berliner, D.C. (2002) *The Impact of High-Stakes Tests on Student Academic Performance: An Analysis of NAEP Results in States with High-Stakes Tests and ACT, SAT, and AP Test Results in States with High School Graduation Exams*. Tempe, AZ: Arizona State University, College of Education, Education Policy Studies Laboratory. Online at http://epsl.asu.edu/epru/documents/EPSL-0211-126-EPRU.pdf, accessed 11 October 2012.

Anishinaabek Mushkegowuk Onkwehonwe Commission of Ontario (2012) *Shatiwennakara:tats Diploma Program/Totahne Language Nest – Tyendinaga's Answer to Declining Mohawk Language Speakers*, 26 February. Online at http://www.amolco.ca/news/shatiwennakaratats-diploma-program-totahne-language-nest–tyendinaga's-answer-declining-mohawk-, accessed 6 June 2012.

Arbuthnot, B.R. (1984) Kahnawake Survival School: A community based case study in bicultural education. Unpublished master's thesis, Concordia University.

Archuleta, M.L, Child, B.J. and Lomawaima, K.T. (eds) (2000) *Away from Home: American Indian Boarding School Experiences 1879–2000*. Phoenix, AZ: The Heard Museum.

Arias, M.B. and Faltis, C. (eds) (2012) *Implementing Educational Language Policy in Arizona: Legal, Historical and Current Practices in SEI*. Bristol: Multilingual Matters.

Arizona Department of Education (ed.) (1988) *Proceedings of the Eighth Annual Native American Language Issues Institute: 'Strengthening Native Languages through Unity and Commitment'*. Choctaw, OK: Native American Language Issues Institute.

Arizona Proposition 203 (2000) English Language Education for Children in Public Schools. Online at http://www.azsos.gov/election/2000/info/PubPamphlet/english/prop203.htm, accessed 6 June 2012.

Arviso, M. and Holm, W. (1990) Native American language immersion programs: Can there be bilingual education when the language is going (or gone) as a child language? *Journal of Navajo Education* 8 (1), 39–47.

Arviso, M. and Holm, W. (2001) Tséhootsooídi Ólta'gi Diné bizaad bíhoo'aah: A Navajo immersion program at Fort Defiance, Arizona. In L. Hinton and K. Hale (eds) *The Green Book of Language Revitalization in Practice* (pp. 203–215). San Diego, CA: Academic Press.

Ash, A., Fermino, J.L.D. and Hale, K. (2001) Diversity in local language maintenance and restoration: A reason for optimism. In L. Hinton and K. Hale (eds) *The Green Book of Language Revitalization in Practice* (pp. 19–35). San Diego, CA: Academic Press.

Assembly of Alaska Native Educators (1998) *Alaska Standards for Culturally Responsive Schools*. Anchorage, AK: Alaska Native Knowledge Network.

Assembly of Alaska Native Educators (2001) *Guidelines for Strengthening Indigenous Languages*. Anchorage, AK: Alaska Native Knowledge Network.

Atherton, K. (2010) Back from the brink: Learning the Yurok language. *The Triplicate*, 18 October. Online at http://www.triplicate.com/index2.php?option=com_content&task=view&id=110520&pop=1&page=0&itemid=199, accessed 19 October 2010.

Atkins, J.D.C. (1887[1992]) Barbarous dialects should be blotted out.... In J. Crawford (ed.) *Language Loyalties: A Source Book on the Official English Controversy* (pp. 47–51). Chicago, IL: University of Chicago Press.

Austin, P.K. (ed.) (2008) *One Thousand Languages: Living, Endangered, and Lost*. Berkeley, CA: University of California Press.

Austin, P.K. and Sallabank, J. (eds) (2011) *The Cambridge Handbook of Endangered Languages*. Cambridge: Cambridge University Press.

Baker, C. (2006) *Foundations of Bilingual Education and Bilingualism* (4th edn). Clevedon: Multilingual Matters.

Baldwin, D. (2003) Miami language reclamation: From ground zero. Lecture presented by the Center for Writing and the Interdisciplinary Minor in Literacy and Rhetorical Studies, Speaker Series 24. Minneapolis, MN: University of Minnesota. Online at http://writing.umn.edu/lrs/assets/pdf/speakerpubs/baldwin.pdf, accessed 6 June 2012.

Baldwin, D. and Costa, D.J. (2005) *myaamia neehi peewaalia kaloosioni mahsinaakani: A Miami-Peoria Dictionary*. Miami, OK: Miami Nation.

Baldwin, D. and Olds, J. (2007) Miami Indian language and cultural research at Miami University. In D.M. Cobb and L. Fowler (eds) *Beyond Red Power: American Indian Politics and Activism since 1900* (pp. 280–290). Santa Fe, NM: School for Advanced Research Press.

Ball, S.J. (2006) What is policy? Texts, trajectories, and toolboxes. In S.J. Ball, *Education Policy and Social Class: The Selected Works of Stephen J. Ball* (pp. 43–53). London: Routledge.

Balter, A. (2006) Toward an ethnographic analysis of federal education policy: The effects of the No Child Left Behind Act on language and culture education in Navajo public schools. Unpublished honors thesis, Swarthmore College.

Balter, A. and Grossman, F.D. (2009) The effects of the No Child Left Behind Act on language and culture education in Navajo public schools. *Journal of American Indian Education* 48 (3), 19–46.

Banks, J.A. (2006) Series foreword. In K.T. Lomawaima and T.L. McCarty, *'To Remain an Indian': Lessons in Democracy from a Century of Native American Education* (pp. xi–xv). New York: Teachers College Press.

Barnhardt, R. and Kawagley, A.O. (2005) Indigenous knowledge systems and Alaska Native ways of knowing. *Anthropology and Education Quarterly* 36 (1), 8–23.

Battiste, M. (1986) Cognitive assimilation and Micmac literacy. In J. Barman, Y. Hébert and D. McCaskill (eds) *Indian Nations in Canada: The Legacy*, Vol. 1 (pp. 23–41). Vancouver: University of British Columbia Press.

Bauer, E. (1970) Bilingual education in BIA schools. *TESOL Quarterly* 4 (3), 223–229.

Baugh, J. (2000) *Beyond Ebonics: Linguistic Pride and Racial Prejudice*. Oxford: Oxford University Press.

Bauman, J.J. (1982) *Guide to Issues in Indian Language Retention*. Washington, DC: Center for Applied Linguistics.

Bean, L.J. and Vane, S.B. (1997) The California culture area. In M.R. Mignon and D.L. Boxberger (eds) *Native North Americans: An Ethnohistorical Approach* (2nd edn) (pp. 309–350). Dubuque, IO: Kendall/Hunt.

Bear Nicholas, A. (2009) Reversing language shift through a Native language immersion teacher training programme in Canada. In T. Skutnabb-Kangas, R. Phillipson, A.K. Mohanty and M. Panda (eds) *Social Justice through Multilingual Education* (pp. 220–237). Bristol: Multilingual Matters.

Beatty, W.W. (1953) *Education for Cultural Change: Selected Articles from Indian Education, 1944–1951*. Chilocco, OK: US Department of the Interior, Bureau of Indian Affairs.

Beaulieu, D. (2006) A survey and assessment of culturally based education programs for Native American students in the United States. *Journal of American Indian Education* 45 (2), 50–61.

Beaulieu, D. (2011) Statement of Dr. David Beaulieu, professor of education policy and director of the Electa Quinney Institute for American Indian Education, University of Wisconsin. In Committee on Indian Affairs, United States Senate, 11th Congress, Second Session, *Indian Education: Did the No Child Left Behind Act Leave Indian Students Behind?* (pp. 46–54). Washington, DC: US Government Printing Office.

Beaulieu, D. (2012) The Obama Administration's blaming of American Indians as policy. *Indian Country Today*, 9 July. Online at http://indiancountrytodaymedianetwork.com/ict_sbc/the-obama-administration's-blaming-of-american-indians-as-policy, accessed 9 July 2012.

Beaulieu, D., Sparks, L. and Alonzo, M. (2005) *Preliminary Report on No Child Left Behind in Indian Country*. Washington, DC: National Indian Education Association.

Begay, S., Dick, G.S., Estell, D.W., Estell, J., McCarty, T.L. and Sells, A. (1995) Change from the inside out: A story of transformation in a Navajo community school. *Bilingual Research Journal* 19 (1), 121–139.

Belgarde, M.J. (2004) Native American charter schools: Culture, language, and self-determination. In E. Rofes and L.M. Stulberg (eds) *The Emancipatory Promise of Charter Schools: Toward a Progressive Politics of School Choice* (pp. 107–124). Albany, NY: State University of New York Press.

Benally, A. and Viri, D. (2005) *Diné bizaad* (Navajo language) at a crossroads: Extinction or renewal? *Bilingual Research Journal* 29 (1), 85–108.

Benjamin, R., Pecos, R. and Romero, M.E. (1996) Language revitalization efforts in the Pueblo de Cochiti: Becoming 'literate' in an oral society. In N.H. Hornberger (ed.) *Indigenous Literacies in the Americas: Language Planning from the Bottom Up* (pp. 115–136). Berlin: Mouton de Gruyter.

Benton, N.A. and Kinsland, J.E. (1953) *Please Fill the Tank*. Ogden, UT: Defense Printing Service for the US Department of the Interior, Bureau of Indian Affairs, Branch of Education.

Bergstrom, A., Cleary, L.M. and Peacock, T.D. (2003) *The Seventh Generation: Native Students Speak about Finding the Good Path*. Charleston, WV: ERIC Clearinghouse on Rural Education and Small Schools.

Bielenberg, B.T. (2002) 'Who will sing the songs?' Language renewal among Puebloan adolescents. Unpublished PhD dissertation, Graduate School of Education, University of California, Berkeley.

Biemiller, L. (2011) Cherokee for beginners: The long road back, starting on campus. *The Chronicle of Higher Education*, 9 January. Online at http://chronicle.com/article/Cherokee-for-Beginners-the/125881/, accessed 11 June 2012.

Blommaert, J. (2008) Artefactual ideologies and the textual production of African languages. *Language and Communication* 28 (4), 291–307.
Blommaert, J. (2010) *The Sociolinguistics of Globalization*. Cambridge: Cambridge University Press.
Boyarin, J. (1992) Introduction. In J. Boyarin (ed.) *The Ethnography of Reading* (pp. 1–9). Berkeley, CA: University of California Press.
Bradley, D. (2011) A survey of language endangerment. In P.K. Austin and J. Sallabank (eds) *The Cambridge Handbook of Language Endangerment* (pp. 66–77). Cambridge: Cambridge University Press.
Bragdon, K.J. (1997) The Northeast culture area. In M.R. Mignon and D.L. Boxberger (eds) *Native North Americans: An Ethnohistorical Approach* (2nd edn) (pp. 113–158). Dubuque, IO: Kendall/Hunt.
Brandt, E.A. (1988) Applied linguistic anthropology and American Indian language renewal. *Human Organization* 47 (4), 322–329.
Brayboy, B.M. and Deyhle, D. (2000) Insider–outsider: Researchers in American Indian communities. *Theory into Practice* 39 (3), 163–169.
Brayboy, B.M.J., Faircloth, S.C., Lee, T.S., Maaka, M.J. and Richardson, T. (2013) *Indigenous Education in the 21st Century*. Washington, DC: American Educational Research Association (in press).
Breinig, J. (2006) Alaskan Haida stories of language growth and regeneration. *American Indian Quarterly* 30 (1–2), 110–118.
Briggeman, K. (2007) Keeping a language alive: Co-founder of Blackfoot immersion school in Browning visits UM. *The Missoulian*, March. Online at http://www.pieganinstitute.org, accessed 22 July 2008.
Brill de Ramírez, S.B. and Zuni Lucero, E. (2009) Introduction: Simon J. Ortiz, a poetic legacy of Indigenous continuance, belonging, and commitment. In S.B. Brill de Ramírez and E.Z. Lucero (eds) *Simon J. Ortiz: A Poetic Legacy of Indigenous Continuance* (pp. 1–71). Albuquerque, NM: University of New Mexico Press.
Brossy, C. (2007) New media for Diné: Translators help develop language-learning software. *Navajo Times*, 31 December, n.p.
Brunden, J. (2009) Ten teens study to guard their Native language. National Public Radio *Weekend Edition*, 19 July. Online at http://www.npr.org/templates/story/story.php?storyId=106783656, accessed 12 June 2012.
Bucholtz, M. (2002) Youth and cultural practice. *Annual Review of Anthropology* 31, 525–552.
Camino Vérité Films (2012) The Young Ancestors. Online at http://www.theyoungancestors.com/TheYoungAncestors/Home.html, accessed 26 June 2012.
Canagarajah, A.S. (ed.) (2005) *Reclaiming the Local in Language Policy and Practice*. Mahwah, NJ: Lawrence Erlbaum.
Canagarajah, S. (2006) Ethnographic methods in language policy. In T. Ricento (ed.) *An Introduction to Language Policy: Theory and Method* (pp. 153–169). Malden, MA: Blackwell.
Castagno, A.E. and Brayboy, B.M.J. (2008) Culturally responsive schooling for Indigenous youth: A review of the literature. *Review of Educational Research* 78 (4), 941–993.
Castellanos, D. (1992) A polyglot nation. In J. Crawford (ed.) *Language Loyalties: A Source Book on the Official English Controversy* (pp. 13–19). Chicago, IL: University of Chicago Press.
Cazden, C.B. and Snow, C.E. (guest eds) (1990) English plus: Issues in bilingual education. (Special issue.) *Annals of the American Academy of Political and Social Science*, 508 (March).
Center for American Indian Languages (2011) Shoshone/Goshute Youth Language Apprenticeship Program. SYLAP 2011. Online at http://www.cail.utah.edu/?pageid=5750, accessed 30 May 2012.

Chafe, W. (1962) Estimates regarding the present speakers of North American Indian languages. *International Journal of American Linguistics* 28 (3), 162–171.
Chafe, W. (1965) Corrected estimates regarding speakers of Indian languages. *International Journal of American Linguistics* 31 (4), 345–346.
Charles, W. (2005) *Qaneryaramta egmiucia*: Continuing our language. *Anthropology and Education Quarterly* 36 (1), 107–111.
Charles, W. (2011) Dynamic assessment in a Yugtun L2 intermediate adult classroom. Unpublished PhD dissertation, School of Education, University of Alaska Fairbanks.
Chen, E.M. (2001) Statement on the civil liberties implications of Official English legislation before the United States Senate Committee on Governmental Affairs, December 6, 1995. In R.D. González and I. Melis (eds) *Language Ideologies: Critical Perspectives on the Official English Movement. Vol. 2: History, Theory, and Policy* (pp. 30–62). Urbana, IL and Mahwah, NJ: National Council of Teachers of English and Lawrence Erlbaum.
Cherokee Nation Language Planning Committees (2008) *Ga-du-gí: A Vision for Working Together to Revitalize the Cherokee Language*. Tahlequah, OK: Cherokee Nation Culture Resource Center.
Cherokee Phoenix (2011) *Cherokee Phoenix Annual Report 2011*. Tahlequah, OK: Cherokee Phoenix.
Chew, K. (2012) Minority births outpace White births in the U.S. *Care2make a difference*, 17 May. Online at http://www.care2.com/causes/minority-births-outpace-white-births-in-the-us.html, accessed 12 June 2012.
Child, B.J. (1998) *Boarding School Seasons: American Indian Families 1900–1940*. Lincoln, NE: University of Nebraska Press.
Chrismer, S.S., Hodge, S.T. and Saintil, D. (2006) Assessing NCLB: Perspectives and prescriptions. (Special issue.) *Harvard Educational Review*, 76 (4).
Cobb, D.M. and Fowler, L. (2007) Introduction. In D.M. Cobb and L. Fowler (eds) *Beyond Red Power: American Indian Politics and Activism since 1900* (pp. x–xx). Santa Fe, NM: School for Advanced Research.
Cochran-Smith, M. (2005) No Child Left Behind: 3 years and counting. *Teacher Education* 56 (2), 99–103.
Coley, M-E. (2005) A message from the chair. In S. Tulloch (compiler) *1st Inuit Circumpolar Youth Symposium on the Inuit Language Summary Report* (p. 4). Iqaluit, Nunavut: Inuit Circumpolar Youth Council. Online at http://www.gordonfn.org/resfiles/ICYC-LanguageReport-English.pdf, accessed 6 September 2012.
Collier, J. Jr (1988) Survival at Rough Rock: A historical overview of Rough Rock Demonstration School. *Anthropology and Education Quarterly* 19 (3), 253–269.
Combs, M.C. (1999) Public perceptions of Official English/English Only: Framing the debate in Arizona. In T. Huebner and K.A. Davis (eds) *Sociopolitical Perspectives on Language Policy and Planning in the USA* (pp. 131–153). Amsterdam: John Benjamins.
Combs, M.C. and Nicholas, S.E. (2012) The effect of Arizona language policies on Arizona Indigenous students. *Language Policy* 11 (1), 101–118.
Conklin, P. (1967) Good day at Rough Rock. *American Education*, February, 4–9.
Cooper, J. and Gregory, R. (1976) Can community control of Indian education work? *Journal of American Indian Education* 15 (3), 7–11.
Cooper, R. (1989) *Language Planning and Social Change*. Cambridge: Cambridge University Press.
Coronel-Molina, S.M. and McCarty, T.L. (2011) Language curriculum design and evaluation for endangered languages. In P.K. Austin and J. Sallabank (eds) *The Cambridge Handbook of Endangered Languages* (pp. 354–370). Cambridge: Cambridge University Press.
Costa, D.J. (1994) The Miami–Illinois language. Unpublished PhD dissertation, University of California, Berkeley.

Costa, D.J. (ed., trans.) (2010) *myaamia neehi peewaalia aacimoona neehi aalhsoohkaana. Myaamia and Peoria Narratives and Winter Stories.* Miami Nation, OK: Miami Tribe of Oklahoma and Peoria Tribe of Oklahoma.
Crawford, J. (ed.) (1992) *Language Loyalties: A Source Book on the Official English Controversy.* Chicago, IL: University of Chicago Press.
Crawford, J. (1995a) Endangered Native American languages: What is to be done, and why? *Bilingual Research Journal* 19 (1), 17–38.
Crawford, J. (1995b) *Bilingual Education: History, Politics, Theory, and Practice.* Los Angeles, CA: Bilingual Educational Services.
Crawford, J. (2000) Seven hypotheses on language loss. In *At War with Diversity: US Language Policy in an Age of Anxiety* (pp. 66–83). Clevedon: Multilingual Matters.
Crawford, J. (2004a) *No Child Left Behind: Misguided Approach to School Accountability for English Language Learners.* Takoma Park, MD: Institute for Language and Education Policy. Online at http://www.elladvocates.org/documents/nclb/Crawford_NCLB_Misguided_Approach_for_ELLs.pdf, accessed 23 June 2008.
Crawford, J. (2004b) *Educating English Learners: Language Diversity in the Classroom* (5th edn). Los Angeles, CA: Bilingual Educational Services.
Crystal, D. (1992) *An Encyclopedic Dictionary of Language and Languages.* Cambridge, MA: Blackwell.
Cultural Survival (2012) The Wôpanâak (Wampanoag) Language Reclamation Project. Online at http://www.culturalsurvival.org/current-projects/native-language-revitalization-campaign/partners-links, accessed 6 September 2012.
Cummins, J. (1989) *Empowering Minority Students.* Sacramento, CA: California Association for Bilingual Education.
Dauenhauer, N.M. and Dauenhauer, R. (1998). Technical, emotional, and ideological issues in reversing language shift: Examples from Southeast Alaska. In L.A. Grenoble and L.J. Whaley (eds) *Endangered Languages: Language Loss and Community Response* (pp. 57–98). Cambridge: Cambridge University Press.
Davis, K.A. (1999) The sociopolitical dynamics of Indigenous language maintenance and loss: A framework for language policy and planning. In T. Huebner and K.A. Davis (eds) *Sociopolitical Perspectives on Language Policy and Planning in the USA* (pp. 67–97). Amsterdam: John Benjamins.
Davis, K.M.A. (2008) Implementation of language and cultural objectives at Kawenni:io/Gaweni:yo School. Unpublished master's thesis, Brock University.
Deloria, P.J. (2011) On leaking languages and categorical imperatives. *American Indian Culture and Research Journal* 35 (2), 173–181.
Dementi-Leonard, B. and Gilmore, P. (1999) Language revitalization and identity in social context: A community-based Athabascan language preservation project in western interior Alaska. *Anthropology and Education Quarterly* 30 (1), 37–55.
Demmert, W.G. (2011) *Indigenous Culture-Based Education Rubrics Training Manual.* Bellingham, WA: Education Northwest, Kamehameha Schools, 'Aha Pūnana Leo, and Western Washington University.
DeVoe, J.F., Darling-Churchill, K.E. and Snyder, T.D. (2008) *Status and Trends in the Education of American Indians and Alaska Natives: 2008.* Washington, DC: US Department of Education, National Center for Education Statistics, Institute of Education Sciences.
Dick, G.S. (1998) I maintained a strong belief in my language and culture: A Navajo language autobiography. *International Journal of the Sociology of Language* 132, 23–25.
Dick, G.S. and McCarty, T.L. (1996). Reclaiming Navajo: Language renewal in an American Indian community school. In N.H. Hornberger (ed.) *Indigenous Literacies in the Americas: Language Planning from the Bottom Up* (pp. 69–94). Berlin: Mouton de Gruyter.
Dinwoodie, D.W. (1998) Authorizing voices: Going public in an Indigenous language. *Cultural Anthropology* 13 (2), 193–223.

Dorian, N.C. (1981) *Language Death: The Life Cycle of a Scottish Gaelic Dialect*. Philadelphia, PA: University of Pennsylvania Press.
Dorian, N.C. (1989) *Investigating Obsolescence: Studies in Language Contraction and Death*. Cambridge: Cambridge University Press.
Dorian, N.C. (1998) Western language ideologies and small-language prospects. In L.A. Grenoble and L.J. Whaley (eds) *Endangered Languages: Current Issues and Future Prospects* (pp. 3–21). Cambridge: Cambridge University Press.
Duchêne, A. and Heller, M. (eds) (2007) *Discourses of Endangerment: Ideology and Interest in the Defence of Languages*. London: Continuum.
Dunsmore, R. (2009) Simon Ortiz and the lyricism of continuance: 'For the sake of the people, for the sake of the land'. In S.B. Brill de Ramírez and E. Zuni Lucero (eds) *Simon J. Ortiz: A Poetic Legacy of Indigenous Continuance* (pp. 205–212). Albuquerque, NM: University of New Mexico Press.
Eisenlohr, P. (2004) Language revitalization and new technologies: Cultures of electronic mediation and the refiguring of communities. *Annual Review of Anthropology* 33, 21–45.
Ellis, C. (1996) *To Change Them Forever: Indian Education at the Rainy Mountain Boarding School, 1893–1920*. Norman, OK: University of Oklahoma Press.
Emerson, G. (1983) Navajo education. In A. Ortiz (volume ed.) and W.C. Sturtevant (general ed.) *Handbook of North American Indians. Vol. 10: Southwest* (pp. 659–671). Washington, DC: Smithsonian Institution.
Endangered Language Fund (2011) Breath of life archival institute for Indigenous languages, Washington, DC, 13–24 June. Online at http://www.endangeredlanguagefund.org/BOL.php, accessed 10 February 2012.
Esther Martinez Native American Languages Preservation Act (2006). Online at http://www.gpo.gov/fdsys/pkg/BILLS-109hr4766enr/pdf/BILLS-109hr4766enr.pdf, accessed 6 July 2012.
Evers, L. and Molina, F.S. (1987) *Yaqui Deer Songs, Maso Bwikam: A Native American Poetry*. Tucson, AZ: Sun Tracks and the University of Arizona Press.
Evers, L. and Zepeda, O. (eds) (1995) *Home Places: Contemporary Native American Writing from Sun Tracks*. Tucson, AZ: University of Arizona Press.
Evers, L., with Dozier, A., Lopez, D., Molina, F., Perkins, E.T., Sekaquaptewa, E. and Zepeda, O. (1983) *The South Corner of Time: Hopi, Navajo, Papago, and Yaqui Tribal Literature*. Tucson, AZ: University of Arizona Press.
Executive Order 13096 (1998) American Indian and Alaska Native education. *Federal Register*, 11 August, 63 (154), 42681–42684.
Fairclough, N. (2001) *Language and Power* (2nd edn). London: Longman.
Fasold, R.W. (1984) *Sociolinguistics of Society*. Oxford: Basil Blackwell.
Feldman, O. (2001) Inspired by a dream. *Spectrum IIX* (2). Online at http://spectrum.mit.edu/articles/normal/inspired-by-a-dream, accessed 11 October 2012.
Field, M.C. and Kroskrity, P.V. (2009) Introduction: Revealing Native American language ideologies. In P.V. Kroskrity and M.C. Field (eds) *Native American Language Ideologies* (pp. 3–28). Tucson, AZ: University of Arizona Press.
Fife, G. (2010) Cherokee Nation creates syllabary keypad. *Native American Times*, 1 March. Online at http://www.nativetimes.com/index.php?option=com_content&view=article&id=3152:cherokee-nation-creates-syllabary-keypad&catid=50&Itemid=26, accessed 11 June 2012.
Fillerup, M. (2000) Racing against time: A report on the Leupp Navajo Immersion Project. In J. Reyhner, J. Martin, L. Lockard and W.S. Gilbert (eds) *Learn in Beauty: Indigenous Education for a New Century* (pp. 2–34). Flagstaff, AZ: Northern Arizona University. Online at http://jan.ucc.nau.edu/~jar/LIB/LIBconts.html, accessed 12 June 2012.
Fillerup, M. (2002) The Leupp Navajo Immersion Program. *NABE News* 25(6), 17, 44. Online at http://jan.ucc.nau.edu/~jar/OtherNABE.html, accessed 12 June 2012.

Fillerup, M. (2005) Keeping up with the Yazzies: The impact of high stakes testing on Indigenous language programs. *Language Learner*, September/October, 14–16.

Fillerup, M. (2008) Building bridges of beauty between the rich languages and cultures of the American Southwest: Puente de Hózhǫ́ Trilingual Magnet School. Online at http:// www.puentedehozho.org/puenteschool.htm, accessed 6 June 2012.

Fillerup, M. (2011) Building a 'bridge of beauty': A preliminary report on promising practices in Native language and culture teaching at Puente de Hózhǫ́ Trilingual Magnet School. In M.E. Romero-Little, S.J. Ortiz, T.L. McCarty and R. Chen (eds) *Indigenous Languages Across the Generations – Strengthening Families and Communities* (pp. 145–164). Tempe, AZ: Arizona State University Center for Indian Education.

Fishman, J.A. (1991) *Reversing Language Shift: Theoretical and Empirical Foundations of Assistance to Threatened Languages*. Clevedon: Multilingual Matters.

Fishman, J.A. (ed.) (2001) *Can Threatened Languages Be Saved? Reversing Language Shift, Revisited: A 21st Century Perspective*. Clevedon: Multilingual Matters.

Fishman, J.A. (2002) Commentary: What a difference 40 years make! *Journal of Linguistic Anthropology* 12 (2), 144–149.

Fishman, J.A. (2012) Cultural autonomy as an approach to sociolinguistic power-sharing: Some preliminary notions. *International Journal of the Sociology of Language* 213, 11–46.

Fixico, D. (2002) Federal and state policies and American Indians. In P. Deloria and N. Salisbury (eds) *A Companion to American Indian History* (pp. 379–396). Malden, MA: Blackwell.

Fox, S. (2012) What BIE students got from No Child Left Behind. Unpublished policy brief.

Francis, N. and Reyhner, J. (2002) *Language and Literacy Teaching for Indigenous Education: A Bilingual Approach*. Clevedon: Multilingual Matters.

Franciscan Fathers (1910) *An Ethnologic Dictionary of the Navajo Language*. St Michael's, AZ: St Michael's Press.

Freeman, C. and Fox, M. (2005) *Status and Trends in the Education of American Indians and Alaska Natives*. Washington, DC: National Center for Education Statistics, US Department of Education.

Gándara, P. and Hopkins, M. (2010) The changing linguistic landscape of the United States. In P. Gándara and M. Hopkins (eds) *Forbidden Language: English Learners and Restrictive Language Policies* (pp. 7–19). New York: Teachers College Press.

Gándara, P. and Orfield, G. (2010) Moving from failure to a new vision of language policy. In P. Gándara and M. Hopkins (eds) *Forbidden Language: English Learners and Restrictive Language Policies* (pp. 216–226). New York: Teachers College Press.

Garcia, D.R. (2008) Mixed messages: American Indian achievement before and since the implementation of *No Child Left Behind*. *Journal of American Indian Education* 47 (1), 136–154.

García, O. (1992) Societal bilingualism and multilingualism. In H. Byrnes (ed.) *Languages for a Multicultural World in Transition. Northeast Conference Reports on the Teaching of Languages* (pp. 1–27). Lincolnwood, IL: National Textbook Co.

García, O. (2009) *Bilingual Education in the 21st Century: A Global Perspective*. Malden, MA: Wiley-Blackwell.

García, O. and Fishman, J.A. (2012) Power-sharing and cultural autonomy: Some sociolinguistic principles. *International Journal of the Sociology of Language* 213, 143–147.

García, O., Bartlett, L. and Kleifgen, J. (2007) From biliteracy to pluriliteracies. In P. Auer and L. Wei (eds) *Handbook of Applied Linguistics, Vol. 5: Multilingualism* (pp. 207–228). Berlin: Mouton de Gruyter.

García, O., Skutnabb-Kangas, T. and Torres-Guzmán, M.E. (eds) (2006) *Imagining Multilingual Schools: Languages in Education and Glocalization*. Clevedon: Multilingual Matters.

Gee, J.P. (2012) *Social Linguistics and Literacies: Ideology in Discourses* (4th edn). New York: Routledge.

Gegeo, D.W. and Watson-Gegeo, K.A. (1999) Adult education, language change, and issues of identity and authenticity in Kwara'e (Solomon Islands). *Anthropology and Education Quarterly* 30 (1), 22–36.

Gegeo, D.W. and Watson-Gegeo, K.A. (2012) The critical villager revisited: Continuing Transformation of language and education in the Solomon Islands. In J.W. Tollefson (ed.) *Language Policies in Education: Critical Issues* (2nd edn). New York: Routledge.

Gilmore, P. and Wyman, L.T. (2013) An ethnographic long look: Language and literacy over time and space in Alaska Native communities. In K. Hall, T. Cremin, B. Comer and L.C. Moll (eds) *The Wiley Blackwell International Handbook of Research on Children's Literacy, Learning, and Culture*. London: Wiley Blackwell (in press).

Goddard, I. (1996a) Introduction. In I. Goddard (volume ed.) and W.C. Sturtevant (general ed.) *Handbook of North American Indians Vol. 17: Languages* (pp. 1–16). Washington, DC: Smithsonian Institution.

Goddard, I. (1996b) The description of the Native languages of North America before Boas. In I. Goddard (volume ed.) and W.C. Sturtevant (general ed.) *Handbook of North American Indians Vol. 17: Languages* (pp. 17–42). Washington, DC: Smithsonian Institution.

Goddard, I. (1996c) The classification of the Native languages of North America. In I. Goddard (volume ed.) and W.C. Sturtevant (general ed.) *Handbook of North American Indians Vol. 17: Languages* (pp. 290–323). Washington, DC: Smithsonian Institution.

Goddard, I. and Bragdon, K. (1988) *Native Writings in Massachusett*. Philadelphia, PA: American Philosophical Society.

González, R.E., with Melis, I. (eds) (2001a) *Language Ideologies: Critical Perspectives on the Official English Movement Vol. 1: Education and the Social Implications of Official Languages*. Urbana, IL and Mahwah, NJ: National Council of Teachers of English and Lawrence Erlbaum.

González, R.E., with Melis, I. (eds) (2001b) *Language Ideologies: Critical Perspectives on the Official English Movement Vol. 2: History, Theory, and Policy*. Urbana, IL and Mahwah, NJ: National Council of Teachers of English and Lawrence Erlbaum.

González, N., Moll, L.C. and Amanti, C. (eds) (2005) *Funds of Knowledge: Theorizing Practices in Households, Communities, and Classrooms*. Mahwah, NJ: Lawrence Erlbaum.

Goodman, Y.M. and Wilde, S. (eds) (1992) *Literacy Events in a Community of Young Writers*. New York: Teachers College Press.

Gordon, R.G. Jr (ed.) (2005) *Ethnologue: Languages of the World* (15th edn). Dallas, TX: SIL International.

Grant, A. (1996) *No End of Grief: Indian Residential Schools in Canada*. Winnipeg, MB: Pemmican Publications.

Grenoble, L.A. (2011) Language ecology and endangerment. In P.K. Austin and J. Sallabank (eds) *The Cambridge Handbook of Language Endangerment* (p. 27–44). Cambridge: Cambridge University Press.

Grenoble, L.A. and Whaley, L.J. (eds) (1998) *Endangered Languages: Current Issues and Future Prospects*. Cambridge: Cambridge University Press.

Grenoble, L.A. and Whaley, L.J. (2006) *Saving Languages: An Introduction to Language Revitalization*. Cambridge: Cambridge University Press.

Greyeyes, W. (2011) Welcome to the Navajo Nation's Department of Education. Presentation at the Navajo Nation and Māori Delegation Meeting, 20 September, Department of Diné Education, Navajo Nation, Window Rock, AZ.

Greymorning, S. (2001) Reflections on the Arapaho language project, or when Bambi spoke Arapaho and other tales of Arapaho language revitalization efforts. In L. Hinton and K. Hale (eds) *The Green Book of Language Revitalization in Practice* (pp. 287–297). San Diego, CA: Academic Press.

Grigg, W., Moran, R. and Kuang, M. (2010) *National Indian Education Study – Part I: Performance of American Indian and Alaska Native Students at Grades 4 and 8 on NAEP*

2009 Reading and Mathematics Assessments (NIES 2010-462). Washington, DC: National Center for Education Statistics, Institute of Education Sciences, US Department of Education.

Grillo, R.D. (1989) *Dominant Languages: Language and Hierarchy in Britain and France.* Cambridge: Cambridge University Press.

Grimes, B. (ed.) (1996) *Ethnologue Language Name Index to the Thirteenth Edition of the Ethnologue.* Dallas, TX: Summer Institute of Linguistics.

Grinwald, C. and Bert, M. (2011) Speakers and communities. In P.K. Austin and J. Sallabank (eds) *The Cambridge Handbook of Endangered Languages* (pp. 45–65). Cambridge: Cambridge University Press.

Grounds, R. (2011) Youth bridging the gap: The hope for language revitalization. In M.E. Romero-Little, S.J. Ortiz, T.L. McCarty and R. Chen (eds) *Indigenous Languages Across the Generations – Strengthening Families and Communities* (pp. 97–105). Tempe, AZ: Arizona State University Center for Indian Education.

Gumperz, J. and Hymes, D. (eds) (1972) *Directions in Sociolinguistics: The Ethnography of Communication.* New York: Holt, Rinehart and Winston.

Gutiérrez, K.D., Asato, J., Pacheco, M., Moll, L.C., Olson, K., Horng, E.L., Ruiz, R., García, E. and McCarty, T.L. (2002) 'Sounding American': The consequences of new reforms on English language learners. *Reading Research Quarterly* 37 (3), 328–343.

Haile, B. (ed.) (1912) *Vocabulary of the Navajo Language.* St Michael's, AZ: Franciscan Fathers.

Haile, B. (1929) *Manual of Navaho Grammar.* St Michael's, AZ: St Michael's Mission.

Haile, B. (1942–1949) *Learning Navaho* (Vols 1–4). St Michael's, AZ: St Michael's Mission.

Haile, B. (1951) *A Stem Vocabulary of the Navaho Language.* St Michael's, AZ: St Michael's Press.

Hale, K. (1995) Universal grammar and the roots of linguistic diversity. Edward Sapir Lecture presented at the Linguistic Society of America Linguistic Institute, 28 June, University of New Mexico, Albuquerque, NM.

Hale, K. (1997) Reasons to be optimistic about local language maintenance and restoration. Paper prepared for the Linguistic Association of the Southwest (LASSO) Conference, Los Angeles, CA.

Hale, K. (2001a) The Navajo language: I. In L. Hinton and K. Hale (eds) *The Green Book of Language Revitalization in Practice* (pp. 83–85). San Diego, CA: Academic Press.

Hale, K. (2001b) The Navajo Language: II. In L. Hinton and K. Hale (eds) *The Green Book of Language Revitalization in Practice* (pp. 199–201). San Diego, CA: Academic Press.

Harrison, K.D. (2007) *When Languages Die: The Extinction of the World's Languages and the Erosion of Human Knowledge.* Oxford: Oxford University Press.

Haugen, E. (1972) *The Ecology of Language.* Stanford, CA: Stanford University Press.

Haugen, E. (1983) The implementation of corpus planning: Theory and practice. In J. Cobarrubias and J. Fishman (eds) *Progress in Language Planning: International Perspectives* (pp. 269–290). Berlin: Mouton de Gruyter.

Heath, S.B. (1982) Protean shapes in literacy events: Ever-shifting oral and literate traditions. In D. Tannen (ed.) *Spoken and Written Language: Exploring Orality and Literacy* (pp. 91–117). Norwood, NJ: Ablex.

Heath, S.B. (1983) *Ways with Words: Language, Life, and Work in Communities and Classrooms.* New York: Cambridge University Press.

Hermes, M. (2005) 'Ma'iingan is just a misspelling of the word wolf': A case for teaching culture through language. *Anthropology and Education Quarterly* 36 (1), 43–56.

Hermes, M. (2007) Moving toward the language: Reflections on teaching in an Indigenous-immersion school. *Journal of American Indian Education* 46 (3), 54–71.

Heugh, K. and Skutnabb-Kangas, T. (eds) (2010) *Multilingual Education Works: From the Periphery to the Centre.* New Delhi: Orient BlackSwan.

Hill, J.H. (1993) Structure and practice in language shift. In K. Hyltenstam and A. Viberg (eds) *Progression and Regression in Language: Sociocultural, Neuropsychological and Linguistic Perspectives* (pp. 68–93). Cambridge: Cambridge University Press.

Hill, J. (2002) 'Expert rhetorics' in advocacy for endangered languages: Who is listening, and what do they hear? *Journal of Linguistic Anthropology* 12 (2), 119–133.

Hinton, L. (1991) The Native American Languages Act. *News from Native California*, February/April, 22–23.

Hinton, L. (1994) *Flutes of Fire: Essays on California Indian Languages*. Berkeley, CA: Heyday Books.

Hinton, L. (1998) Language loss and revitalization in California: Overview. *International Journal of the Sociology of Language* 132, 83–93.

Hinton, L. (2001a) Language revitalization: An overview. In L. Hinton and K. Hale (eds) *The Green Book of Language Revitalization in Practice* (pp. 3–18). San Diego, CA: Academic Press.

Hinton, L. (2001b) Language planning. In L. Hinton and K. Hale (eds) *The Green Book of Language Revitalization in Practice* (pp. 51–59). San Diego, CA: Academic Press.

Hinton, L. (2001c) The Master–Apprentice Language Learning Program. In L. Hinton and K. Hale (eds) *The Green Book of Language Revitalization in Practice* (pp. 217–226). San Diego, CA: Academic Press.

Hinton, L. (2001d) Sleeping languages: Can they be awakened? In L. Hinton and K. Hale (eds) *The Green Book of Language Revitalization in Practice* (pp. 413–417). San Diego, CA: Academic Press.

Hinton, L. (2003) Language revitalization. *Annual Review of Applied Linguistics* 23, 44–57.

Hinton, L. (2011) Revitalization of endangered languages. In P.K. Austin and J. Sallabank (eds) *The Cambridge Handbook of Endangered Languages* (pp. 291–311). Cambridge: Cambridge University Press.

Hinton, L. (ed.) (2013) *Bringing Our Languages Home – Language Revitalization for Families*. Berkeley, CA: Heyday Books (in press).

Hinton, L. and Watahomigie, L.J. (1984) *Spirit Mountain: An Anthology of Yuman Story and Song*. Tucson, AZ: Sun Tracks and the University of Arizona Press.

Hinton, L., Vera, M. and Steele N. (2002) *How to Keep Your Language Alive: A Commonsense Approach to One-on-One Language Learning*. Berkeley, CA: Heyday Books.

Hixson, L., Hepler, B.B. and Kim, M.O. (2012) *The Native Hawaiian and Other Pacific Islander Population: 2010. 2010 Census Briefs*. Washington, DC: US Department of Commerce Economics and Statistics Administration, US Census Bureau. Online at http://www.census.gov/prod/cen2010/briefs/c2010br-12.pdf, accessed 11 June 2012.

Hohepa, M.K. (2006) Biliterate practices in the home: Supporting Indigenous language regeneration. *Journal of Language, Identity, and Education* 5 (4), 293–301.

Hollingsworth, S., Gallego, M.A., Clandinin, D.J., Morrell, P., Portes, P., Rueda, R. and Welch, O. (guest eds) (2007) No Child Left Behind. (Special issue.) *American Educational Research Journal* 44 (3), 454–629.

Holm, A. and Holm, W. (1990) Rock Point, a Navajo way to go to school: A valediction. *Annals of the American Association of Political and Social Science* 508, 170–184.

Holm, A. and Holm, W. (1995) Navajo language education: Retrospect and prospects. *Bilingual Research Journal* 19 (1), 141–167.

Holm, W. (1996) On the role of 'YounganMorgan' in the development of Navajo literacy. *Journal of Navajo Education* 8 (2), 4–11.

Holm, W. (2006) The 'goodness' of bilingual education for Native American children. In T.L. McCarty and O. Zepeda (eds) *One Voice, Many Voices – Recreating Indigenous Language Communities* (pp. 1–46). Tempe, AZ: Arizona State University Center for Indian Education.

Holton, G. (2011) The role of information technology in supporting minority and endangered languages. In P.K. Austin and J. Sallabank (eds) *The Cambridge Handbook of Endangered Languages* (pp. 371–399). Cambridge: Cambridge University Press.

Hoover, M.L. and Kanien'kehaka Raotitiohkwa Cultural Center (1992) The revival of the Mohawk language in Kahnawake. *Canadian Journal of Native Studies* 12 (2), 269–287.
Hornberger, N.H. (1988) *Bilingual Education and Language Maintenance: A Southern Peruvian Quechua Case*. Berlin: Mouton de Gruyter.
Hornberger, N.H. (1994) Literacy and language planning. *Language and Education* 8 (1–2), 87–94.
Hornberger, N.H. (1995) Ethnography in linguistic perspective: Understanding school processes. *Language and Education* 9 (4), 233–248.
Hornberger, N.H. (1996) Indigenous literacies in the Americas. In N.H. Hornberger (ed.) *Indigenous Literacies in the Americas: Language Planning from the Bottom Up* (pp. 3–16). Berlin: Mouton de Gruyter.
Hornberger, N.H. (2002) Multilingual language policies and the continua of biliteracy: An ecological approach. *Language Policy* 1 (1), 27–51.
Hornberger, N.H. (ed.) (2003) *Continua of Biliteracy: An Ecological Framework for Educational Policy, Research, and Practice in Multilingual Settings*. Clevedon: Multilingual Matters.
Hornberger, N.H. (2006a) *Nichols* to *NCLB*: Local and global perspectives on US language education policy. In O. García, T. Skutnabb-Kangas and M.E. Torres-Guzmán (eds) *Imagining Multilingual Schools: Languages in Education and Glocalization* (pp. 223–237). Clevedon: Multilingual Matters.
Hornberger, N.H. (2006b) Frameworks and models in language policy and planning. In T. Ricento (ed.) *An Introduction to Language Policy: Theory and Method* (pp. 24–41). Malden, MA: Blackwell.
Hornberger, N.H. (ed.) (2008) *Can Schools Save Indigenous Languages? Policy and Practice on Four Continents*. New York: Palgrave Macmillan.
Hornberger, N.H. and Johnson, D.C. (2007) Slicing the onion ethnographically: Layers and spaces in multilingual language education policy and practice. *TESOL Quarterly* 41 (3), 509–532.
Hornberger, N.H and Johnson, D.C. (2011) The ethnography of language policy. In T.L. McCarty (ed.) *Ethnography and Language Policy* (pp. 273–289). New York: Routledge.
Hornberger, N.H and King, K.A. (1996) Bringing the language forward: School-based initiatives for Quechua language revitalization in Ecuador and Bolivia. In N.H. Hornberger (ed.) *Indigenous Literacies in the Americas: Language Planning from the Bottom Up* (pp. 299–319). Berlin: Mouton de Gruyter.
Hornberger, N.H and Swinehart, K.F. (2012) Not just *situaciones de la vida*: Professionalization and Indigenous language revitalization in the Andes. *International Multilingual Research Journal* 6 (1), 35–49.
Horne, E.B. and McBeth, S. (1998) *Essie's Story: The Life and Legacy of a Shoshone Teacher*. Lincoln, NE: University of Nebraska Press.
House, D. (2002) *Language Shift among the Navajos: Identity Politics and Cultural Continuity*. Tucson, AZ: University of Arizona Press.
Hull, T. (2010) Arizona teachers claim law against Mexican-American Studies unconstitutional. *Courthouse News Service*, 21 October. Online at http://www.firstamendmentcoalition.org/2010/10/arizona-teachers-claim-law-against-mexican-american-studies-unconstitutional, accessed 22 June 2011.
Hymes, D. (1964) Introduction: Toward ethnographies of communication. *American Anthropologist* 66 (6; Part 2: The Ethnography of Communication), 1–34.
Hymes, D. (1974) *Foundations in Sociolinguistics: An Ethnographic Approach*. Philadelphia, PA: University of Pennsylvania Press.
Hymes, D. (1980) What is ethnography? In D. Hymes, *Language in Education: Ethnolinguistic Essays* (pp. 86–103). Washington, DC: Center for Applied Linguistics.

Indian Country Today (2011) Native American students helping preserve language, 22 June. Online at http://indiancountrytodaymedianetwork.com/2011/06/22/native-american-students-helping-preserve-language-39595, accessed 10 May 2012.

Institute of Social and Economic Research (1998–2004) Athabaskan Languages and the Schools. Online at http://www.alaskool.org/language/Athabaskan/Athabas_Lng.htm, accessed 7 June 2012.

International Labour Organisation (1989) C169: Indigenous and Tribal Peoples Convention, 1989. Online at http://www.ilo.org/ilolex/cgi-lex/convde.pl?C169, accessed 7 June 2012.

Iokepa-Guerrero, N. (2008) Raising a child in the Pūnana Leo: Everyone (men and women) play an important role. *Exchange: The Early Childhood Leaders' Magazine* May/June, 30–32.

Iverson, P. (2002) *Diné: A History of the Navajos*. Albuquerque, NM: University of New Mexico Press.

Jacob, B.A. (2004) Accountability, incentives and behavior: The impact of high-stakes testing in the Chicago Public Schools. NBER Working Paper no. 8968. Online at http://www.nber.org/papers/w8969.pdf, accessed 23 August 2005.

Jacobs, K.A. (1998) A chronology of Mohawk language instruction at Kahnawá:ke. In L.A. Grenoble and L.J. Whaley (eds) *Endangered Languages: Language Loss and Community Response* (pp. 117–125). Cambridge: Cambridge University Press.

Jaffe, A. (2011) Critical perspectives on language-in-education policy: The Corsican example. In T.L. McCarty (ed.) *Ethnography and Language Policy* (pp. 205–229). New York: Routledge.

Jim, R.L. (1998) *Dúchas/Táá Kóó Diné: A Trilingual Poetry Collection in Navajo, Irish, and English*, Diarmuid O'Breaslin, Irish trans. Belfast: An Clochán.

Johnson, B.H. (1968) *Navaho Education at Rough Rock*. Rough Rock, AZ: Rough Rock Demonstration School, D.I.N.E. Inc.

Johnson, B.H. and Roessel, R. (eds) (1973) *Navajo Stories of the Long Walk Period*. Tsaile, Navajo Nation, AZ: Navajo Community College Press.

Johnson, C. (2003) *myaamiaki piloohsaki amahsinaakanemawe iilaataweenki. A Miami Children's Language Curriculum*. Miami Nation, OK: Miami Tribe of Oklahoma.

Johnson, D.C. (2009) Ethnography of language policy. *Language Policy* 8 (2), 139–159.

Johnson, F.T. and Legatz, J. (2006) Tséhootsooí Diné Bi'ólta' [Fort Defiance Navajo Immersion School]. *Journal of American Indian Education* 45 (2), 26–33.

Johnson, F.T. and Wilson, J. (2004) Embracing change for student learning. Diné language immersion school. Presentation at the 25th Annual American Indian Language Development Institute, 23 June, University of Arizona, Tucson.

Jojola, T., Lee, T.S., Alcántara, A., Belgarde, M., Bird, C., Lopez, N. and Singer, B. (2010) *Indian Education in New Mexico, 2025*. Santa Fe and San Juan Pueblo, NM: New Mexico Public Education Department and Eight Northern Indian Pueblos Council, Inc.

Juan, M.J.B. (2003) *Modern Nomad*, September, *110°*, 26–30.

Kageleiry, J. (2001) Wampanoag 101. *Yankee Magazine*, October, 18–19.

Kahnawake Survival School (n.d.) Home page. Online at http://kss.qc.com/ accessed 3 September 2012. www.aboriginal/survive, accessed 18 July 2006.

Kamanā, K. (2011) Moʻokiʻina Hoʻoponopono: Ke O O Kaʻike Kuʻuna Hawaiʻi Ma Ke Kula ʻO Nāwahīokalaniʻpuʻu [The continuity of traditional Hawaiian conflict resolution at Ke Kula ʻO Nāwahīokalaniʻōpuʻu]. Unpublished PhD dissertation, Program in Hawaiian and Indigenous Language and Culture Revitalization, University of Hawaiʻi–Hilo.

Kaomea, J. (2004) Dilemmas of an Indigenous academic: A Native Hawaiian story. In K. Mutua and B.B. Swadener (eds) *Decolonizing Research in Cross-Cultural Contexts: Critical Personal Narratives* (pp. 27–44). Albany, NY: State University of New York Press.

Kaplan, R.B. and Baldauf, R.B. Jr (1997) *Language Planning: From Practice to Theory.* Clevedon: Multilingual Matters.

Kehoe, A.B. (2001) Real Speak: Language revival among the Montana Blackfeet. *World and I*, October. Online at http:// www.pieganinstitute.org, accessed 22 July 2008.

King, C.S. (1956) *The Flag of My Country: Shikéyah Bidah Na'at'a'i.* (Navajo text by Marian Nez.) Phoenix, AZ: Phoenix Indian School for the US Indian Service.

King, K.A. (2000) Language ideologies and heritage language education. *International Journal of Bilingual Education and Bilingualism* 3 (3), 167–184.

King, K.A. (2001) *Language Revitalization Processes and Prospects: Quichua in the Ecuadorian Andes.* Clevedon: Multilingual Matters.

King, K. and Ganuza, N. (2005) Language, identity, education, and transmigration: Chilean adolescents in Sweden. *Journal of Language, Identity, and Education* 4 (3), 179–199.

Kipp, D.R. (2000) *Encouragement, Guidance, Insights, and Lessons for Native Language Activists Developing Their Own Tribal Language Programs.* Browning, MT: Piegan Institute's Cut-Bank Language Immersion School.

Kloss, H. (1998) *The American Bilingual Tradition.* Washington, DC and McHenry, IL: Center for Applied Linguistics and Delta Systems.

Kouritzin, S.G. (1999) *Face[t]s of First Language Loss.* Mahwah, NJ: Lawrence Erlbaum.

Kral, I. (2011) Youth media as cultural practice: Remote Indigenous youth speaking out loud. *Australian Aboriginal Studies. Journal of the Australian Institute of Aboriginal and Torres Strait Islander Studies* 1, 4–16.

Krauss, M. (1992) The world's languages in crisis. *Language* 68 (1), 4–10.

Krauss, M. (1997) The Indigenous languages of the North: A report on their present state. *Northern Minority Languages: Problems of Survival. Ethnological Studies* 44, 1–34.

Krauss, M. (1998) The condition of Native North American languages: The need for realistic assessment and action. *International Journal of the Sociology of Language* 132, 9–21.

Kroskrity, P.V. (2000) Language ideologies in the expression and representation of Arizona Tewa identity. In P.V. Kroskrity (ed.) *Regimes of Language: Ideologies, Polities, and Identities* (pp. 329–359). Santa Fe, NM: School of American Research Press.

Kroskrity, P.V. (2011) Facing the rhetoric of language endangerment: Voicing the consequences of linguistic racism. *Journal of Linguistic Anthropology* 21 (2), 179–192.

Kroskrity, P.V. and Field, M.C. (eds) (2009) *Native American Language Ideologies: Beliefs, Practices, and Struggles in Indian Country.* Tucson, AZ: University of Arizona Press.

Kroupa, K.T. (2013) Efforts of the Ree-volution: Revitalising Arikara language in an endangered community context. In L.T. Wyman, T.L. McCarty and S.E. Nicholas (eds) *Beyond Endangerment: Language in the Lives of Indigenous Youth.* New York: Routledge (in press).

Kulick, D. (1992) *Language Shift and Cultural Reproduction: Socialization, Self, and Syncretism in a Papua New Guinean Village.* Cambridge: Cambridge University Press.

Lambert, W.E., Hodgson, R.C., Gardner, R.C. and Fillenbaum, S. (1960). Evaluational reactions to spoken language. *Journal of Abnormal and Social Psychology* 60, 44–51.

Langer, E. (2008) Famous are the flowers: Hawaiian resistance then – and now. *The Nation*, 15 (28 April), 17–29.

Lapahie, H. Jr (2001) Fort Defiance (Tséhootsooí – Meadow in Between the Rocks). Online at http://www.lapahi.com/Fort_Defiance.cfm, accessed 18 July 2008.

Leap, W.L. (1988) Indian language renewal. *Human Organization* 47 (4), 283–291.

Leap, W.L. (1991) Pathways and barriers to Indian language literacy-building on the Northern Ute reservation. *Anthropology and Education Quarterly* 22 (6), 21–41.

Leap, W.L. (1993) *American Indian English.* Salt Lake City, UT: University of Utah Press.

Lee, L.L. and Lee, T.S. (2012) Navajo cultural autonomy. *International Journal of the Sociology of Language* 213, 119–126.

Lee, T. (2012) No Child Left Behind Act: A bust in Indian Country. *Indian Country Today*. Online at http://indiancountrytodaymedianetwork.com/2012/03/07/101597-101597, accessed 7 June 2012.

Lee, T.S. (1999) Sources of influence over Navajo adolescent language attitudes and language use. Unpublished PhD dissertation, Stanford University, School of Education, Stanford, CA.

Lee, T.S. (2007) 'If they want Navajo to be learned, then they should require it in all schools': Navajo teenagers' experiences, choices, and demands regarding Navajo language. *Wicazo Sa Review*, Spring, 7–33.

Lee, T.S. (2009) Language, identity, and power: Navajo and Pueblo young adults' perspectives and experiences with competing language ideologies. *Journal of Language, Identity, and Education* 8 (5), 307–320.

Lee, T.S. (2013) Critical language awareness among Native youth in New Mexico. In L.T. Wyman, T.L. McCarty and S.E. Nicholas (eds) *Beyond Endangerment: Language in the Lives of Indigenous Youth*. New York: Routledge (in press).

Lee, T. and McLaughlin, D. (2001) Reversing Navajo language shift, revisited. In J.A. Fishman (ed.) *Can Threatened Languages Be Saved? Reversing Language Shift, Revisited: A 21st Century Perspective* (pp. 23–43). Clevedon: Multilingual Matters.

Leibowitz, A.H. (1974) Language as a means of social control. ERIC Document no. 093168. Charleston, WV: ERIC Clearinghouse.

Leonard, B. (2009) Deg Xinag oral traditions: Reconnecting Indigenous language and education through traditional narratives. Unpublished doctoral thesis, University of Alaska Fairbanks.

Leonard, W.Y. (2007) Miami language reclamation in the home: A case study. Unpublished PhD dissertation, University of California Berkeley.

Leonard, W.Y. (2008) When is an 'extinct' language not extinct? Miami, a formerly sleeping language. In K.A. King, N. Schilling-Estes, L. Fogle, J.J. Lou and B. Soukup (eds) *Sustaining Linguistic Diversity: Endangered and Minority Languages and Language Varieties* (pp. 23–33). Washington, DC: Georgetown University Press.

Leonard, W.Y. (2011) Challenging 'extinction' through modern Miami language practices. *American Indian Culture and Research Journal* 35 (2), 135–160.

Levinson, B.A.U. and Sutton, M. (2001) Introduction: Policy as/in practice – A sociocultural approach to the study of educational policy. In M. Sutton and B.A.U. Levinson (eds) *Policy as Practice: Toward a Comparative Sociocultural Analysis of Educational Policy* (pp. 1–22). Westport, CT: Ablex.

Link, M.A. (ed.) (1968) *Navajo: A Century of Progress 1868–1969*. Window Rock, AZ: Navajo Tribe.

Lipka, J. and McCarty, T.L. (1994) Changing the culture of schooling: Navajo and Yup'ik cases. *Anthropology and Education Quarterly* 25 (3), 266–284.

Lipka, J., with Mohatt, G.V. and the Ciulistet Group (1998) *Changing the Culture of Schools: Yup'ik Eskimo Examples*. Mahwah, NJ: Lawrence Erlbaum.

Littlebear, D. (1990) Effective language education practices and Native language survival. In J. Reyhner (ed.) *Effective Language Education Practices and Native Language Survival* (pp. 1–8). Choctaw, OK: Native American Languaage Issues, NALI Board of Executors. Online at http://jan.ucc.nau.edu/~ jar/NALI1.html, accessed 9 July 2012.

Littlebear, R.E. (2000) To save our languages, we must change our teaching methods. *Tribal College Journal* 11 (3), 18–20.

Littlebear, R.E. (2004) One man, two languages: Confessions of a freedom-loving bilingual. *Tribal College Journal* 15 (3), 11–12.

little doe, j. (2000) The 're-awakening' of the Wôpanâak language. *Native Language Network*, Winter, 3.

Lockard, L. (1996) New paper words: Historical images of Navajo literacy. *Journal of Navajo Education* 8 (2), 40–48.

Lomawaima, K.T. (1993) Domesticity in the federal Indian schools: The power of authority over mind and body. *American Ethnologist* 20 (2): 1–14.
Lomawaima, K.T. (1994) *They Called It Prairie Light: The Story of Chilocco Indian School*. Lincoln, NE: University of Nebraska Press.
Lomawaima, K.T. (1995) Educating Native Americans. In J. Banks (ed.) *Handbook of Research on Multicultural Education* (pp. 331–347). New York: Macmillan.
Lomawaima, K.T. (guest ed.) (1996) Boarding School Experience. (Special issue.) *Journal of American Indian Education* 35 (3).
Lomawaima, K.T. (2000) Tribal sovereigns: Reframing research in American Indian education. *Harvard Educational Review* 70 (1), 1–21.
Lomawaima, K.T. (2002) American Indian education: *By* Indians vs. *for* Indians. In P. Deloria and N. Salisbury (eds) *A Companion to American Indian History* (pp. 422–440). Malden, MA: Blackwell.
Lomawaima, K.T. (2003) Educating Native Americans. In J. Banks (ed.) *Handbook of Research on Multicultural Education* (2nd edn) (pp. 441–446). New York: Jossey-Bass.
Lomawaima, K.T. (2012) Speaking from Arizona: Can scholarship about education make a difference in the world? *Journal of American Indian Education* 51 (2), 3–21.
Lomawaima, K.T and McCarty, T.L. (2002a) When tribal sovereignty challenges democracy: American Indian education and the democratic ideal. *American Educational Research Journal* 39 (2), 279–305.
Lomawaima, K.T and McCarty, T.L. (2002b) *Reliability, Validity, and Authenticity in American Indian and Alaska Native Research*. ERIC Digest EDO-RC-02-4. Charleston, WV: ERIC Clearinghouse on Rural Education and Small Schools. Online at http://www.eric.ed.gov:80/ERICDocs/data/ericdocs2sql/content_storage_01/0000019b/80/1a/96/0e.pdf, accessed 15 July 2009.
Lomawaima, K.T and McCarty, T.L. (2006) *'To Remain an Indian': Lessons in Democracy from a Century of Native American Education*. New York: Teachers College Press.
López, L.E. (2008) Top-down and bottom-up: Counterpoised visions of bilingual intercultural education in Latin America. In N.H. Hornberger (ed.) *Can Schools Save Indigenous Languages? Policy and Practice on Four Continents* (pp. 42–65). New York: Palgrave Macmillan.
Luke, A., McHoul, A.W. and Mey, J.L. (1990) On the limits of language planning: Class, state and power. In R.B. Baldauf Jr and A. Luke (eds) *Language Planning and Education in Australasia and the South Pacific* (pp. 25–44). Clevedon: Multilingual Matters.
MacArthur Fellows Program (2010) *Jessie Little Doe Baird, Indigenous Language Preservationist*, 25 January (video). Online at http://www.macfound.org/fellows/24/, accessed 7 June 2012.
Makepeace, A. (2011) *We Still Live Here. Âs Nutayuneân* (film). Oley, PA: Bullfrog Films.
Manuelito, K. (2004) An Indigenous perspective on self-determination. In K. Mutua and B.B. Swadener (eds) *Decolonizing Research in Cross-Cultural Contexts: Critical Personal Narratives* (pp. 235–253). Albany, NY: State University of New York Press.
Manuelito, K. (2005) The role of education in American Indian self-determination: Lessons from the Ramah Navajo Community School. *Anthropology and Education Quarterly* 36 (1), 73–87.
Manuelito, K.D., Bird, C.P. and Belgarde, M. (2011) Language and educational initiatives in Southwest Indigenous communities. In M.E. Romero-Little, S.J. Ortiz, T.L. McCarty and R. Chen (eds) *Indigenous Languages Across the Generations – Strengthening Families and Communities* (pp. 304–320). Tempe, AZ: Arizona State University Center for Indian Education.
Maracle, I., Hill, K., Maracle, T. and Brown, K. (2011) Rebuilding our language foundation through the next generation. In M.E. Romero-Little, S.J. Ortiz, T.L. McCarty and R. Chen (eds) *Indigenous Languages Across the Generations – Strengthening Families and Communities* (pp. 83–94). Tempe, AZ: Arizona State University Center for Indian Education.

Marlow, P.E. (2006) The Denaqenage Career Ladder Program: The University of Alaska's role in language revitalization. In T.L. McCarty and O. Zepeda (eds) *One Voice, Many Voices – Recreating Indigenous Language Communities* (pp. 395–405). Tempe, AZ: Arizona State University Center for Indian Education.

Mato Nunpa, C. (2006) The Dakota–English Dictionary Project: A Minnesota collaborative effort. In T.L. McCarty and O. Zepeda (eds) *One Voice, Many Voices – Recreating Indigenous Language Communities* (pp. 205–217). Tempe, AZ: Arizona State University Center for Indian Education.

Matua, K. and Swadener, B.B. (eds) (2004) *Decolonizing Research in Cross-cultural Contexts: Critical Personal Narratives*. Albany, NY: State University of New York Press.

May, S. (1991) Making the difference for minority children: The development of an holistic language policy at Richmond Road School, Auckland, New Zealand. *Language, Culture, and Curriculum* 4, 201–217.

May, S. (1994) *Making Multicultural Education Work*. Clevedon and Toronto, CA: Multilingual Matters and Ontario Institute for Studies in Education.

May, S. (2012) *Language and Minority Rights: Ethnicity, Nationalism and the Politics of Language* (2nd edn). New York: Routledge.

McBroom, P. (1995) Saving tribal tongues: California's Native Americans are in a race against time. *Berkleyan* 3 (1). Online at http://www.berkeley.edu/news/berkeleyan/1995/0301/tribal.html, accessed 8 February 2012.

McCarty, T.L. (1993) Federal language policy and American Indian education. *Bilingual Research Journal* 17 (1–2), 13–34.

McCarty, T.L. (2002a) Between possibility and constraint: Indigenous language education, planning, and policy in the United States. In J.W. Tollefson (ed.) *Language Policies in Education: Critical Issues* (pp. 285–307). Mahwah, NJ: Lawrence Erlbaum.

McCarty, T.L. (2002b) *A Place To Be Navajo – Rough Rock and the Struggle for Self-Determination in Indigenous Schooling*. Mahwah, NJ: Lawrence Erlbaum.

McCarty, T.L. (2003) Revitalising Indigenous languages in homogenising times. *Comparative Education* 39 (2), 147–163.

McCarty, T.L. (2004) Dangerous difference: A critical–historical analysis of language education policies in the United States. In J.W. Tollefson and A.B.M. Tsui (eds) *Medium of Instruction Policies: Which Agenda? Whose Agenda?* (pp. 71–93). Mahwah, NJ: Lawrence Erlbaum.

McCarty, T.L. (ed.) (2005) *Language, Literacy, and Power in Schooling*. Mahwah, NJ: Lawrence Erlbaum.

McCarty, T.L. (2006) Voice and choice in Indigenous language revitalization. *Journal of Language, Identity, and Education* 5 (4), 308–315.

McCarty, T.L. (2008a) Native American languages as heritage mother tongues. *Language, Culture and Curriculum* 21 (3), 201–225.

McCarty, T.L. (2008b) Schools as strategic tools for Indigenous language revitalization: Lessons from Native America. In N.H. Hornberger (ed.) *Can Schools Save Indigenous Languages? Policy and Practice on Four Continents* (pp. 161–179). New York: Palgrave Macmillan.

McCarty, T.L. (2008c) Evaluating images of groups in your curriculum. In M. Pollock (ed.) *Everyday Antiracism: Getting Real about Race in School* (pp. 180–185). New York: The New Press.

McCarty, T.L. (guest ed.) (2008d) American Indian, Alaska Native, and Native Hawaiian education in the era of standardization and NCLB. (Special issue.) *Journal of American Indian Education* 47 (1).

McCarty, T.L. (2009) The impact of high-stakes accountability policies on Native American learners: Evidence from research. *Teaching Education* 20 (1), 1–23.

McCarty, T.L. (2010) Native American languages in the USA. In K. Potowski (ed.) *Language Diversity in the USA* (pp. 47–65). Cambridge: Cambridge University Press.

McCarty, T.L. (ed.) (2011a) *Ethnography and Language Policy*. New York: Routledge.
McCarty, T.L. (2011b) Preface. In T.L. McCarty (ed.) *Ethnography and Language Policy* (pp. xii–xiii). New York: Routledge.
McCarty, T.L. (2011c) Entry into conversation: Introducing ethnography and language policy. In T.L. McCarty (ed.) *Ethnography and Language Policy* (pp. 1–28). New York: Routledge.
McCarty, T.L. (2012) Language planning and cultural continuance in Native America. In J.F. Tollefson (ed.) *Language Policies in Education: Critical Issues* (2nd edn) (pp. 255–277). New York: Routledge.
McCarty, T.L. (2013a) Indigenous literacies: Continuum or divide? In M. Hawkins (ed.) *Framing Languages and Literacies: Socially Situated Views and Perspectives*. New York: Routledge (in press).
McCarty, T.L. (2013b) Indigenous languages and cultures in Native American student achievement: Promising practices and cautionary findings. In B. Klug (ed.) *Standing Together: Indigenous Education as Culturally Responsive Pedagogy*. Lanham, MD: Rowman and Littlefield (in press).
McCarty, T.L and Dick, G.S. (2003) Telling The People's stories: Literacy practices and processes in a Navajo community school. In A.I. Willis, G.E. García, R.B. Barrera and V.J. Harris (eds) *Multicultural Issues in Literacy Research and Practice* (pp. 101–122). Mahwah, NJ: Lawrence Erlbaum.
McCarty, T.L. and Watahomigie, L.J. (2004) Language and literacy in American Indian and Alaska Native communities. In B. Pérez (ed.) *Sociocultural Contexts of Language and Literacy* (pp. 79–110). Mahwah, NJ: Lawrence Erlbaum.
McCarty, T.L. and Wyman, L. (2009) Introduction: Indigenous youth and bilingualism – Theory, research, praxis. *Journal of Language, Identity, and Education* 8 (5), 279–290.
McCarty, T.L., Watahomigie, L.J., Yamamoto, A.Y. and Zepeda, O. (2001) Indigenous educators as change agents: Case studies of two language institutes. In L. Hinton and K. Hale (eds) *The Green Book of Language Revitalization in Practice* (pp. 371–383). San Diego, CA: Academic Press.
McCarty, T.L., Romero, M.E. and Zepeda, O. (2006a) Reimagining multilingual America: Lessons from Native American youth. In O. García, T. Skutnabb-Kangas and M. Torres-Guzmán (eds) *Imagining Multilingual Schools: Languages in Education and Glocalization* (pp. 91–110). Clevedon: Multilingual Matters.
McCarty, T.L., Romero, M.E. and Zepeda, O. (2006b) Reclaiming the gift: Indigenous youth counter-narratives on Native language loss and revitalization. *American Indian Quarterly* 30 (1–2), 28–48.
McCarty, T.L., Romero-Little, M.E. and Zepeda, O. (2006c) Native American youth discourses on language shift and retention: Ideological cross-currents and their implications for language planning. *International Journal of Bilingual Education and Bilingualism* 9 (5), 659–677.
McCarty, T.L., Romero-Little, M.E., Zepeda, O. and Warhol, L. (2007) *The Impact of Native Language Shift and Retention on American Indian Students' English Language Learning and School Achievement*. Final report submitted to the US Department of Education, Institute of Education Sciences, Washington, DC, 15 October.
McCarty, T.L., Skutnabb-Kangas, T. and Magga, O-H. (2008) Education for speakers of endangered languages. In B. Spolsky and F.M. Hult (eds) *The Handbook of Educational Linguistics* (pp. 297–312). Malden, MA: Blackwell.
McCarty, T.L., Romero-Little, M.E., Warhol, L. and Zepeda, O. (2009a) Indigenous youth as language policy makers. *Journal of Language, Identity, and Education* 8 (5), 291–306.
McCarty, T.L., Romero-Little, M.E., Warhol, L. and Zepeda, O. (2009b) 'I'm speaking English instead of my culture': Portraits of language use and change among Native

American youth. In M. Farr, L. Seloni and J. Song (eds) *Ethnolinguistic Diversity and Education: Language, Literacy, and Culture* (pp. 69–98). New York: Routledge.

McCarty, T.L., Romero-Little, M.E., Warhol, L. and Zepeda, O. (2011) Critical ethnography and Indigenous language survival: Some new directions in language policy research and praxis. In T.L. McCarty (ed.) *Ethnography and Language Policy* (pp. 31–51). New York: Routledge.

McCarty, T.L., Nicholas, S.E. and Wyman, L.T. (2012) Re-emplacing place in the 'global here and now' – Critical ethnographic case studies of Native American language planning and policy. *International Multilingual Research Journal* 6 (1), 50–63.

McCoy, T., Ironstrack, G., Baldwin, D., Strack, A.J. and Olm, W. (2011) *ašiihkiwi neehi kiišikwi myaamionki. Earth and Sky – The Place of the Myaamiaki*. Miami, OK: Miami Tribe of Oklahoma.

McLaughlin, D. (1992) *When Literacy Empowers: Navajo Language in Print*. Albuquerque, NM: University of New Mexico Press.

Mead, N., Grigg, W., Moran, R. and Kuang, M. (2010) *National Indian Education Study 2009 – Part II: The Educational Experiences of American Indian and Alaska Native Students in Grades 4 and 8* (NCES 2010-463). Washington, DC: National Center for Education Statistics, Institute of Education Sciences, US Department of Education.

Medicine, B. (2001) Contemporary cultural revisitation: Bilingual and bicultural education. In B. Medicine and S-E. Jacobs (eds) *Learning To Be an Anthropologist and Remaining 'Native': Selected Writings* (pp. 50–57). Urbana, IL: University of Illinois Press.

Meek, B.A. (2007) Respecting the language of elders: Ideological shift and linguistic discontinuity in a Northern Athapascan community. *Journal of Linguistic Anthropology* 17 (1), 23–43.

Meek, B.A. (2010) *We Are Our Language: An Ethnography of Language Revitalization in a Northern Athabaskan Community*. Tucson, AZ: University of Arizona Press.

Meek, B.A. (2011) Failing American Indian languages. *American Indian Culture and Research Journal* 35 (2), 43–60.

Menezes de Souza, L.M.T. (2002). A case among cases, a world among worlds: The ecology of writing among the Kashinawá in Brazil. *Journal of Language, Identity, and Education* 1 (4), 261–278.

Menken, K. (2008) *English Learners Left Behind: Standardized Testing as Language Policy*. Clevedon: Multilingual Matters.

Meriam, L., Brown, R.A., Roe Cloud, H., Dale, E.E., Duke, E., Edwards, H.R., McKenzie, F.A., Mark, M.L., Ryan, W.C. and Spillman, W.J. (1928) *The Problem of Indian Administration*. Baltimore, MD: Johns Hopkins Press for the Institute for Government Research.

Messing, J.H.E. (2009) Ambivalence and ideology among Mexicano youth in Tlaxcala, Mexico. *Journal of Language, Identity, and Education* 8 (5), 350–364.

Messing, J.H.E. and Rockwell, E. (2006) Local language promoters and new discursive spaces: Mexicano in and out of schools in Tlaxcala. In M. Hidalgo (ed.) *The Mexican Indigenous Languages at the Dawn of the 21st Century* (pp. 249–280). Berlin: Mouton de Gruyter.

Metz, A. (2008) School immerses Mohawk children in traditional language. *Orlando Sentinel*, 26 June. Online at http://www.orlandosentinel.com/topic/ny-mohawk1109,0,1520752.story, accessed 26 June 2008.

Meyer, L.M. (2012) Fishman's cultural autonomy as an approach to sociolinguistic power-sharing. *International Journal of the Sociology of Language* 213, 127–142.

Miami Tribe of Oklahoma (2008) *myaamiaki eemamwiciki. Miami Awakening* (DVD). Miami, OK: Miami Tribe of Oklahoma.

Mifflin, J. (2008) Saving a language. *Technology Review*, May/June. Online at http://www.technologyreview.com/article/20629/, accessed 30 January 2012.

Mignon, M. and Boxberger, D. (eds) (1997) *Native North Americans: An Ethnohistorical Approach* (2nd edn). Dubuque, IO: Kendall/Hunt.

Mithun, M. and Chafe, W.L. (1987) Recapturing the Mohawk language. In T. Shopen (ed.) *Languages and Their Status* (pp. 1–34). New York: Winthrop.

Mohanty, A., Panda, M., Phillipson, R. and Skutnabb-Kangas, T. (eds) (2009) *Multilingual Education for Social Justice: Globilising the Local*. New Delhi: Orient BlackSwan.

Mohawk Council of Kahnawá:ke (2008) Mohawks of Kahnawá:ke. Online at http:/// www.kahnawake.com, accessed 18 July 2006.

Moll, L.C. (2004) Rethinking resistance. *Anthropology and Education Quarterly* 35(1), 126–131.

Moore, K. (2011) Statement of Keith Moore, director, Bureau of Indian Education, US Department of the Interior. In Committee on Indian Affairs, United States Senate, 111th Congress, Second Session, *Indian Education: Did the No Child Left Behind Act Leave Indian Students Behind?* (pp. 6–11). Washington, DC: US Government Printing Office.

Moore, R.E. (1999) Endangered. *Journal of Linguistic Anthropology* 9 (1–2), 65–68.

Moore, R.E., Pietikäinen, S. and Blommaert, J. (2010) Counting the losses: Numbers as the language of endangerment. *Sociolinguistic Studies* 4 (1), 1–26.

Moran, R., Rampey, B.D., Dion, G. and Donahue, P. (2008) *National Indian Education Study 2007 Part I: Performance of American Indian and Alaska Native Students at Grades 4 and 8 on NAEP 2007 Reading and Mathematics Assessments*. Washington, DC: US Department of Education, National Center for Education Statistics, Institute of Education Sciences.

Moriarty, M. (2011) New roles for endangered languages. In P.K. Austin and J. Sallabank (eds) *The Cambridge Handbook of Endangered Languages* (pp. 446–458). Cambridge: Cambridge University Press.

Mühlhäusler, P. (1996) *Language Change and Linguistic Imperialism in the Pacific Region*. London: Routledge.

Mühlhäusler, P. (2000) Language planning and language ecology. *Current Issues in Language Planning* 1 (3), 306–367.

Mühlhäusler, P. (2003) *Language of Environment – Environment of Language. A Course in Sociolinguistics*. London: Battlebridge.

Mutua, K. and Swadener, B.B. (eds) *Decolonizing Research in Cross-Cultural Contexts: Critical Personal Narratives*. Albany, NY: State University of New York Press.

Myaamia Project (2009) Statement of purpose. Online at http://www.myaamiaproject. org/mission.html, accessed 6 July 2012.

National Alliance to Save Native Languages (2007) House Appropriations Subcommittee recommends near doubling of Native language program funding. Press Release, 8 June. Online at http://search.yahoo.com/search?ei=utf-plw&p=National+Alliance+ to+Save+Native+Languages,+house + appropriations+subcommittee+recommends+ near+doubling+of+Native+language+program+funding, accessed 12 June 2012.

National Caucus of Native American State Legislators (2008) *Striving to Achieve: Helping Native American Students Succeed*. Denver, CO: National Conference of State Legislatures.

National Clearinghouse for English Language Acquisition (2002) *How Many Indigenous American Languages are Spoken in the United States? By How Many Speakers?* Washington, DC: Office of English Language Acquisition, Language Enhancement and Academic Achievement, US Department of Education. Online at http://www.ncela.gwu.edu/ expert/faq/20natlang.html, accessed 25 July 2007.

Native American Languages Act (1990) *P.L. 101–477*. Online at http://www.nabe.org/ files/NALanguagesActs.pdf, accessed 7 June 2012.

Native Hawaiian Education Council and Ka Haka 'Ula O Ke'elikōlani College of Hawaiian Language (2002). *Nā Honua Mauli Ola. Hawai'i Guidelines for Culturally Healthy and*

Responsive Learning Environments. Hilo, HI: Native Hawaiian Education Council and Ka Haka 'Ula O Ke'elikōlani College of Hawaiian Language, University of Hawai'i at Hilo.

Native Networks (2011) 2011 Native American Film + Video Festival March 31–April 3, 2011. Online at http://www.nativenetworks.si.edu/eng/blue/nafvf_11.html, accessed 11 January 2012.

Navajo Nation Washington Office (2005) Navajo Nation Profile. Online at http://www.nnwo.org/nnprofile.htm, accessed 26 July 2006.

Navajo Sovereignty in Education Act (NSIEA) (2005) *Navajo Sovereignty in Education Act of 2005*. Window Rock, AZ: Navajo Nation: 20th Navajo Nation Council. Online at http://www.odclc.navajo-nsn.gov/PDF/Resolution%20CJY%2037%2005%20Navajo%20Sovereignty%20in%20Education%20Act%20of%202005.pdf, accessed 8 June 2012.

NEA-Alaska (2012) Legislature passes bill to protect Alaska Native languages. Juneau: Alaska State Capitol. Online at http://www,neaalaska.org/nea.node/951, accessed 21 May 2012.

Nettle, D. and Romaine, S. (2000) *Vanishing Voices: The Extinction of the World's Languages*. Oxford: Oxford University Press.

Neundorf, A. (1987) Bilingualism: A bridge to power for interpreters and leaders in the Navajo Tribal Council. Unpublished PhD dissertation, University of New Mexico.

New London Group (1996) A pedagogy of multiliteracies: Designing social futures. *Harvard Educational Review* 66 (1), 60–92.

Ngai, P. and Koehn, P. (2010) Implementing Montana's Indian-Education-for-All initiative in a K-5 public school: Implications for classroom teaching, education policy, and Native communities. *Journal of American Indian Education* 49 (1–2), 50–68.

Ng-Osoro, J. and Tibbetts, K.A. (2010) *Department of Education Update 2010: The R&E Annual Update Series*. Honolulu, HI: Kamehameha Schools Research and Evaluation.

Nicholas, S. (2005) Negotiating for the Hopi way of life through literacy and schooling. In T.L. McCarty (ed.) *Language, Literacy, and Power in Schooling* (pp. 29–46). Mahwah, NJ: Lawrence Erlbaum.

Nicholas, S.E. (2008) Becoming 'fully' Hopi: The role of the Hopi language in the contemporary lives of Hopi youth – A Hopi case study of language shift and vitality. Unpublished PhD dissertation, University of Arizona.

Nicholas, S.E. (2009) 'I live Hopi, I just don't speak it': The critical intersection of language, culture, and identity for contemporary Hopi youth. *Journal of Language, Identity, and Education* 8 (5), 321–334.

Nicholas, S.E. (2011) 'How are you Hopi if you can't speak it?' An ethnographic study of language as cultural practice among contemporary Hopi youth. In T.L. McCarty (ed.) *Ethnography and Language Policy* (pp. 53–75). New York: Routledge.

Nichols, S.L. and Berliner, D.C. (2008) *Collateral Damage: How High-Stakes Testing Corrupts America's Schools*. Cambridge, MA: Harvard Education Press.

Nichols, S.L., Glass, G.V. and Berliner, D.C. (2006) High-stakes testing and student achievement: Does accountability pressure increase student learning? *Education Policy Analysis Archives* 14 (1). Online at http://epaa.asu.edu/ojs/article/view/72, accessed 6 September 2012.

Nielson, J. (2011) *Population Update 2011: The R&E Annual Update Series*. Honolulu, HI: Kamehameha Schools Research and Evaluation.

No Child Left Behind Act (2001) *Title III: Language Instruction for Limited English Proficient and Immigrant Students. Public Law 107-110, January 8, 2002*. Washington, DC: US Department of Education, Office of English Language Acquisition, Language Enhancement and Academic Achievement for Limited English Proficient Students.

No Child Left Behind Act (2001) *Title VII: Indian, Native Hawaiian, and Alaska Native Education. Public Law 107-110, January 8, 2002*. Washington, DC: US Department of Education, Office of English Language Acquisition, Language Enhancement and Academic Achievement for Limited English Proficient Students.

Noley, G. (1979) Choctaw bilingual and bicultural education in the nineteenth century. In American Indian Studies Center (ed.) *Multicultural Education and the American Indian* (pp. 25–39). Los Angeles, CA: University of California American Indian Studies Center.

Norrell, B. (2005) Education reform elevates status of Navajo-controlled education. *Indian Country Today*, 12 August. Online at http://www.arizonaenergy.org/News%2005/News%20Aug05/Education%20reform%20elevates%20status%20of%20Navajo-controlled%20education.htm, accessed 23 October 2012.

Norris, T., Vines, P.L. and Hoeffel, E.N. (2012) *The American Indian and Alaska Native Population: 2010*. Washington, DC: US Department of Commerce Economics and Statistics Administration, US Census Bureau. Online at http://www.census.gov/prod/cen2010/briefs/c2010br-10.pdf, accessed 11 June 2012.

Nott, R. (2010) Student films aim to bring Native tongues back to life. *Santa Fe New Mexican*, 5 March. Online at http://www.santafenewmexican.com/Local%20News/Bringing-language-back-to-life, accessed 19 June 2012.

Obama, B. (2008) *Barack Obama's Principles for Stronger Tribal Communities*. Online at http://www.ncai.org/attachments/Consultation_ZxLDLvebLpHLIquwsPua UjkPNQdszcmkjgHRsoUzxiLEqvcxaLY_Barack%20Obama%27s%20Principles%20for%20Stronger%20Tribal%20Communities.pdf, accessed 4 September 2012.

O'Brien, M. and Walton, M. (2011) New home movies resurrect endangered American Indian language. *Science Nation*, 21 November. Online at http://www.nsf.gov/news/special_reports/science_nation/savingtriballanguages.jsp, accessed 7 June 2012.

O'Connor, B. and Brown, G. (2013) Just keep expanding outwards: Embodied space as cultural critique in the life and work of a Navajo hip hop artist. In L.T. Wyman, T.L. McCarty and S.E. Nicholas (eds) *Beyond Endangerment: Language in the Lives of Indigenous Youth*. New York: Routledge (in press).

Ogunwole, S.U. (2006) *We the People: American Indians and Alaska Natives in the United States*. Washington, DC: US Department of Commerce Economics and Statistics Administration, US Census Bureau.

Olsen, L., Bhattacharya, J., Chow, M., Jaramillo, A., Tobiassen, D.P., Solorio, J. and Dowell, C. (2001) American Indian Language Development Institute, Tucson, Arizona. In C. Dowell (ed.) *And Still We Speak… Stories of Communities Sustaining and Reclaiming Language and Culture* (pp. 46–53) Oakland, CA: California Tomorrow.

Ó Riagáin, D. (2006) Language planning – An outline introduction. Unpublished manuscript.

O'Rourke, B. and Walsh, J. (2012) New speakers of Irish: Shifting identities and new allegiances. Paper Presented at Sociolinguistics Symposium 19, Berlin, August 21.

Ortiz, S.J. (1992) *Woven Stone*. Tucson, AZ: University of Arizona Press.

Ortiz, S.J. (1993) The language we know. In P. Riley (ed.) *Growing Up Native American: An Anthology* (pp. 29–38). New York: Morrow.

Ortiz, S.J. (1994) *After and Before the Lightning*. Tucson, AZ: University of Arizona Press.

Ovando, C.J. and Combs, M.C. (2012) *Bilingual and ESL Classrooms: Teaching in Multicultural Contexts* (5th edn). New York; McGraw-Hill.

Paris, D. (2011) 'A friend who understand fully': Notes on humanizing research in a multiethnic youth community. *International Journal of Qualitative Studies in Education*, 24 (2), 137–149.

Paris, D. and Winn, M. (eds) (2013) *Humanizing Research: Decolonizing Qualitative Research with Youth and Their Communities*. Thousand Oaks, CA: SAGE (in press).

Parsons-Yazzie, E. (1996) Perceptions of selected Navajo elders regarding Navajo language attrition. *Journal of Navajo Education* 13 (2), 51–57.

Parsons-Yazzie, E. (1996/1997) Niha'áłchíní dayistł'ó nahalin. *Journal of Navajo Education* 14 (1–2), 60–67.
Parsons-Yazzie, E. and Speas, M. (2008) *Diné Bizaad Bináhoo'aah: Rediscovering the Navajo Language*. Flagstaff, AZ: Salina Bookshelf.
Parsons-Yazzie, E. and Yazzie, B. Sr (2008) *Diné Bizaad Bináhoo'aah: Rediscovering the Navajo Language Correlated Workbook*. Flagstaff, AZ: Salina Bookshelf.
Patrick, D. (2003) *Language, Politics, and Social Interaction in an Inuit Community*. Berlin: Mouton de Gruyter.
Patrick, R. (2008) Perspectives on change: A continued struggle for academic success and cultural relevancy at an American Indian school in the midst of No Child Left Behind. *Journal of American Indian Education* 47 (1), 65–81.
Paulston, C.B., Chen, P.C. and Connerty, M.C. (1992) Language regenesis: A conceptual overview of language revival, revitalization and reversal. *Journal of Multilingual and Multicultural Development* 14 (4), 274–286.
Payne, N.A., Wallace, L. and Shorten K.S. (1953) *Be a Good Waitress*. Brigham City, UT: Intermountain School for the US Department of the Interior, Bureau of Indian Affairs, Branch of Education.
PBS Newshour (2011) 'We Still Live Here' Details Effort to Restore Wampanoag Language, 10 November. Online at http://www.pbs.org/newshour/bb/social_issues/july-dec11/efp_11-10.html, accessed 2 February 2012.
Pecos, R. and Blum-Martinez, R. (2001) The key to cultural survival: Language planning and revitalization in the Pueblo de Cochiti. In L. Hinton and K. Hale (eds) *The Green Book of Language Revitalization in Practice* (pp. 75–82). San Diego, CA: Academic Press.
Penfield, S.D. and Flores, A. (2006) Preservation strategies: A translation paradigm. In T.L. McCarty and O. Zepeda (eds) *One Voice, Many Voices – Recreating Indigenous Language Communities* (pp. 219–233). Tempe, AZ: Arizona State University Center for Indian Education.
Pennycook, A. (2001) Lessons from colonial language policies. In R.D. González and I. Melis (eds) *Language Ideologies: Critical Perspectives on the Official English Movement. Vol. 2: History, Theory, and Policy* (pp. 198–223). Urbana, IL and Mahwah, NJ: National Council of Teachers of English and Lawrence Erlbaum.
Peter, L. (2007) 'Our beloved Cherokee': A naturalistic study of Cherokee preschool language immersion. *Anthropology and Education Quarterly* 38 (4), 323–342.
Philips, L. (2011) Unexpected languages: Multilingualism and contact in eighteenth- and nineteenth-century America. *American Indian Culture and Research Journal* 35 (2), 19–41.
Phillipson, R. and Skutnabb-Kangas, T. (eds) (1996) *Linguistic Human Rights*. Berlin: Mouton de Gruyter.
Piatt, B. (1990) *¿Only English? Law and Language Policy in the United States*. Albuquerque, NM: University of New Mexico Press.
Platero, P. (2001) Navajo Head start language study. In L. Hinton and K. Hale (eds) *The Green Book of Language Revitalization in Practice* (pp. 67–97). San Diego, CA: Academic Press.
Prucha, F.P. (1984) *The Great Father: The United States Government and the American Indians* (abridged edn). Lincoln, NE: University of Nebraska Press.
Pye, C. (1992) Language loss among the Chilcotin. *International Journal of the Sociology of Language* 93, 75–86.
Qin-Hilliard, D.B., Feinauer, E. and Quiroz, B.G. (2001) Introduction. *Harvard Educational Review* 71 (3), v–ix.
Ramanathan, V. (2005) *The English–Vernacular Divide: Postcolonial Language Politics in Practice*. Clevedon: Multilingual Matters.
Read, J., Spolsky, B. and Neundorf, A. (1975) Socioeconomic implications of bilingual education on the Navajo reservation. Paper presented at the Annual Meeting of the American Educational Research Association, March, Washington, DC.

Reese-Miller, J. (1998) Stages in the obsolescence of certain eastern Algonquian languages. *Anthropological Linguistics* 40 (4), 535–569.

Reeves, A.G. (2006) To us they are butterflies: A case study of the educational experience at an urban Indigenous-serving charter school. Unpublished PhD dissertation, University of Arizona.

Reyhner, J.A. (2004) *Education and Language Restoration*. Philadelphia, PA: Chelsea House.

Reyhner, J.A. and Eder, J. (2004) *American Indian Education: A History*. Norman, OK: University of Oklahoma Press.

Reyhner, J. and Hurtado, D.S. (2008) Reading First, literacy, and American Indian/Alaska Native students. *Journal of American Indian Education* 47 (1), 82–93.

Rhodes, J. (1953) *Shoe Repairing Dictionary*. Brigham City, UT: Materials Preparation Department, Intermountain Indian School.

Ricento, T. (2000). Historical and theoretical perspectives in language policy and planning. *Journal of Sociolinguistics* 4 (2), 196–213.

Ricento, T. (2006) Theoretical perspectives in language policy: An overview. In T. Ricento (ed.) *An Introduction to Language Policy: Theory and Method* (pp. 4–23). Malden, MA: Blackwell.

Ricento, T.K. and Burnaby, B. (eds) (1998) *Language and Politics in the United States and Canada: Myths and Realities*. Mahwah, NJ: Lawrence Erlbaum.

Ricento, T.K. and Hornberger, N.H. (1996) Unpeeling the onion: Language planning and policy and the ELT professional. *TESOL Quarterly* 30 (3), 401–427.

Rinehart, M.A. (2006) Miami Indian language shift and recovery. Unpublished PhD dissertation, Michigan State University.

Rockwell, E. (2005) Indigenous accounts of dealing with writing. In T.L. McCarty (ed.) *Language, Literacy, and Power in Schooling* (pp. 5–27). Mahwah, NJ: Lawrence Erlbaum.

Rockwell, E. and Gomes, M.R. (2009) Introduction to the special issue: Rethinking Indigenous education from a Latin American perspective. *Anthropology and Education Quarterly* 40 (2), 97–109.

Roessel, C.M. (2007) Navajo education in and out of the classroom: A photographic case study of Rough Rock Community School. Unpublished doctoral dissertation, Arizona State University.

Roessel, M. (2011) 'Preserving the past to secure the future': The Center for Indian Education – The next 50 years. *Journal of American Indian Education* 50 (2), 13–23.

Roessel, R.A. (1977) *Navajo Education in Action: The Rough Rock Demonstration School*. Chinle, AZ: Navajo Curriculum Center, Rough Rock Demonstration School.

Romaine, S. (2006) Planning for the survival of linguistic diversity. *Language Policy* 5, 441–473.

Romero, M.E. (2003) Perpetuating the Cochiti way of life: A study of child socialization and language shift in a Pueblo community. Unpublished PhD dissertation, University of California Berkeley.

Romero-Little, M.E. (2010) How should young Indigenous children be prepared for learning? A vision of early childhood education for Indigenous children. *Journal of American Indian Education* 49 (1–2), 7–27.

Romero-Little, M.E. (2012) Globalization from the bottom up, inside out, and outside in: Indigenous language planning and policy from an Indigenous perspective. *International Multilingual Research Journal* 6 (1), 79–81.

Romero-Little, M.E. and McCarty, T.L. (2006) *Language Planning Challenges and Prospects in Native American Communities and Schools*. Tempe, AZ: Arizona State University Education Policy Studies Laboratory, College of Education. Online at http://nepc.colorado.edu/files/Report-EPSL-0602-105-LPRU.pdf, accessed 6 September 2012.

Romero-Little, M.E., McCarty, T.L., Warhol, L. and Zepeda, O. (2007) Language policies in practice: Preliminary findings from a large-scale study of Native American language shift. *TESOL Quarterly* 41 (3), 607–618.

Romero-Little, M.E., Ortiz, S.J., McCarty, T.L. and Chen, R. (eds) (2011) *Indigenous Languages Across the Generations – Strengthening Families and Communities.* Tempe, AZ: Arizona State University Center for Indian Education.

Rosier, P. and Farella, M. (1976) Bilingual education at Rock Point: Some early results. *TESOL Quarterly* 10 (4), 379–388.

Rosier, P. and Holm, W. (1980) *Bilingual Education Series: 8, The Rock Point Experience: A Longitudinal Study of a Navajo School Program (Saad Naaki Bee Na'nitin).* Washington, DC: Center for Applied Linguistics.

Ruiz, R. (1988). Orientations in languages planning. In S.L. McKay and S.-C. Wong (eds) *Language Diversity: Problem or Resource? A Social and Educational Perspectives on Language Minorities in the United States* (pp. 3–25). Boston, MA: Heinle and Heinle.

Sallabank, J. (2011) Language policy for endangered languages. In P.K. Austin and J. Sallabank (eds) *The Cambridge Handbook of Endangered Languages* (pp. 277–290). Cambridge: Cambridge University Press.

Scheirbeck, H.M., Barlow, E.J., Misiaszek, L.F., McKee, K., and Patterson, K.J. (1976) *Report on Indian Education. Task Force Five: Indian Education. Final Report to the American Indian Policy Review Commission.* Washington, DC: US Government Printing Office.

Schiffman, H. (1996) *Linguistic Culture and Language Policy.* London: Routledge.

Schiffman, H. (2006) Language policy and linguistic culture. In T. Ricento (ed.) *An Introduction to Language Policy: Theory and Method* (pp. 111–125). Malden, MA: Blackwell.

Seidman, I.E. (2006) *Interviewing as Qualitative Research* (3rd edn). New York: Teachers College Press.

Shohamy, E. (2006) *Language Policy: Hidden Agendas and New Approaches.* London: Routledge.

Shonerd, H.G. (1990) Domesticating the barbarous tongue: Language policy for the Navajo in historical perspective. *Language Problems and Language Planning* 14 (3), 193–208.

Shortman, I. (2011) TinkrLabs releases Navajo Toddler HD 1.0 for the iPad, November. Online at http://prmac.com/release-id-33418.htm, accessed 18 December 2011.

Siebens, J. and Julian, T. (2011) *Native North American Languages Spoken at Home in the United States and Puerto Rico: 2006–2010. American Community Survey Briefs,* December. Washington, DC: US Department of Commerce Economics and Statistics Administration, US Census Bureau. Online at http://www.census.gov/prod/2011pubs/acsbr10-10.pdf, accessed 11 June 2012.

Silentman, I. (1995) Navajo bilingual education in the 1970s: A personal perspective. Unpublished manuscript.

Silentman, I. (1996a) An interview with Dr. Robert W. Young. *Journal of Navajo Education* 8 (2), 14–20.

Silentman, I. (guest ed.) (1996b) In Honor of Robert Young and William Morgan. (Theme issue.) *Journal of Navajo Education* 8 (2).

Silverstein, M. (1996) Dynamics of linguistic contact. In I. Goddard (volume ed.) and W.C. Sturtevant (general ed.) *Handbook of North American Indians Vol. 17: Languages* (pp. 609–643). Washington, DC: Smithsonian Institute.

Sims, C. (1998) Community-based efforts to preserve Native languages: A descriptive study of the Karuk Tribe of northern California. *International Journal of the Sociology of Language* 132, 95–113.

Sims, C. (2001) Native language planning: A pilot process in the Acoma Pueblo community. In L. Hinton and K. Hale (eds) *The Green Book of Language Revitalization in Practice* (pp. 63–73). San Diego, CA: Academic Press.

Sims, C.P. (2005) Tribal languages and the challenges of revitalization. *Anthropology and Education Quarterly* 36 (1), 104–106.
Sims, C.P. (2006) Language planning in American Indian Pueblo communities: Contemporary challenges and issues. *Current Issues in Language Planning* 7 (2), 251–268.
Sims, C.P. (2008) Assessing the language proficiency of tribal heritage language learners: Issues and concerns for American Indian Pueblo languages. *Current Issues in Language Planning* 9 (3), 327–343.
Sims, C.P. (2011) Teaching Indigenous languages: Perspectives from American Indian Pueblo communities. *Educación Comunal*, July (4–5), 153–163.
Skutnabb-Kangas, T. (2000) *Linguistic Genocide in Education – Or Worldwide Diversity and Human Rights?* Mahwah, NJ: Lawrence Erlbaum.
Skutnabb-Kangas, T. (2008) Human rights and language policy in education. In S. May and N.H. Hornberger (eds) *Encyclopedia of Language and Education Vol. 1: Language Policy and Political Issues in Education* (2nd edn) (pp. 107–119). New York: Springer.
Skutnabb-Kangas, T. (2012) Indigenousness, human rights, ethnicity, language and power. *International Journal of the Sociology of Language* 213, 87–104.
Skutnabb-Kangas, T., Bear Nicholas, A. and Reyhner, J. (forthcoming) Linguistic human rights and language revitalization: Canada and the United States. In S. Coronel-Molina and T.L. McCarty (eds) *Indigenous Language Revitalization in the Americas*. New York: Routledge.
Skutnabb-Kangas, T. and McCarty, T.L. (2008) Key concepts in bilingual education: Ideological, historical, epistemological, and empirical foundations. In J. Cummins and N.H. Hornberger (eds) *Encyclopedia of Language and Education. Vol. 5: Bilingual Education* (pp. 3–17). New York: Springer Science+Business Media.
Skutnabb-Kangas, T., Phillipson, R., Mohanty, A.K. and Panda, M. (eds) (2009) *Social Justice through Multilingual Education*. Bristol: Multilingual Matters.
Slate, C. (2001) Promoting advanced Navajo language scholarship. In L. Hinton and K. Hale (eds) *The Green Book of Language Revitalization in Practice* (pp. 389–410). San Diego, CA: Academic Press.
Smith, L.T. (1999) *Decolonizing Methodologies: Research and Indigenous Peoples*. London: Zed Books.
Smith, L.T. (2007) Welcoming remarks. Presentation at the International Conference on Language, Education and Diversity, 21 November, University of Waikato, Hamilton, NZ.
Snipp, C.M. (2002) *American Indian and Alaska Native Children in the 2000 Census*. Baltimore, MD and Washington, DC: The Annie E. Casey Foundation and the Population Reference Bureau.
Solórzano, R.W. (2008) High-stakes testing: Issues, implications, and remedies for English language learners. *Review of Educational Research* 78 (2), 260–329.
Spack, R. (2002) *America's Second Tongue: American Indian Education and the Ownership of English, 1860–1900*. Lincoln, NE: University of Nebraska Press.
Spicer, E.H. (1962) *Cycles of Conquest: The Impact of Spain, Mexico, and the United States on the Indians of the Southwest, 1533–1960*. Tucson, AZ: University of Arizona Press.
Spolsky, B. (1972) *The Situation of Navajo Literacy Projects*. Navajo Reading Study Progress Report No. 17. Albuquerque, NM: University of New Mexico.
Spolsky, B. (1974) *American Indian Education*. Navajo Reading Study Progress Report No. 24. Albuquerque, NM: University of New Mexico.
Spolsky, B. (1975) Linguistics in practice: The Navajo Reading Study. *Theory into Practice* 14 (5), 347–352.
Spolsky, B. (2002) Prospects for the survival of the Navajo language: A reconsideration. *Anthropology and Education Quarterly* 33 (2), 139–162.
Spolsky, B. (2004) *Language Policy*. Cambridge: Cambridge University Press.

Spolsky, B. (2009) Language management for endangered languages: The case of Navajo. In P.K. Austin (ed.) *Language Documentation and Description Vol. 6* (pp. 117–131). London: SOAS.

Spolsky, B., Green, J.B. and Read, J. (1974) *A Model for the Description, Analysis, and Perhaps Evaluation of Bilingual Education*. Navajo Reading Study Progress Report No. 23. Albuquerque, NM: University of New Mexico.

Spring, J. (1996) *The Cultural Transformation of a Native American Family and Its Tribe 1763–1995, A Basket of Apples*. Mahwah, NJ: Lawrence Erlbaum.

Stairs, A., Peters, M. and Perkins, E. (1999) Beyond language in Indigenous language immersion schooling. *Practicing Anthropology* 20 (2), 44–47.

Stancavage, F.B., Mitchell, J.H., Bandeira de Mello, V., Gaertner, F.E., Spain, A.K. and Rahal, M.L. (2006) *National Indian Education Study Part II: The Educational Experiences of Fourth- and Eighth-Grade American Indian and Alaska Native Students*. Washington, DC: US Department of Education, National Center for Education Statistics, Institute of Education Sciences.

St Clair, R.N. (1982) What is language renewal? In R. St Clair and W. Leap (eds) *Language Renewal among American Indian Tribes: Issues, Problems, and Prospects* (pp. 3–17). Washington, DC: National Clearinghouse for Bilingual Education.

Strack, A.J., Baldwin, D. and Dorey, M. (2011a) *myaamiaki iši meehtohseeniwiciki: How the Miami People Live*. Miami, OK: Miami Tribe of Oklahoma.

Strack, G., Ironstrack, G., Baldwin, D., Fox, K., Olds, J., Abbitt, R. and Rinehart, M. (2011b) *myaamiaki aancihsaaciki. A Cultural Exploration of the Myaamia Removal Route*. Miami, OK: Miami Tribe of Oklahoma.

Street, B.V. (2001) *Literacy and Development: Ethnographic Perspectives*. London: Routledge.

Street, B.V. (2008) New literacies, new times: Developments in literacy studies. In B.V. Street and N.H. Hornberger (eds) *Encyclopedia of Language and Education Vol. 2: Literacy* (2nd edn) (pp. 3–14). New York: Springer.

Suárez-Orozco, M. (2001) Globalization, immigration, and education: The research agenda. *Harvard Educational Review* 71 (3), 345–365.

Supahan, T. and Supahan, S.E. (2001) Teaching well, learning quickly: Communication-based language instruction. In L. Hinton and K. Hale (eds) *The Green Book of Language Revitalization in Practice* (pp. 195–197). San Diego, CA: Academic Press.

Sutton, M.Q. (2004) *An Introduction to Native North America* (2nd edn). Boston, MA: Pearson.

Sydney Morning Herald (2010) Apple includes Cherokee language in iPods. *The Sydney Morning Herald*, 24 December. Online at http://www.smh.com.au/digital-life/digital-life-nes/apple-includes-cherokee-language-in-ipods-20101223-19 6op.html, accessed 27 December 2010.

Szasz, M. (1974) *Education and the American Indian: The Road to Self-Determination, 1928–1973*. Albuquerque, NM: University of New Mexico Press.

Szasz, M. (1988) *Indian Education in the American Colonies, 1607–1783*. Albuquerque, NM: University of New Mexico Press.

Talking Alaska (2012) Alaska legislature passes bill to protect Alaska Native languages, 12 April. Online at http://talkingalaska.blogspot.com/2012/04/alaska-legislature-passes-bill-to.html, accessed 21 May 2012.

Tapahonso, L. (1987) *A Breeze Swept Through: Poetry by Luci Tapahonso*. Albuquerque, NM: West End Press.

Task Force on Aboriginal Languages and Cultures (2005) *Towards a New Beginning: A Foundational Report for a Strategy to Revitalize First Nation, Inuit and Métis Languages and Cultures*. Ottawa, Canada: Aboriginal Languages Directorate, Aboriginal Affairs Branch, Department of Canadian Heritage.

The Regents of the University of California (2009–2010) Breath of Life – Survey of California and other Indian languages. Online at http://linguistics.berkeley.edu/~survey/activities/breath-of-life.php, accessed 13 June 2012.

The White House (2011) Executive Order 13592. Improving American Indian and Alaska Native Educational Opportunities and Strengthening Tribal Colleges and Universities, 2 December. Online at http://www.whitehouse.gov/the-press-office/2011/12/02/ executive-order-improving-american-indian-and-alaska-native-educational-, accessed 11 June 2012.

Thornton, R. (1987) *American Indian Holocaust and Survival: A Population History since 1492*. Norman, OK: University of Oklahoma Press.

Thornton, R. (2002) A Rosebud reservation winter count, circa 1751–1887. *Ethnohistory* 49 (4), 725–742.

Tirado, M. (2001) Left behind: Are public schools failing Indian kids? *American Indian Report*, September, 12–15.

Todeva, E. and Cenoz, J. (eds) (2009) *The Multiple Realities of Multilingualism: Personal Narratives and Researchers' Perspectives*. Berlin: Mouton de Gruyter.

Tohe, L. (2005) *Tseyi, Deep in the Rock*. Tucson, AZ: University of Arizona Press.

Tollefson, J.W. (1991) *Planning Language, Planning Inequality: Language Policy in the Community*. London: Longman.

Tollefson, J.W. (ed.) (2002a) *Language Policies in Education: Critical Issues*. Mahwah, NJ: Lawrence Erlbaum.

Tollefson, J.W. (2002b) Introduction: Critical issues in educational language policy. In J.W. Tollefson (ed.) *Language Policies in Education: Critical Issues* (pp. 3–15). Mahwah, NJ: Lawrence Erlbaum.

Tollefson, J.W. (2006) Critical theory in language policy. In T. Ricento (ed.) *An Introduction to Language Policy: Theory and Method* (pp. 42–59). Malden, MA: Blackwell.

Tollefson, J.W. (2012) *Language Policies in Education: Critical Issues* (2nd edn). New York: Routledge.

Trennert, R.A. Jr (1988) *The Phoenix Indian School: Forced Assimilation in Arizona, 1891–1935*. Norman, OK: University of Oklahoma Press.

Trumbell, J.H. (1903) *Natick Dictionary: A New England Indian Lexicon*. Bureau of American Ethnology Bulletin 25. Washington, DC: Bureau of American Ethnology.

Tsunoda, T. (2005) *Language Endangerment and Language Revitalization: An Introduction*. Berlin: Mouton de Gruyter.

Tulloch, S. (2004) Inuktitut and Inuit youth: Language attitudes as a basis for language planning. Unpublished doctoral dissertation, University of Laval.

Tulloch, S. (2013) Igniting a youth language movement: Inuit youth as agents of circumpolar language planning. In L.T. Wyman, T.L. McCarty and S.E. Nicholas (eds) *Beyond Endangerment: Language in the Lives of Indigenous Youth*. New York: Routledge (in press).

Underhill, R. (1956) *The Navajos*. Norman, OK: University of Oklahoma Press.

UNESCO Ad Hoc Expert Group on Endangered Languages (2003) *Language Vitality and Endangerment*. Paris: UNESCO Intangible Cultural Heritage Unit. Online at http://www.unesco.org/endangeredlanguages, accessed 18 July 2006.

US Census Bureau (2007) *The American Indian Community – American Indians and Alaska Natives: 2004*. Washington, DC: US Department of Commerce Economics and Statistics Administration, US Census Bureau.

US Commission on Civil Rights (2004) *Closing the Achievement Gap: The Impact of Standards-based Education Reform on Student Performance. Draft Report for Commissioner's Review*. Washington, DC: US Commission on Civil Rights.

US Congress, Senate Committee on Labor and Public Welfare, Special Subcommittee on Indian Education (1969) *The Study of the Education of Indian Children, Part 3* (Kennedy Report). Washington, DC: US Government Printing Office.

US Department of Education (n.d.) *Stronger Accountability: Adequate Yearly Progress*. Washington, DC: US Department of Education. Online at http://www.ed.gov/nclb/ accountability/ayp/ epicks.html, accessed 16 June 2008.

US Department of Education (2011) *The Growing Numbers of English Learner Students 1998/99–2008/09*. Online at http://www.ncela.gwu.edu/files/uploads/9/growing LEP_0809.pdf, accessed 22 October 2012.

US Department of the Interior (2004) *Learn Today Lead Tomorrow. Fingertip Facts 2004*. Washington, DC: US Department of the Interior, Bureau of Indian Affairs, Office of Indian Education Programs.

US Senate Committee on Indian Affairs (2011) *Indian Education: Did the No Child Left Behind Act Leave Indian Students Behind?* Hearing before the Committee on Indian Affairs, United States Senate, 111th Congress, Second Session, 17 June 2010. Washington, DC: US Government Printing Office.

Valenzuela, A., Prieto, L. and Hamilton, M.P. (guest eds) (2007) No Child Left Behind (NCLB) and minority youth: What the qualitative evidence suggests. (Special issue.) *Anthropology and Education Quarterly* 38 (1).

Vasquez Heilig, J. and Darling-Hammond, L. (2008) Accountability Texas-style: The progress and learning of urban minority students in a high-stakes testing context. *Educational Evaluation and Policy Analysis* 30 (2), 75–110.

Vogelin, C.F., Vogelin, F.M. and Schutz, N.W. Jr (1967) The language situation of Arizona as part of the Southwest cultural area. In D. Hymes and W.E. Bittle (eds) *Studies in Southwestern Ethnolinguistics: Meaning and History in the Languages of the American Southwest* (pp. 11–32). The Hague: Mouton.

Warhol, L. (2011) Native American language education as policy-in-practice: An interpretive policy analysis of the Native American Languages Act of 1990/1992. *International Journal of Bilingual Education and Bilingualism* 14 (3), 279–299.

Warhol, L. (2012) Creating official language policy from local practice: The example of the Native American Languages Act 1990/1992. *Language Policy* 11 (3), 235–252.

Warner, S.L.N. (1999a) *Kuleana*: The right, responsibility, and authority of Indigenous peoples to speak and make decisions for themselves in language and cultural revitalization. *Anthropology and Education Quarterly* 30 (1), 68–93.

Warner, S.N. (1999b) Hawaiian language regenesis: Planning for intergenerational use of Hawaiian beyond the school. In T. Huebner and K.A. Davis (eds) *Sociopolitical Perspectives on Language Policy and Planning in the USA* (pp. 313–330). Amsterdam: John Benjamins.

Warner, S.L.N. (2001) The movement to revitalize Hawaiian language and culture. In L. Hinton and K. Hale (eds) *The Green Book of Language Revitalization in Practice* (pp. 133–144). San Diego, CA: Academic Press.

Watahomigie, L.J. (1998) The Native language is a gift: A Hualapai language autobiography. *International Journal of the Sociology of Language* 132, 5–7.

Watahomigie, L.J. and McCarty, T.L. (1996) Literacy for what? Hualapai literacy and language maintenance. In N.H. Hornberger (ed.) *Indigenous Literacies in the Americas: Language Planning from the Bottom Up* (pp. 95–113). Berlin: Mouton de Gruyter.

Waterman, S. and Arnold, P. P. (2010) The Haudenosaunee flag raising: Cultural symbols and intercultural contact. *Journal of American Indian Education* 49 (1–2), 125–144.

wa Thiong'o, N. (2009) *Something Torn and New: An African Renaissance*. New York: Basic*Civitas* Books.

Watson-Gegeo, K.A. and Gegeo, D.W. (1999) Culture, discourse, and Indigenous epistemology: Transcending current models in language planning and policy. In T. Huebner and K.A. Davis (eds) *Sociopolitical Perspectives on Language Policy and Planning in the USA* (pp. 99–130). Amsterdam: John Benjamins.

Watson-Gegeo, K.A. and Gegeo, D.W. (2011) Divergent discourses: The epistemology of healing in an American medical clinic and a Kwara'ae village. *Anthropology of Consciousness* 22 (2), 209–233.

Webster, A.K. (2011) 'Please read loose': Intimate grammars and unexpected languages in contemporary Navajo literature. *American Indian Culture and Research Journal* 35 (2), 61–86.

Webster, A.K. and Peterson, L.C. (2011) Introduction: American Indian languages in unexpected places. *American Indian Culture and Research Journal* 35 (2), 1–18.

Weitzman, E.A. (2000) Software and qualitative research. In N.K. Denzin and Y.S. Lincoln (eds) *Handbook of Qualitative Research* (2nd edn) (pp. 803–820). Thousand Oaks, CA: SAGE.

Wetzel, C. (2006) Neshnabemwen renaissance: Local and national Potawatomi language revitalization efforts. *American Indian Quarterly* 30 (1–2), 61–86.

White, L. (2009) Free To Be Kanien'kehaka: A case study of educational self-determination at the Akwesasne Freedom School. Unpublished PhD dissertation, University of Arizona.

White House Native Languages Working Group (2010) Discussion Draft Executive Order White House Initiative on Native American Language Revitalization. Online at http://www.lsadc.org/info/documents/2011/resolutions/executive-order-draft.pdf, accessed 6 July 2012.

Wiley, T.G. and Wright, W.E. (2004) Against the undertow: Language-minority education policy and politics in the 'age of accountability'. *Educational Policy* 18 (1), 142–168.

Wilkins, D.E. and Lomawaima, K.T. (2001) *Uneven Ground: American Indian Sovereignty and Federal Law*. Norman, OK: University of Oklahoma Press.

Williams, C. (1994) Arfarniad o Ddulliau Dysgu ac Addysgu yng Nghyd-destun Addysg Uwchradd Ddwyieithog. Unpublished PhD thesis, University of Wales.

Williamson, V. (1954) *I Am a Good Citizen*. Brigham City, UT: Defense Printing Service for the US Department of the Interior, Bureau of Indian Affairs, Branch of Education.

Wilson, W.H. (1998) I ka 'ōlelo Hawai'i ke ola, 'Life is found in the Hawaiian language'. *International Journal of the Sociology of Language* 132, 123–137.

Wilson, W.H. (1999) The sociopolitical context of establishing Hawaiian-medium education. In S. May (ed.) *Indigenous Community-Based Education* (pp. 95–108). Clevedon: Multilingual Matters.

Wilson, W.H. (2008) Language fluency, accuracy, and revernacularization in different models of immersion. *NIEA News* 39 (2), 40–42.

Wilson, W. H. (2012) USDE violations of NALA and the testing boycott at Nāwahīokalani'ōpu'u School. *Journal of American Indian Education* 51 (3), 30–45.

Wilson, W. H. (2013) Hawaiian – A Native American language official for a state. In T.G. Wiley, J. Peyton, D. Christian, N. Liu, and S.C. Moore (eds), *Handbook of Heritage, Community, and Native American Languages in the United States*. New York: Routledge (in press).

Wilson, W.H. and Kamanā, K. (2001) '*Mai loko mai o ka 'i'ini*: Proceeding from a dream': The 'Aha Pūnana Leo connection in Hawaiian language revitalization. In L. Hinton and K. Hale (eds) *The Green Book of Language Revitalization in Practice* (pp. 147–176). San Diego, CA: Academic Press.

Wilson, W.H. and Kamanā, K. (2006) 'For the interest of the Hawaiians themselves': Reclaiming the benefits of Hawaiian-medium education. *Hūlili: Multidisciplinary Research on Hawaiian Well-Being* 3 (1), 153–178.

Wilson, W.H. and Kamanā, K. (2009) Indigenous youth bilingualism from a Hawaiian activist perspective. *Journal of Language, Identity, and Education* 8 (5), 369–375.

Wilson, W.H. and Kawai'ae'a, K. (2007) I kumu; i lālā: 'Let there be sources; let there be branches': Teacher education in the College of Hawaiian Language. *Journal of American Indian Education* 46 (3), 37–53.

Wilson, W.H., Kamanā, K. and Rawlins, N. (2006) Nāwahī Hawaiian Laboratory School. *Journal of American Indian Education* 45 (2), 42–44.

Winstead, T., Lawrence, A., Brantmeier, E.J. and Frey, C.J. (2008) Language, sovereignty, cultural contestation, and American Indian schools: No Child Left Behind and a Navajo test case. *Journal of American Indian Education* 47 (1), 46–54.

Wolcott, H.F. (2008) *Ethnography: A Way of Seeing* (2nd edn). Lanham, MD: AltaMira Press.
Wong, K.L. (1999a) Language varieties and language policy: The appreciation of Pidgin. In T. Huebner and K.A. Davis (eds) *Sociopolitical Perspectives on Language Policy and Planning in the USA* (pp. 205–222). Amsterdam: John Benjamins.
Wong, K.L. (1999b) Authenticity and the revitalization of Hawaiian. *Anthropology and Education Quarterly* 30 (1), 94–115.
Wong, K.L. (2011) Keynote address: Language, fruits, and vegetables. In M.E. Romero-Little, S.J. Ortiz, T.L. McCarty and R. Chen (eds) *Indigenous Languages Across the Generations – Strengthening Families and Communities* (pp. 3–16). Tempe, AZ: Arizona State University Center for Indian Education.
Wong Fillmore, L. (2011) An ecological perspective on intergenerational language transmission. In M.E. Romero-Little, S.J. Ortiz, T.L. McCarty and R. Chen (eds) *Indigenous Languages Across the Generations – Strengthening Families and Communities* (pp. 19–48). Tempe, AZ: Arizona State University Center for Indian Education.
Woolard, K.A. (1998) Introduction: Language ideology as a field of inquiry. In B.B. Schieffelin, K.A. Woolard and P.V. Kroskrity (eds) *Language Ideologies: Practice and Theory* (pp. 3–47). New York: Oxford University Press.
Wôpanâak Language Reclamation Project (2010a) Project History. Online at http://wlrp.org/History.html, accessed 22 June 2012.
Wôpanâak Language Reclamation Project (2010b) Language Program Class Schedules – Summer 2012. Online at http://wlrp.org/Schedules.html, accessed 22 June 2012.
Wôpanâak Language Reclamation Project (2010c, September 24) Press Release: Wôpanâak Language Reclamation Project (WLRP) Awarded Two Year Grant from the Administration for Native Americans to Conduct Language Apprentice Program. Online at http://www.wlrp.org/ANA_Grant_Press_Release.pdf, accessed 13 June 2012.
Worthy, L. (n.d.) The *Cherokee Phoenix* (and *Indian Advocate*). Online at http://ngeorgia.com/history/phoenix.html, accessed 20 December 2007.
Wright, S. (2004) *Language Policy and Planning: From Nationalism to Globalisation*. New York: Palgrave Macmillan.
Wright, W.E. (2002) The effects of high-stakes testing on an inner-city elementary school: The curriculum, the teachers, and the English language learners. *Current Issues in Education* 5 (5). Online at http://cie.asu.edu/volume5/number5, accessed 23 June 2008.
Wurm, S.A. (ed.) (2001) *Atlas of the World's Languages in Danger of Disappearing* (2nd edn). Paris: UNESCO.
Wyman, L.T. (2004) Language shift, youth culture, and ideology: A Yup'ik example. Unpublished PhD dissertation, School of Education, Stanford University.
Wyman, L.T. (2009) Youth, linguistic ecologies and language endangerment: A Yup'ik example. *Journal of Language, Identity, and Education* 8 (5), 335–349.
Wyman, L. (2012) *Youth Culture, Language Endangerment, and Linguistic Survivance*. Bristol: Multilingual Matters.
Wyman, L., Marlow, P., Andrew, F.C., Miller, G.S., Nicholai, C.R. and Rearden, Y.N. (2010a) Focusing on long-term language goals in challenging times: A Yup'ik example. *Journal of American Indian Education* 49 (1–2), 28–49.
Wyman, L., Marlow, P., Andrew, C.F., Miller, G., Nicholai, C.R. and Rearden, Y.N. (2010b) High stakes testing, bilingual education and language endangerment: A Yup'ik example. *International Journal of Bilingual Education and Bilingualism* 13, 701–721.
Wyman, L., Marlow, P., Andrew, C.F., Miller, G., Nicholai, C.R. and Rearden, Y.N. (2011) Focusing communities and schools on Indigenous language maintenance: A Yup'ik example. In M.E. Romero-Little, S.J. Ortiz, T.L. McCarty and R. Chen (eds), *Indigenous Languages Across the Generations – Strengthening Families and Communities* (pp. 262–280). Tempe, AZ: Arizona State University Center for Indian Education.

Wyman, L.T., McCarty, T.L and Nicholas, S.E. (eds) (2013) *Indigenous Youth and Bi/multilingualism*. New York: Routledge (in press).

Yamamoto, A. (2007) Endangered languages in USA and Canada. In M. Brenzinger (ed.), *Language Diversity Endangered* (pp. 87–122). Berlin: Mouton de Gruyter.

Young, R.W. (1972) *Written Navajo: A Brief History*. Navajo Reading Study Progress Report No. 19. Albuquerque, NM: University of New Mexico.

Young, R.W. (1983) Apachean languages. In A. Ortiz (vol. ed.) and W.C. Sturtevant (general ed.) *Handbook of North American Indians. Vol. 10: Southwest* (pp. 393–400). Washington, DC: Smithsonian Institution.

Young, R.W. (2000) *The Navajo Verb System: An Overview*. Albuquerque, NM: University of New Mexico Press.

Young, R.W. and Morgan, W. Sr (1980) *The Navajo Language: A Grammar and Colloquial Dictionary*. Albuquerque, NM: University of New Mexico Press.

Young, R.W. and Morgan, W. Sr (1987) *The Navajo Language: A Grammar and Colloquial Dictionary* (revised edn). Albuquerque, NM: University of New Mexico Press.

Young, R.W., Morgan, W., Sr and Midgette, S. (1991) *Analytical Lexicon of Navajo*. Albuquerque, NM: University of New Mexico Press.

Zepeda, O. (1990) American Indian language policy. In K.L. Adams and D.T. Brink (eds) *Perspectives on Official English: The Campaign for English as the Official Language of the USA* (pp. 247–256). Berlin: Mouton de Gruyter.

Zepeda, O. (1995a) The continuum of literacy in American Indian communities. *The Bilingual Research Journal* 19 (1), 5–15.

Zepeda, O. (1995b) *Ocean Power: Poems from the Desert*. Tucson, AZ: University of Arizona Press.

Zepeda, O. (1997) *Jewed 'I-hoi: Earth Movements*. Tucson, AZ: Kore Press.

Zepeda, O. and Hill, J. (1992) The condition of Native American languages in the United States. In R.H. Robins and E.M. Ehlenbeck (eds) *Endangered Languages* (pp. 135–155). New York: Berg.

Zimmerman, T. (1997) *Plessy v. Ferguson*. Online at http://www.bgsu.edu/departments/acs/1890s/plessy/plessy.html, accessed 13 July 2007.

Zinn, H. (2003) *A People's History of the United States*. New York: Perennial Classics.

Zrioka, P. (2012) Cultural conservation: Keeping Indigenous languages alive. *Cultural Survival Quarterly*, 10 April. Online at http://www.culturalsurvival.org/news/cultural-conservation-keeping-indigenous-languages-alive, accessed 11 June 2012.

Author Index

Adams, D.W. 48, 50–52, 185, 221
Adley-SantaMaria, B. 41, 221
'Aha Pūnana Leo 130–133, 221
Aikman, S. 41, 221
Amrein, A. 191, 221
Archuleta, B. 48, 53, 221
Arias, M.B. 191, 221
Arviso, M. 71–72, 140–141, 221–222
Ash, A. 106–107, 110–111, 154, 183, 222
Assembly of Alaska Native Educators 195–196, 222
Austin, P.K. 36, 222, 224–225, 229–231, 240, 245, 247

Baker, C. 198, 222
Baldauf, R. 33, 234, 236
Baldwin, D. xxiii, 25, 30, 91–102, 104–105, 150, 160–161, 222, 239, 247
Ball, S. 36, 222
Balter, A. 189, 194, 222
Banks, J.A. 192, 222, 236
Barnhardt, R. 195–196, 222
Battiste, M. 13, 222
Baugh, J. 35, 223
Bauman, J.J. 19, 223
Bear Nicholas, A. 30, 223, 246
Beatty, W.W. 56, 223
Beaulieu, D. 188–190, 201–202, 223
Begay, S. 45, 223
Belgarde, M. 29, 202, 223, 233, 236
Benally, A. 22, 69, 71, 73, 88, 223
Benjamin, R. xxii, 16, 22–23, 223
Benton, N.A. 53, 223
Bergstrom, A. 183, 223
Berliner, D. 191, 221, 241
Bielenberg, B.T. 159–160, 223
Bird, C. 180–181, 233, 236
Blommaert, J. xxiii, 92, 153, 224, 240

Bradley, D. 9, 224
Bragdon, K.J. 108, 120, 224, 229
Brandt, E.A. 88, 224
Brayboy, B.M.J. xxi, 28, 143, 188, 190, 202, 224
Brill de Ramírez, S.B. 178, 224, 227
Brown, G. 161, 242
Bucholtz, M. 156, 224

Canagarajah, A.S. (S.) 41, 224
Castagno, A.E. 190, 224
Cazden, C.B. 191, 224
Chafe, W. 46, 120–122, 150, 225
Charles, W. 41, 151, 225
Cherokee Nation Language Planning Committees 13, 152, 225
Child, B.J. 52, 221, 225
Cobb, D.M. 123, 222, 225
Coley, M-E. 183, 225
Collier, J. 74–75
Collier, J. Jr 79–80, 225
Combs, M.C. 191–192, 194, 225, 242
Conklin, P. 81, 225
Cooper, J. 58, 225
Cooper, R. 33, 39–40, 225
Coronel-Molina, S.M. 154, 225
Costa, D.J. 26, 92, 95–97, 102, 222, 225–226
Crawford, J. 38, 53, 61, 69, 185–186, 191, 222, 224, 226
Crystal, D. 35, 226
Cummins, J. 72, 226, 246

Dauenhauer, N.M. 200, 226
Dauenhauer, R. 200, 226
Davis, K.A. 41, 225–226, 249, 251
Deloria, P.J. 24–25, 179, 226, 228, 236
Dementi-Leonard, B. 151, 154, 226
Demmert, W.G. 190, 226
Deyhle, D. xxi, 224

Dick, G.S. 45–47, 53, 56–57, 65, 79, 86–87, 223, 226, 238
Dinwoodie, D.W. 14, 226
Dorian, N.C. 37, 169, 184–185, 227
Duchêne, A. 36, 227
Dunsmore, R. 157, 178, 227

Eder, J. 48, 52, 244
Eisenlohr, P. 25–27, 227
Ellis, C. 52–53, 227
Emerson, G. 68, 83, 227
Endangered Language Fund 117, 227
Esther Martinez Native American Languages Preservation Act (EM-NALPA) 62
Evers, L. 24, 47, 227

Faircloth, D. 224
Faltis, C. 191, 221
Feldman, O. 108–109, 227
Field, M.C. 35–36, 227, 234
Fillerup, M. 143–150, 155, 194, 227–228
Fishman, J.A. xix, 19–20, 37–38, 61, 152, 201, 228, 230, 235, 239
Fowler, L. 123, 222, 225
Fox, S. 186, 228
Francis, N. 14, 45, 228
Freeman, C. 228

Gándara, P. 192, 228
Garcia, D.R. 189, 228
García, O. 48, 73, 167, 179, 200, 201, 228, 230, 232, 238
Gee, J.P. xxii, 77, 228
Gegeo, D.W. 42, 229, 249
Gilmore, P. 151, 154, 226, 229
Glass, G.V. 88, 241
Goddard, I. 9–10, 48–50, 69, 106, 108, 112, 119–120, 229, 245
González, R.E. 191, 225, 229
González, N. 80, 229
Goodman, Y. xxiii, 229
Grant, A. 53, 229
Grenoble, L. 9, 17, 19–20, 36, 38, 122, 129–130, 226–227, 229, 233
Greymorning, S. 25, 229
Grigg, W. 28, 187, 229, 239
Grimes, B. 230
Grinwald, C. 11, 230
Grounds, R. 152, 156, 230
Gumperz, J. 41, 230
Gutiérrez, K.D. 191, 230

Haile, B. 74, 230
Hale, K. xix, 65, 69, 75, 81, 106–110, 132, 222, 229–231, 238, 243, 245–247, 249–250
Harrison, K.D. xix, xx, 36, 159, 230
Haugen, E. 33–34, 39, 230
Heath, S.B. xxiii, 230
Heller, M. 36, 227
Hermes, M. 25, 42, 152, 200, 230
Heugh, K. 200, 230
Hill, J. xx, xxiii, 9, 37, 179, 231, 236, 252
Hinton, L. 24, 36, 38, 61, 111–115, 117–118, 132, 138, 154, 185, 222, 229–231, 238, 243, 245–247, 249–250
Hohepa, M.K. 38, 231
Holm, A. 58, 78–79, 81, 85–86, 140–142, 231
Holm, W. 23, 58–59, 66, 71–79, 81, 83, 85–86, 90, 140–143, 154–155, 182, 200, 221–222, 231, 245
Hoover, M.L. 121–122, 154, 232
Hopkins, M. 192, 228, 239
Hornberger, N.H. xx, xxvi, 31–34, 36, 39, 41, 77, 82, 92, 99, 108, 113–114, 138, 150, 161, 178, 185, 187, 197, 223, 226, 232, 236–237, 244, 246–247, 249
Horne, E.B. 52, 56–57, 232
House, D. 41, 88, 232
Hymes, D. 41, 230, 232, 249

International Labour Organisation 2, 233
Iokepa-Guerrero, N. 130, 138, 233
Ironstrack, G. 92, 100, 104–105, 239, 247
Iverson, P. 68, 74, 233

Jacobs, K.A. 121–122, 233
Jaffe, A. xix, xx, 233
Jim, R.L. 24, 233
Johnson, B.H. 58, 79, 233
Johnson, F.T. 142, 143, 194, 233
Jojola, T. 2, 233

Kamanā, K. xviii, 42, 128–133, 135, 138, 155, 159, 233, 250
Kanien'kehaka Raotitiohkwa Cultural Center 121–122, 154, 232
Kaomea, J. xxi, 233
Kaplan, R.B. 33, 234
Kawagley, A.O. 195–196, 222
King, K. A. 8, 35, 38, 41, 49, 76, 107, 157, 168, 178, 232, 234–235
Kloss, H. 50, 234

Kouritzin, S. 37, 157, 234
Kral, I. 181, 234
Krauss, M. 8–9, 17–19, 25, 36–37, 60, 69, 166, 234
Kroskrity, P.V. xvii, xix, xxv, 23, 35–36, 227, 234, 251
Kroupa, K.T. 179–180, 234
Kulick, D. 158, 234

Lambert, W.E. 35, 234
Lapahie, H. Jr 139, 234
Leap, W.L. 12, 16, 32, 45, 234, 247
Lee, L.L. 42, 89, 159–160, 179, 187, 224, 235
Lee, T.S. 89, 201, 234
Legatz, J. 142–143, 233
Leibowitz, A.H. 42–43, 52–53, 193, 235
Leonard, B. 41–42, 235
Leonard, W.Y. xxiii, 18, 20–21, 25, 28, 36, 38, 42, 91–92, 94, 97, 99–100, 105, 154, 160–161, 173, 235
Levinson, B.A. 36, 235
Link, M.A. 139, 235
Lipka, J. 45, 235
Littlebear, R.E. xix, xx, 63, 235
little doe, j. 106, 108–111, 235–236
Lockard, L. 73–75, 77, 227, 235
Lomawaima, K.T. xxiv, xxv, 1–4, 30, 42–45, 48, 50–52, 55–56, 58, 61, 63, 76, 140, 183, 192–193, 195–196, 202, 221–222, 236, 250
López, L.E. 133, 149, 151, 176, 194, 200, 227, 233, 236
Luke, A. 33, 39–40, 236

Makepeace, A. 106, 110–111, 236
Manuelito, K. 42, 82, 88, 202, 236
Maracle, I. 119, 126–128, 236
Marlow, P.E. 151, 237, 251
Mato Nunpa, C. 26, 237
May, S. 39, 41, 237, 246, 250
McBeth, S. 52, 56, 232
McCarty, T.L. xxi, xxiv, xxv, 2, 4, 9–10, 24, 29–32, 37, 40–45, 47–48, 51–56, 58–61, 63, 68, 76–77, 79, 81, 83, 86–88, 90, 137, 142–143, 145–148, 153–154, 156, 159, 163, 179, 182, 189, 192, 195–196, 199–200, 202, 222–223, 225–226, 228, 230–239, 241–246, 248–249, 251–252
McLaughlin, D. 23, 77, 235, 239
Mead, N. 188, 239

Medicine, B. 1, 9, 11, 21, 30, 55, 239
Meek, B. xxvi, 157, 163, 182, 239
Menezes de Souza xxiii, 31, 239
Menken, K. 185, 239
Meriam, L. 53, 55, 239
Messing, J.H.E. 153, 179, 239
Meyer, L.M. 153, 239
Miami Tribe of Oklahoma 94–97, 99–100, 104–106, 226, 233, 239, 247
Mithun, M. 120–122, 150, 240
Mohanty, A. 165, 200, 223, 240, 246
Molina, F. 24, 154, 225, 227
Moll, L. 193, 229–230, 240
Moore, R. xxiii, 8, 186, 189, 202, 240, 250
Moran, R. 28, 187, 229, 239–240
Morgan, W. Sr 73–76, 83, 89, 252
Moriarty, M. 26–27, 240
Mühlhäusler, P. 34, 240
Mutua, K. 233, 236, 240
Myaamia Project 91, 95–96, 98–99, 101, 103–105, 154, 240

National Caucus of Native American State Legislators xviii, 240
National Clearinghouse for English Language Acquisition 69, 240
Native American Languages Act (NALA) 61, 203, 207, 240
Native Hawaiian Education Council and Ka Haka 'Ula O Ke'elikōlani College of Hawaiian Language 135, 240, 241
Navajo Sovereignty in Education Act 68–69, 194, 241
Nettle, D. 36, 241
Neundorf, A. 22, 241, 243
New London Group, xxii, 241
Nicholas, S.E. 23, 42, 159–160, 192, 194, 225, 234–235, 239, 241–242, 248, 252
Nichols, S.L. 191, 232, 241
No Child Left Behind Act (NCLB) 187, 241, 242
Noley, G. 50, 242
Norris, T. 4, 6–8, 31, 242

Obama, B. 62, 201, 223, 242
O'Connor, B. 161, 242
Olds, J. 30, 94, 222, 247
Orfield, G. 192, 228
Ó Riagáin, D. 33, 242
O'Rourke, B. xxiv, 11, 242
Ortiz, S.J. xxvi, xxvii, 47, 157, 178, 184, 224,

227–228, 230, 236, 242, 245, 251–252
Ovando, C. 191, 242

Paris, D. 42, 242, 248, 251
Parsons-Yazzie, E. 24–25, 88, 158, 182, 242–243
Patrick, D. 41, 243
Patrick, R. 189, 243
Paulston, C.B. 38, 243
Peacock, T.D. 223
Pecos, R. 16, 223, 243
Penfield, S. 26, 243
Pennycook, A. 40, 243
Peter, L. 22–23, 152, 243
Phillipson, R. 40, 223, 240, 243, 246
Platero, P. 71, 88–89, 243
Prucha, F.P. 63–64, 243
Pye, C. 157–158, 170, 243

Ramanathan, V. 41, 243
Read, J. 81–82, 84–85, 243, 247
Reese-Miller, J. 244
Reeves, A.G. 195, 244
Reyhner, J.A. 14, 48, 52, 132, 187, 227–228, 235, 244, 246
Ricento, T. 32–34, 36, 39, 224, 232, 244–245, 248
Rinehart, M.A. 92–93, 230, 244, 247
Rockwell, E. xx, xxii, 153, 239, 244
Roessel, M. (C.M.) 197, 244
Roessel, R.A. Jr 58, 79, 80, 244
Romaine, S. 20, 36, 241, 244
Romero, M.E. 16, 23, 42, 223, 238, 244
Romero-Little, M.E. 36–37, 60, 132, 156, 163, 228, 230, 236, 238–239, 244–245, 251
Rosier, P. 71, 81, 85, 245
Ruiz, R. xix, 34–35, 230, 245

Scheirbeck, H.M. 57, 59, 86–87, 245
Schiffman, H. 34, 61, 245
Seidman, I.E. 162, 245
Shohamy, E. 73, 245
Shonerd, H.G. 185, 245
Silentman, I. 75–76, 83–84, 245
Silverstein, M. 48, 245
Sims, C. P. 16, 22–23, 42, 47, 112, 116, 245–246
Skutnabb-Kangas, T. xxi, xxiv, 32, 37–38, 40, 49, 153, 200, 223, 228, 230, 232, 238, 240, 243, 246
Slate, C. 30, 66–69, 88, 246

Smith, L.T. 5, 29, 42, 186, 200, 225, 246
Snipp, M. 3, 246
Snow, C.E. 191, 224
Solórzano, R.W. 186, 246
Spack, R. 52–53, 246
Spicer, E.H. 49–50, 246
Spolsky, B. xvii, xxi, 22–23, 33–34, 59–60, 71, 82, 84, 86, 238, 243, 246–247
Spring, J. 48, 50–51, 185, 247
Stairs, A. 123, 125, 247
Stancavage, F.B. 28, 188, 247
St Clair, R.N. 39, 247
Strack, A.J. 102, 239, 247
Strack, G. 92–93, 102, 247
Street, B.V. xxii, xxiii, 77, 247
Suárez-Orozco, M. 192, 247
Supahan, S.E. 116–117, 247
Supahan, T. 116–117, 247
Sutton, M. 36, 120, 235, 247
Swadener, B.B. 42, 233, 236–237, 240
Szasz, M. 48–49, 55–56, 59, 247

Task Force on Aboriginal Languages and Cultures xix, 19, 183, 247
The White House 201, 248
Thornton, R. 4, 31, 248
Tirado, M. 29, 248
Tollefson, J.W. 35, 39–40, 229, 237–238, 248
Trennert, R.A. Jr 52, 248
Trumbell, J.H. 248
Tulloch, S. 160, 179, 225, 248

Underhill, R. 139, 248
UNESCO Ad Hoc Expert Group on Endangered Languages 19, 153, 248
US Census Bureau, 5, 13
US Commission on Civil Rights, 191, 248
US Congress, 57, 90, 191, 248
US Department of Education 186, 192, 248–249
US Senate Committee on Indian Affairs 189, 201, 249

Valenzuela, A. 167, 202, 249
Vasquez Heilig, J. 186, 249
Vogelin, C.F. 34, 249

Walsh, J. xxiv, 11, 242
Warhol, L. 61, 156, 238–239, 245, 249

Warner, S.N. xviii, xx, 42, 128–130, 136, 138, 158, 249
Watahomigie, L.J. xix, 9–10, 24, 60, 63, 231, 238, 249
wa Thiong'o, N. xix, xxii, 249
Watson-Gegeo, K.A. 42, 229, 249
Webster, A.K. 11–12, 25, 249–250
Weitzman, C. 163, 250
White, L. 119, 122–126, 155, 250
White House Native Languages Working Group 62–63, 250
Wiley, T.G. 187, 228–229, 250
Wilkins, D.E. xviii, xxiv, 1–3, 30, 140, 250
Wilson, J. 194, 233
Wilson, W.H. xxiv, 2, 4, 21, 24, 30, 62, 128–136, 138, 151, 155, 159, 194–195, 233, 250
Winstead, T. 69, 89, 194, 250
Wolcott, H.F. 41–42, 251
Wong, K.L. 12, 42, 129–130, 138, 251
Wong Fillmore, L. 193–194, 251
Woolard, K.A. 35, 251
Wôpanâak Language Reclamation Project 106–111, 251
Wright, W.E. 191, 251
Wright, S. 32, 251
Wurm, S.A. 19, 251
Wyman, L.T. 37, 41, 159–160, 182, 190, 197, 229, 234–235, 238–239, 242, 248, 251–252

Yamamoto, A.Y. 9, 238, 252
Young, R.W. 69, 73–76, 245, 252

Zepeda, O. xix, xxi, xxiii, 9, 16–17, 24, 47, 156, 227, 231, 237–239, 243, 245, 252
Zrioka, P. 181, 252
Zuni Lucero, E. 178, 224, 227

Subject Index

Abenaki 10, 106
accountability 87, 185, 186, 188, 190, 191 (*see also* high-stakes accountability/testing)
Acoma 5, 22, 23, 47
  scholar-activist-educator Christine Sims 16, 47
  writer Simon Ortiz 47 (*see also* Keres; Pueblo)
acquisition planning 33, 38, 58, 60, 65, 82, 84, 121, 185
Ádahooníłígíí (Events, Occurrences) 24, 75
additive bilingualism xv, 85, 198, 200
adequate yearly progress (AYP) 149, 186, 189, 190, 194, 197
Advocates for Indigenous California Language Survival (AICLS) 114, 116, 118
'Aha Pūnana Leo (Hawaiian language nest) 130, 131, 132, 133, 138, 142, 144, 151, 152
affective enculturation 160
Akimel O'odham (River People, Pima) 12, 58
Akwesasne (Land Where the Partridge Drums) 120, 152, 154, 155;
  Freedom School 122–126, 154
  lands/settlements 5, 120, 121, 122
  Mohawk Council of 123, 155 (*see also* Mohawk; St Regis)
alpha language xvii
Alaska Native
  bilingual–bicultural education programs 59, 197
  definition of xxi, 30
  Guidelines for Strengthening Indigenous Languages 196
  lands 4, 5
  Language Preservation and Advisory Council 3
  languages 3, 10, 59
  people(s) xxi, 2, 3, 4, 7
  population 6, 7, 8, 66
  Rural Systemic Initiative 195, 196
  speakers 9
  standards for cross-cultural education 195, 196
  students 27, 28, 29, 187, 188, 189, 190, 201
  village(s) 28 (*see also* Deg Xinag; Lower Kuskokwim School District; Yup'ik)
Albers, Elaina Supahan 117
Albers, Phil Jr 117, 118
Aleut 4, 5, 6, 10, 50, 59
Algonquian 10, 13, 49, 50, 92, 106, 110, 117, 120
American Indian
  definition of 31
  education xxv, 3, 56, 81, 201
  lands 5
  languages 10–13
  people(s) xxi, 2, 4, 6–8, 56
  policy xxv
  population 6, 7, 66
  students 28
American Indian Language Development Institute xvii, ix, xxii, 153
Anishinaabe 183 (*see also* Ojibwe)
Apache
  lands 5
  language(s) 10, 12, 69
  population 6
  White Mountain 41
Apalachee 49
Arakmbut 41
Arapaho
  lands 5
  language 10
  language revitalization program 25
  population 6

Arikara 10, 179, 180
Arviso, Marie 140–141
Arviso–Holm typology of multilingual
    competencies 72
assimilation/assimilationist 52, 55, 56,
    57, 63, 76, 123
  linguistic 34, 37, 129, 199
Athabaskan
  Alaskan 6
  communities 151
  language(s) 10, 59, 69, 70, 73, 74, 151
Atkins, John D.C. 53, 60

Baird, Mae Alice 111 (*see also* Little
    Doe Baird, Jessie; Wampanoag;
    Wôpanâak)
Baldwin, Daryl xxvi, 91, 92, 93, 94,
    96, 98, 99, 105 (*see also* Miami;
    Myaamia)
Baldwin, Karen 97, 160
Beatty, Williard 56
bilingual–bicultural education 14, 24, 34,
    46, 58, 59, 65, 71, 78, 83, 85, 86, 145,
    149, 175, 187, 191, 193
  scholar Lily Wong Fillmore 194
Bilingual Education Act of 1968 xiv, 57,
    58, 113, 144, 187
biliteracy xvii, 31, 87, 198
Blackfeet 156
  immersion schools 152
  lands 5
  language 10
  Nation 152
  population 6 (*see also* Kipp, Darrell;
      Piegan Institute)
Blackwater community and school 58
Board of Indian Commissioners 51
boarding schools 50–56, 59, 64, 65, 75, 94,
    112, 139, 158, 172, 194
Borrego Pass School (Dibé Yázhi Habitiin
    Ólta') 82
bottom-up language planning 36, 40, 66,
    113, 153
Breath of Life
  Archival Institute for Indigenous
      languages 116, 117
  workshop 116, 117, 153
*Brown v. Topeka, Kansas Board of
    Education* 57
Bureau of Indian Affairs (BIA) xiii, 3, 24,
    53–58, 60, 64, 75, 79, 81, 82, 83, 85,
    89, 90, 201, 222

Bureau of Indian Education (BIE) 28, 29,
    30, 68, 186, 189, 194, 195, 202
Burke, Bobbe 97, 98 (*see also* Miami;
    Myaamia)

Caddoan
  lands 5
  languages 10
California Master–Apprentice Language
    Learning Program (MALLP)
    111–117, 152, 154 (*see also* Native
    California[n])
Castillo, Winona (cover photo), iv
Cayuga 5, 119
charter school(s) 28, 29, 195, 202
Cherokee
  'All Things Cherokee', 26
  Chief Chad Smith 29
  community 24
  lands 5
  language 10, 12, 13, 22, 25, 50, 59
  language immersion/revitalization 22,
      23, 29
  people 22, 23
  Nation 4, 13, 29
  Oklahoma 22
  population 4, 6
  speaker David Brown 50
  speakers 25
  syllabary 13, 14, 26 (*see also* Sequoyah)
  Trail of Tears 31
Cherokee Phoenix 13, 14, 15, 23, 24, 26, 31
Cheyenne
  identity xv
  language xiii, xiv, xix, 12, 59, 63
  people xvi
  population 6
  speaking community, xiv, xvi
  warriors xvi
  words xiv
Chickasaw
  lands 5
  language 10
  population 6
Chilcotin 10, 157, 158
Chimakuan 10
Chinook
  Jargon 9
  Tsimshian language family 10
Chippewa
  language 10, 59
  population 6 (*see also* Ojibwe)

Chitimacha
　lands 5
　language 26
Choctaw xvii
　Code Talkers 21
　lands 5
　language 10, 12, 59
　Mississippi Band xvii, 184
　population 6 (*see also* Thompson, Roseanna)
Civilization Fund Act of 1819 50
Civil Rights Act of 1964 57
Civil Rights Movement 57, 130
Cleveland, Grover 129
Cochiti 16, 22, 42 (*see also* Keres; Pueblo)
code-switching 22
Code Talkers 21, 148, 174
Collier, John 55, 56
colonial
　language xvii
　schooling 50–56 (*see also* boarding schools)
colonization 2, 37, 48, 112, 178
Comanche
　Code Talkers 21
　lands 5
　language 11
　leader Quanah Parker 23
communicative repertoire(s) 156, 157, 166, 171, 179, 182, 199 (*see also* language repertoire[s])
community research collaborator(s) (CRC[s]) 162, 163, 175, 179, 182
computer-assisted language learning (CALL) 26
continua of biliteracy 31
continuance (cultural and linguistic) xxi, xxvi, 157, 178, 179, 182, 184
corpus planning 33, 38
Costa, David 95, 102 (*see also* Miami, Myaamia)
Cree
　language 10, 46, 48, 59
　population 6
Creek
　language 12
　population 6
creole(s) 9, 11
critical sociocultural perspective 32, 39–42
Crow
　language 12, 59
　population 6

Dakota
　language 11, 12, 26
　population 6
dangerous
　bilingual education 195
　difference xxv, 42, 43, 48, 52, 57, 184
　diversity 192, 193
　ideological mechanisms 202
　languages 61
　policies and practices 57
decolonization/decolonizing xxi, 33, 42
Deg Xinag 42
dialect(s) 8, 61
diaspora(ized) xx, 11
Diaz, Natalie iv, 181
Dick, Ernest 86, 87
Dick, Galena Sells 46, 47, 53, 56
Diné
　artist Shonto Begay 146, 147, 150
　bilingual–bicultural education 66, 145
　citizens and communities 66, 84
　College 29–30, 68, 88
　Department of Education 69, 89
　educator Gloria Emerson 68
　educators/teachers xvii, 144, 146–148
　heritage 47
　immersion 141–144
　language 65, 72, 74, 142, 148, 150, 151
　language and culture program(s) 148, 149, 197
　linguist Paul Platero 71
　poet Luci Tapahonso 47
　scholars 89
　sociolinguist Alyse Neundorf 22
　speakers 77
　students 68, 144
　The People 65, 66, 89
　values xxii (*see also* Navajo)
Diné Bikeyah (Navajo Country, Navajoland) 66, 67, 147, 148
Diné Bi'ólta' Association 82
Diné Bizaad Bínáhoo'aah (Rediscovering the Navajo Language) 25, 88
discrimination (racial and linguistic) 35, 57, 63, 130, 158, 178
Dodge, Chee 73
'dormant' language(s) 18, 36
'dysfluency' xxvi, 163

Economic Opportunity Act of 1964 57
Elementary and Secondary Education Act (ESEA) of 1965 87, 186

Elementary and Secondary School Improvement Amendments of 1988 (PL 100–297) 87
Eliot Bible xi, 49, 63, 107 (see also Wampanoag)
Eliot, John 49, 107
Endangered Language Program 26
English Language Acquisition, Language Enhancement, and Academic Achievement Act 187
English-only xxvi, 44, 51, 53, 85, 87, 130, 140, 143, 149, 157, 169, 185, 191, 192, 194
Eskimoan 10
Esther Martinez 62
Esther Martinez Native American Languages Preservation Act (EM-NALPA) of 2006 2, 62, 132, 153, 193, 211–213
ethnographic 23, 24, 41, 42, 66, 77, 97, 123, 143, 159, 160, 162, 170
ethnography
  critical 41, 42
  of communication 41
  of language policy 41
Euchee (Yuchi)
  language 11
  Language Project 152
  youth language activist Renée Grounds 156
Executive Order(s) 62, 63
  1998 Executive Order 161
  2004 Executive Order 187
  2011 Executive Order 201
expedient tolerance xxv, 50
'extinct' language(s)/language extinction 17, 19, 20, 94, 96, 173, 184, 202

family language policy/language policy of the home 158, 161, 177, 179
Fielding, Fidelia 106 (see also Wampanoag)
Fillerup, Michael 143–150, 155
First Nations xix, xxi, 3
  Technical Institute, 127
Fort Berthold 179
Fort Defiance 155, 71, 73, 74
  Diné (Navajo) immersion program 140–142
  Elementary School 72, 140
  location 67 (see also Tséhootsooí Diné Bi'ólta')
Fort Mojave 181 (see also Mojave)

'four-fold empowerment' 86
Franciscan(s) 49, 74, 75, 89
funds of knowledge 80

Gamble, Chief Thomas vi
General Allotment Act of 1887 (Dawes Act) 51
genocide 37, 139, 178
Gila River Indian Reservation 5, 58
Goshute
  lands 5
  language 180 (see also Shoshone)
Graded Intergenerational Disruption Scale (GIDS) 19, 20
Gray, Lorinda 77
Great Law of Peace 119, 124

Haida 59
Haile, Father Berard 74
Hale, Kenneth 106–110
Harvard Indian College 107
Haudenosaunee (People of the Longhouse) 119, 120
  Thanksgiving Address (*Ohonten Kariwahtekwa*) 124 (see also Iroquois; Mohawk)
Hawai'i/Hawaiian xxvi
  annexation 30
  Apology Act 155
  Hawaiian Creole English 9, 130
  ho'oponopono (conflict resolution)
  language 2, 9, 11, 12, 21, 47, 48, 128–138, 151, 158
  language newspaper(s) 24
  language revitalization 42, 128–138, 159
  medium schooling x, xviii, 42, 128–138, 151, 155, 195
  monarchy/Kingdom 21, 129
  'renaissance' 130, 132
  statehood 4
  students 28, 29
  syllabary 133
  takeover by US 129, 155 (see also Native Hawaiian)
heritage language/heritage mother tongue v, xi, xxiv, xxv, 11, 17, 18, 20, 27, 46, 52, 89, 94, 111, 132, 142, 143, 150, 157, 159, 161, 162, 163, 166, 169, 170, 173, 188, 195
Hermes, Mary 25, 152
heteroglossia/heteroglossic xxiii, 12, 73, 179

Hiawatha Belt 119 (*see also* Great Law of Peace)
high-stakes accountability/testing 87, 185, 186, 188, 190, 192
hip-hop 161
Hokan 10
Holm, Wayne 23, 59, 66, 71, 83, 86, 89, 90, 140, 155
hooghan (Navajo dwelling) 46, 75, 174
Hopi
  culture 23, 160
  identity 160
  lands 5, 67
  language 11, 12, 160
  population 6
  scholar Sheilah Nicholas 23
  youth 42, 159, 160
House Bill 2281 (Arizona's Mexican American Studies ban) 193, 194
Hualapai
  Bilingual–Bicultural Education Program, ix
  educator Lucille Watahomigie xix
  lands 5
  language 10, 59, 60
  youth 60
human rights 40, 61
Hwéeldi (Fort Sumner, NM) 139, 148
hybridity xxiii, xxvi, 12, 157, 163, 179

identity(ies) xv, xxi, xxiv, 1, 2, 35, 39, 42, 76, 100, 104, 123, 125, 160, 161, 172, 173, 181
ideological
  basis of language planning and policy 39, 40
  clarification 28, 200
  management 49
  mechanisms 202
  model of literacy xxii
  notion of racial superiority 51
  orientations 179
  resources 151
  transformation 105, 179
  valuations 26
'ideological and implementational spaces' xxvi, 77, 92, 99, 108, 113, 138, 185, 197
ideology(ies) xix, 17, 25, 26, 33, 34, 8, 40, 42, 47, 49, 51, 55, 56, 66, 89, 100, 102, 105, 156, 159, 160, 161, 163, 173, 190
  definition of 35
  'of contempt' 185 (*see also* ideological)
Improving American Indian and Alaska Native Educational Opportunities and Strengthening Tribal Colleges and Universities (2 December 2011 Executive Order) 201, 214–220
Indian Citizenship Act of 1924 30
Indian Education Act (federal) 58, 64, 82, 204
Indian Education Act (New Mexico) 2
Indian Education for All Act (Montana) 2
Indian 'New Deal' 56
Indian 'praying town' 49
Indian Removal Act of 1830 31
Indian Self-Determination and Educational Assistance Act (PL 93-638) 44, 58
Indian Territory 31, 51, 93, 94
Indigenous Language Institute xxii, 153, 181, 182
  director Inée Slaughter 27, 182
inequality(ies) xviii, xxv, 35, 39
intergenerational language transmission 17, 19, 20, 38, 59, 169, 171
Inuit xix, 3, 10, 41, 160, 179
  Circumpolar Youth Council 179, 183
Inupiaq 4, 6, 10, 26, 59
Inuktitut 26, 160
Inupik 12
Ironstrack, George xxvi, 92, 95, 101, 104 (*see also* Miami; Myaamia)
Iroquois
  Confederacy/League 119, 120
  lands 5, 120
  languages 10, 47, 48
  people 119, 120
  population 6, 120 (*see also* Haudenosaunee; Mohawk)

Jesuit(s) 49, 92, 94
Johnson, Florian Tom 142–143
Johnson, Lyndon B. 57, 89
Journal of American Indian Education 58, 189
Journal of Navajo Education 24

Ka Lama Hawai'i 24
Ka Haka 'Ula O Ke'elikōlani College of Hawaiian Language 133, 135, 136
Kahnawà:ke (Kahnawake) 120, 125, 154
  Education Center 122

land/settlements 120, 121
  Mohawk Council of 154
  Survival School 121–122 (*see also* Mohawk)
Kahuawaiola Indigenous Teacher Education Program 134–135
Kamanā, Kauanoe 133
Kanehsatake 127
Kanienkeha (Kanienke:ha) 119–123, 125, 126, 128 (*see also* Kanienkehaka; Mohawk)
Kanienkehaka (People of the Flint) 120, 123
  lands/settlements 120, 121 (*see also* Lazore, Dorothy; Mohawk)
Karuk
  lands 5
  language 10, 117, 113, 118
  language activists Terry and Sarah Supahan 116, 117 (*see also* Albers, Elaina Supahan; Albers, Phil)
Kaska 157
Ke Kula Kauapuni Hawai'i (Hawaiian surrounding environment) 131
Ke Kula Kaiapuni 'O Ānuenue School 136, 137
Kennedy, Edward (Ted) 57
Kennedy, John F. 57
Kennedy, Robert 57
Keres (Keresan) 12, 22, 59 (*see also* Acoma; Cochiti; Pueblo)
Kinaaldá (Navajo girl's puberty ceremony) 147
Kiowa
  language 11
  population 6
Kipp, Darrell 152, 156 (*see also* Blackfeet; Piegan Institute)
Klamath–Sahaptin 10
Kōhanga Reo (Māori language nest preschool) 130

Lakota
  anthropologist-activist Beatrice Medicine 1
  Code Talkers 21
  federal agent to 52
  lands 5
  population 6
  language 11, 12, 59
  'Life Readers' 55
  missionary to 51
  winter count 31

language
  abandonment 37, 53, 158, 173
  attitude(s) 34, 35, 42, 89, 160, 161
  documentation 14, 17, 18, 27, 36, 38, 92, 94, 96, 97, 100, 107, 108, 109, 117, 150, 180, 181
  endangerment xxi, xxiii, 1, 9, 17, 18, 21, 35, 36, 37, 94, 159
  garden(s) 48
  ideology(ies) 17, 25, 33–35, 66, 94, 100, 105, 159, 160, 173 (*see also* ideology[ies])
  loss 37
  maintenance 20, 22, 38, 45, 59, 160, 197
  orientation(s) 34–35
  planning (approach, definitions) xxv, 32–45
  pods approach to revitalization 118
  policy (approach, definitions) xxv, 32–45
  practices xiv, xviii, xxiii, xxvi, 25, 28, 33, 35, 40, 73, 89, 156, 157, 159, 161, 162, 163, 166, 172, 182, 190
  reclamation xxi, xxvi, 14, 38 (definition of), 42, 105, 106, 108, 109, 111, 113, 121, 140, 154, 157, 173, 178, 179, 181, 201
  regeneration 17, 38 (definition of), 39, 73, 97, 125, 150, 151, 152, 153, 154
  regenesis 35, 38, 59, 91–155
  renewal 35, 45
  repatriation xx
  repertoire(s) 59, 72 (*see also* communicative repertoire[s])
  restrictionism/restrictive policies 42, 43, 184, 186–192
  revitalization xx, xxiii, xxv, xxvi, 14, 20, 35, 38
  revival 59
  rights xxi, xviii, 42, 61, 153, 193
  shift xv, xvii, xvii, xix, xx, xxiv, xxvi, 17, 19, 37, 38, 41, 43, 60, 71, 73, 88, 89, 91, 92, 122, 129, 130, 153, 156, 157, 158, 159, 160, 161, 182, 185, 1990, 195
  vitality xxiii, xiv, 1, 17–20, 153, 207
Language Is Life Conference 114
Lazore, Dorothy 46, 125, 126, 128, 131, 132, 152
Legatz, Jennifer 142–143
Leonard's revised view of the language endangerment continuum 20, 21

limited English proficient xviii, 160, 163
linguicide 37, 135, 185
linguistic
 abilities/competencies xviii, 11, 37, 160, 163
 assimilation 37, 129 (*see also* assimilation/assimilationist)
 classification 1, 17–21
 continuance 178, 179
 culture 34
 difference 43, 56, 193
 diversity xviii, xix, 9, 34, 45, 48, 112, 191
 ecology(ies) 34, 65, 162, 170
 enumeration xxiii–xxiv, 1, 8, 69
 identity(ies) 156–157, 182
 inequality 35
 justice xxvii, 42
 profiling 35
 repertoire 72, 140 (*see also* communicative repertoire[s])
 rights xxv, 36, 61 (*see also* language rights)
 self-determination xxi, 26, 30, 44, 84, 138, 146, 153
 sovereignty xxvi, 2, 3, 40, 200, 201
 tip 37, 160, 169, 157 (*see also* language shift)
Linn, Mary 180
literacy/literacies
 alphabetic xxii, xxiii, 13, 49, 66, 73, 107, 119
 continuum 31
 definition and approach xxii-xxiii
 digital 24–28
 events xxii
 Indigenous 65
 multimodal xii, 12–17, 119
 practices xxiii
 print xxii, xxiii, 12–17, 48–50, 66, 73, 74, 77, 107, 119, 129, 139, 199
Littlebear, Richard xix, 63
Little Doe Baird, Jessie 106, 108–111 (*see also* Wampanoag; Wôpanâak)
Lower Kuskokwim School District 190, 197
Lumbee 6

Maliseet 30
magnet school 139, 155 (*see also* Puente de Hózhǫ́ Trilingual Magnet School)

Margolin, Malcolm 113, 114
Massachusett 49, 63, 106, 107, 108, 109
Matthews, Washington 73
McCord, Hubert (cover photo), iv, 181
medium of instruction xxv, 61, 195, 205
Menominee
 lands 5
 language 59
 population 6
Meriam Report 53, 55
Métis xix, 3
Mexicano (Nahuatl) 153
Miami
 Chief Thomas Gamble vi, 99
 Heritage Award 100
 lands 5, 92, 93
 language xxii, xxv, xxvi, 10, 20, 21, 26, 36, 30, 91–107, 112, 150, 154, 160, 161
 language reclamation 42, 92–106, 160, 161
 linguist Wesley Leonard xxiii, 20, 21, 28, 42, 99, 100
 people 25, 92–106, 150
 population 94
 removal 92–94
 Tribal Business Committee 99
 Tribe of Oklahoma 98
 University 96–99, 105
 youth camps 100–101 (*see also* Myaamia)
Miccosukee 59
Micronesian 11
Mi'kmaq 13, 30
missionary schooling 49, 50, 51
'mixed messages' 159, 179
Mobilian Jargon 9
Mohawk
 Council of Akwesasne 155
 lands 5, 120, 121
 language 10, 26, 46, 119–128
 Language Certificate Program 126–127
 Language Diploma Program 127
 language revitalization 119, 128, 132
 Nation 121, 122, 126
 people 119, 123, 126
 schools xxvi, 121–126, 131 (*see also* Akwesasne; Kahnawa:ke; Tyendinaga)
Mohegan–Pequot 106, 109

Mojave (Mohave) iv, 181
  lands 5
  language 10, 26, 113
Moore, Keith 186, 189
moribund language(s)/moribundity xx, 19, 36, 37, 91
mother tongue(s) xxiv, xix, xx, xxv, xxvi, 17, 20, 21, 24, 34, 41, 47, 53, 60, 85, 127, 128, 150, 156, 160, 166, 175, 193
Muskogean 10, 49 (*see also* Creek)
Myaamia
  Heritage Museum 93, 95
  language 20, 25
  ideology 102
  Language Project xxiii, 91, 95, 96, 98, 99, 101, 103, 104, 105, 154
  myaamiaki eemamwiciki (Miami awakening), 94, 95
  people 91, 92, 104
  population centers 95 (*see also* Miami)

Nā Honua Mauli Ola Hawai'i Guidelines for Culturally Healthy and Responsive Learning Environments 135
Narragansett 106, 109
Natchez 10
Natick 106, 108
National Assessment of Education Progress (NAEP) 187, 188
National Indian Bilingual Center xvii
National Indian Education Association 62, 188
National Indian Education Study 187, 188
National Museum of the American Indian 27
Native American Church 23, 88
Native American Film + Video Festival 26
Native American Language Issues Institute 64
Native American Languages Act (NALA) 2, 44, 61, 62, 64, 97, 99, 111, 114, 118, 132, 153, 193, 194, 203–210
Native American Materials Development Center (NAMDC) 83
Native American Youth Language Fair 180
Native California(n)
  lands 5
  languages xxvi, 10, 112, 113
  language revitalization 111–118
  Network (NCN), 114

  peoples 111, 112, 114, 150 (*see also* California Master–Apprentice Language Learning Program)
Native Hawaiian(s)
  ancestry 7
  children and youth 28, 159
  definitions of xxi, 31, 204
  education/language revitalization xviii, 128–138
  Homelands 4, 7, 31
  people(s) xxi, 2, 3, 4, 128, 129, 130
  political incorporation into US system 30, 129
  population 4, 7, 8
  students 28, 29, 188
  youth 159 (*see also* Hawai'i/Hawaiian; Ka Haka 'Ula O Ke'elikōlani College of Hawaiian Language; *Ke Kula Kauapuni Hawai'i;* Ke Kula Kaiapuni 'o Ānuenue School; Nāwahīokalani'ōpu'u Laboratory School)
Native Language Shift and Retention Study 157, 161–178, 182, 185, 190, 195
Navajo
  bilingual–bicultural education 41, 59, 65–90
  Blessingway ceremony, xxii
  case study 65–90
  Code Talkers 21, 74, 148
  Community College (Diné College), 29, 68, 88
  community-controlled schools 66, 78–87
  Country xxvi 66, 67, 73 (*see also* Diné Bikeyah)
  Curriculum Center 83
  curriculum specialist Don Mose 27
  elder(s) 39
  immersion 139–150, 194, 197
  lands 5, 67
  language xxv, xvii, xxv 10, 12, 13, 22, 25, 26, 27, 30, 46, 59, 65–90
  lands 5, 67
  'Life Readers' 55, 56
  linguist William Morgan 24, 75, 83
  linguist Mary Willie 76
  linguistics 30
  Long Walk 139, 172
  Nation xxii, xxv, 4, 5, 22, 29, 41, 65, 66, 67, 68, 69–73, 87–89, 112, 19, 151, 155, 158, 171, 176, 182, 189, 194
  population 4, 6

print literacy (written Navajo) 23, 29,
    30, 37, 38, 65, 73–79
Reading Study 71, 84
religion 23
reservation 5, 58, 66, 67
Sovereignty in Education Act (NSIEA)
    3, 68, 69, 89, 151, 194
speakers 9, 12
Technical College 68
Tribal Council 22
youth 42, 159, 160, 161, 171
Nāwahīokalaniʻōpuʻu (Nāwahī)
    Laboratory School 132–134, 194, 195
new speakers xxiv, 11, 37, 38
News from Native California 113, 114
Nixon, Richard M. 57, 90
Nizipuhwahsin (Real Speak) 152
No Child Left Behind Act of 2001
    (NCLB) 44, 87, 162, 168, 186–194,
    197, 201, 202
'No Indian Talk' rule 52
Nunavik 41
Nunavut 160
    location 70

Official English 191 (*see also* English-only)
Ojibwe
    immersion 42, 152
    language 10, 12
    people (Anishinaabe), 25, 183 (*see also*
        Chippewa)
Olds, Julie xxvi, 92, 94, 97, 98
Onandaga 10, 119
Oneida
    lands 5
    language 10, 59, 119
    people 119
O'odham
    lands 5
    language 11, 12, 59
    parent 60
    population 6 (*see also* Akimel
        O'odham; Tohono O'odham)
oral tradition(s) xxvi, 3, 42, 46, 47, 79,
    160, 183
orature xxii, xxiii, 128, 181
Osage
    lands 5
    language 11
    population 6
Other Pacific Islander(s) 4, 7, 8
    definition of 31

Paiute
    lands 5
    language 11, 113
    population 6
Parker, Quanah 23
pidgin(s) 9, 11, 130
Piegan Institute 152, 156
Plains Sign Language 48
Plessy v. Ferguson 64
Polynesian 11, 128
Pomo/Pomoan 10, 59, 113
Potawatami
    lands 5, 153
    language 59, 153
    people 153
    population 6
power x, xx, xxii, xxiii, xxiv, xxv, 2, 3, 22,
    27, 28, 32, 35, 36, 37, 38, 39, 40, 44, 51,
    65, 68, 77, 78, 79, 86, 88, 89, 91, 122,
    123, 125, 129, 142; 149, 150, 152, 153,
    157, 173, 181, 182, 184, 185, 200, 202
    Power of Two 145
    Red Power 123
Principles for Stronger Tribal Communities 201
Proposition 203 ('English for the Children',
    Arizona) 145, 191, 192 (*see also*
    English-only)
Proposition 227 ('English for the Children',
    California) 191 (*see also* English-only)
Pueblo
    communities 16, 22, 42
    culture(s), 23
    language programs 16
    population 6
    students 16
    theocratic societies 22, 23
    youth 42, 159, 181 (*see also* Acoma;
        Cochiti; Hopi; Keres; Tewa; Tiwa;
        Zuni)
Puente de Hózhǫ́ Trilingual Public
    Magnet School 139, 143–150, 151,
    194, 195, 200
    student outcomes 149–150
Puritan(s) 49, 107

Quechua 41, 45, 161
Quichua 35, 41, 45

Ratt, Soloman ix, 46
reversal of language shift (RLS) 19, 38,
    66, 122
Ramah community and school 42, 81, 82
    location 5, 67

Richmond Road School 41
Rock Point community and school 59, 71, 81, 82, 85, 86, 89, 90, 155, 200
  location 67
Roessel, Monty (C. Monty) 197
Roessel, Robert A. Jr 81
Roessel, Ruth 80
Rosetta Stone 26, 27
Rough Rock community and school xvii, 29, 41, 46, 58, 71, 77–89, 90, 197, 200
  Demonstration School 5, 8, 71, 78, 81, 83
  English–Navajo Language Arts Program (RRENLAP) 85–86
  location 67
  school board 79, 90
  school director Dillon Platero 82, 88
  teachers xvii, 77, 197

safety zone/safety zone theory xxv, 42–46, 52, 55, 56, 60, 61, 63, 66, 77, 86, 139, 156, 184, 185, 193, 194, 195, 200, 201, 202
Salinian–Seri–Shastan 10, 113
Salishian 10
self-determination xx, xxiv, xxv, 1, 2, 27, 30, 42, 44, 57, 58, 59, 60, 78, 86, 87, 90, 138, 146, 153, 192, 201, 203, 204 (*see also* linguistic self-determination)
Seminole
  lands 5
  language 10, 59
  population 6
segregation 57, 64, 166, 192
Senate Bill 130 (Alaska) 3
Senate Bill 1070 (Arizona) 193
Senate Special Subcommittee on Indian Education 57
Seneca 119
  lands 5
  language 10
Sequoyah (George Guess or Gist) 13, 14, 24, 25, 50
seventh generation xxvi, 183, 184, 202
Shoshone
  educator Esther Burnett Horne 56
  lands 5
  language 12
  population 6
  master teachers 180
  students 180

Sioux/Siouan
  language 11, 12, 180
  population 6
'sleeping' languages(s) xxvi, 18, 19, 21, 36, 91, 111, 173
social justice xxvii, 40, 42
sociolinguistic nexus 1, 12, 17, 21, 30
sovereign(ty) xix, xxi, xxii, xiv, xxvi, 61, 192, 202
  definition of 2
  educational and linguistic xxvi, 3, 40 (*see also* linguistic sovereignty)
  Indigenous 61
  Navajo Sovereignty in Education Act (*see* Navajo)
  tribal xxiv, 2, 3, 30, 35, 44, 58, 68, 122, 154, 188, 200, 201
speakerhood 1, 173
St Regis
  lands/settlements 5, 120, 122
  Mohawk Tribe 155 (*see also* Akwesasne; Mohawk)
standardization xx, xxvi, 33, 184, 186–194, 196
status planning 33, 77, 185
Still Smoking, Dorothy 152
Strack, Andrew J. 98, 102 (*see also* Miami; Myaamia)
subtractive bilingualism xviii, 190, 198, 200
syllabary
  Cherokee 13, 14, 24, 25, 26, 29, 60 (*see also* Sequoyah)
  Hawaiian 131, 133

Tanoan 11
Teller, Lynda 77
Tewa
  Arizona 23
  lands 5
  language 11, 12, 59, 62
termination policy 57, 63, 64, 76
Thompson, Roseanna xvii, 184, 185
Timicua 49
Tiwa 11, 12
Tlingit 10, 59
Tohono O'odham (Desert People)
  lands 5
  language 59
  linguist Ofelia Zepeda 16
  population 6 (*see also* O'odham)
top-down language planning 36, 44, 66, 113
Totahne (Mohawk immersion preschool) 127

transitional bilingual education 140, 199, 200
translanguaging(er) 73, 167
treaties/treaty-making 51, 93, 94, 96, 112, 122, 129, 139, 140
tribal/community-controlled schools xxv, 29, 66, 78–87
tribal colleges and universities (TCUs) 30, 201
tribal–federal relationship 3, 4 76 (*see also* trust responsibility/relationship)
Tribally Controlled Colleges and Universities Assistance Act (1978 Tribally Controlled College or University Assistance Act) 68
Trubakoff, Dawn 146
trust responsibility/relationship 3, 63, 86, 112, 140 (*see also* sovereignty; tribal–federal relationship)
Tsalagi Ageyui (Our Beloved Cherokee) 152
Tséhootsooí Diné Bi'ólta' (TDB, The Navajo School at the Meadow Between the Rocks) 139–143, 149, 195, 200
Tsi Tyonnheht Onkwawenna (TTO) Language Circle 126–128 (*see also* Tyendinaga)
Tyendinaga (Placing the Wood Together) 120, 126–128
  Band Council 127
  location 121

Unami 50
United Nations *Declaration on the Rights of Indigenous Peoples* 153, 201
University of California Los Angeles Civil Rights Project 192
University of Hawai'i–Hilo College of Hawaiian Language 132, 135
University of Utah Center for American Indian Languages 180
Unquachog 50
US Census Bureau/Census data 3, 4, 5 9, 31
US Department of Education xii, 62, 161
US Office of Bilingual Education and Minority Languages Affairs 187
US Office of English Language Acquisition, Language Enhancement, and Academic Achievement for Limited English Proficient Students 187

Ute
  population 6
  Southern Ute language 59
Uto-Aztecan 11

Waadookodaading Immersion School 152
Wampanoag
  Aquinnah 5, 108, 109, 110
  Assonet Band 109
  Bible 107 (*see also* Eliot Bible)
  Herring Pond 5, 109
  lands 5
  language 106, 107, 111
  linguist Jessie Little Doe Baird (*see* Little Doe Baird)
  literacy 108
  Mashpee 5, 108, 109, 110
  Nation 63, 106, 109, 111, 118, 154
  people 106, 107, 111 (*see also* Wôpanâak)
War on Poverty 79, 89
White House Initiative on Native American Language Revitalization 62, 63
White House Native Languages Working Group 62, 63
Winnebago
  educator Henry Roe Cloud 55
  lands 5
  language 11, 59
Wôpanâak (Wampanoag)
  classes 109, 110
  communities/Nation 109, 111
  dictionary 109
  documentation 107, 108
  language 10, 36, 92, 106, 107, 111, 112, 154
  Language Reclamation Project 106, 108, 110, 150
  language reclamation/revival x, 106–111, 154, 184
  speakers 108 (*see also* Wampanoag)

Yakima
  lands 5
  language 10
  population 6
Yaqui (Yoeme)
  lands 5
  language xix, 11
  population 6
  tribal language policy, xix

Young Ancestors Project 181, 182
Young and Morgan dictionary 74–76
    orthography 75
Young, Robert 24, 69, 75
youth iv, xv, xvi, xxi, xxvi, xxvii, 26, 27, 35, 41, 42, 52, 60, 61, 69, 76, 88, 89, 98, 100 103, 104, 116, 123, 151, 153, 156–182, 183, 185, 190, 195, 201
Yuchi *see* Euchee
Yuman
    languages 10
    population 6
Yup'ik
    language 4, 10, 12, 13, 37, 41, 50, 59, 160, 190, 197
    Language Institute 151
    people(s) 4
    population 6
    scholar-practitioner Walkie Charles 151
    teacher-researchers 197
    villages 197
    youth 41, 160, 190
Yurok
    lands 5
    language 113, 116, 118

Zuni
    lands 5
    language 12, 59

For Product Safety Concerns and Information please contact our EU Authorised Representative:

Easy Access System Europe

Mustamäe tee 50

10621 Tallinn

Estonia

gpsr.requests@easproject.com